Small Business Management

4th Edition

David Stokes

THOMSON

Australia • Canada • Mexico • Singapore • Spain • United Kingdom • United States

Small Business Management

Copyright © 2002 David Stokes

The Thomson logo is a registered trademark used herein under licence.

For more information, contact Thomson Learning, High Holborn House, 50-51 Bedford Row, London WC1R 4LR or visit us on the World Wide Web at:
http://www.thomsonlearning.co.uk

British Library Cataloguing-in-Publication Data
A catalogue record for this book is available from the British Library

ISBN 0-82645-679-0

First edition 1992 by D P Publications
Second edition 1995 by Letts
Reprinted 1997 by Letts
Third edition 1998 by Letts
Fourth edition 2002 by Continuum
Reprinted 2002 by Continuum
Reprinted 2003 by Thomson Learning

Typeset by KAI, Nottingham
Printed in the UK by TJ International, Padstow, Cornwall

Contents

Section A Exploring small business

Part I The small business contex

Part II The small business choice

Part III The small business in action

Section B Planning a new venture

Stage I The feasibility study

Contents

About the author

Dr David Stokes is Assistant Director of the Small Business Research Centre and Principal Lecturer at Kingston Business School, Kingston University. Educated at Oriel College, Oxford, and the City University Business School, his career in management has involved both larger and smaller enterprises in the private and public sectors. He combines both an academic and a practical involvement with small and medium-sized enterprises (SMEs). The subject of his PhD thesis was small enterprise development in the public sector, and he has been involved in many research studies into diverse aspects of small business management, including marketing, critical survival factors and raising finance. He is directly involved with a number of smaller enterprises as a director or an adviser, having been an active manager in business ventures of his own. He is chairman of the Academy of Marketing's special interest group in entrepreneurship and marketing. He is also the author of *Marketing*, by the same publishers.

Dedication

This book is dedicated with all my love to my parents,

Charles and Florence Stokes.

Preface

Purpose of this book

The principal aim of this book is to provide a course of study in the management of the smaller business or enterprise.

It is intended to be used in the classroom on a variety of business and management courses at undergraduate, and post graduate level. It can also be used by those who wish to study the subject on their own. The material in the book has been developed from the teaching of, and feedback from, small business components in HND, BA (Business Studies), Certificate in Management, Diploma in Management Studies, and MBA courses, as well as workshops for intending or practising small business managers.

Need

This book aims to fill a gap. There are many publications targeted at would-be entrepreneurs and existing small business owners, which give general and detailed advice on how to set up and run a small enterprise. There are also many articles and books of a more academic nature which survey the small business scene, investigating crucial topics such as the role of the small business in the economy and society, or detailing the common experiences of small businesses in a wide variety of management contexts and situations.

This book is intended to give the student one main source of reference on small business management. Firstly, it aims to help the student understand more about the specific management issues involved in setting up and running a small enterprise. Secondly, it aims to provide the student with a summary of some of the research studies and debate on the small business sector, in order to develop an individual perspective in a wider context.

Approach and structure

The book is structured around a case study approach. Although a considerable amount of information is given in the book, the aim is to impart skills and knowledge by engaging the reader in interesting tasks and activities which build on existing understanding.

There are two main sections.

Section A Exploring small business

This section gives the reader the necessary information to understand the relevance of the small business sector in a wider economic and social context, and to explore the management aspects which particularly affect the success or failure of a small enterprise.

It is sub-divided into 3 Parts made up of 14 Units which link directly to the activities in Section B:

Part I, The small business context, Units 1–5, evaluates the role that small businesses play in our economy and society, and the environment in which small business managers operate.

Part II, The small business choice, Units 6–8, explores the diversity of small business forms, looking at start ups, franchises, buying a business and the legal forms.

Part III, The small business in action, Units 9–14, considers how small businesses work in practice, focusing on successful strategies particularly in the areas of the management of people, marketing and money.

Each Unit contains student exercises to be completed during, and at the end of, the reading of the Unit:

Activities: These are intended to provoke thoughts around the subject matter before it is read so that the reader discovers as much as possible for themselves.

Case studies: A specific small enterprise situation is described, and issues and problems specified as activities for the reader to undertake. In Part I, the cases follow two different small business ideas through various stages towards start up. In Parts II and III the cases illustrate a wider range of small business types.

Extended tasks: An activity is suggested at the end of each Unit which is designed to develop understanding of the subject of the Unit through observation of small enterprises in action.

The 3 Parts and 14 Units of Section A 'Exploring small business' link directly to the Stages and Steps in Section B, Planning a new venture.

Section B Planning a new venture

To build on understandings developed in Section A, the student is asked to undertake various steps towards a business plan for a new venture. This can form the basis of assessed work if required. This section is based around the choice of an enterprise or business idea by the student, and the development of that idea in three main stages.

Stage I: The feasibility study This is divided into a series of sequential steps in which the student chooses and evaluates an area of opportunity to a preliminary level which indicates the likelihood of success or failure. Each Step links to a Unit in Part I of Section A.

Stage II: The route to market entry The student is asked to evaluate the alternative methods for developing their selected opportunity. This involves looking at franchising, buying existing businesses, as well as starting up from scratch. The alternative legal forms are also considered. Each Step links to a Unit in Part II of Section A.

Stage III: The business plan The student is asked to complete the detailed planning for their idea as a business plan. A suggested format and stages are identified to help the reader draw up this important document. Each Step links to a Unit in Part III of Section A.

How to use this book

This book can be used as a workbook in the classroom, as a guide for less supervised study, or a mixture of both.

However they are used, the activities in Section A and in Section B are the basis for the learning process. The student should work through these in the order indicated, with support where necessary from the text and other recommended works of reference.

Section A *Exploring small business*	Section B *Planning a new venture*
Part I The small business context ⟶	*Stage I The feasibility study*
Unit 1 Small business in the economy ⟶	Step 1.1 Outlining the process
Unit 2 The entrepreneur and the owner ⟶ manager	Step 1.2 Know thyself
Unit 3 The small business environment ⟶	Step 1.3 Identifying the opportunity area
Unit 4 Innovation and the market place ⟶	Step 1.4 Selecting the idea
Unit 5 Information and help ⟶	Step 1.5 Researching the idea
	Step 1.6 Summary of the feasibility study
Part II The small business choice ⟶	*Stage II The route to market entry*
Unit 6 Start-ups and franchises ⟶	Step 2.1 Start-up or franchise?
Unit 7 Buying an existing business ⟶	Step 2.2 Buying an existing business
Unit 8 Legal identities ⟶	Step 2.3 Selecting the form
Part III The small business in action ⟶	*Stage III The business plan*
Unit 9 The business plan ⟶	Step 3.1 Outlining the plan
Unit 10 Successful small business strategies ⟶	Step 3.2 Deciding the strategy
Unit 11 Management of resources ⟶	Step 3.3 Managing the resources
Unit 12 Marketing ⟶	Step 3.4 Planning the marketing
Unit 13 Money ⟶	Step 3.5 Forecasting the money
Unit 14 Further case studies ⟶	Step 3.6 Summary of the business plan

Note to the fourth edition

The fourth edition builds upon the popular three previous editions with findings from recent research and updated information, case studies and references. In particular, it contains new information and ideas concerning business closures, the impact of the Internet and the financing of small businesses. Government initiatives, particularly the launch of the Small Business Service, are also taken into account.

David Stokes, October 2001

Section A

Exploring small business

How to use this section

1. This section is divided into Parts I, II and III, a total of 14 Units which link directly with those in Section B, Planning a new venture. They are referenced to specific stages and steps in the process of putting together a business plan.

2. Each Unit contains information around a major subject area, which can be read in total, or in part as specific help to activities in Sections A and B.

3. At the beginning of each Unit is a list of contents which summarises the topics covered and the numbering system.

4. Activities are designed to stimulate your thoughts and experiences of the topic under discussion. Understanding and retention of information is more likely if it is related to what you already know and have experience of, so it is important to attempt to answer these questions. As you are working through the text have pen and paper to hand and formulate your answers, before reading on.

5. Case studies are used to describe a situation illustrating some of the topic areas under consideration. Whilst they are fictional situations, and fictional characters, they are drawn from real-life examples of small business and enterprises. A number of Activities are also listed at the end of each case.

6. At the end of each Unit in Section A there is an Extended Activity. This is a general activity, designed to provide more understanding of the subject of the Unit through observation of small enterprises in action. Where the reader is undertaking the Steps in Section B, Planning a new venture, it may not be necessary to undertake every Extended Activity.

7. At the end of each Unit, it is important to consolidate the learning of the Unit by tackling the relevant Step of Section B.

Part I

The small business context

This Part comprises Units 1 to 5. It evaluates the role that small businesses play in our economy and society, and the environment in which small business managers operate. Each Unit links to a Step in Stage I (The feasibility study) of Section B, as shown below. Each Step should be considered immediately following your completion of the relevant Unit.

Section A Exploring small business	Section B Planning a new venture
Part I The small business context ⟶	*Stage I The feasibility study*
Unit 1 Small business in the economy ⟶	Step 1.1 Outlining the process
Unit 2 The entrepreneur and the owner-⟶ manager	Step 1.2 Know thyself
Unit 3 The small business environment ⟶	Step 1.3 Identifying the opportunity area
Unit 4 Innovation and the marketplace ⟶	Step 1.4 Selecting the idea
Unit 5 Information and help ⟶	Step 1.5 Researching the idea
	Step 1.6 Summary of the feasibility study

Contents

1 Small business in the economy

This Unit investigates the significance of small business to national economies. Small businesses form a very diverse sector which is difficult to define and measure, but, after a period of decline and neglect, they are recognised today as a key element in national economic growth. Although there are underlying structural reasons for this revival, small firms remain a turbulent part of the economy.

Contents

Activity 1 What is a small business?

How would you define a small business? Attempt to write your own definition of a small business, compared to a medium-sized or large one, before comparing your answer to the definitions given below.

5

1 What is a small business?

1.1 Problems of definition

Definition is a fundamental issue facing those who wish to understand more about small businesses. What exactly is a small business, and when does it become medium-sized or large? We use the terms 'small business sector', and 'small business management' to describe a certain group of enterprises, and how they are run. This implies that these enterprises have certain characteristics and management issues in common, which distinguish them from other organisations because of their size. In practice, it is hard to define these characteristics, and even harder to draw a precise line which separates small from large firms. Small businesses do not conform to any neat parameters. Much depends on the industry in which they operate and the personalities and aspirations of those that run them. These factors vary from manufacturers to retailers, professional managers to husband and wife teams, high growth, high tech start ups funded by venture capitalists to self-financed tradesmen content just to make a living. It is this diversity which makes generalisations of any kind, including a definition of the sector, extremely difficult, and often unwise.

1.2 Bolton Report definition

The Committee of Inquiry on Small Firms, set up by the UK government under its chairmanship of J. E. Bolton, recognised this diversity in their influential report, published in 1971, which became known as the Bolton Report[1]:

> *'Small firms are present in virtually every industry and the characteristics they share as small firms are sometimes not as apparent because of the differences arising from the contrasting conditions of the different industries. There is also extreme variation . . . as regards efficiency, methods of operation, the nature of the market served and the size of the resources employed. Thus, a manufacturing business employing up to 200 people has very little in common with a small shop owned and run by a married couple.'*

The Report proposed that a small firm had three essential characteristics:

- ❏ A small firm is managed by its owner(s) in a personalised way.
- ❏ It has a relatively small share of the market in economic terms.
- ❏ It is independent in the sense that it does not form part of a larger enterprise and its ownership is relatively free from outside control in its principal decisions.

As well as these general qualities, small firms were defined by more specific, quantitative measurements. The diversity of the sector was recognised as definitions depended on the industry type. For example:

Small firm type	Definition used
manufacturing	200 employees or less
construction	25 employees or less

Small firm type	Definition used
road transport	5 vehicles or less
retailing	£50,000 p.a. turnover or less
miscellaneous services	£50,000 p.a. turnover or less

(Turnover thresholds are subject to inflation: since 1971 about 20 times.)

Although these definitions have formed the basis of subsequent research in the UK, they are open to several criticisms including:

❐ low market share is not always a characteristic; small firms can operate in highly specialised niches, or limited geographic markets, where they have a relatively high share;

❐ independence is difficult to measure. Bolton's definition excluded franchises for example, which do form part of a larger enterprise, but included sub-contractors very dependent on one customer;

❐ whilst different size measures are very justifiable (50 employees makes a small manufacturer, but makes a large consultancy or retailer for instance), they have bedevilled statistical comparisons, especially internationally, as countries employ different definitions.

The 1985 Companies Act simplified and updated Bolton's definition.

A 'small' or 'medium' business satisfies a minimum of two of the following criteria:

	Small	Medium
Sales turnover up to	£2.8m	£11.2m
Balance sheet value up to	£1.4m	£5.6m
Employees up to	50	250

1.3 Other definitions

Small firms may be difficult to define precisely on paper, but most are easy to recognise once they are seen in operation. There seem to be fundamental differences in practice which enable us to distinguish between small and large firms.

❐ Wynarczyk and others[2] identified three key aspects in which small and large firms differ: uncertainty, innovation and evolution. Uncertainty is a persistent feature of small firms which tend to have small customer bases and limited resources. The innovation of either very new products, or marginal differences to well established ones, is a key factor in the success or failure of new business start ups. Evolution refers to the state of constant structural and market changes which small firms are likely to experience as they struggle to survive and develop.

❐ Curran and others[3] have argued against over-general notions of the 'small firm sector' because it does consist of an exceptionally mixed bag of businesses, engaged in a wide range of activities, whose managers often have little in common with each other. Instead they use more detailed, pragmatic definitions derived from sources within a trade or activity type. Thus a 'small' public house (free house) business is defined as having one outlet, an unspecified number of employees but not brewery owned, whilst a 'small' employment agency can have up to two outlets and ten employees.

❏ The European Commission (EC) initiated a set of definitions of the 'small and medium-sized enterprise' (SME). These are also the statistical parameters adopted by the Department of Trade and Industry (DTI) and the Small Business Service (SBS) in the UK. The SME sector consists of:

○ Micro enterprises – from 0 to 9 employees.

○ Small enterprises – from 10 to 49 employees.

○ Medium enterprises – from 50 to 249 employees.

(These definitions exclude agriculture, hunting, forestry and fishing.)

Whilst the EC definitions oversimplify matters, they do reflect the changing management environment of an enterprise as it reaches key stages in its growth; businesses with less than 10 employees rarely need a middle management structure, but over that size there is often pressure on the owner-manger to delegate more of the decision-making.

1.4 Definitions used in this book

This book does not take such precise quantitative definitions to define its scope. Small business management is different in several respects to management in larger organisations, because of social structures and relationships, and because of the levels of resources available. Whilst these differences may derive from the numbers of employees and size of turnover, it is the management implications of these differences that will be our primary concern. For example, the manager who has no specialist departments to turn to for advice, who takes phone calls from creditors emphasising the shortage of cash and who has to choose between keeping an appointment with a customer or attending to an important production issue, is facing situations typical of small, rather than large, business management.

In this sense small business management can be extended to small 'enterprise' management to bring in the many types of small organisations which are not traditionally regarded as businesses, but which share many of the management issues of a small firm. Small non-profit making units may be influenced by the 'smallness' of their operation in ways which are similar to small business. A doctor in a small medical practice, the head teacher of a primary school, or the manager of a small charity may work in a similar management environment, and face similar management decisions as the owner-manager of a small firm. Whilst such organisations may not fit with accepted definitions of a small business, the management environment can still be typical of a small enterprise.

It is this peculiar management environment of the small enterprise which defines the parameters of this book, rather than any precise threshold level above which a small firm automatically becomes medium sized or large.

Activity 2 Why are small businesses important to the economy?

What contributions to the health of the economy do small businesses make? Write down as many factors as you can think of before reading on.

2 Why bother with small business?

2.1 Shifting perceptions of small business

Guided by politicians and management theorists, public perceptions of the small business have shifted in recent times from the extremes of neglect and ignorance to hype and over-expectation. In the 1950s and 60s, small firms were written off as out-of-date forms of economic activity. By the late 1970s and 80s they were hailed as the new saviours of ailing western economies and by the 1990s, SMEs were recognised as the key to fuller employment.

❐ **Small firm neglect**

The industrial revolution of the nineteenth century first threatened the pre-dominance of the small enterprise after centuries in which it had been the basic economic unit. Technological and marketing changes seemed to be sounding its death-knell by the middle of the twentieth century, by which time several factors were working in favour of larger industrial units:

○ Economies of scale lowered costs for manufacturers big enough to use mass production techniques.

○ New products from electrical goods to pharmaceutical drugs were transforming the buying habits of society, but the research and development costs were very high and affordable only by larger companies.

○ Protectionist trade barriers fell away as the marketplace became increasingly global to the advantage of big businesses with international marketing and distribution resources.

Social scientists and policy makers devoted their attention to large units of production, which they believed would be the increasingly predominant form of industrial organisation. There was a wide-spread belief that the small firm was rather superfluous to economic growth and the spate of mergers and take-overs in the 1950s and 60s seemed to confirm this view: global marketing had handed the key to economic prosperity to the multi-national corporation and modern technology demanded a concentration of resources, confining small firms to a peripheral role supporting the dominant position of larger organisations.

Management theory and education focused its attention on the manager working in a large company. Small firm owners were seen in a rather inferior light, managing limited resources with backward technologies in an amateur way. The major publications on business disciplines such as marketing, finance and strategy were written in the context of large organisations and the new business schools which began to develop at this time used case studies of large firms, almost exclusively[4].

☐ **The 'entrepreneurial economy'**

During the late 1970s and 80s the situation changed. Research into the behaviour of small enterprises dramatically increased. The literature boomed[5], with written material published on virtually every aspect of the small business. Regular newspaper columns[6] began to give advice to small business owners and information on their environment.

Politicians of differing ideologies in many countries developed a remarkable enthusiasm for the small firm. All three major political parties in the UK supported policies promoting small businesses. In the 1980s leaders on both sides of the Atlantic proclaimed the dawn of a new age of enterprise, led by an army of entrepreneurs working in small firms.

In 1985, Peter Drucker, one of the most influential writers of the era when management theory was based on big business practice, acknowledged the new climate by welcoming the shift from a managerial to an entrepreneurial economy in which growth was being fuelled by small and medium-sized enterprises[7].

2.2 Bolton Report, 1971

In the UK, a watershed in the perceptions of the small firm was the highly influential Bolton Report[1]. This was the outcome of the Committee of Inquiry on Small Firms, under the chairmanship of J. E. Bolton, set up in 1969 by the Labour government and reporting to the Conservative government in 1971. During its two years of research, it commissioned many reports which have formed the basis for the large body of work carried out since. It represented the first significant attempt to assess the importance and functions of the small firms sector in the UK.

The report recognised that small enterprises made a special contribution to the health of the economy, identifying eight important roles:

☐ a productive outlet for enterprising and independent individuals (some of whom may be frustrated under-achievers in a larger, more controlled environment);

☐ the most efficient form of business organisation in some industries or markets where the optimum size of the production unit or sales outlet is small;

☐ specialist suppliers, or sub-contractors to larger companies;

☐ contributors to the variety of products and services made available to customers in specialised markets, too small for larger companies to consider worthwhile;

☐ competition to the monopolistic tendencies of large companies;

☐ innovators of new products, services and processes;

☐ the breeding ground for new industries; and

❐ the seedbed from which tomorrow's larger companies will grow, providing entry points for entrepreneurial talent who will become the industrial captains of the future.

These important roles were underpinned by the conclusion of the Committee that small firms could be extremely efficient, having the advantage of the commitment of their owner-managers, plus the ability in certain circumstances to better exploit business opportunities than their larger brethren.

However, the Committee provided evidence of the decline of the small business sector in the UK economy, concluding that further weakening of small firms was inevitable due to the economics of scale of larger firms. In view of the actual and potential contribution of small firms to the overall health of the economy, the major recommendation of the Report was therefore the creation of a Small Firms Division under a Minister for Small Firms. This was implemented by the establishment of the Small Firms Service within the Department of Industry.

The particular concern of the Report was that government policies should encourage and support the sector, not accelerate its decline through an unfair burden of regulations, paperwork and taxes:

> 'We believe that the health of the economy requires the birth of new enterprises in substantial numbers and the growth of some to a position from which they are able to challenge and supplant the existing leaders of industry...This seedbed function, therefore, appears to be a vital contribution of the small firms sector to the long-run health of the economy. We cannot assume that the ordinary working of market forces will necessarily preserve a small firm sector large enough to perform this function in future.' [1]

Activity 3 Inevitable decline?

Do you agree with Bolton's view that the small business sector is subject to long-term decline? What do you think the trends are today and how long will they last?

3 The revival of small enterprise

In fact, the Bolton Report proved unduly pessimistic about the immediate future for small firms. If their survival as an organisational form was the issue in 1971, the concern today is that the expectations have been too high. Small firms are now heralded as leaders in providing employment and growth in a restructuring of advanced economies. In retrospect, we can see that the tide was turning before the Bolton Report.

3.1 The American experience

In the USA, small enterprises began their revival in the 1960s. Since the late 1960s, the creation of new jobs has shifted from the country's largest organisations, to small and medium-sized firms, many of them new businesses[7]. The growth in employment in the USA between the mid-60s and mid-80s was phenomenal. The total workforce grew from 71 million in 1965 to 106 million in 1985, an increase of 50 per cent, or 35 million new jobs. Yet at the same time the traditional power-houses of the American economy, the largest businesses (the Fortune 500), were actually shedding jobs, an estimated loss of 5 million permanent jobs by 1985. In other words, taking into account this loss, 40 million new jobs were created in the two decades to 1985 by small and medium-sized businesses. Much of the growth has come from new enterprises, with an estimated 600,000 new businesses being started every year during the boom times of the 1980s.

3.2 The UK statistics

The pick-up of small enterprises in the UK may have come later but has been no less impressive. Figure 1.1 illustrates the growth in numbers of firms since the 1980s and Table 1.1 shows their share of total employment and turnover. Between 1980 and 1990, there was a substantial jump in the total number of firms in the UK. Their numbers rose by 58 per cent in the decade[8].

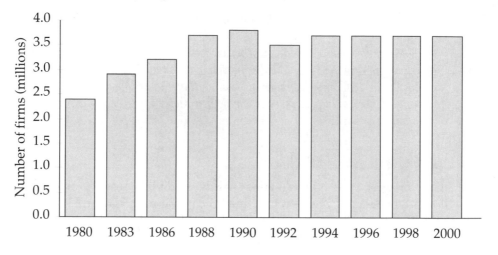

Source: SME Statistics for the UK, 2000, *Small Business Service, 2001*

Figure 1.1 Number of UK firms 1980-2000

Although the numbers of firms fell in the recession of the early 1990s, they have since increased back up to 3.7 million. The great majority of these are small firms, employing either no-one else or only a handful of people each. Table 1.1 shows that of the 3.7 million businesses in the UK in 2000, almost 95 per cent had fewer than 10 employees; 2.6 million businesses, over two-thirds of the total, had no employees at all, representing the large number of 'one-man band' businesses. Micro firms of under 10 employees accounted for just over 25 per cent of employ-ment in the private sector and over 20 per cent of turnover. Those employing under 50 people accounted for 9.5 million jobs (44 per cent of non-government employment) and almost 40 per cent of turnover. Although there were only approximately 7,500 large enterprises employing over 250 people, they made up 45 per cent of employment and 50 per cent of turnover. However, the total SME sector of firms employing less than 250 people now contributes 55 per cent of employment and 50 per cent of turnover in the UK.

A sector which had been largely ignored or dismissed as an out-of-date irrelevance by business and management analysts in the 1960s has grown to represent half of total UK sales, and over half of total private sector employment.

Table 1.1 Profile of the UK business population, 1999 and 2000

		Percentages				
Size (No. of employees)	No. of businesses		Employment		Turnover	
	1999	2000	1999	2000	1999	2000
None	63.2	69.6	12.5	13.5	4.2	7.4
1 – 9	31.7	25.3	17.7	16.7	15.2	15.4
10 – 49	4.3	4.1	13.7	13.3	13.3	14.4
50 – 249	0.6	0.6	11.4	11.4	12.0	13.9
250 +	0.2	0.2	44.6	44.9	55.2	48.8

Source: SME Statistics for the UK, *Small Business Service, 2000*

3.3 Self-employment and part-time businesses

It is noticeable from Table 1.1 that the largest proportion of small firms is in the very smallest category, that is firms of sole traders or partners without employees. Of the 3.7 million firms, under one third (1.2 million), employ other people. It is important to make a distinction between self-employment and the creation of a small business; the former could be just another form of working for larger organisations with no prospects of directly creating employment for others. For example, many professional specialists or skilled workers have become self-employed as consultants or tradesmen. Often they work for larger firms on a fee or a subcontract basis. This has become a particular feature of recessionary times when employers try to maintain the maximum flexibility over the costs of employment, by using self-employed labour. Some welcome the opportunity for self-employment in this way. Others – it has been suggested up to one-third[9] – accept self-employment reluctantly because of redundancy or lack of alternative employment.

The total number of self-employed rose steeply in the UK in the 1980s, from 1.9 million in 1979 to 3.6 million by 1990, and has since stabilised around the 3.3 million level. Of these, only around one-quarter employ other people[10].

It is also important to recognise that many businesses do not even employ the owner on a full-time basis. Many ventures are started as a part-time activity to supplement employment elsewhere, either because the owner regards them as a 'sideline' activity, or because they are testing out a business idea before committing fully to it by leaving their jobs. For this reason, 'mainstream' firms, defined as 'full time sole occupation businesses', were estimated to total 2.8 million in 2000, considerably less than the total stock of 3.7 million[11].

3.4 International comparisons

❐ **Global revival**

The UK experience in the 1980s mirrored that of the USA: large companies shed jobs, whilst smaller ones created them. Total employment in the UK fell by 0.5 million between 1979 and 1986. But large businesses employing 1,000 people or more reduced their workforces by 3.5 million, whilst smaller companies of under 1,000 people increased their total employment by 3 million.

International comparisons of statistics on small firms are very difficult because of the lack of common definitions and data sources[12]. However, the increase in employment in small firms seems to have been a common feature of the economies of many industrialised countries in the 1980s just as most had shown a decline in the sector prior to 1970. One report[13] concluded that small firms of less than 100 employees had increased their overall share of total employment in France, Germany, Italy, Japan, the UK and the USA, which 'signifies the reversal of a substantial downward trend in the employment shares of small units that had prevailed for many decades', although the rate of increase had varied by country and industrial sector. Similarly, the numbers of self-employed in OECD (Organisation for Economic Co-operation and Development) countries declined as a percentage of total employment until the late 1970s from which time they have increased steadily. SMEs now account for 60 to 70 per cent of jobs in most OECD countries[14].

❐ **UK and Europe**

The Bolton Report showed that the concentration of resources in large companies had gone further in the UK than anywhere else in Europe; only the USA had more multinationals in the world's top 500 companies than Britain in the 1960s. The increase in small firms and in self-employment in the UK has subsequently been greater than in many industrialised nations as the contribution of small firms to both employment and output in the UK still lagged behind that of leading economies such as the USA, Japan and Germany.

Since the 1990s, the UK has had a more average profile compared to its European neighbours, although employment is still slightly more concentrated in larger firms. Figure 1.2 indicates that the UK and Europe (19 states) have a similar profile of numbers of firms with under 50 employees – 98.6 per cent of UK businesses compared to 98.9 per cent of European businesses. However, UK employment is lower than the European average in those firms – 45.9 per cent of the UK workforce compared to 52.1 per cent across Europe. This reflects the higher number of very small firms (including those employing no-one else) in the UK compared to some European countries. Larger firms also have a higher than average share of employment in the UK.

The 'average' business in Europe employs six people. In the UK, it is five. Some countries have a more fragmented profile, such as Greece (average three employees per enterprise), Iceland (three), Italy (four) and Portugal (four).

Other countries are more concentrated, such as Luxembourg (average 12 employees per enterprise), Austria (11), Ireland (11), Netherlands (10), and Germany (8).

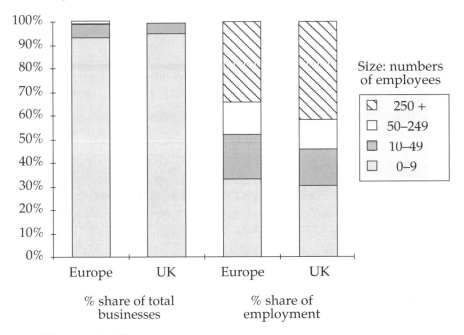

Total firms: 17 million

Source: The European Observatory for SMEs, Annual Report, 1997

Figure 1.2 Profile of European business population

'Europe' here comprises 19 states: the 15 EU members plus Iceland, Liechtenstein, Norway and Switzerland.

❑ **USA and Japan**

Employment in the USA, and to a lesser extent the UK, is still more concentrated in larger companies than the European average and Japan. Table 1.2 compares the percentages of people employed in firms in the USA, UK, Europe and Japan[12]. This shows considerable variation in the percentages employed in smaller (less than 100 employees) and larger firms (over 500 employees). The USA concentrates 49 per cent of its workforce in larger companies whilst Japan has only 26 per cent. In Japan 56 per cent of people work in firms of less than 100 employees, close to the European average, but more than in the USA and UK.

Table 1.2 International comparisons of employment by firm size

	Share of national employment by size of firm		
Numbers employed in firm	Less than 100	100 to 499	Over 500
USA	37%	14%	49%
UK	47%	18%	35%
Europe	55%	16%	29%
Japan	56%	18%	26%

Source: Storey, D. Understanding the Small Business Sector[12]

One trend that has emerged in recent years is that small firms are getting smaller. Although the overall numbers of businesses have tended to stabilise in most developed countries, there has been a steady increase in the numbers of firms who employ no other people, or which fall into the micro category of less than 10 employees. Micro enterprises are particularly common in Denmark, France, Ireland and New Zealand, where they make up at least 90 per cent of all businesses[14]. In the UK, there has been an increase in the number of firms comprising only the self-employed owner-manager which now make up over two-thirds of all businesses.

Activity 4 Why the revival?

Why do you think small enterprises have increased in number, reversing the previous decline? List as many contributory factors as you can, before reading on.

4 Interpretations of the small business revival

4.1 Three theories

By the 1980s the small firm found itself at centre stage of a political and economic debate which offered radically different interpretations over its role, and its recent revival. The contenders in this debate have been classified by Goss[15] into three distinct camps.

❐ **Free Market theory**

Right-wing governments in the UK and the USA simultaneously seized upon the small firm as a symbol of the new order of 'Enterprise Culture', which was ushering out an age of collectivism and government economic intervention. President Reagan hailed the small business as the economic saviour of America, whilst Prime Minister Thatcher pronounced them a barometer of freedom, insisting that 'the freer the society, the more small businesses there will be'.

The free market economy promoted by the Right relies on the widespread competition provided by new ventures and smaller companies to prevent the monopolistic distortions of large organisations. Entrepreneurial action, stemming from an 'on your bike', self-sufficient philosophy, is seen as the antidote to the adversity of job loss and regional economic realignment. The virtues of innovation and job creation in small enterprises is contrasted to the lethargy and stagnation of large nationalised industries.

❑ **Marxian analysis**

According to Marxist theory, capitalism degenerates into economies dominated by a small number of monopolistic companies, as society polarises between those that own the large units of production and those that work in them. Far from being inconvenient evidence, the revival of the small firm is explained as part of this inevitable tendency. Small firms represent a subtler form of economic domination by the large firms, and another instrument for the exploitation of labour. Central to this argument is the dependent status of small business on larger organisations which only allow them to thrive when it is more profitable that way.

So, for example, the growth in small firms in the 1980s is seen as part of a strategy by which large firms effectively sub-contract their less profitable activities to smaller firms in difficult times. These can operate on a lower cost base because of their lack of unionisation, and poorer terms and conditions of work. The tendency for small firm formation to increase during recessions illustrates that the core sector of big business is merely using small business as a secondary sector, to cushion itself against market fluctuations. Moreover this secondary sector only survives because it can exploit its unorganised, non-unionised labour with lower pay, poorer working conditions and safety records.

❑ **The Green Movement**

Over-production, bureaucracy, centralisation, and short-term material gain are symptoms of a deepening crisis in industrial society which only a return to a more natural order can reverse. This is the language of many 'alternative' movements which have also put small business to the forefront of their ideology. The 'small is beautiful' slogan of Fritz Schumacher[16] has been taken up, representing the feeling that the quality of life must come before the materialistic motives of big business. Small enterprises are seen as more democratic and responsive to society than large remote organisations following strategies of high growth, which take little account of their effects either on the world environment or local communities.

4.2 Reasons for the small business revival

Whatever the political interpretations, several inter-linking factors have influenced the growth of small businesses:

❐ **Growth of the service sector**

The vast majority of all small firms operate in the service and construction sectors of the economy. Eighty-five per cent of UK firms employing less than 50 people are in services and construction[17], as shown in Table 1.3.

There has been a strong structural shift in the economy away from manufacturing-based industries and towards services; services have expanded to over 70 per cent of GDP (gross domestic product, a measure of the total outputs of an economy). Hence small firms are most active in the most dynamic sector of the economy.

Small firms have competitive advantages in many service sectors, which accounts for their strong representation in this area of business. Many services, such as communication and professional advice services (e.g. advertising, accounting, computer services and other consultancies), rely on a personalised, tailor-made service very suited to the flexibility and responsiveness of small business.

Other services involve consumption at the point of purchase (restaurants, wine bars, free houses), which favours smaller, localised outlets, requiring individual management.

Table 1.3 Small business by sector

	Manufacturing	Construction	Services	Agriculture, mining & energy	
Percentage of small firms (under 50 employees)	8.6%	18.6%	66.9%	5.1%	100% = 3.7 million

Source: SME Statistics for the UK, 2000, *Small Business Service, 2001*

❐ **Information technology**

Many of the new small firms are in the business of providing information services. A key growth area in the formation of new ventures recently has been in computers, the Internet and related services such as web design. As the industry is relatively young, the enterprises involved tend to be small. In the first half of this century, there was an upsurge in the numbers of companies supplying and servicing the new products of that era – motor cars, radios and other electrical goods, chemical and pharmaceutical products. As these industries have matured and consolidated into fewer, larger organisations in the latter part of the century, new technology has provided the opportunity for new enterprise to develop and spread once again. This cyclical view of industrial development infers that the new businesses of today will also tend to amalgamate into larger units as markets mature – until new technologies and other developments give rise to new markets which shift the balance towards smaller businesses again.

❐ **'Flexible specialisation' and networks**

A different interpretation of these trends in the provision of goods and services considers changes to patterns of demand as well as supply. Consumers now expect individual preferences to be catered for in detail as business managers have learned the value of segmenting markets to differentiate their products. A walk down any high street, past shops specialising in socks, expensive chocolates, video games and doorknobs, confirms this point. Fundamental changes have happened in the economy, as the mass production methods of large companies become less appropriate to new patterns of demand.

At the same time new technology has reduced the fixed costs of some manufacturing processes, so that production can profitably be based in smaller, more flexible units. For example, traditional printing methods involved capital intensive equipment, operated by expensive skilled labour, which became very uneconomic for short run, or one-off jobs. New printing technology, with more flexible presses and computerised text setting, has allowed instant printing to flourish by offering shorter economic print quantities, and faster availability.

It has also been claimed that co-operation between networks of specialised small businesses can make them even more competitive. Some 'industrial districts' have emerged in which independent small firms operating in the same geographic area and industrial sector, combine by performing one or two stages of the production process to offer a highly competitive, flexible service. Small firms manufacturing footwear and textiles in Northern Italy and the hi-tech and software companies around Cambridge in the UK have been held up as models of this flexible specialisation approach. These local economic networks of small businesses which can deliver flexibly whilst retaining the economies of larger organisations have been seen by some commentators as the natural successor to the old industrial model which depended on scale economies from the production of standardised products. The limited number and impact of these industrial districts indicate that these high hopes have yet to be fulfilled[18].

However, this 'flexible specialisation' model of economic development implies a long-term trend in favour of small business. Driven by consumer preferences, the marketplace has become increasingly specialised into 'niches' of one-off products and services which small businesses using technological advances can now deliver.

❐ **Sub-contracting and fragmentation**

The cycle of recessions since the early 1980s stimulated a fragmentation of production and services as larger firms reorganised themselves. Leaner and fitter became the watchwords as companies adjusted to the new economic realities. In an effort to reduce fixed costs and develop flexibility to cope with fluctuations in demand, some larger organisations have sub-contracted part of their activities to smaller enterprises. In other cases, large companies have withdrawn altogether from some activities to concentrate on what they see as their core business, selling off or closing down peripheral businesses. This is fundamentally different to the 'flexible specialisation' interpretation as it denies there is a long-term shift towards small business[19]. Large organisations still retain primary control over economic activity but it has served their interests to shift some employment and output to smaller firms. It does not therefore represent a fundamental, long-term realignment of forces in favour of smaller business, but a strategy to increase the profitability and flexibility of larger ones (along the lines of Marxian analysis described in section 4.1). This fragmentation model of industry sees small firms as still very dependent on larger ones.

❐ **Public sector reorganisation**

The public sector in the UK has been subject to constant reorganisations, some of which have provided opportunities for SME involvement. A variety of measures has caused public bodies to open up some of the services they purchase to private sector involvement. The creation of internal markets – a clearer distinction between departments that purchase services and those that provide them – and compulsory competitive tendering for some functions hitherto provided internally, has meant more sub-contracting possibilities for small firms. For example, grounds maintenance and cleaning and catering services in schools and hospitals are now contracted out to the lowest bidder. Independent architects, solicitors, trainers and consultants have all benefited from additional work from public bodies which have cut back their own internal departments previously providing these professional services. Private/public partnerships have been seen as a way to improve the efficiency of the public sector and thereby reduce the burden on taxpayers.

Privatisation and deregulation have become common themes in other economies, too, as governments have considered the levels and effectiveness of public expenditure. For example, New Zealand has gone even further with its radical reforms in the public sector than the UK. First the Labour government from 1984 privatised large parts of the state sector, and then the National Party government from 1990 required central and local government to put more services out to contract to the private sector.

❐ **Unemployment**

The revival of self-employment and small business ownership in developed countries coincided with a period of recession and high levels of unemployment from the late 1970s, through the early 1980s. There does seem to have been a link between the rate of unemployment and entry into business ownership in the UK. Redundancy, especially with a golden handshake, has pushed many reluctant entrepreneurs into self-employment, and provided the stimulus for others who had already considered starting their own business, but were reluctant to give up the security of their employment.

Whilst this does seem to have been a factor in the early 1980s, unemployment has since fallen with little slackening in the rate of new business formations[20].

❐ **The Enterprise Culture**

A rare consensus has emerged in British politics, as all three major political parties have proclaimed their support for a healthy small business sector.

In keeping with their market economy ideology, the Conservative administration which came to power in 1979 introduced a series of measures designed to stimulate new businesses. These ranged from investment incentives to information and advice (see Unit 5, Information and help).

As the revival of the small firm was well under way before 1979, this policy served to further stimulate or prolong growth, not initiate it. But the estimated £1 billion spent by the Exchequer between 1980 and 1985, through over 200 policy measures in support of small firms, clearly had a positive effect on the growth of the sector. The Labour administrations in the 1990s continued these policies with attempts to concentrate fragmented support agencies under the single umbrella of the Small Business Service (SBS).

How far the government has succeeded in establishing an 'enterprise culture', which encourages and values entrepreneurial attitudes and self-employment, is more debatable. One survey[21] found that although young people were very aware of entrepreneurial opportunities they were cautious over the risks involved.

❐ **The New Age**

The growth in numbers of small firms has coincided with an increased awareness of environmental and lifestyle issues, heralded as a 'New Age' in the values of society. Endorsing the philosophies of the Green Movement, people have sought to further the cause through employment. A whole new variety of self-employment possibilities have been created including:

○ practitioners of alternative medicine from reflexology to rolfing massage;

○ health and organic food producers, wholesalers and retailers;

○ trainers, counsellors, writers, publishers and retailers selling courses, books, magazines, video and audio cassettes on 'New Age' themes; and

○ producers and retailers of alternative beauty products.

Whilst no statistics are available on the level of self-employment created by the popularity of these activities, their impact has been noticeable in some small business areas; for example, the growth in number of worker co-operatives is partially explained by 'alternative' movements, (see Unit 8, Legal identities).

Activity 5 A rough ride?

The next section describes the small business sector as 'turbulent'. What do you think is meant by this? How has it affected the growth in small business numbers?

5 A turbulent sector

Although many new enterprises are born every year and others expand, a large number also close and disappear. Small business is a turbulent sector with huge movements in and out. Even in years when the economy is performing relatively well, many firms close as well as start up, as shown in Table 1.4.

Table 1.4 Business start ups and closures, 1997–2000

000s of businesses	1997	1998	1999	2000
Total business stock	3708	3658	3677	3723
Business starts	477	455	438	439
Starts to total stock	12.9%	12.4%	11.9%	11.8%
Business closures	443	389	382	393
Closures to total stock	11.9%	10.6%	10.3%	10.5%

Sources: SME Statistics for the UK 2000, *Small Business Service, 2001*; Barclays Business Starts and Closures Survey, 2001

Every year, large numbers of businesses are born and an almost equally large number disappear. The statistics above indicate that over 400,000 firms start up each year, and a similar number close representing an annual attrition rate of over 10 per cent of the business stock[10]. Small businesses have provided independence and employment for some, but changing fortunes for others. (The factors behind these births and closures are discussed in Unit 3, The small business environment.)

6 Case studies and activities

Case studies *First thoughts*

The use of case studies in this book

The two cases below are about people facing decisions which relate to some of the themes of this Unit. Taken from actual events, the cases in Part I illustrate the process which would-be entrepreneurs might go through before starting up a small business. The story is developed through the five Units of Part I so that each situation can be followed through to subsequent stages. Whilst this continuation of the story may indicate what happened next, do not assume that the decisions described are examples of 'best practice', or that they are the best possible decisions in the circumstances. Your advice may well be wiser!

Case 1 Andrea thinks small

Andrea Clarey had a decision to make about her career. She was the manager in charge of the payroll function in the accounts department of a government authority. Although no formal announcement had been made, it was strongly rumoured that the authority would soon be contracting out more of its central services, and that the payroll would be one of them. When this had happened in other areas, the options for individuals in Andrea's position were usually either to seek transfer to another department within the authority, take redundancy and look for employment elsewhere, or form an organisation to put in a bid for the work that was being contracted out. Andrea had been employed by the authority for a few years and would qualify for some redundancy. However she was a qualified bookkeeper and her management qualities were appreciated by other departmental heads, some of whom had already approached her unofficially to see if she would be interested in moving into their departments. Whilst she liked the security of her monthly pay cheque, pension scheme, health insurance and other benefits, Andrea found her current work lacking in real challenges and she disliked the impersonal, bureaucratic methods of the organisation and its political in-fighting. The independence of running her own business had some real attractions for her, especially if she could win the authority's contract to give her a flying start.

To Andrea's surprise, when she discussed the idea with her husband, John, he was immediately supportive of it.

'Its about time you got out of the rut you're in at work. If I could get a big enough redundancy package I'd join you myself. Quite a few of my colleagues have become self-employed as consultants or specialist suppliers to large organisations. It's a major trend in the way we work – the days of working for large organisations and multinational corporations for life are over. Now we can become entrepreneurs, putting our own ideas into action, creating work for ourselves – not waiting for someone else to do it for us', John said.

'Yes, but I'll be earning less to begin with', Andrea had started to explain when her father came in to see them.

After Andrea outlined her options to him, he took a less sympathetic line towards self-employment. 'It's out of the frying pan into the fire. You'll end up working for a big organisation whatever you do – either as supplier or employee. Either way they stay in control of you, small business or not. The only difference working in a small firm is that you'll get paid less for it, and have to work harder. No unions. No negotiating power if your suppliers want to put up their prices. Big business will have you where they want you.'

Andrea was confused further when she met an old school friend who had started her own business. 'My only advice is don't do it unless you can test the idea in some way to make sure it will work. Otherwise it's just not worth the risk. I am just about making ends meet now, and this is my second attempt. All that I have to show from my first business is a much larger mortgage.'

Andrea began to realise that small business could lead to some big issues.

Case 2 Kit thinks beautiful

Kit Hugos was a sales engineer in a large company supplying electronic components. Previously he had worked for a small business, TronTech, involved in the design and manufacture of specialised electronic circuitry. Although he had enjoyed the flexibility and informality of the working environment, he had become very uncertain of the longer term viability of TronTech after a failed diversification attempt and a struggle for power between the two principal shareholders. Rather than wait for what he considered to be the inevitable collapse of the business, Kit had decided to try a more conventional career in a large 'blue chip' organisation.

But his past re-visited him when Robin Davidson rang one day. He was one of the founders of TronTech, who had evidently been ousted by the other shareholders. 'Are you interested in running your own business?' Davidson asked. 'I want to set up in business again but I need a partner, someone to run the business on a day-to-day basis, as I am going to take a less active role.'

The two agreed to meet to discuss the idea. It had always been Kit's long-term aim to have his own business – but with a difference. He had seen how groups of hi-tech companies in some areas worked together to compete with larger companies. These networks of small firms each provided a complete stage in the production process, but their individuality and small size made them more flexible in responding to customers' requirements. When he explained this concept to Davidson, he was less enthusiastic. 'In principle it's a nice idea. But in my experience it doesn't work as ideally as you describe. There can be co-operation between small firms, but in our industry we still tend to work for larger companies who make and market the final product. It's with them you have to co-operate first and foremost. Anything else is a bonus.'

Kit had another ideal. He wanted his own business to operate in an environmentally friendly way and not use some of the damaging processes he had seen elsewhere. Again Davidson took a more pragmatic approach. 'Sure – as long as it doesn't push our prices up and lose business.'

Kit wondered if small was going to be less than beautiful.

Activities

i) From these two cases draw up a 'balance sheet' of the pros and cons of running a small business. List on one side what you consider to be the positive aspects and on the other, the negative.

ii) Advise Andrea and Kit on what to do next. How should they go about assessing their various options?

iii) If you were in their positions what would your decision be – to stay in large organisations or to make the move into small business?

Extended activity *Food and drink*

The use of extended activities in this book

Below is an activity which, unlike earlier activities, is not designed to be done whilst reading the book or sitting at a desk. It extends beyond the classroom or home as it requires you to investigate the world of small enterprise in your local environment, for example, by investigating your local community and the small businesses within it.

Consider the local community with which you are most familiar. Draw up a list of the types of businesses which provide food and drink to this community. This should include take-away food and drink which is to be consumed in the home or elsewhere, as well as food and drink consumed on the premises. For example, your list should include such categories as supermarkets, fast-food restaurants, off-licences, and other business types.

In each of the categories you have listed, write down the names of some of the businesses actually operating in this category.

Now try to divide them into small or large enterprises (you may also need a medium-sized category).

This data can be used in subsequent activities, so try to include as many local businesses as possible. Now try to answer the following questions:

i)   In each of your categories, which is the predominant business size – small or large? What are the trends in terms of size – towards smaller or larger enterprises?

ii) What are the particular contributions which those small businesses make to the local economy? Are these contributions increasing or decreasing in importance in your experience?

iii) Try and talk to some of the small business owners and ask for their views on the competition they have from larger companies, (for example the corner-shop trader's view of the major supermarkets).

In conclusion

At the end of this Unit it is recommended that you go to Section B, Planning a new venture, and read Step 1.1, Outlining the process.

7 References and further reading

References and further information

1.   Bolton Report, *Committee of Inquiry on Small Firms*, HMSO, Cmnd 4811, 1971.

2.   Wynarczyk, P., Watson, R., Storey, D. J., Short, H. and Keasey, K. *The Managerial Labour Market in Small and Medium-sized Enterprises*, Routledge, 1993.

3.   Curran, J., Blackburn, R. and Woods, A. *Profiles of the Small Enterprise in the Service Sector*, ESRC Centre for Research on Small Service Sector Enterprises, Kingston Polytechnic, 1991.

4.   Curran J. and Stanworth, J. 'The small firm – a neglected area of management' in Cowling, A., Stanworth, M., Bennett, R., Curran, J. and Lyons, P. (eds) *Behavioural Sciences for Managers*, Edward Arnold, 1987.

5. A summary is provided by the London Business School Small Business Bibliography published by the London Business School.

6. For example the *Guardian* carried a 'New Business' section every Monday, edited by Clive Woodcock.

7. Drucker, P. *Innovation and Entrepreneurship*, Heinemann, 1986.

8. Bannock, G. and Daly, M. *Small Business Statistics*, PCP, 1994. This book contains a series of articles of useful statistics on UK small business including numbers, job creation, and bankruptcies.

9. Hakim, C. 'New recruits to self-employment in the 1980s', in *Employment Gazette*, HMSO, June, 1989.

10. Small Business Service *Small and Medium Enterprise (SME) Statistics for the United Kingdom, 1999,* Research and Evaluation Unit, URN 00/92, September 2000. The SBS now provide essential information on the small business sector which can be accessed via their web site on *www.sbs.gov.uk/statistics*

11. Barclays Bank Small Business Bulletin *Barclays Business Starts and Closures Survey,* 2000. Reports can be viewed on the Barclays Bank web site *www.smallbusiness.barclays.co.uk*

12. Storey, D. *Understanding the Small Business Sector*, International Thompson Business Press, 1998. Chapter 2 has a summary of recent international comparisons.

13. Sengenberger, W., Loveman, G. and Priore, M. *The Re-emergence of Small Enterprises: Industrial Re-structuring in Industrialised Countries*, International Labour Organisation, Geneva, 1990.

14. OECD Publications, *OECD Small and Medium Enterprise Outlook,* 2000.

15. Goss, D. *Small Business and Society*, Routledge, 1991. See Chapter 1 'Theories of small business and society'.

16. Schumacher, F. *Small is Beautiful*, Abacus, 1974.

17. Curran, J. *The Role of the Small Firm in the UK Economy*, SBRC, Kingston University, 1997.

18. Curran, J. and Blackburn, R. *Small Business and Local Economic Networks*, PCP, 1994.

19. For a full summary of the debate see Curran, J. and Blackburn, R. (eds), *Paths of Enterprise, The Future of Small Business*, Routledge, 1991.

20. Johnson, S. 'Small Firms and the UK Labour Market', in Curran, J. and Blackburn, R. (eds), *Paths of Enterprise, The Future of Small Business*, Routledge, 1991.

21. Blackburn, R. and Curran, J. *The Future of the Small Firm: Attitudes of Young People to Entrepreneurship*, paper to 12th UK Small Firms Policy and Research Conference, 1989.

Recommended further reading

❏ Carter, S. and Dylan-Jones, D. *Enterprise and Small Business: Principles, Practice and Policy*, FT Prentice Hall, 2000. Chapters 2 & 3.

❏ The Small Business Service and Barclays Bank publish statistics on the SME sector which can be accessed via their web sites on *www.sbs.gov.uk/statistics*, *www.smallbusiness.barclays.co.uk* and *www.businesspark.barclays.com*

❏ Storey, D. J. *Understanding the Small Business Sector*, 2nd edn, International Thompson Business Press, 1998. Chapter 2.

❏ Burns, P. *Entrepreneurship and Small Business*, Palgrave, 2001.

❏ Goss, D. *Small Business and Society*, Routledge, 1991. Chapter 2, 'The Empirical Investigation of UK Small Business'.

2 The entrepreneur and the owner-manager

The success or failure of a small business relies significantly on the people who start and manage it. This Unit looks at the personality and backgrounds of entrepreneurs and owner-managers to see if a model of an ideal 'entrepreneurial type' exists to guide those who wish to enter the small business sector. After considering the definitions of entrepreneur and owner-manager, the Unit explores their personality traits, motivations and backgrounds, before summarising some of the key influences and characteristics in theory and in practice.

Contents

Activity 1 Entrepreneur or owner-manager?

What do you think the terms 'entrepreneur' and 'owner-manager' mean? What do you consider to be the similarities and differences between the terms?

1 Entrepreneur and owner-manager: some definitions

The terms 'entrepreneur' and 'owner-manager' are often used to describe somebody who is engaged in the management of a small business. They are sometimes interchanged as though they have the same meaning: anyone who starts up in business is labelled an entrepreneur, and entrepreneurship is inextricably linked to small business management.

Yet strictly speaking these terms have different meanings. There is great diversity among those engaged in managing small enterprises and, in order to understand them better, it is necessary to define how we label them more clearly.

1.1 'Entrepreneur': a brief history

The word 'entrepreneur' derives from the French, literally meaning someone who 'takes between' or 'goes between'. The earliest use of the term reflected this sense of the 'middleman' who directed resources provided by others. In the Middle Ages, an entrepreneur was someone who managed large projects on behalf of a landowner or the church, such as the building of a castle or a cathedral. In the 17th century the concept was extended to include some element of risk and profit. Entrepreneurs were those who contracted with the state to perform certain duties, such as the collection of revenues or the operation of banking and trading services. As the price was fixed, the entrepreneur could profit – or lose – from their performance of the contract.

Richard Cantillon introduced the word into economic literature in 1734 when he described three types of agents in the economy: the 'landowner' who as the proprietor of land provided the primary resource; 'entrepreneurs', including farmers and merchants who organised resources and accepted risk by buying 'at a certain price and selling at an uncertain price'; and 'hirelings' who rented their services. J. B. Say, a French economist writing in the early 1800s, distinguished between the profits of those who provided capital and the profits of entrepreneurs who used it. He defined an entrepreneur as 'someone who consciously moves economic resources from an area of lower, and into an area of higher, productivity and greater yield'. In other words, the entrepreneur takes existing resources, such as people, materials, buildings and money, and redeploys them in such a way as to make them more productive and give them greater value.

This definition implies changing what already exists; it sees the entrepreneur as an instrument of change, someone who does not seek to perfect, or optimise existing ways of doing things, but searches instead for new methods, and new markets – different ways of doing things. In the mid-20th century, Joseph Schumpeter[1] took up this theme of the entrepreneur as a necessary destabilising force. According to Schumpeter, economic equilibrium, which optimises what already exists, does not create healthy economies. A dynamic economy takes as its norm the disequilibrium brought about by the constant change of innovation and entrepreneurship.

In the 1980s Peter Drucker[2] developed these earlier ideas, seeing the emergence of an entrepreneurial economy in the USA as a 'most significant and hopeful event'. He defined an entrepreneur as someone who 'always searches for change, responds to it, and exploits it as an opportunity'. He thus made innovation a necessary part of entrepreneurship. In doing so, he focused on the management processes involved in what an entrepreneur does. Others have taken up this theme of entrepreneurship as a process, an action-oriented management style which takes innovation and change as the focus of thinking and behaviour[3]. A more recent definition by Hisrich summarises this approach:

> *'Entrepreneurship is the process of creating something different with value by devoting the necessary time and effort, assuming the accompanying financial, psychic, and social risks, and receiving the resultant rewards of monetary and personal satisfaction[4].'*

1.2 Entrepreneurship in different contexts

Entrepreneurship is commonly linked directly to small business management. However, this presents several problems.

❐   Most small business owners do not innovate or seek out change in a continuous or purposeful way in line with more recent definitions of entrepreneurship. Some do of course. There are inventive people – labelled 'boffin business men' by some researchers[5] – who seek to exploit new ideas through commercial activity. But these are the exceptions: most small businesses are founded on existing ideas and practices. The couple that open their own wine bar, the redundant employee who forms a training consultancy or the craftsman who starts up a joinery firm, are all taking risks but only by doing what has been done many times before. They do not necessarily attempt to innovate or seek out change, but base their business on hopes of increased consumption of the same products or services also on offer elsewhere.

Many small firms lack creative spirit. The majority of start ups are based on established industries. Research into the choice of product for a new business in relation to the owner-manager's previous experience showed that the vast majority stuck to the same industry. Only 4 per cent had innovated a new product or technique in one survey[6]. There seems to be a natural tendency to play safe, staying with known business areas, when considering a new business.

Once established, small firms can also lack innovative entrepreneurship. Owner-managers are invariably close to the day-to-day problems of their business as it grows – often too close to see opportunities or the need for change. Small business management can easily become a reactive process in which new ideas are pushed out by the need to cope with more pressing realities. In these circumstances, the entrepreneur has to adapt and react, rather than direct and create. From its innovative origins, entrepreneurship has been watered down to imply adaptability and constant manoeuvring to fit the circumstances of the day. Entrepreneurs have taken on a wheeler-dealer image in which creativity is used only for survival rather than progress.

❑ Entrepreneurs can exist in large as well as small economic units, and in the public as well as the private sector. Small business does not have a monopoly of entrepreneurial talent. There is a perception, to some extent confirmed by research, that small business is more innovative, and therefore more entrepreneurial, than larger organisations. (The role of innovation in small business is discussed more fully in Unit 4, Innovations and the marketplace.) The lack of policy and rules in a small, informal structure can provide a more creative environment than a large, hierarchical organisation. Many large organisations, however, exhibit more sustained entrepreneurial tendencies than small business. Some have deliberately tried to remain entrepreneurial by encouraging managers to innovate rather than administer. Companies such as 3M have a track record of innovative entrepreneurship which is hard to match in any business sector. Because the word entrepreneur has been so linked to small business the term, 'intrapreneur', was coined to describe someone who behaves in an entrepreneurial fashion in a larger organisation. 'Intrapreneurship', or entrepreneurship in an existing business structure, has been encouraged by corporate developments such as 'downsizing' and delegation of powers to smaller, strategic business units (SBUs).

❑ The public services have been through an era of upheaval in how they are managed in many developed economies. The introduction of market forces and increased delegation of management responsibilities have been common themes in these changes, which have tended to encourage more entrepreneurial management behaviour. For example, head teachers of schools in the English state system have a double reason to become more opportunistic and innovative: they have won much more control over the funds allocated to their school, and these funds are mainly dependent on the numbers of pupils they attract – direct incentives to become more entrepreneurial in their marketing activities.

In summary, entrepreneurial activity can be found in many different types of private and non-profit organisations. It is neither exclusive to, nor always present in, small businesses.

1.3 The 'heroic' entrepreneur

Entrepreneurs are frequently presented as heroic individuals. Asked to picture an entrepreneur, we tend to think of an individual who masters the odds stacked against them, single-handedly overcoming traditional barriers until, by sheer force of personality, they manage to change what exists and offer the customer the something different that they really wanted all along. The enterprise culture promoted by successive governments in the UK certainly encouraged this portrayal. Economic policy was developed on the premise that individuals needed only the right environment to become entrepreneurs, and that the economy could be led by heroic individuals whose entrepreneurial talent would lead the way to a new era of growth in British industry. The likes of Richard

Branson and Lord Hanson were seen as examples for small business managers to emulate.

The reality is that whilst large numbers of new small businesses have been started, only a tiny minority will grow into substantial enterprises. Many will cease after only a few years' trading, as the heroic vision fades. The substantial growth in numbers of small businesses has masked an even greater amount of activity in and out of the sector. The growth in overall numbers has only been achieved through a high level of new entrants to small business who quickly returned to other types of employment, or sadly unemployment.

1.4 The owner-manager

The term 'owner-manager' is also commonly used to describe those involved in running a small business. It encapsulates a condition which is typical of many small firms – the predominant role of the owner as manager. The majority of small businesses are very small; of the approximate 3.7 million firms in the UK in 2000, 3.5 million (99 per cent) of them employed only 50 people or less, and 2.6 million (70 per cent) of them employed no-one else (see Unit 1, Table 1.1: Profile of the UK business population). The owners of these firms are predominantly the managers as well, and likely to be the only manager. The 'owner-manager' describes the reality for a large number of small firms which are totally reliant on, and dominated by, their owner.

Although less confusing than 'entrepreneur' to describe small business managers, owner-manager is also a limiting term which implies a uniformity of management which does not exist in practice. Owner-managers are not an homogeneous group which can be easily classified, or expected to behave in certain ways.

Activity 2 Classifying owner-managers

Write down a list of some small businesses that you know or have heard about – it could be a shop, restaurant or service that you use, for example. (The list of local businesses you developed in the Extended activity: Food and drink, Unit 1, may be useful here.) Consider the differences in how the owners run these businesses and their motivations for doing so. How would you classify them as types of owner-managers or entrepreneurs?

2 Types of owner-managers and entrepreneurs

The diversity of types of owner-managers and entrepreneurs has led to many attempts to classify them. Early studies by industrial sociologists[7] simply split them into craftsmen and opportunists, to reflect the different backgrounds and aspirations of these types. More recent work[8] has extended this to three distinct types:

❏ The craftsman – small business owners ranging from joiners to hairdressers who themselves directly provide a product or service, and who enjoy doing it.

❏ The promoter – the archetypal 'wheeler-dealer' who does deals, often starting, growing and selling several different businesses in the pursuit of personal wealth.

❏ The professional manager – the owner who adopts a more structured approach to building an organisation on the lines of a 'little big business'.

This basic typology has been extended by other writers to lengths which indicate the great diversity of small business managers. Figure 2.1 below illustrates a list of entrepreneurial types, adapted from a publication[9] which offers self-assessment profiles to judge the reader's suitability to entrepreneurial activity.

1. Soloist	A self-employed person operating alone, for example in a specific trade or profession.
2. Key partner	One stage on from the soloist, as an autonomous individual, but with a partner in the background, sometimes as a financial backer only.
3. Grouper	Those who prefer working in small groups with other partners who share the decision making; for example craftsmen working in their own firm as equals.
4. Professional	Self-employed experts; e.g. traditional professionals (accountants, solicitors, doctors, architects etc.). Whilst not traditionally considered to be entrepreneurs they do tend to work in small firms.
5. Inventor-researcher	Creative inventors, who may, or may not, have the practical skills to turn creativity into innovation.
6. High-tech	New technological developments have created opportunities for those with the technical expertise, e.g. in computers and Internet developments.
7. Workforce builder	The delegator who manages the labour and expertise of others in an effective way; e.g. in the building trade.
8. Inveterate initiator	The start-up expert who only really enjoys the challenge of initiating new enterprises, then loses interest, often selling the business in order to start another.
9. Concept multiplier	Someone who identifies a successful concept that can be duplicated by others, for example through franchising, or licensing arrangements.
10. Acquirer	Those that prefer to take over a business that already exists, rather than start from scratch.

11. Speculator	There are many property based opportunities to buy and sell at a profit, as well as collectables such as art, stamps and antique furniture which have spawned many dealers as owner-managers of small firms.
12. Turn-about artist	An acquirer who buys small businesses with problems, but which have potential for profit.
13. Value manipulator	An entrepreneur who acquires assets at a low price and who then, through manipulation of the financial structure, is able to sell at a higher price.
14. Lifestyle entrepreneur	Small business is a means to the end of making possible the 'good-life' however this is defined. Consistent cash flow is the primary business requirement rather than high growth which might involve too much time commitment.
15. Committed manager	The small business is regarded as a lifetime's work, something to be built up carefully. Personal satisfaction comes from the process of nurturing the fledgling firm through all its various stages of growth.
16. Conglomerator	An entrepreneur who builds up a portfolio of ownership in small businesses, sometimes using shares or assets of one company to provide the financial base to acquire another.
17. Capital aggregator	A business owner with the necessary financial leverage to acquire other substantial attractive businesses.
18. Matriarch or patriarch	The head of a family-owned business, which often employs several members of the family.
19. Going public	Entrepreneurs who start up in business with the clear aim of achieving a quotation on the stock exchange, usually via an unlisted securities market in the first instance.
20. The alternative entrepreneur	Alternative new age beliefs in a return to simpler, more environmentally sound lifestyles may be expressed in a wish to avoid conventional employment. Commercial activities have developed in areas such as health foods, alternative healing and medicines, alternative beauty products, and new age publications and audiotapes.

Adapted from The Entrepreneur's Complete Self-Assessment Guide, by Douglas Gray[9].

Figure 2.1 Entrepreneurial types

Activity 3 Who becomes a successful entrepreneur?

What does it take to become a successful entrepreneur? Write down a list of personality traits that you would expect to find in a typical entrepreneur. Which do you consider to be the most important characteristics for the successful management of a new venture?

3 The search for the entrepreneurial archetype

3.1 Entrepreneurial traits

Is there a typical person who becomes a successful entrepreneur, an archetype on which we can base our judgements about someone's aptitude to entrepreneurship? Can anyone become a small business manager, or does it require a certain type of person to make it really work? If it does require certain attributes, are they innate or can we acquire them – in other words are successful entrepreneurs and owner-managers born or made?

The influence of the owner-manager on a small business is crucial. Particularly in the early days, enterprises are inseparable from their owner-managers; they are conceived by them, born of their labours, and survive because of their dedication. In later stages of growth, a management team may emerge which makes the enterprise more autonomous, capable of continuity without the originating force.

But it is the owner-manager who has to grow the enterprise to the stage where it has the critical mass to survive as an entity in its own right. As this impact is so vital, it would be very helpful to identify personality types who are more likely to succeed, in order to encourage those who are the right fit and discourage others who do not have the necessary characteristics.

A number of traits or personality characteristics have been put forward as important influences in successful entrepreneurship.

❐ **Need for achievement**

A well-known investigation into the entrepreneurial personality, by McClelland[10], concluded that the driving force is need for achievement. Parental influences are significant in the development of this need for achievement personality. According to this study, entrepreneurs are likely to have parents who expected them to be self-reliant at an early age, whilst remaining supportive and not rejecting of their offspring. An entrepreneur's need for achievement manifests itself in a number of ways:

○ risk taking;

○ confidence of success;

○ desire for independence;

○ energy in pursuing goals;

○ measurement of success by wealth.

◻ **The 'dark side' of entrepreneurship**

Kets de Vries[11] also concluded that family background and experiences were significant in forming an entrepreneurial personality, but from a very different perspective. He painted a picture of hardships endured in childhood which leave an adult troubled by images of the past, leading to low self-esteem, insecurity and lack of confidence. Such people often exhibit driving ambition and hyperactivity, but linked to a non-conformist and rebellious nature. They are thus driven to self-employment through lack of acceptance in conventional employment. The entrepreneur who comes from such a background is therefore driven by a need to escape from their roots, but their aggressive, impulsive behaviour, which does not accept the authority of others, means they have to create their own organisation to succeed. Whilst an inner compulsion may lead to some business success, longer-term problems are likely to emerge as a result of these deviant personality traits.

◻ **Self-determination**

Successful entrepreneurs, according to some research studies, are convinced that they can control their own destinies. Behavioural scientists describe those who believe they have the ability to control their environment as having an *internal locus of control*, compared to others with an *external locus of control* who believe that their lives are dominated by chance and fate. One study[12] concluded that small business survival and success is linked to the internal locus of control beliefs of the owner-managers. The stronger commitment to self-determination has enabled some owner-managers to overcome difficulties which defeated others.

◻ **Risk taking**

Without a significant level of belief in themselves, owner-managers are unlikely to have taken the initial risk of starting their own business. Entrepreneurs are often characterised as risk-takers who instinctively know that gains do not accrue to those who always play safety first.

However, there is debate over the levels of risk taken, which highlights a distinction between the entrepreneur and the owner-manager. At one extreme there is the opportunist entrepreneur who relentlessly pursues every possibility with little regard to the resources available to them at the time. According to the Kets de Vries' version of their personality, this compulsive competitiveness stems from their deep insecurity which drives them to prove themselves time and time again by taking risks. Others might argue that their internal locus of control gives them the self-confidence to take on any challenge.

At the other end of the spectrum is the conservative owner-manager, who took some risk to establish their business, but whose only aim now is to preserve what they have achieved. Risks are to be avoided for this type of small business manager, whose traits match those of an administrator more than an entrepreneur.

In between there are many shades of risk taking, from the reckless to the calculated, which depend on the context as well as an individual's character. A young, unemployed person with no family would be seen as taking less risk in starting a new venture than an older person in a secure job with a family.

☐ **Desire for independence**

A trait which is commonly recognised as prevalent among entrepreneurs and owner-managers alike is their strong desire for independence, the freedom to create their own futures. This can be linked to their internal locus of control: belief in their ability to control their own destiny can lead to a desire for the necessary independence to make it happen their way.

☐ **Innovation**

Definitions developed earlier (in section 1, Entrepreneur and owner-manager: some definitions) singled out innovative activity as a hallmark of entrepreneurship, but not necessarily of the owner-manager. Innovative behaviour according to many commentators is key to the entrepreneurial personality. Can this be learned or are we born with, or without, an ability to innovate? Drucker insists that we can develop our innovation skills.

He regards entrepreneurship and innovation as tasks that can be and should be organised in a purposeful, systematic way. In other words, they are part of any manager's job, whether he or she works in a small or a large enterprise. The entrepreneurial manager is constantly looking for innovations, not by waiting for a flash of inspiration, but through an organised and continuous search for new ideas. Drucker presents entrepreneurs, not as people who are born with certain character traits, but as managers who know where to look for innovation, and how to develop it into useful products or services once they have found it. (See Unit 4 Innovation and the marketplace.)

Drucker's entrepreneurship is not so much a knack that you either have, or you don't, but rather a practice which you constantly follow or you choose to ignore. It can thus be developed, and learned; its core activity is innovation and a continuous, purposeful search for new ideas, and their practical applications.

3.2 Limitations of the trait approach

The attempt to find single personality traits that characterise either entrepreneurs or owner-managers is useful in providing insights into some entrepreneurial types. But although the ideas discussed above do describe certain types of entrepreneurs or owner-managers, none can claim general application. Criticisms of this so-called 'trait approach' include:

☐ Over-emphasis on finding the one key trait which characterises the entrepreneur. Some writers[13] have tried to overcome this problem by looking for clusters of desirable attitudes and behaviours. The most widely-used scale of entrepreneurial activity developed by Covin and Slevin is based around three behavioural dimensions of risk taking, innovation and proactive response[14].

❑ The implication that entrepreneurial traits are formed during childhood, so that the would-be adult entrepreneur either has them, or not, and cannot acquire them later.

❑ The lack of recognition that the needs of a business venture change during its life cycle, and so the characteristics of successful entrepreneurship will likewise change. The personal attributes which can bring a new venture to life are unlikely to be the same as those which can manage it as a more mature business. As a firm grows, other managers have a greater impact on the likelihood of success, as the influence of the original founder diminishes.

In order to overcome some of these criticisms, Chell and others[15] put forward the following profile of the archetypal entrepreneur:

❑ opportunistic;

❑ innovative;

❑ proactive rather than reactive;

❑ high-profile image maker;

❑ restless and easily bored.

Their model also recognised three distinct phases in how an entrepreneur might organise business activities:

❑ post-start up;

❑ established;

❑ professionally managed.

However, the diversity of types of entrepreneurs (who, as we have seen, are not limited to small businesses, nor the private sector) means that there can be no rules without significant exceptions.

Activity 4 Why become an owner-manager?

Why do you think people start their own business? Write down a list of possible motives, indicating which you consider to be positive reasons and those which you consider to be more negative.

4 Motivations for starting a business

Some of the reasons for the difficulties in classifying those involved in small business management is the wide variety of motives for their involvement in small firms. The reasons for small firm formation can be divided between 'pull' and 'push' influences[16].

4.1 'Pull' influences

Some individuals are attracted towards small business ownership by positive motives such as a specific idea which they are convinced will work. Pull motives include:

❒ *Desire for independence:* this features prominently in several research studies[16] as the key motivator. The Bolton Report singled out the need to gain and keep independence as a distinguishing feature of small business owner-managers. A study of female entrepreneurs in Britain found that women were motivated particularly by the need for autonomy, which had been frustrated by the individuals' prior training and background[17].

❒ *Desire to exploit an opportunity:* the identification of a perceived gap in the marketplace through personal observation or experience is also a common reason for starting a business. For example, a study of new manufacturing firms in South Hampshire[16] reported that 60 per cent of founders quoted their desire to exploit a perceived market. Whilst other studies have shown lower percentages, the wish to satisfy a perceived market gap remains a powerful motive. Entrepreneurs may seek to exploit this opportunity through specialist knowledge, product development or they may hire the appropriate technology and skills.

❒ *Turning a hobby or previous work experience into a business:* many new entrepreneurs seek fulfilment by spending more time involved in a cherished hobby, or part of their work that they particularly enjoy. Although research confirms that founders tend to establish businesses in activities of which they have direct prior experience, this is often precipitated by a push motive, such as redundancy (see 4.2 below), rather than part of a considered decision process.

❒ *Financial incentive:* the rewards of succeeding in your own business can be high, and are well publicised by those selling 'how to succeed' guides to would-be entrepreneurs. The promise of long-term financial independence can clearly be a motive in starting a new firm, although it is usually not quoted as frequently as other factors.

4.2 'Push' influences

Many people are 'pushed' into founding a new enterprise by a variety of factors including:

❒ *Redundancy:* this has proved a considerable push into entrepreneurship particularly when accompanied by a generous handshake in a locality where other employment possibilities are low.

❒ *Unemployment (or threat of):* job insecurity and unemployment varies in significance by region, and by prevailing economic climate. A study reported that 25 per cent of business founders in the late 1970s were pushed in this way, whilst later research showed a figure of 50 per cent when unemployment nationally was much higher[16].

❏ *Disagreement with previous employer:* Uncomfortable relations at work has also pushed new entrants into small business.

The dividing line between those pulled and those pushed is often blurred. Many people considering an opportunity or having a desire for independence still need some form of push to help them make their decision.

What is clear is that the diversity of motivations for starting a business will influence the owner-manager once they have set up. For example, the desire for independence may inhibit growth, as this can be seen as a threat to autonomy; once a firm becomes less than small it might take on some of the characteristics of larger organisations from which the owner-manager is trying to escape. Entrepreneurial tendencies to develop the business through new opportunities may therefore conflict with an owner-manager motivation to retain control by remaining small.

Activity 5 Origins of the owner-manager

Are some origins and backgrounds more likely to produce entrepreneurs or induce self-employment than others? Give your responses to the possible factors below before reading on.

❏ Age: which age group most commonly enters self-employment or owner-management?

❏ Gender: are men or women more likely to start a small business?

❏ Marital status: does marriage help or hinder owner-management?

❏ Social class: which social class provides most owner-managers?

❏ Education: are owner-managers above or below average education levels?

❏ Ethnicity: which ethnic group has the highest propensity towards self-employment in the UK?

5 Owner-manager backgrounds

There has been considerable research interest recently into the backgrounds of owner-managers. Whilst the results for the UK reveal some interesting overall trends, there are significant differences common to owner-managers in different industry sectors.

❏ **Age**

There seems to be two age-windows for self-employment and owner-management: the first is in the 35 to 50 age group and the second after normal retirement at 65[18]. It seems that owner-managers need the experience, stable background and capital assets (especially home ownership) that is more likely to come with middle-age – over 40 per cent of the self-employed are in the 35 to 50 age range.

The post retirement peak is caused by twin influences: the self-employed needing to continue working past retirement because of pension insufficiencies; and the employed who wish to work but who are compulsorily retired from their jobs.

Types of enterprise will influence age ranges, however. Recent research into the profiles of small enterprises in different service sectors found that younger sectors such as computer services and video hire attracted relatively younger owner-managers, whereas established business types such as plant and equipment hire, free houses, wine bars and restaurants were owned by relatively older managers[19].

❑ **Gender**

Women are under-represented in small business ownership. Although they represent over 40 per cent of the employed workforce in the UK, they account for only a quarter of the self-employed, and under 25 per cent of small business owners who employ others[17]. Recently women have been entering self-employment at nearly twice the rate of men, but mostly without employees so the ratio of male to female owner-managers who employ others has not changed significantly. Women are much more likely to go into service sector enterprises than manufacturing, being strongly represented in such businesses as employment, secretarial and training agencies.

❑ **Marital status**

Marriage, it would seem, is good for small business ownership as single people are less likely to be owner-managers or self-employed than those who are married. This reflects not only the more mature age range of small business owners, but also the possibilities of either husband–wife teams in business partnership, or one supporting the other whilst a new venture is formed.

❑ **Social and class backgrounds**

The lower middle-classes provide more small business owners than other social backgrounds. This is partly explained by attempts at upward mobility by manual and routine white collar employees, who may see self-employment as the means for advancement in society, especially if they lack formal educational qualifications.

It is also influenced by the fact that those born into families of small business owners tend to follow in their parents' footsteps. This overall trend is however subject to considerable variation by types of business; longer established forms of small enterprise such as free houses, wine bars and restaurants are much more likely to be owned by the children of self-employed parents, than more recent types of small business such as advertising and computer services[19].

❑ **Education**

There is a traditional view that small business management requires an aptitude for practical activities in which formal educational qualifications are less relevant. In this sense owner-management was seen as an alternative route for advancement for those who had more practical and less academic skills. The

Bolton Report[20] quoted data which supported this view by suggesting that small business owner-managers were less well educated than the average in the population. Recent research has painted a much more complicated picture, as this qualification gap seems to have significantly narrowed, with changing attitudes towards small business and the growth of knowledge-based small enterprises in the service sectors. Owner-managers involved in high-tech industries such as computer services, or those in marketing and design sectors, are likely to be well qualified with A level or equivalent qualifications, or degrees[19].

❏ **Ethnicity**

Some ethnic minorities turn to self-employment and entrepreneurial activities because of inequality of opportunity in the jobs market. Whilst research[18] has generally confirmed this view, there are significant variations among non-white groups. Those of Afro-Caribbean origin in fact have a self-employment rate of about half that for Whites, whilst those from the Indian sub-continent have a self-employment rate of about twice that of Whites. Those originally from the Mediterranean region are top of the list, representing the group with the highest propensity towards self-employment.

Activity 6 Branson vs Sugar

Read the brief portraits of Richard Branson and Alan Sugar below. List the similarities and contrasts in their personal backgrounds and approach to business. Can you make any generalised comments about what makes a successful entrepreneur from these examples? (If possible read more about these and other fascinating entrepreneurs in articles or books – see References 21 and 22.)

6 Towards successful entrepreneurship

6.1 Portraits of the entrepreneur as a young man

The history of well-known owner-managers can provide clues and inspiration for those that wish to follow the entrepreneurial path. But their backgrounds and characteristics exhibit many contrasts, as well as similarities, as these two examples of well-known British entrepreneurs illustrate.

❏ *Richard Branson*[21] was born in 1950 into the privileged classes of the English establishment. Three generations of judges on his father's side laid the foundations for his secure and comfortable early years in a leafy Surrey village. He showed little inclination for academic studies during his years at private boarding schools and he left with 6 O levels at the age of 17 to start his first venture, which was the magazine *Student*. An extrovert with a liking for practical jokes and a flair for publicity, Branson has proven to be a restless entrepreneur. After the success of Virgin Music, he sold the company in 1992 to concentrate on his airline, Virgin Atlantic. He has been involved in ventures as diverse as commercial radio, video games, condoms and insurance, and has experienced failure – for example, movies produced by Virgin Visions, the sinking of his powerboat, Challenger 1, in its attempt on the Blue Riband, and an embarrassing public flotation and private repurchase of Virgin shares – as well as his much publicised successes. He has become as well known for his personal exploits as for his business ventures. Branson thrives on public recognition and his smile and dress habits are as recognisable as any filmstar's.

☐   *Alan Sugar*[22] was born in 1947 into a working-class Jewish family in Hackney, in London's East End. The devastation of the war and the aftermath of rationing and shortages made his childhood on a council housing estate tough and devoid of luxuries. His father was a semi-skilled worker in the garment trade, a very insecure job where lay-offs without pay at a moment's notice were common. After failing his 11+ exam for a state grammar school, Sugar attended a secondary technical school where he was described by his teachers as quiet, introverted and 'very average'. He left at 16 with a few O levels to become a civil servant in the statistics department of the Ministry of Education and Science. His entrepreneurial inclinations soon led him out of this bureaucratic environment to a job selling tape recorders, and then into his own one-man business selling car aerials and other electrical goods to London retailers. Through Amstrad (Alan Michael Sugar's Trading Company) he developed a consistent formula which made him Britain's most successful seller of electrical consumer goods: design simple products by cutting out unwanted features, have them produced by the cheapest source of supply world-wide, and use large-scale advertising campaigns and extensive distribution to develop mass markets for them. He became an icon for popular capitalism in the 1980s through his self-confident belief in value-for-money goods, made possible by hard work and lack of frills – a reflection of his own values and lifestyle. He has developed a love–hate relationship with established institutions from the City of London to the Football Association through his attitude towards anyone whom he believes owes their position to privilege rather than to hard work, or to working the system rather than making a valid contribution to it. Few lifestyle changes followed his growth in personal wealth as he prefers personal privacy to the company of the rich and famous.

Investigations into the types, characteristics and backgrounds of entrepreneurs and owner-managers reveal a very mixed picture. Clearly, there is no simple answer to the question: 'What makes the difference between really successful entrepreneurs and run of the mill owner-managers?'

6.2 The model entrepreneur

Whilst no clear 'identikit' of a successful entrepreneur emerges, a list of skills and characteristics which form the 'building blocks' of successful entrepreneurship can be attempted. Figure 2.2 below summarises these into three categories of technical skills, management competencies and personal attributes. Whilst it can be argued that technical skills and management competencies are required in any context, most commentators agree that the difference between the successful entrepreneur and the also-rans lies in the area of personal attributes.

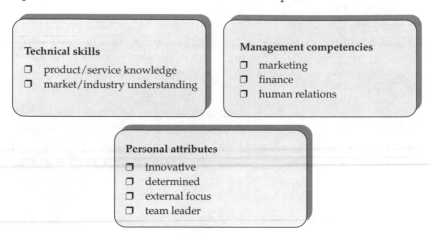

Technical skills

❏ product/service knowledge
❏ market/industry understanding

Management competencies

❏ marketing
❏ finance
❏ human relations

Personal attributes

❏ innovative
❏ determined
❏ external focus
❏ team leader

Figure 2.2 The building blocks of successful entrepreneurship

❏ **Technical skills**

Technical skills relate to an understanding of the products or services on offer and the market and industry environment in which they exist. Whilst the successful entrepreneur may not be a technical expert in their chosen field, they have an intuitive feel for their chosen marketplace and develop business relationships with those who do have the necessary expertise.

❏ **Management competencies**

Management competencies relate to managing key functions of the enterprise. Research indicates that problems in young firms are most likely to arise in the areas of marketing, finance and the management of people, (see Unit 10, Successful small business strategies, for a fuller discussion). The competency to deal with these areas depends particularly on the entrepreneur in the early years of their venture when they are less likely to employ specialists. The model entrepreneur has all-round competency in these key management functions.

❏ **Personal attributes**

Personal attributes make the difference between entrepreneurial and other styles of management and form the basis of a successful approach to owner-management. They cover many of the areas already discussed:

○ *Innovative*: innovation is needed if a business is to develop that is different from the competition, and continues to seek advantages over other firms. This requires a constant search for tangible benefits for the customer, not just in terms of new products or services, but more efficient and effective ways of making them available in the marketplace.

Characteristics which help innovation include the creativity to spot new ideas, allied to a practical and adaptable mind which can convert them to productive use.

As new ideas are unlikely to be immediately successful, the entrepreneur needs the conviction to cope with failure, and the shrewdness to minimise its impact on the survival chances of the enterprise.

○ *Determined*: a common motive which pulls entrepreneurs into a small business is a desire for independence and control over their own destinies. To succeed, this needs translating into a single-minded determination to ride the inevitable ups and downs which this freedom brings. Such resolve and commitment give the necessary motivation and self-belief to cope with the inevitable risks, hard work and failures that follow. It demonstrates itself in an enthusiasm to make the enterprise succeed, and a determination to organise the resources necessary for success. It also manifests itself in the high energy levels and pro-active, rather than reactive, decision making which flow from a sense of purpose and personal motivation.

It has been suggested that innovation, the first of the key entrepreneurial influences, sometimes stems from an 'unreasonable conviction based on inadequate evidence'. This flavour of energetic perseverance and decisiveness flows from a whole-hearted determination to make an enterprise work.

○ *External focus*: entrepreneurs who start a successful venture, and continue to grow it, maintain an external focus in what they do. The pressure on owner-managers in the early years is on the day-to-day running of the enterprise. This may become so all-consuming that they take their eye off the external environment as they concentrate on internal operations and become internally focused.

An external focus maintains the foresight to identify and exploit new opportunities on a continuous basis. It helps retain flexibility in the face of changing market forces.

It may manifest itself as a network of acquaintances and contacts in the trade, an aptitude for selling and personal contact with customers, or a high image profile which draws new ideas and concepts to the entrepreneur. Alan Sugar developed new electrical products, not from formalised research into consumer needs, but through his knowledge of the trade which he built up whilst selling to retailers. Richard Branson was presented with the plans for Virgin Atlantic by Randolph Fields, who developed the idea following the collapse of Laker Airways in 1982 and thought Branson would be the best person to exploit his concept.

However they receive their ideas, successful entrepreneurs like Sugar and Branson never forget that the marketplace is full of opportunities.

○ *Team leader*: whilst some owner-managers seem lonely figures relying only on their own abilities, successful entrepreneurs know that long-term growth relies on leading a team of people who influence the enterprise.

The lone owner-manager is unable to develop a business beyond a certain size, if it is reliant totally on his or her efforts. Effective delegation, and training of others are important prerequisites for sustained growth.

The team does not stop at the internal members of an enterprise; other stakeholders in the business, such as financial backers, banks, suppliers, key customers, the immediate family of both entrepreneur and employees all exert an influence which have to be managed and encouraged in positive directions. The entrepreneur requires leadership qualities to maintain this team, supporting the individuals within it, to ensure successful outcomes for the tasks in hand.

6.3 The realities of owner-management and networking

In practice owner-managers are highly unlikely to exhibit all of these skills and characteristics. Some have inadequate technical skills when they start up; many are lacking management competency in key areas. Most do not constantly seek new opportunities through innovation. Their determination is variable, as the large-scale movements in and out of small businesses and self-employment show. The external focus required to set up a successful enterprise is soon forgotten in the daily details of running it. Autocratic styles rather than team leadership are more common, with most small firms remaining very small (with under five employees). The heroic, high growth entrepreneur is a rare species, indicating that most owner-managers need help and support in order to survive.

The idea of *networking*, in which owner-managers give each other mutual support, collaborate with larger organisations and gain assistance from local institutions such as Chambers of Commerce and Business Links, has been put forward as a way of dealing with these deficiencies[23]. Personal contact networks (PCNs) – the relationships and alliances which individuals develop with others – are particularly useful to managers who have few, or no, colleagues internally that they can turn to for consultation and advice. PCNs can work well for owner-managers who collect information and make decisions in a relatively unstructured, intuitive way. Inter-organisational relationships (IORs) are an obvious route for small enterprises which do not have the resources to accomplish their objectives alone. Whilst the number of support bodies available to owner-managers has increased substantially in recent years, the advantages of these networks have been minimised by another characteristic of small business owners: they are not joiners, preferring to keep themselves and their business problems to themselves. (Networking is discussed further in Units 4, 10 and 12.)

7 Case studies and activities

Case studies *Making it personal*

Case 1 Andrea's strengths

Andrea Clarey was finding the first stage towards setting up her own business both unexpected and difficult. She had decided to take the plunge by taking redundancy from her local government employer and setting up her own payroll service. Excited by her decision, she had begun to write a list of everything she needed to do from buying equipment to registering a company. She decided to visit a small business advisor to help her with some of the details. His advice about what to do first surprised her: 'Your first step towards self-employment should be self-analysis. Start by writing down what you consider to be your personal strengths and weaknesses. Then test your conclusions by asking other people if they agree – we can fool ourselves sometimes,' he had advised her.

Andrea had always found critical self-evaluation difficult and was reluctant to follow his advice. 'I wonder what good this navel-gazing can do', she thought. 'I'd rather just get on with the job.' She had worked in payroll services for over 10 years in various types of public bodies from an education department to a local council. When she had left school at 17, she drifted through several clerical jobs until she married a few years later and started a family. Returning to work when her two children entered school, she realised that she needed more formal qualifications and studied bookkeeping on a part-time basis in the evening. Despite the pressures of raising a young family and an increasingly demanding job, she was determined to have at least one qualification to her name. This was partly to compensate for disappointing examination results at school where she had found most subjects too academic and lacking in practical application.

'My strengths are fairly obvious', Andrea thought. 'I know the payroll system inside out, and I know the public services which will provide me with at least two-thirds of the business I need to set up. I enjoy working with other people – as long as it doesn't involve too many meetings or time-wasting chitchat. My staff have always stuck by me – I think I know how to manage my department well. But what are my weaknesses?'

Case 2 Kit's weakness

Kit Hugos had not given too much thought to the invitation from his former employer, Robin Davidson, to set up in business on their own. He had agreed almost immediately. 'What are the next steps?' he asked after agreeing in principle to become co-owner and managing director of a new electronics business. 'First we need to raise more money than I suspect we have between us', said Davidson. 'And to do that we need a business plan, which I have already begun to draft. One section you need to write is some details about yourself – career to date, personal strengths, that sort of thing. Banks and investors always seem to ask for it so we may as well be prepared. You joined TronTech straight from University didn't you?'

'More or less,' replied Hugos. 'Although I did do some research in the electronic engineering department first. I had some interesting ideas in the field of circuit miniaturisation and the University said I should register for a postgraduate degree – they even offered me a place as a Ph.D. student. But I couldn't get any grant, and my parents couldn't support me. So I came to work for you instead. I had hoped to follow up my ideas at TronTech, but you gave me too much work to do!'

'What would you cite as your strengths then?' asked Davidson.

'I'm ambitious, work hard and know the electronics trade, especially from a sales perspective.' He went on to explain that since leaving TronTech four years previously he had worked for three larger electronic companies in sales or technical support. 'I enjoy selling', he explained. 'You can work on your own without worrying about who to watch or who's watching you. And I have built up lots of good contacts on my travels – in and out of the industry.'

'Yes, quite a few people have mentioned seeing you at exhibitions and conferences. Any weakness that potential investors may pick up on?' Davidson asked.

'I'll need some financial training as I've always been hopeless at budgeting. And I can lose my temper faster than some. What do you think?'

Activities

i)   Why did Andrea's small business advisor start with self-analysis? Why is it important to Davidson's bankers and investors?

ii) Summarise Andrea's and Kit's strengths and weaknesses in relation to the technical skills, management competencies and personal attributes which they may need as owner-managers (see section 6.2 The model entrepreneur).

iii) How would you rate their chances of success in running a small business? What training or personal development needs would you suggest for each?

iv) Once they have completed their critical self-analysis, what should they do next?

Extended activity *Local entrepreneurs and owner-managers*

Consider some small businesses with which you are familiar, and their owners and managers. (If you completed the Extended activity in Unit 1 you can use the list of small businesses you drew up for that.)

i)   Which do you consider to be entrepreneurial? What sets them apart from other small businesses in respect of their entrepreneurship?

ii) Considering the owners, can you guestimate their ages, gender, marital status, social backgrounds, likely education and ethnicity? How do these compare to the information given in Unit 2, 5, Owner-manager backgrounds?

iii) What do you consider were the main influences which pushed or pulled these owners to set up their own business?

To answer these questions in detail it is preferable to interview some owner-managers. Where this is not possible, observation and previous knowledge can reveal a considerable amount of information.

In conclusion

At the end of this Unit, it is recommended that you go to Section B, Planning a new venture, and undertake Step 1.2, 'Know thyself'.

8 References and further reading

References and further information

1. Schumpeter, J. *The Theory of Economic Development*, Harvard University Press, 1934.

2. Drucker, P. *Innovation and Entrepreneurship*, Heinemann, 1986.

3. Cunningham, J. and Lischeron, J. 'Defining Entrepreneurship', *Journal of Small Business Management*, 29(1), 1991.

4. Hisrich, R. and Peters, M. *Entrepreneurship*, Irwin, 1995.

5. See Storey, D. *Entrepreneurship and the New Firm*, Croom Helm, 1982.

6. Binks, M. and Jennings, A. 'New Firms as a Source of Industrial Regeneration', in Scott, M., Gibb, A., Lewis, J. and Faulkner, T. (eds), *Small Firms' Growth and Development*, Gower, 1986.

7. Smith, N. *The Entrepreneur and His Firm: The Relationship between Type of Man and Type of Company*, Michigan State University Press, 1967.

8. See a summary by Hornaday, R. 'Dropping the E-words from Small Business Research', *Journal of Small Business Management*, 28(4), 1990.

9. Gray, D. *The Entrepreneur's Complete Self-Assessment Guide*, Kogan Page, 1987.

10. McClelland, D. *The Achieving Society*, Van Nostrand, 1961.

11. Kets de Vries, M. 'The Dark Side of Entrepreneurship', *Harvard Business Review*, Nov–Dec, 1985.

12. Brockhaus, R. and Horwitz, P. 'The Psychology of the Entrepreneur', in Sexton, D. and Smilor, R. (eds), *The Art and Science of Entrepreneurship*, Ballinger, 1986.

13. Timmons, J. *New Venture Creation*, Irwin, 1990.

14. Covin, J. G. and Slevin, D. P. (1988) 'The Influence of Organizational Structure on the Utility of an Entrepreneurial Top Management Style', *Journal of Management Studies*, 25, pp. 217–37.

15. Chell, E., Haworth, J. and Brealey, S. *The Entrepreneurial Personality: Concepts, Cases and Categories*, Routledge, 1991.

16. See Mason, C. and Lloyd, P. 'New Manufacturing Firms in a Prosperous UK Sub-region: The Case of South Hampshire', and Binks, M. and Jennings, A. 'New Firms as a Source of Industrial Regeneration', both in Scott, M., Gibb, A., Lewis, J. and Faulkner, T. (eds), *Small Firms' Growth and Development*, Gower, 1986.

17. See 'Labour Market Trends' from the Office of National Statistics. Also Watkins, D. and Watkins, J. 'The Female Entrepreneur in Britain', in Scott, M., Gibb, A., Lewis, J. and Faulkner, T. (eds), *Small Firms' Growth and Development*, Gower, 1986.

18. Curran, J., and Burrows, R. *Enterprise in Britain: A National Profile of Small Business-Owners and the Self-Employed*, Small Business Research Trust, 1988.

19. Curran, J., Blackburn, R. and Woods, A. *Profile of the Small Enterprise in the Service Sector*, ESRC Centre for Research on Small Service Sector Enterprises, Kingston Business School, 1991.

20. Bolton Report, *Committee of Inquiry on Small Firms*, HMSO, Cmnd 4811, 1971.

21. See Brown, M. *Richard Branson, The Inside Story*, Headline, 1992.

22. See Thomas, D. *Alan Sugar, The Amstrad Story*, Pan Books, 1991.

23. Carson, D., Cromie, S., McGowan, P. and Hill, J. *Marketing and Entrepreneurship in SMEs*, Prentice Hall, 1995.

Recommended further reading

❏ Carter, S. and Dylan-Jones, D. *Enterprise and Small Business: Principles, Practice and Policy*, FT Prentice Hall, 2000. Chapters 8, 10 and 11.

❏ Chell, E. *Entrepreneurship, Globalisation, Innovation and Development*, Thomson Learning, 2000.

❏ Chell, E., Haworth, J. and Brealey, S. *The Entrepreneurial Personality: Concepts, Cases and Categories*, Routledge, 1991.

❏ Burns, P. *Entrepreneurship and Small Business*, Palgrave, 2001. Chapters 2 and 3.

❏ Hisrich, R. and Peters, M. *Entrepreneurship*, Irwin, 1995.

❏ Goss, D. *Small Business and Society*, Routledge, 1991. Chapter 3.

❏ Brown, M. *Richard Branson, The Inside Story*, Headline, 1992.

❏ Thomas, D. *Alan Sugar, The Amstrad Story*, Pan Books, 1991.

3 The small business environment

Survival rates amongst small businesses are low and so it is important to understand which factors in the environment influence the likelihood of success. After considering the influences on the births and closures of small firms, this Unit investigates why some environments are more hostile than others and which external factors are critical for survival.

Contents

Activity 1 External influences

Which external factors in the small business environment will influence:

a)   the likelihood of a new venture starting up?

b)   its chances of survival thereafter?

51

1 A matter of life and death

In Unit 1 we saw that small businesses form a turbulent part of the national economy because of the large-scale movements in and out of the sector. Many new ventures are created every year but an almost equally large number of businesses close.

In Unit 2 we considered the backgrounds and personalities of entrepreneurs and owner-managers whose skills and characteristics play such a significant role in determining the fate of these businesses. They provide the motive force for the establishment of a new venture, and strongly influence how it is managed thereafter.

In this Unit, we consider factors in the business environment which affect the births and deaths of small firms but which are to some extent beyond the control of the owner-managers.

It is a combination of these less controllable, external factors together with the more controllable, internal factors, arising from the personal attributes and skills of the owner-manager, which influence:

❐ The likelihood of a new firm starting up – there are many environmental as well as personal influences on the formation of small firms.

❐ Its chances of survival – once established it is vulnerable to circumstances beyond its control as well as the possibility of internal mis-management.

This is illustrated in Figure 3.1.

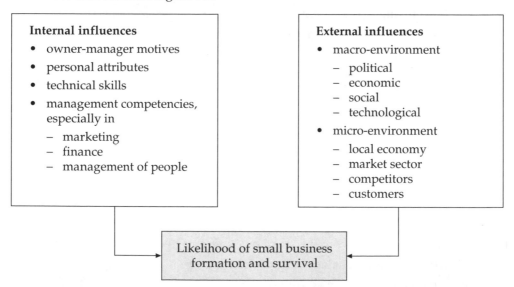

Figure 3.1 Influences on small firm formation and survival

Internal influences stem from the motivations, attributes, skills and competencies of the owner-manager(s) who sets up the business in the first instance. As we saw in Unit 2, motives vary from those which 'pull' someone into starting their own business, such as a desire for independence, to other motives which 'push' a person into self-employment, such as the lack of employment alternatives elsewhere. Once set up, the personal attributes, skills and competencies of the owner largely determine how the firm is managed in crucial functional areas. A review of research into the management problems faced by young, small firms revealed that they experience problems particularly in the areas of marketing, accounting and finance, and the management of people[1]. (See Unit 2, Figure 2.2; we shall return also to this theme in Unit 10, Successful small business strategies.)

External influences can be considered in two main categories: the macro- and micro-environment.

❑ The macro-environment consists of factors which tend to have an impact on all firms nationally and sometimes internationally. It includes:

  ○ political and regulatory factors, such as levels of taxation and health and safety regulations;

  ○ economic conditions such as the rate of inflation or levels of unemployment;

  ○ social and demographic influences such as the age profile of the population;

  ○ technological changes, for example, in information handling and communications.

❑ The micro-environment refers to more local factors which influence particular firms. It includes:

  ○ local socio-economic conditions, such as the relative prosperity and population profile of a specific catchment area;

  ○ the market development of a particular sector or industry;

  ○ the competitive environment;

  ○ customer needs and the structure of demand for individual products and services.

These factors are obviously dynamic – their impact changes over time. They do not necessarily apply in the same way to the formation of new ventures as they do to their likelihood of survival. Some factors which are crucial to the setting up of a small business may not be such a significant consideration in whether or not it survives[2]. We shall therefore consider the 'births' and 'deaths' of small businesses separately in the following sections.

Activity 2 Birth rates

The birth rates of new firms vary considerably according to the time period, location and the industrial or market sector in which they are set up. Can you give examples of when, where and in which sectors you would expect to see high rates of small business births?

2 The birth of new businesses

2.1 Data on business births

In the 1980s new businesses were born at an average rate of over 200,000 per year in the UK, and over 600,000 in the USA. Although these birth rates were considered high, they have increased since; currently nearly two million new businesses are born each year in Europe, of which 450,000 are in the UK[3]. This high birth rate means that a significant percentage of the total stock of firms in the economy are very young: in any one year, between 10 and 20 per cent of all businesses are probably less than one year old[4].

The rates of new business formation are by no means uniform[5]. Birth rates of small firms vary according to:

- ○ *When* – the time period in which they are set up.
- ○ *Where* – the geographic location.
- ○ *Which sector* – the industrial or market sector in which they are set up.

❑ *When:* birth rates vary over time. In the UK, birth rates were relatively low in the 1960s and 70s but grew rapidly in the 1980s. They seem to have been highest in 1981–2 and in 1988–9, then dropped between 1989 and 1991. Rates increased again to a peak of over 475,000 in 1996, and have since stabilised at around 440,000 new business starts each year[2] (see Table 3.1).

❑ *Where:* births also vary according to location. Rates differ by geographic regions both across national boundaries and within more local areas. Within Europe some countries have higher rates of new business formation than others: Denmark and the UK have had relatively high rates and Portugal and Holland relatively low rates. Within the UK, London and the South East accounted for 145,000 new businesses (a third of all start ups) in 2000, but this represented a decline over the 1995 figure of 172,000 new businesses, (36 per cent of all new start ups). Other areas are now growing more rapidly; for example, business starts in the South West have grown from 49,000 in 1995 to 59,000 in 2000; the North recorded 21,000 starts in 1995, and 24,000 in 2000[3].

❑ *Which sector:* some business sectors attract more new firms than others. Table 3.1 illustrates some of the differences and trends by industry sectors. For example, the production, wholesale and transport sectors have reported declines in new businesses over recent years, whereas property and catering firms are increasingly popular start ups.

The reasons behind these differences ought to be of interest to would-be entrepreneurs as they give clues as to when, where and in what sector they should consider setting up their venture.

Table 3.1 Business start ups by industry sector, 1998–2000

	000s of firms		
Sector	*1998*	*1999*	*2000*
Production	84	70	68
Wholesale	11	9	9
Transport	16	15	14
Retail	82	81	83
Property/Finance	11	13	18
Catering	27	28	29
Motor trades	30	24	25
Construction	34	28	31
Business and professional	70	81	77
Government/community	27	26	26
Leisure services	61	61	59
TOTAL (England and Wales)	455	438	439

Source: Barclays Bank Small Business Bulletin, Barclays Business Starts and Closures Survey, *2000*

2.2 When to set up

Small firms are most vulnerable in their early years. Research suggests that nearly one half cease trading within the first three years, and between 15 and 20 per cent do not even last one year[3]. The timing of business closures is strongly affected by movements of the economic cycle; one year survival rates were higher in 2000, a year of relative economic prosperity, than they were a decade earlier in the recessionary years of the late 1980s and early 1990s. Therefore, in order to have the best possible chance of long-term survival, a new venture is best formed at a time when economic conditions are most helpful. Established firms have a much better chance of surviving recessions than young firms whose vulnerable early years need the benefit of a favourable business climate[6].

In a review of research into influences on the timing of new business births, Storey[2] identified several possible factors:

❐ *Levels of unemployment.* As we saw in Unit 2, unemployment, and lack of alternative employment possibilities, is an important factor which pulls people into self-employment and so times of relatively high unemployment are associated with higher rates of new firm formations.

❐ *Government policies.* Successive governments in the UK and elsewhere have introduced measures such as the Enterprise Allowance Scheme to encourage new business start ups; (these and other aspects of government policy are described more fully in Unit 5, Information and help).

❐ *Profitability.* When income from self-employment is higher, more people will be attracted by this option.

- *Interest rates.* When real interest rates are high, new owner-managers find it more difficult to obtain finance and are less willing to borrow.

- *Personal savings and assets.* Personal savings or borrowings guaranteed by personal assets are the most common form of finance for a new business. Periods when the value of houses, the most common form of personal guarantee, are high favour business start ups.

- *Consumer expenditure.* The highest number of new firms are in consumer services, so during times of growing consumer expenditure, more opportunities for new ventures appear in this sector.

- *Structural change.* Some structural changes in the economy favour the small business, such as the movement from manufacturing to service industries. When these changes occur, more new firms are likely to appear.

Whilst these factors may induce more new business start ups, they do not all represent positive forces in the business environment which are likely to help the new owner-manager. Some are potentially negative factors which can push people into new ventures for the wrong reasons.

- *Potential negative factors.* Unemployment, and government initiatives to reduce unemployment through self-employment, may encourage many people into a new venture, but this is no guarantee of a friendly business environment. The opposite is more likely to be true as high unemployment is likely to depress levels of demand, and therefore potential customer expenditure with a new business. High house prices, which make more finance available through personal bank guarantees, can increase the penalty for failure through the potential loss of a key personal asset without necessarily reducing the risks of it happening.

- *Potential positive factors.* Periods when real interest rates are low and consumer expenditure is growing are likely to be good times to start a new business, providing demand is not too dependent on a healthy economy. The high failure rates in the early 1990s in the UK indicate that many young firms were only viable in a strong economy and were not flexible enough to deal with more recessionary times. Times of structural change create opportunities for new ventures; for example, new types of business services have emerged to support changing work patterns following the development of new methods of communication and information processing. The successful entrepreneur is alert to underlying structural changes which can be rich sources of innovation and new business ideas (see Unit 4, Innovation and the marketplace).

2.3 Where to set up

Storey[2] cites eight possible factors that may lead to higher rates of new firm formation within a given geographic area:

- *Population growth* – high population growth or high levels of immigration into an area.

- *Unemployment* – higher levels of local unemployment.

- *Wealth* – high income area with more disposable income to spend, especially on services.

- *Workforce qualifications* – more managerial qualifications, leading to more wealth and more confidence to go it alone.

- *Business size* – large numbers of small firms already existing in an area may indicate low entry barriers into the predominant business types of the area. A local small business culture may also encourage more of the workforce into their own new venture by example and familiarity.

- *Housing* – high levels of owner-occupancy and house prices in a region, giving more access to capital.

- *Local government* – higher levels of spending by local authorities which create more demand in the region.

- *Government policy* – some small business incentives and development schemes are targeted regionally.

These factors, with the possible exception of unemployment, can represent positive factors that help the new venture. Most small businesses begin trading within a very limited geographic area so the local, micro-environment is likely to be a more significant factor in its success than wider macro-environmental influences. Obvious advice to a would-be owner-manager is to select a geographic area that exhibits as many as possible of the positive factors listed above. Historically such advice has been largely unheard. The vast majority of owner-managers select the area in which to establish their business based on where they live, not on considerations of which location represents the most favourable business environment[7].

Activity 3 Barriers to entry

An entrepreneur wanted to open a wine bar. Which particular barriers to market entry do you think will be encountered?

2.4 Which sector to choose

Starting a new business is more difficult in some industry sectors than others. The data on new business start ups discussed above (see section 2.1, Data on business births, and particularly Table 3.1, Business start ups by industry sector) indicates trends favouring some sectors over others. Anyone wishing to start up in a given marketplace encounters a series of issues, or potential problems, whose impact varies according to the industry sector. These form 'barriers to entry' for the small business which help determine the attractiveness of a specific sector to a potential new entrant. They are summarised in Figure 3.2.

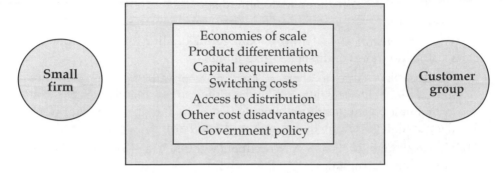

Source: adapted from Porter, M. Competitive Strategy. Techniques for Analysing Industries and Competitors, The Free Press, 1980

Figure 3.2 Barriers to market entry for a small firm

Before a small firm can do business with its chosen customer group, it must face the following competitive, structural and regulatory issues (illustrated in Figure 3.2), which are discussed in more detail below:

❐ **Economies of scale**

Where significant cost reductions result from high levels of output in an industry, then small firms find it difficult to compete. It was believed that the increasing existence of such economies in mass markets would lead to the inevitable decline of smaller firms. Certainly a large firm enjoying economies of scale can use this cost advantage in a number of ways. By establishing low market prices, large companies can force competitors to operate on low margins which make it an unattractive market to new entrants. If prices are kept up, then the additional profits enjoyed by the supplier can be reinvested in marketing, or research and development of new products, again reducing the competitiveness of new entrants. It is for such reasons that the economies of scale created by automation in car manufacturing have effectively blocked entry to smaller companies.

However, although an industry may be subject to economies of scale, particular operations or processes within it may not. Many small firms exist as suppliers to car manufacturers who find it more efficient to subcontract some specialised areas, such as design and development. For example, a small firm won an award for its innovative design of a supercharger, licensed to the large car manufacturers[8a].

In relying on economies of scale, the larger company can have problems which can be successfully exploited by the smaller firm:

○ To achieve scale economies, the larger firm may have to sacrifice differentiation of products or services. It may not go as far as Henry Ford's famous restriction on the colour range of the Model T ('You can have any colour as long as it's black') but it may encourage a standardisation of products or services leaving niche markets open to less uniform treatment.

For example, the cosmetic and toiletries industry is dominated by some very large organisations, such as Unilever, Proctor and Gamble, Avon and Revlon, who achieve significant economies in production, distribution and marketing.

A small firm[8b] has successfully entered this market by offering soaps shaped and decorated in the image of favourite children's characters (such as Minnie Mouse and Winnie the Pooh). Such specialised products do not easily lend themselves to large-scale production, partly because of their individual shapes and colours, but also because of their life span. The average life of these character-based concepts is short, so the need for a constant flow of new up-to-date designs is more important than the efficiency of production in this particular market segment.

○ Scale economies may be achieved by a larger firm using an existing technology, which makes them less flexible in adapting to new technologies, or blind to the changes which are taking place. Far reaching changes in industries are often generated from without by new small firms, rather than by the existing participants in the industry for this very reason. The move away from large, mainframe computers into smaller, high volume personal computers was triggered not by the well established giants, but by a complete newcomer, Apple Computers. A novice in the floor cleaning industry, James Dyson, introduced an innovative carpet cleaner based on 'cyclone' technology, and his success eventually forced the established brands to abandon their old methods reliant on replaceable bags.

❐ **Product differentiation**

Established companies build up loyalty with customers who identify with their particular product, or service. This differentiation takes time (to prove the reliability of a product or service) and money (for advertising, packaging, signage, branding), and therefore represents a significant barrier for any new entrant to overcome.

Direct competition with nationally branded products, supported by the resources of large companies, is not feasible for smaller firms. Nevertheless there are always segments less affected by large-scale loyalty, as we have already seen in the example of the small toiletries firm.

The Body Shop successfully overcame the brand loyalty of the cosmetic giants by rejecting the basic ideas of beauty products on which that loyalty was based. Their cheap plastic containers and simple descriptions appealed by their contrast to the lifestyle image approach of established brands, and provided the perfect market entry for a small firm with no resources to compete head on.

Small firms also build up their own loyalties which differentiate them sufficiently to deter new competitors. Allegiances to an existing small business are sometimes sufficiently great, and the local market sufficiently small, to make market entry impossible except by purchasing the business. Well liked publicans in small communities effectively differentiate their public houses by their own character, thereby blocking new entrants through personal loyalties.

In fact the brewing industry is a good example of large-, and small-scale product differentiation. At a national and regional level the large brewers have created differentiated, branded products which, coupled with economies of scale in production and distribution, have established high barriers. At the local level public houses and other outlets are differentiated by location, management and environment, which often works to the benefit of an owner-manager.

❐ Capital requirements

A very tangible barrier into some markets is the large set-up cost involved. Industry classifications with a low representation of small firms are usually those requiring substantial start-up investment, often those involved in production and manufacturing. This barrier can be reduced by the availability of second-hand plant and equipment. Bankruptcy and trading difficulties increase the availability of second-hand machinery, often sold cheaply through auction, which is a further factor in the higher level of small business starts during times of recession[7].

❐ Switching costs

When buyers switch from one company's product to another, they may incur one-off switching costs. These might be in the retraining of staff; for example the most significant costs in changing computer software may be in the retraining needed for the users. Other switching costs could be incurred by a manufacturer changing supplier of raw materials which involves product redesign, or increased stock obsolescence. Where significant costs exist, the potential new supplier has to offer more than just marginal benefits to persuade a buyer to change.

Some firms deliberately exploit switching costs as a marketing ploy to attract and retain existing customers. For example, suppliers of coffee offer commercial customers the free loan of coffee making equipment, immediately establishing a barrier to any competitors.

For small firms, switching costs often represent a real, but hidden, barrier. A concept which has been researched only hypothetically may not pass the ultimate test of being purchased in place of a competitive product, because of the emotional switching costs of severing a relationship with an existing supplier. Sales training emphasises the need to build strong personal relationships with existing customers so these emotional switching costs will be increased, and the temptation to buy elsewhere decreased.

❐ Access to distribution channels

Another market barrier, sometimes overlooked in the concept stage of a small business, is the need to have access to established channels of distribution. For example, anyone wishing to publish a consumer magazine will have to persuade retailers to give their new publication shelf space – not an easy task as space is limited and fiercely fought over by many publications.

A small business marketing a new food product will similarly face an uphill struggle to win space on the shelves of the major retailers.

❏ **Other cost disadvantages**

Some cost advantages enjoyed by established companies are independent of scale. Perhaps the two most significant of these for smaller firms are:

○ *Learning curve*. Improvements come with experience, and this can be translated into cost economies. Manufacturers will often benefit from higher machine productivity for example, as they gain production experience. A restaurant owner will learn how to reduce food waste by serving a particular menu only with time and practice. The new business can expect higher unit costs in its early days than its more established competitors.

○ *Location*. In many markets, location of premises is a crucial marketing factor. Existing firms often have good locations which will be expensive for the new entrant to equal. For example leasehold retail premises in good locations can command a premium when they change hands; that is, the incoming tenant pays the outgoing one for the privilege of taking over the lease. Established companies may have paid no such premium because they were an original tenant, or the location had not been popular when they moved in.

❏ **Government policy**

Certain industries are controlled by national or local government regulations, which create total or partial barriers to entry. Some postal delivery services have only recently been opened up to new business entrants, whilst other areas still remain prohibited. The licensing laws present barriers to entrants who wish to open a restaurant, run a public house, or operate an off-licence.

Other regulations increase the capital costs of market entry. Conforming to Health and Safety regulations often requires expenditure in adapting premises, for example, in the provision of toilets and fire escapes. Hygiene regulations lay down strict requirements on food preparation for public consumption, which increases the start-up and ongoing costs for several types of small business, from exclusive restaurants to sandwich bars.

Owners of small businesses often complain that conforming to government regulations gives larger firms an unfair economy of scale; the costs of conforming to the paperwork of tax returns, for example, is a relatively fixed cost, which the larger firm can amortise over higher sales turnover than the small firm. Since the Bolton Report, the UK government has become increasingly aware of these problems, and a number of measures have been taken to try and level the playing field (see Unit 5 for fuller details of government policy).

Ninety per cent of small businesses operate in the services sector of the economy where barriers to entry are generally lower than for manufacturing sectors. More specific sectors in which barriers to entry are relatively low, and new business start ups more numerous, include (see also Table 3.1):

○ construction;

○ retail distribution;

○ transport and communications;

○ finance and insurance;

○ business services;

○ other services.

2.5 Impact of the Internet

The Internet promised to offer ways in which new enterprises could by-pass some of these barriers to entry and overthrow the established order in many markets. Some commentators forecast that the relatively low entry costs of selling internationally via the Internet could challenge some market leaders and that it could also create new market niches for entrepreneurial companies to exploit. In some industries, Internet-related technologies have indeed begun to upset the status quo and allow new ventures to compete on equal terms with larger firms.

For example, the music industry is dominated by five companies world-wide. In the UK market, EMI is the market leader with over 25 per cent of album sales, helped by the acquisition of Virgin and Chrysalis and the success of artists such as the Spice Girls and Robbie Williams. The other big companies, BMG, Sony, Time Warner and Polygram, represent a further 55 per cent share of the UK market between them. Independent record labels and music publishers such as Telstar and Beggars Banquet have been successful, but they are few in number, and make up only 20 per cent of the market as the big five have tended to buy up any promising newcomers.

New technology has threatened to destabilise these established positions and create opportunities for new ventures. Music can be digitised and downloaded onto computers, which means that musical products can be distributed directly over the Internet. Digital recordings of music can be encoded on the Internet using the MP3 format, compressed and distributed across computer networks. This means that music can be copied and quickly distributed anywhere in the world. The big five music companies tried to ignore the new technology until Napster was founded in September 1999 to allow users to swap music files amongst themselves. As the service quickly developed, with a huge following of 70 million users world-wide, the market leaders' first reaction to this threat was legal action. Napster's operation was declared illegal in 2001 as it violated copyright laws. Recognising that the threat will not disappear, one of the big five, BMG, is now backing Napster in a legitimate, paid-for service. Many in the industry believe the future for music distribution will be 'streaming' – instant access to any music via pocket computers and advances in telephony. This opens up new opportunities for the industry which may be exploited by entrepreneurs who are more agile than the established corporations.

It was not only the music industry that seemed destined for a surge in new ventures. The early wave of Internet entrepreneurs setting up innovative new services such as eBay and lastminute.com seemed to indicate that traditional larger organisations in many sectors could be challenged by newcomers. Since then, the pace of change has slowed. The domination of markets by existing brands and organisations now seems less at risk for a number of reasons:

❑ Sales of £13.5 billion were made over the Internet in the UK in 2000[9]. However most of these transactions were business-to-business, as existing organisations adopted the Internet as a purchasing mechanism. Sales to end-users, or business-to-consumer transactions, are still relatively small over the Internet, representing about 15 per cent of the total e-commerce sales, and less than 2 per cent of all retail sales. New ventures have yet to make substantial inroads into our shopping habits via the Internet.

❑ Existing major brands sold by large organisations are popular on the Internet because consumers are concerned about Internet shopping security, and choose known brands to reduce the perceived risk.

❑ Existing, larger, companies may not have been the first to realise the potential of e-commerce, but they are likely to take advantage of subsequent developments on the Internet. Well-publicised casualties amongst new technology companies, such as the demise of Boo.com, have made investors more wary of Internet shares. New investment is likely to come from existing competitors buying into the new technology. The music industry model of a market leader (BMG) supporting an Internet newcomer (Napster) is becoming more common.

Activity 4 Closure rates

Ten entrepreneurs set up in business in the same year. If they suffer the average closure rates of small firms in the UK, how many would you expect to remain in business at the end of:

❑ Year 1?

❑ Year 3?

❑ Year 6?

3 Sink or swim

3.1 Small business closure rates

A key feature which distinguishes small business from large business is the much higher closure rates of small firms.

Recent statistics in the UK have cautioned against the euphoria of the enterprise culture of the 1980s, which heralded a new wave of small business start ups as the beginning of a new economic dawn. Whilst the 1980s was a decade of rapid rise in self-employment the recession of the early 1990s witnessed record failure rates, with nearly 22,000 reported company insolvencies in 1991, the majority of them small firms, and over 25,000 individual bankruptcies, many the result of small business activity[10]. By 1992, company and individual insolvencies were running at a combined total of 58,000 a year, or over 1000 per week. This has since declined; by the late 1990s Dun & Bradstreet reported that insolvencies as a result of business activities were running at around 40,000. Many more firms close without leaving behind bad debts.

Business closures almost match the rate of business start ups, but the knowledge we have of these two processes is very uneven. Despite high rates of new business formation, the total stock of 3.7 million businesses has been relatively stable since the mid-1990s because closure rates have been similarly high. Between 350,000 and 400,000 businesses, or approximately 10 per cent of the total stock, close each year (see Table 3.2). Most businesses that close are micro or small firms because these constitute the most numerous and the most vulnerable sector.

Table 3.2 Business lifespan

Months since start up	Percentage still surviving
6	90.9
12	79.4
24	58.3
36	45.6
48	36.9
60	30.6

Source: SME Statistics for the UK, *Small Business Service, 2001*[4]

Only a small percentage stay in business in the long-term[2]: less than one in three business start ups survive for five years, a half may last two to three years. Twenty per cent close within a year, nearly ten per cent after only six months.

Internationally, the picture is broadly similar. Increasing rates of small business formation are associated with a higher likelihood of closure – high birth rates are followed by high death rates. In Germany, birth and death rates are broadly similar to the UK; in the USA they are even higher, whilst in France they are somewhat lower.

However we should not assume that a closed business equates to a failed business. Closures occur for a variety of reasons, some negative but others more positive, such as retirement or sale of the firm. A recent study carried out by Kingston University[11] indicated that only half of closed businesses are discontinued because they have failed financially or they no longer meet their owners' objectives. The other half are effectively continued; they are either sold-on or they are businesses that close and then re-open for technical reasons such as the change of a sole trader to a limited company. These types of closures are summarised in Figure 3.3.

Discontinued		Continued	
Financial failures	*Not meeting owners' objectives*	*Technical closures*	*Sold on*
20%	30%	15%	35%
Insoluble financial problems often resulting in bad debts	Not meeting owners' current objectives. Closed with neither significant debts nor sold on for a consideration	Closed for business objectives and re-opened in a different form. For example, upgrade of sole trader to limited company or changes to partnership	Sold for a consideration to third parties, existing managers, family members or friends

Source: Small Business Research Centre, Kingston University, 2001[11]

Figure 3.3 Types of business closures

Other patterns emerge from the statistics on closed firms:

❒ The young are more likely to die than the old – closure rates are highest in the early months and years.

❒ The smallest are most vulnerable – micro-firms employing less than 10 people close at a much higher rate than small firms employing up to 50 people, which in turn are more likely to close than medium-sized companies.

❒ Those that grow are less likely to close than those that do not. Treading water is not a good survival strategy.

In summary, as a firm becomes larger and older its chances of survival improve. Statistically this has been calculated in one survey as a 1 per cent change in firm size leads to a 7 per cent change in the probability of survival, and a 1 per cent change in age leads to a 13 per cent change in the probability of survival[12].

3.2 Adjusting to uncertainty

Small business owners are described sometimes as being at the mercy of a hostile environment which threatens them from many directions. Unfair competition from larger firms, the burden of government regulations, penal bank charges, high interest rates and the recession, all contribute to make life in the small business a constant struggle. Smallness, and therefore lack of resources, seems to mean that small firms will always be the most vulnerable members of the business community. Certainly the declining numbers of small firms up to the 1970s was attributed to external influences, just as their revival has been put down to changes in the social, economic and political environment. A major concern of the Bolton Committee was to protect the small business sector, which it saw as unable to fully sustain itself without government help.

Uncertainty is a key feature of the small business environment. Some researchers see it as one of the central distinctions between small and large firms[13]. They identify the inability to control prices because of lack of market power and dependency on a relatively small customer base as major factors which make the management environment in small firms more uncontrollable, and therefore more uncertain, than in larger organisations.

We discussed earlier (in sub-section 1, A matter of life or death) some of the influences on small business survival, dividing them into internal and external factors. The internal factors revolve around the motivations and characteristics of the owner-manager. The external factors, which are largely outside the control of the owner-manager, were divided into the macro-environment and the micro-environment.

An insight into how owner-managers view these external factors, and how their perceptions shift with changes in the macro-environments, is provided by the Small Business Quarterly Survey that reports regularly on the opinions of a panel of small business owners on the problems they face. Issues listed include:

❏   interest rates;
❏   cash flow and payments;
❏   low turnover;
❏   lack of skilled employees;
❏   total tax burden;
❏   premises, rent and rates;
❏   inflation;
❏   government regulations and paperwork;
❏   access to finance;
❏   competition from big business;
❏   high rates of pay.

Changes to the business environment are reflected in how important these issues are perceived to be. In the 1980s when the economy was booming and unemployment falling, the availability of premises and skilled employees became key problems. At the end of 1990, interest rates were seen as the single biggest issue, followed by cash flow and late payments, with low turnover in third place. By the end of 1991, the effects of the recession and lowering of interest rates were reflected in a shift in the order as low turnover became the largest problem with cash flow and late payments in second place. By 2000, lack of skilled employees was back to the top of a list that reflected the key issues of the 1980s. Whatever the business environment, it seems to create problems of some sort for the small firm.

Lack of resources and lack of market power make small firms particularly vulnerable to these problems. Those with least resources and market power – the very young, and the very small businesses – have least defence against changes in the business environment.

How can small firms best cope with the uncertain and changing environment? Some research[2] indicates that adjustment is the key. Those firms that are most active in making adjustments in what they do, and how they do it, seem to have a greater chance of survival than those who carry on as before.

Important adjustments to consider include:

- ❏ market development;
- ❏ production processes;
- ❏ employment and labour processes;
- ❏ ownership;
- ❏ location.

However, the key adjustment was found to be in the area of market development: a continuous search for new market opportunities and broadening the customer base of the business. The nature and frequency of these market adjustments, and the potential for a small firm to make them, depends on the market sector in which the owner-manager has chosen to operate – some are more hostile than others. (These issues are discussed in more detail in Unit 10, Successful small business strategies.)

Activity 5 Popular small business sectors

Write down some industrial or market sectors which have a high proportion of small businesses operating within them, (for example, hairdressing). Why do you think small is the popular size of business for each of the examples you have given?

4 Hostile and benign environments

4.1 Sector analysis

Small enterprises operate in virtually every market or industry, but in some sectors small firms are more commonplace than others. This is not by chance. Smallness is the most appropriate size of trading unit in certain markets, where the environment, far from being hostile, favours small firms. In other areas, larger firms have distinct advantages and the small business has to find a niche in order to survive.

Table 3.3 illustrates the differences between the major sectors of the UK economy in terms of the numbers and typical size of the firms operating within them.

The business services sector has the highest number of small businesses, followed by the construction industry, which has a particularly high level of micro-enterprises employing under 10 people. Many small businesses operate in the services sectors and this is reflected in the high proportion of small firms in the distributive, business and other service categories. The number of manufacturing firms continues to decline; in 1993 there were over 400,000 compared to the current figure of 330,000.

Table 3.3 Number of UK firms by size and sector, 2000

Size: percentage of size band (by number of employees) in each sector	Number of firms (000s)	One-person firm (none)	Small (1–49)	Medium (50–249)	Large (250+)
Agriculture/forestry	190	69.2	30.7	0.1	0.0
Mining, energy and water	4	57.0	36.3	3.9	2.8
Manufacturing	332	62.2	34.5	2.5	0.7
Construction	679	81.8	18.0	0.2	0.0
Wholesale and retail	536	51.3	47.8	0.8	0.2
Catering and hotels	157	34.3	64.6	1.0	0.2
Transport	228	80.6	18.6	0.6	0.2
Finance	59	70.7	27.7	1.0	0.6
Business and prof.	826	69.6	29.8	0.5	0.1
Education/training	111	89.9	9.7	0.4	0.1
Health and social	207	75.3	23.5	1.0	0.3
Personal services	393	79.3	20.4	0.3	0.1
Total UK	3722	69.6	29.5	0.7	0.2

Source: Small Business Service, *SME Statistics for the UK, 2000*[4]

4.2 Structural analysis

The underlying structure of an industry or market sector determines how favourable it is towards large-, medium- or small-sized units, and therefore whether it will provide a relatively hostile or relatively benign environment for small firms.

Porter's well-known model[14] of the forces which drive industry competition can be used to assess the structural features which influence an industry's suitability to the small business form. See Figure 3.4.

These five forces of entry, rivalry, substitutes, buyers and suppliers jointly govern the intensity of competition, and profit potential for a small and large firm in a given industry or market sector.

❐ **Entry**

The potential for a small business to enter a given industry sector is determined initially by the barriers to entry that exist, as we have already discussed more fully in sub-section 2.4. Barriers to entry work both ways for small firms: at first, high entry barriers act to keep a new venture out, but once a small firm has entered a market, they can protect it from too many new competitors.

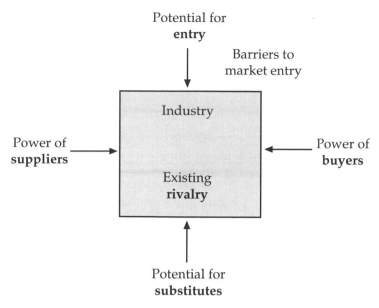

Figure 3.4 The five forces model of industry competition

❏ **Buyers**

Buyers, or customers, 'compete' with the small firm by trying to get the best possible deal for themselves; they will try to negotiate discounts, additional services, higher quality, more after-sales support and other benefits which are added costs for the supplying business.

Buyers differ in the power they can bring to bear on a small firm, which will in turn condition the attractiveness of doing business with the buyer group of a particular industry.

○ Some buyers have little choice. The costs of switching to another supplier are too great; for example, the existing supplier has locked them in by providing free on-loan equipment to use their product; or the supplier is the only stockist in town, and it is not convenient to travel elsewhere.

○ Other buyers are not inclined to negotiate. The purchase is of such little significance in their cost structure that they are not sensitive to price. Graphic art suppliers, for example, are able to charge high prices because the materials they sell to a designer represent a small fraction of the price charged to the client by the designer.

○ Some buyers are all powerful. They can effectively dictate terms to a small firm which becomes dependent on them. This happens when buying is concentrated in the hands of a small number of large customers, who purchase high volumes from a large number of small suppliers. Superstore retailers have achieved this position. A small firm wishing to supply Sainsbury or Tesco will have little choice over most marketing variables, such as product quality, packaging, delivery times and methods, and even prices.

The buyer groups, or potential customers, to which a small firm can sell, do not usually exercise equal power. Choice of buyer groups is therefore a key decision, which will influence the business environment of the firm. For instance, a garment manufacturer may have a choice of selling large quantities with little marketing control to multiples such as Marks and Spencer, or lower volumes but setting their own strategies through a variety of smaller, fragmented outlets.

❏ **Suppliers**

Suppliers to a small firm also influence its environment in their pricing and other marketing policies. As the small firm is now in the position of buyer, its powers in relation to the supplier mirror the factors considered already. Small firms tend to buy in a fragmented way so their power, relative to large suppliers, tends to be low. Franchising has attempted to overcome this by grouping a large number of outlets into one buying source. A franchisee can therefore expect higher discounts than an independent outlet of similar size.

Other small firms attempt to enhance their power over suppliers by coming together as formal or informal groups. For example, an office equipment company which distributed its products through a series of owner-managed agents throughout the country was able to dictate its own terms when the network was first set up. When the agents had successfully developed their territories they used their improved negotiating position to jointly strike a better deal with the supplier.

❏ **Rivalry**

Rivalry between established firms is evidenced by traditional forms of competition: selling and promotional campaigns, discount offers, new product launches, extending distribution channels and so on. Small firms may do this in spirits of rivalry which range from collaborative and co-operative to fiercely competitive.

The intensity of rivalry is affected by the exit barriers in the industry. These are the factors that keep a firm from quitting altogether, even though returns are inadequate or negative. Exit barriers for small firms can be economic – the costs of liquidation or sale and loss of income – or psychological attachment to the enterprise, loyalty to employees and pride that comes from ownership. Where these barriers are high, then a firm will continue for as long as possible before exiting, thus increasing the intensity of rivalry in the marketplace.

❏ **Threat of substitute products or services**

Substitution of a firm's products or services can come in two ways:

○ a substitute which performs the same function, but in a different way. A taxi service is competing not only with other taxi firms, but also bus companies, for instance;

○ a substitute way of spending money. The competition for disposable income comes from widely differing products and services. For example, a restaurant is competing not only with other restaurants and take-aways, but a whole range of other leisure opportunities from the theatre to the pub. The drop in cinema audiences in 1995 was attributed to cash in the pocket being spent on the National Lottery.

Industries where there are fewer real substitutes tend to be more stable than those that can be easily substituted by other products or services, or those that rely on disposable income. In recessionary times, for example, taxis in areas where cheaper public transport is readily available will be affected more quickly than those that serve a more captive market, such as tourists.

4.3 Fragmented industries

In some industries, large firms will have advantages as buyers, suppliers, or rivals to small firms. In other sectors, however, larger organisations will have little natural advantage, and the common form of business unit will be small.

Industries are fragmented into a large number of smaller firms for a variety of reasons:

- ❐ *Low entry barriers*: most industries with a large population of small firms have low entry barriers. These include many of the service sectors where small enterprises predominate, such as training, recruitment and secretarial agencies, household services, and the construction industry. Low barriers on their own do not always create fragmentation however, as there are usually other forces in favour of the small firm.

- ❐ *Diseconomies of scale*: where customer preferences necessitate constantly changing products and styles, smaller, more flexible firms can be more efficient than larger, bureaucratic companies. Women's clothes, and other industries where fashion is a major ingredient, would be typical here.

- ❐ *High creative content*: architects, interior design firms, and specialist product development companies tend to be small as it is often more difficult to produce conditions of high creativity in large organisations.

- ❐ *Personal service*: where an individualised, personal service is required, for example in consultancy, or picture framing, then small operations tend to be able to offer more responsive, tailor-made services than large firms.

- ❐ *Close local control*: restaurants, wine bars and night clubs are good examples where the close local supervision of an owner-manager often works better than the absentee management of a large company.

- ❐ *Newness*: a new or emerging industry can be fragmented because no companies have been able to take a significant market share. Technological innovations, or shifting consumer needs which create these newly-formed industries are sometimes exploited first by newly-formed small businesses. There are currently many small businesses operating in environmental markets such as solar heating and water filtering.

4.4 Franchising and fragmentation

In some markets, franchising is being used to overcome some of the forces towards fragmentation. For example, where economies of scale potentially exist in production or purchasing, an industry may still remain fragmented because the marketplace demands personal service or local sources of supply. The brewing industry overcame this problem with an early form of franchising, retaining centralised production but using tenants with some autonomy to manage the local outlet.

Format franchising has enabled parts of the retail industry to centralise production or buying, whilst retaining the benefits of local service and location. Fast food chains such as McDonalds and Kentucky Fried Chicken are able to market themselves as providing a convenient, neighbourly service whilst offering the low prices and uniform standards of a larger organisation.

Activity 6 What counts most?

Some influences in the business environment need careful consideration before starting a new venture, as they will have a critical impact on the chances of survival. From what you have read in this Unit, which factors are the most important to take into consideration?

5 Critical survival factors

In summary, the previous sections point to some critical factors in the small business environment which help to determine whether a new venture will sink or swim.

❑ *Where and when*

Some locations and time periods are more favourable for small business start ups than others. The business environment is particularly hostile to the very young business. So the time and place chosen for a new venture need to be as favourable as possible in order to survive these vulnerable early days.

❑ *Growth*

The business environment is least kind to very small firms. Growth is needed to give small firms more resources to deal with the inevitable environmental changes. In particular, small firms need to reach a stage of financial viability as fast as possible so they can use their limited resources to develop the business rather than supporting losses. Standing still may mean the business is going backwards.

❑ *Choice of market sector*

The market sector in which an owner-manager chooses to operate is a decision that will have a continuous impact on the fortunes of the business. Macro-environmental forces, such as government policy and general economic conditions, are of course important. But the micro-business environment largely determines how well a business can cope with changes to these more general forces.

For example, some market sectors are more sensitive to price increases than others. After an increase in VAT or other duties on alcoholic drinks, off-licences usually experience a drop in sales, whilst demand for wines and spirits in restaurants is hardly affected. In some sectors, such as construction, the competitive forces keep profit margins so low that relatively small changes in demand can put many small firms out of business. Prospective owner-managers can increase their chances of survival by choosing markets where it is easier to ride out the storms that inevitably come.

❐ *Barriers to entry*

Although owner-managers are tempted to choose a market sector which is relatively easy to enter because the barriers to small firms are low, they would do well to consider markets which are more difficult to enter. The extra initial effort may be rewarded by less competition once the business has been established.

❐ *Choice of buyer group*

The choice of buyer groups, or market segments, within a sector is also a crucial decision for the owner-manager. Segments or niches of market sectors can provide a favourable business environment even if the general pattern is more hostile.

For example, in the retail sector, the percentage of total sales through single outlets, i.e. small firms, has fallen to less than 28 per cent of the total as the power of the large chains has grown. But single outlet retailers account for 62 per cent of newspapers and periodicals sold, indicating perhaps that the unsociable hours involved in this type of business do not suit the larger multiples. The construction industry was particularly hard hit during the recession of the early 1990s, but developers who targeted the elderly population by providing sheltered housing survived much better than other building companies.

❐ *Adjustments to changing conditions*

The chances of survival of a small firm depend in large measure on how nimbly and skilfully it can adjust to changes in the business environment and particularly to conditions within its market sector. A new venture which is set up to be flexible so that it can make continuous product and market adjustments is more likely to succeed than one which has an inflexible structure and strategy, (we shall return to this theme in Unit 4).

6 Case studies and activities

Case studies *Second thoughts*

Case 1 Andrea adjusts her ideas

Andrea Clarey was having her first doubts since deciding to set up her own business. She had defined her opportunity area as providing a cost effective payroll service to the public sector as this seemed to fit well with her personal skills and experience. But she now recognised that winning the contract for the payroll service of her existing employers, a local government authority, was not going to be as simple as she had first imagined.

'I have seen the terms of the contract they have put out to tender, and I'm not sure it is worth having,' she told her small business advisor. 'It is only for a year in the first instance. So I could spend all my time and money setting up a service only to find that I lose the contract and have no business left. '

'I am also worried about the timing,' she continued. 'Elections are coming up next year and if the colour of the ruling party changes so might their policies of putting administrative services out to tender.'

'What other market sectors could you consider?' the advisor asked.

'I can look at other public services,' said Andrea. 'Many individual schools have become directly responsible for their payroll, for instance. Or I could consider the private sector. I would have to target small business as larger companies tend to run their own payroll. But the competition from accountants and other suppliers is fierce. Payroll software is becoming more user friendly all the time, so it is not difficult to offer a basic service with minimal experience. I have no experience of dealing with these markets so the risks may be greater.'

Andrea was finding that the only certainty in the small business environment was its uncertainty.

Case 2 Kit suggests a new product

Kit Hugos had an important decision to make with his partner Robin Davidson before they continued the planning of their proposed electronics business.

'We have a fundamental choice it seems to me', he explained to Davidson. 'We either act as a design and manufacture service for other companies. Or we make and sell our own products. If we design and manufacture for other manufacturers, they decide what the final product will be and they control all the sales and marketing to their customers. We depend totally on them to make a success of something for which we have probably come up with most of the good ideas. Alternatively, we can design our own products which we market ourselves. Then we are in charge of what we produce and sell. We don't have to rely on others to make our business work.'

'Yes, but if we produce to a customer's order, we don't carry the risk of stock – they do,' countered Davidson. 'Nor do we have to bear the product development, marketing and distribution costs. Also they come up with the initial ideas – which is usually the hard part. I don't know of any products which we can develop and sell ourselves. Do you?'

'Well actually I do,' said Kit. 'I have developed a personal security device. It's basically an electronic tracking system – a small transmitter which you carry on your person, and computerised receivers which can track and locate the transmitter on a digital map at all times. Any trouble, you press a button on your transmitter which alerts security who can pinpoint you straight away. I believe we could sell it direct to organisations with large, open sites – office complexes, conference centres, and universities, for example – to improve their on-site security. No-one else is offering anything quite like what I have in mind and the market is having to become increasingly security conscious.'

Activities

Assess the business environments in which Andrea and Kit are proposing to operate.

i)   What are likely to be the main barriers of market entry?

ii) What do you think will be some of the key macro-environmental factors in each case?

iii) Which competitive forces will be particularly influential in each case?

iv) Advise Andrea on her choice of market sector. What are the arguments for and against the sectors which she is considering?

v)   Advise Kit and Robin Davidson on their choice of market sector. What are the pros and cons of the alternatives raised by Kit?

Extended activity *The five forces*

You have decided to become a wine importer, bringing in wine from the producing countries and selling it on to retailers, restaurants and other licensed outlets. Using the five forces model, analyse the competitive environment you would expect to encounter as a small firm in this market sector. You may find a directory of local businesses such as *Yellow Pages* or other reference books useful in identifying potential buyers, suppliers and substitutes.

In conclusion

Once you have finished this Unit, turn to Section B, Planning a new venture, and complete Step 1.3, Identifying the opportunity area.

7 References and further reading

References and further information

1. Cromie, S. 'The problems experienced by young firms', *International Small Business Journal*, 9, 3, 1991.

2. Storey, D. *Understanding the Small Business Sector*, International Thomson Business Press, 1998. See chapters 3 and 4.

3. Barclays Bank Small Business Bulletin, *Barclays Business Starts and Closures Survey*, 2000. Reports can be viewed on the Barclays web site www.smallbusiness.barclays.co.uk

4. Small Business Service, *Small and Medium Enterprise (SME) Statistics for the United Kingdom*, Research and Evaluation Unit 2001. The SBS now provide essential information on the small business sector which can be accessed via their web site on www.sbs.gov.uk/statistics

5. See Keeble, D., Walker, S. and Robson, M. *New Firm Formation and Small Business Growth: Spatial and Temporal Variations and Determinants in the United Kingdom*, Employment Department Research Series No. 15, September, 1993.

6. Hall, G. *Surviving and Prospering in the Small Firm Sector*, Routledge, 1995.

7. See Binks, M. and Jennings, A. 'New Firms as a Source of Industrial Regeneration', in Scott, M., Gibb, A., Lewis, J. and Faulkner, T. (eds), *Small Firms' Growth and Development*, Gower, 1986.

8. As reported in, *Ten Case Studies of Owner-Managed Businesses*, Department of Employment, 1990.

    a) Fleming Thermodynamics Ltd, an engineering design and development company founded in 1983 with a turnover of £500,000 and 17 employees in 1989. Although the company was originally engaged in manufacture, it withdrew to concentrate on design and development work.

    b) Prelude Concepts and Designs Ltd, designs, markets and manufactures toiletries and textiles, with a turnover of £1.8 million and 40 employees in 1990. The two founders concentrate on new product development, which they consider to be the key to their business, leaving a management team to look after the operational side.

9. Keynote Report, *Internet Usage in Business*, 2000.

10. DTI statistics, as reported in *The Daily Telegraph Business News*, 8 February 1992. Company insolvencies were up 45 per cent and individual bankruptcies up 83 per cent, over 1990. The number of company failures reached a peak of 6072 in the last 3 months of 1992. The 1991 total represented 2.3 per cent of active business on the Companies House Register.

11. Stokes, D. and Blackburn, R. *Unlocking Business Exits: a Study of Businesses that Close*, Small Business Research Centre, Kingston University, 2001.

12. Evans, D. 'The Relationship between Firm Growth, Size and Age', *Journal of Industrial Economics*, pp. 567–82, 1987.

13. Wynarczyk, P., Watson, R., Storey, D. J., Short, H. and Keasey, K. *The Managerial Labour Market in Small and Medium -Sized Enterprises*, Routledge, 1993.

14. Porter, M. *Competitive Strategy: Techniques for Analysing Industries and Competitors*, The Free Press, 1980.

Recommended further reading

❐ Barrow, C. *Essence of Small Business*, FT Prentice Hall, 2000.

❐ Storey, D. *Understanding the Small Business Sector*, International Thomson Press, 1998. See chapters 3 and 4.

❐ Hall, G. *Surviving and Prospering in the Small Firm Sector*, Routledge, 1995.

❐ Stokes, D. *Marketing: A Case Study Approach*, Continuum, 2001. Chapter 3, 'The Marketing Context', and Chapter 4, 'Customers and Competitors'.

❐ Stanworth, J. and Gray, C. (eds), *Bolton 20 Years On: the Small Firm in the 1990s*, PCP, 1991. Chapter 3, 'Problems and Preoccupations'.

❐ Porter, M. *Competitive Strategy: Techniques for Analysing Industries and Competitors*, The Free Press, 1980. See Chapter 9, 'Competitive Strategy in Fragmented Industry'.

❐ The Which? *Guide to Starting Your Own Business*, Consumers Association, 1998. Chapter 14 contains useful profiles of some common small business sectors: booksellers, pubs, newsagents and small shops, and employment agencies.

4   Innovation and the marketplace

This Unit explores the nature of innovative products and services in relation to their intended markets. Although small firms have advantages in innovative activity, they also have disadvantages which some overcome by co-operation and collaboration. Case studies of entrepreneurs and companies illustrate aspects of innovation, including possible misinterpretations of innovation, and how innovative opportunities can be purposefully pursued. The marketplace is the ultimate test for innovative products, so this Unit considers two key questions for new ventures: who will be my customers and why will they buy from me?

Contents

Activity 1 Small versus large innovators

Do small firms have advantages over larger companies in innovating new products or services? What disadvantages do they have?

78

1 Product innovation in small firms

1.1 'Small is innovative'?

The small firm today is seen as playing an important role in the innovation of new products and processes. Small- and medium-sized companies are often regarded as being more innovative than large ones because of their flexibility and willingness to try new approaches[1].

The point is reinforced by well-publicised success stories of innovative entrepreneurs who were forced to start their own new business because their ideas were rejected by large established companies. Hewlett Packard turned down Steve Wozniak's invention of a small portable computer, so he took the idea to his friend Steven Jobs and together they began making Apple computers in a garage.

This notion that small firms contribute relatively more to innovation than larger ones was not always in vogue. In the 1960s, the UK and other European governments encouraged larger companies to form, through merger and acquisition, in order to promote the research and development of new products and technologies. It was thought that only large industrial units could afford the high fixed cost of investment in research and development. The monopoly power and economies of scale of large organisations were thought to be necessary to provide the resources needed for the high costs of new technology.

In practice, there are advantages and disadvantages for the small and large business involved in innovative activity. Figure 4.1 summarises some of these, from the research of Rothwell[2] into the role of small firms in innovation. In summary small firms have advantages in management, internal communications and marketing, stemming from their flexible and opportunist behavioural patterns, especially influenced by entrepreneurial owner-managers. They have the disadvantages of lack of in-depth resources of qualified people and finance. Larger firms have greater material resources which gives them advantages in attracting the necessary staff and funding the growth and other activities to which successful innovation can lead.

❒ **Industrial life cycles**

   In several respects, comparisons between large and small firms ignore the realities of specific industries and market sectors. In the early stages of an industry's life cycle, firms tend to be small and innovative. The technology of an emergent industry is often new and therefore requires participating companies to be innovative. New industries also tend to be fragmented as competitors, including new small businesses, jostle for position.

   As industries mature, the companies involved tend to become bigger through organic growth as well as consolidation amongst competitors. Innovation in established industries usually requires higher costs in development and marketing, thus favouring larger companies.

FUNCTION	SMALL FIRMS		LARGE FIRMS	
	Advantages	*Disadvantages*	*Advantages*	*Disadvantages*
Management	Entrepreneurial managers seeking new opportunities and taking risks	Unable to cope with high growth and adapt to increased complexity	Professional managers controlling complex organisations	Managers become administrators controlled by risk-averse accountants
Personnel		Lack of technical specialists which limits scale of R&D effort	Attract highly skilled specialists. Can support large R&D facility	
Finance		Difficulties in raising risk capital and inability to spread risk over portfolio of projects	Able to raise venture capital, spread risk and fund any resulting diversification	
Communications	Internal communication fast and efficient, able to adapt to solve problems	Difficulties to link with outside sources of expertise	Able to plug into external sources of expertise, and can buy crucial technical information and services	Internal communications bureaucratic and slow to react
Marketing	Fast reaction time to changing market requirements	Lack resources to set up expensive distribution systems	Marketing of existing products with comprehensive distribution and servicing networks	Management remote from marketplace
Patents and legal requirements		Difficult to cope with patents and subsequent litigation. High unit cost of meeting complex regulations in some industries	Able to employ patent and legal specialists. Able to defend patents and spread cost of compliance with complex regulations	

Adapted from Rothwell, R. The Role of Small Firms in Technological Innovation[2]

Figure 4.1 Small vs large firms in innovation – advantages and disadvantages

○ The micro-electronics and computer industry has epitomised this process in the post war years, moving through several phases of growth and maturity which have alternatively favoured small and large firms. In the 1950s and 60s the industry was dominated by a few large mainframe computer manufacturers, such as IBM, who had the resources to invest in research and development. Entrepreneurs, such as those at Apple, played significant roles in establishing new branches of the industry in the 1970s and 1980s. Today the shake out in the personal computer market has swung the balance back to larger firms who are making the innovative running.

1.2 Innovation records

A record of innovations introduced by British companies, giving details of the size of firms involved[3], produced the results shown in Table 4.1.

Table 4.1 Innovation share (per cent) by size of firm in the UK

Period	No. of employees in firm				
	1–199	200–499	500–999	1,000–9,999	10,000+
1965–69	15.4	8.2	8.5	24.2	43.7
1970–74	17.5	9.0	6.3	20.7	46.5
1975–79	19.6	9.6	7.5	16.2	47.2
1980–83	26.8	12.1	4.3	14.9	41.9

Source: Science Policy Research Unit[3]

This shows that small firms with under 200 employees, and those with under 500 employees have significantly increased their share of innovations since 1975, at the expense of firms above 500 employees and particularly those with over 10,000 employees. This implies that small firms became relatively more efficient at innovating than their larger counterparts.

Small business units

Figure 4.3 shows the share of innovations by size of unit, i.e. subsidiary, division or business unit.

Table 4.2 Innovation share (per cent) by size of unit in the UK

Period	No. of employees in firm				
	1–199	200–499	500–999	1,000–9,999	10,000+
1965–69	21.4	14.2	11.4	37.9	15.1
1970–74	24.5	14.0	12.2	34.0	15.3
1975–79	31.3	13.6	13.0	29.8	12.3
1980–83	32.1	17.7	10.1	29.3	10.9

Source: Science Policy Research Unit[3]

This shows an even more marked shift of share of innovations towards small and medium-sized units, with units employing under 500 people accounting for almost half (49.8 per cent) of innovations in the period 1980–83. This perhaps reflects the attempts by larger companies to benefit from the advantages of both large and small firms shown in Figure 3.1: to keep the large firm benefits deriving from their resources, whilst gaining the benefits of flexibility and adaptability by organising their activities into smaller units.

Activity 2 Innovative entrepreneurs

Can you name some innovators? Write down the names of some entrepreneurs, who have been noted for their innovative abilities, and their principal innovations.

2 Entrepreneurs as innovators

2.1 The creative hero

The entrepreneur has tended to take on an heroic mantle in our pursuit of economic prosperity (see Unit 2). This has been particularly emphasised in the role of the entrepreneur as innovator. The idea that small firms are hot beds of creativity compared to large firms which specialise in efficiency and policy but not innovation, has reinforced the myth of the entrepreneurial innovator versus the industrial drone[4].

The myth portrays the entrepreneur as the personification of creativity, coming up with significant new ideas that solve old problems. These entrepreneurial innovators are non-conformists who do not fit into conventional educational patterns or industrial organisations. Large companies constrain their creative talents, which need the freedom of the small firm to fully develop.

Two such innovators have captured the imagination of the British public in recent years.

❑ **Clive Sinclair**

Clive Sinclair's career to date fits well into the archetype of misfit entrepreneurial innovator. He left school at seventeen, with only modest qualifications, starting work as a technical journalist writing handbooks for the electronics hobbyist.

In 1962 he started a company, Sinclair Radionics, which began in business by selling amplifier kits by mail order. It was Sinclair's innovation of cheap pocket calculators that first brought him industrial fame as his company became the UK market leader.

Diversifying quickly into digital watches, pocket television sets and digital metering equipment, Sinclair Radionics ran into financial difficulties and in 1979 Sinclair left.

His innovative genius soon found another outlet when in 1980 his new company, Sinclair Research, launched the ZX81, the inexpensive home computer that temporarily gave the UK world-wide leadership in this market by selling over 1 million units in the first 18 months. Sinclair soon added the equally successful Spectrum and the more sophisticated QL to the range. Then the business suffered from a period of bad publicity over delivery delays, followed by a downturn in the home computer market in 1985. Sinclair's reaction was typical – another innovation, the C5 electric car. The marketing philosophy of the C5 was based on the same principles as his earlier innovations of turning technologically advanced but expensive products into something which could be afforded by mass markets. This time he misjudged the market and the C5 was a financial disaster, forcing Sinclair to sell off his computer assets to Amstrad.

His innovations have not stopped there. In 1987 his new business Cambridge Computer Company launched an early portable computer, the Z88. He also launched a motorised bicycle, again priced to attract mass markets.

❑ Anita Roddick

Anita Roddick's innovations have been in areas far removed from the high technology of electronics and computers. Indeed her basic concept is not to be 'original' at all.

The daughter of Italian immigrants living in coastal Sussex, Anita Roddick had a mixed career before The Body Shop, varying between teacher, traveller and restaurateur. When her husband went off on a long trip to South America, she decided she needed 'just a little shop' to provide her with a living in his absence.

She had long been irritated by the marketing of cosmetics which were sold on a message of hope in expensive packaging.

'One of the great challenges for entrepreneurs is to identify a simple need. People tend not to trust their gut instincts enough, especially about those things that irritate them,' says Roddick in her autobiography[5]. The simple need that she identified had two main aspects. Firstly she saw the need for cosmetics in cheap containers of different sizes with simple labels, which took away the hyped images of fantasy and expectation that characterised conventional perfumery and toiletries. Secondly she believed in products made from natural ingredients, rather than chemically produced cosmetics which often relied on animal testing. In this sense she was a forerunner of the Green Movement, sharing the perceived need of a growing percentage of the population for environmentally sound, 'return-to-nature' style products. She called her shop 'The Body Shop' to reflect this simpler, honest approach to body care, even though it was named after panel-beating garages she had seen on her travels in the USA! The first shop opened in Brighton in 1976 and the second in Chichester six months later.

But fast growth came through use of another innovation, franchising. By using the commitment and cash of franchisees, the franchisor is able to devote their resources to expand the coverage of a business concept much faster than by internal organic growth. In 1984 The Body Shop was floated on the Unlisted

Securities Market; in 1988 there were 200 stores in 33 countries, and franchises were opened in the USA. By 2001 The Body Shop had grown to an international operation of nearly 2,000 outlets with sales of over £300 million.

2.2 Collective creativity

For every Sinclair and Roddick, there are thousands of unheralded owner-managers who have innovated in some way in creating their small enterprise. Their innovation may have been to only adapt existing ideas and practices to a local market; their appetite and talent for innovation may have stopped with their original idea. These are much more common experiences than the individual success story. Whilst the histories of entrepreneurial innovators like Sinclair and Roddick may inspire others to follow in their creative footsteps, it is a myth to suppose that their example can become the rule rather than the exception. Many may try, very few will succeed, and most will remain as small businesses.

To help those that remain small and yet wish to innovate, it has been suggested that co-operation and collaboration among smaller enterprises can help overcome some of their resource disadvantages. The idea of networked innovation has become increasingly popular, at least in concept. At the initiative of the European Commission, 'Business and Innovation Centres' were set up to promote regional development. Targeted on innovative industrial activities, the aim is to promote individual projects by pooling ideas, technology and commercial experiences[6]. The Department of Trade and Industry in the UK also encourage collaborative innovation through a number of initiatives including 'Inside UK Enterprise', an arrangement that enables businesses to visit other companies and exchange ideas[7].

These initiatives are based on the assumption that there is little point in trying to identify which size of business is more suited to the development of innovative products and services. Rather it is better to look for complementary relations in networks of small firms, and collaborations between small and large firms in innovative activities. Firms of different sizes can play different roles in the processes of innovation according to their levels of resources and skills[8].

Whilst new innovative heroes will undoubtedly emerge, the way forward for the majority of small businesses who wish to innovate may lie in collective creativity rather than reliance on one individual talent.

❏ **Family games**

Two families have emerged as central to the development of the games software industry in the UK, the Stampers and the Darlings.

The Stamper brothers: Christopher, Timothy and Stephen Stamper of Rare Ltd are typical of the type of entrepreneur who succeeds by collaboration with larger corporations whilst retaining their independence in a smaller business environment. In 1981, Chris Stamper dropped out of Loughborough University to start a computer programming business in a small terraced house next door to his parents' newsagent shop. He and his brothers, Tim and Stephen, set up a company, 'Ultimate Play The Game', to develop new games for home computers – such as the Sinclair ZX – which were becoming, for the first time, popular. To avoid the problems of piracy in cassette and disc-based computers, they moved into cartridge-based video games which are more difficult to copy, re-naming their company Rare Ltd. This brought them into a market sector dominated by two international corporations, Nintendo of Japan and Sega of the USA.

During the 1980s, Nintendo became the world leader in video games by producing innovative titles, such as the original Mario Bros, in-house. In 1983, when Chris Stamper first asked them to release the programming codes to write Nintendo games under licence, they refused. Stamper spent 6 months cracking the Nintendo code anyway, and offered them a skiing game called Slalom. Nintendo bought the rights to the game and Rare Ltd has gone on to produce many games for Nintendo, including the classic title Donkey Kong Country which has sold over 8 million copies since its launch in 1994, as well as games for other producers, including 'R.C. Pro-Am Racing' and 'Cobra Triangle'. In 1995, Nintendo launched Rare's 'Killer Instinct', and bought a 25 per cent stake in the company to give it more resources for development. Although the size of their business has outgrown the 'small' category, the Stamper brothers still manage it in a highly personalised way from a renovated farmhouse in Warwickshire.

The Darling brothers: David and brother Richard Darling set up Codemasters in 1986, whilst still in their teens. They have developed their business into a substantial company of 400 employees with hit games such as 'TOCA Touring Car' and 'Colin McRae Rally 2', with help from their father, Jim Darling, who is the Chairman. Like Rare Ltd, they believe in collaboration and work extensively with talented external games developers.

Nintendo and other games producers have recognised that they need to harness the innovative skills of independent software developers. Collaboration between the major hardware producers and publishers and UK game-software developers, such as Rare and Codemasters, has reached such a level that it is estimated that 40 per cent of the world's video games are written in Britain[9]. (If you want to find out more about the Stampers or the Darlings and their businesses, visit their web sites on rareware.com and codemasters.com)

Activity 3 Defining innovations

Consider the following businesses and products:

Rank Xerox copiers	The Body Shop
3M Scotch Tape (Sellotape)	Sinclair C5 electric car
Amstrad video recorders	Internet Explorer

1. In what ways were they innovative? Specify for each one what differentiates them from other businesses or products.
2. In what ways were they not innovative?

3 Misinterpretations of innovation

Innovation is widely recognised as a crucial factor in successful small business management and a key entrepreneurial activity. But innovation has been misinterpreted:

❒ **Misinterpretation 1: innovation = invention**

Innovation is strongly linked to invention but, although they overlap, they are not the same. An invention is essentially a creative idea. Innovation takes that idea, and puts it to work. Innovative activity encourages the development of new ideas, but it also turns them into useful products or services which customers need[10].

○ The British have been prolific inventors, but often failed to take their new ideas successfully to the marketplace. Joseph Swan in England developed a light bulb at the same time as Edison in the USA. Edison thought through the system required to generate and distribute power to customers for the light bulb, and developed an industry. Swan produced a superior light bulb (Edison recognised this by buying up his patents), for which others developed a market.

○ The career of Clive Sinclair has highlighted the distinction between invention and innovation. His pocket calculators, digital watches and home computers were highly successful innovations. His electric car remains an invention in search of a market.

❒ **Misinterpretation 2: innovation = new products or services only**

Innovation may result in new products or services, but it is not confined solely to their development. Certainly the most publicised innovations are often related to new product developments. Small companies have become international giants through successful product innovation. For example 3M's 'Scotch Tape', Xerox's plain paper copiers and Microsoft's computer operating system, MS DOS, turned fledgling companies into international corporations.

Innovation does not stop at products. It embraces new developments in other fields including:

○ *New markets*: it is innovative to take existing products or services and sell them into new markets. These new markets may be differentiated by types of end user; for example 3M first launched Scotch Tape in 1930 into the industrial packaging market. Their second and, in terms of company sales, more important innovation came later when Sellotape was launched into the office and domestic markets – essentially the same product but complete with dispenser.

A new market may be differentiated only by geography. Small business often innovates in this way, spotting a geographic market overlooked by larger companies, or using an idea from another town or country before it is widely introduced. Instant print shops, which expanded very quickly in the USA in the 1970s, are an example of this. The success was spotted by several UK entrepreneurs who suitably modified the idea to local conditions, and established a strong market position which the belated launch of the American originators failed to dent.

○ *New marketing methods*: the product or service can remain the same and the market does not change; the key innovation can come from the marketing of the product to the customer.

Like 3M's Scotch Tape, Xerox copiers required two innovations to become successful. When the first plain paper copier was patented, many companies turned down the opportunity to market it. The first machines were expensive the equivalent of about £50,000 today and conventional wisdom said that no-one would pay that kind of money for a gadget to help the office secretary when carbon paper cost practically nothing.

Xerox – then an obscure New York company called Halloid – thought differently. Although they helped develop the machine, their real innovation was in pricing. They sold not the machine, but what it produced – copies. Providing copiers on a rental basis for a few pennies per copy, made plain paper copying widely available at a price which looked like petty cash, not a major capital investment.

Distribution, another key marketing activity, has been fertile ground for innovative change for small businesses, as they have developed more convenient ways of making goods and services available to the customer. Successful innovations in this category include the home delivery of products from pizzas to flowers, or the lunch-time sandwich van visiting business parks.

○ *New methods of operating*: an enterprise can innovate in how it operates internally. It can change its systems or its way of doing business. Although these changes may be internal, their influence can be felt externally in the marketplace.

For example, technology is transforming how we pay for goods or services. Automated till facilities can not only directly debit a purchaser's bank account, but also provide the supplier with very detailed sales records and stock analyses. These innovations can give a business a distinct competitive edge through increased efficiency or customer knowledge.

The small business world has been increasingly affected by another operational innovation – franchising. A wide range of business concepts, from fast food restaurants to energy conservation systems, have been made available in a short time to a very wide audience through the franchising concept.

❑ **Misinterpretation 3: innovation = original**

Innovation does not take place in a vacuum. New ideas always have roots in the old; they start with what already exists, and become original from the unique way in which they combine or connect these existing ideas and knowledge.

The most prolific innovator of all, nature, creates and recreates using different combinations of a very small number of elements; we have so far only discovered just over 90 separate elements in the Universe, and living matter (which includes us) is made from only 16 of them! Although we are all 'unique', we are made from different arrangements of these small numbers of elements.

Creative thinking starts by trying to make connections between concepts that already exist, but that are too far apart for others to see. It has been said that the secret of entrepreneurial success is to use 'OPB' (Other Peoples' Brains). This is not to encourage imitation which does not create anything new. It is accepting that innovators pick up other peoples' ideas, whether old or new, and piece them together to form a unique pattern, which is only original in that no-one else has put them to use in this way before.

Dai Davies, the creator of Letraset, saw the need for faster lettering for graphic artists in order to save them time in creating advertising captions and headlines. He took an existing idea, water-based transfers which had previously been used for children's products, and adapted them for use by the professional graphic artist. Anita Roddick, on her travels, watched the women in Tahiti rub their bodies with cocoa butter, and the women of Morocco wash their hair in mud. These and other natural treatments were to form the basis of the product range of The Body Shop.

☐ **Misinterpretation 4: innovation = one-off inspiration**

Innovation does not rely on one sudden flash of inspiration to give the blueprint for a new development. Innovation is a gradual process which builds into something new and worthwhile over a period of time, through a variety of stages. We have already mentioned 3M's Scotch Tape, and Xerox's plain paper copiers, which became world-wide products, not through one innovation, but several. Similarly, Letraset's development was a process, not one immediate success. The initial water transfers were messy and time consuming to use. The company did not see real success until a second product had emerged – a dry transfer lettering system which could be easily and speedily rubbed down onto the page.

One of the most influential innovations of modern times is the development of the Internet. Although it seems like a recent phenomenon, the Internet is only the latest stage in the history of the development of communications technology which has taken place over many decades and has involved not just one but many innovations. The principles of linking together a decentralised network of independent computers were demonstrated as early as the 1960s. The first email software was developed in 1972, and in 1974 a standard software protocol (TCP/IP) was made available to ensure that independent computers could all communicate together. However, users of the Internet were restricted largely to researchers and academics until the development of the World Wide Web by Tim Berners-Lee in 1989. This innovation was crucial to extending Internet applications as it improved and simplified the distribution and retrieval of information. But it took a further innovation before the system could become popularised. In the early 1990s, the development of a web browser, Netscape Navigator, an application programme that allows users to enter and find their way around the Internet, marked the beginning of the rush for businesses and individuals to set up a web presence.

Bill Gates, founder of Microsoft, was a key innovator in the spread of personal computing. But this far, he had not played a role in the development of the Internet, and was caught somewhat by surprise by this explosion of Internet usage. Microsoft rapidly developed its own web browser, Internet Explorer, and packaged it into Windows software, the industry standard operating system for PCs. Although the US courts subsequently ruled that this move was anti-competitive, it did allow Microsoft to catch the Internet bandwagon and replace Netscape as the most popular browser system. Gates's book, *The Road Ahead*[11], proclaimed the beginning of the 'information super highway', but thus far his contribution had been limited to providing a complete package of computing software which included Internet access. However, he had awoken to the opportunity early enough to capitalise on its success.

The owners of many small enterprises do not follow Gates's example, but stop at the first innovation. A good marketable idea leads to a new business start up, which meets with early success. The founding entrepreneur can perhaps be forgiven for believing that the initial innovation was all that was required. Besides, the 'innovator' has now become a 'manager'. Having conceived the original idea, the founder now has a business to run. Management likes order, not chaos, certainties rather than novelties. Unfortunately creativity thrives on disorder, which throws up more chances for novel combinations between hitherto unconnected parts. The danger for the small business is that the opportunity for continuous innovation becomes stifled by organised management. Policies and rules are drawn up to help keep the business on the rails in the early days but these restrict the creative thinking necessary to feed the innovative growth of the future.

Activity 4 Finding innovations

How can we look for innovations? Suggest some clues in the business environment which may point to innovative opportunities. How can we watch out for them?

4 The seven sources for innovative opportunity

How can the owner-manager ensure a continuous, systematic search for innovation? The would-be innovator can look at changes in what already exists to give clues to what opportunities may exist in future.

Innovation uses and builds on changes that are already taking place. The Wright Brothers aeroplane exploited the earlier invention of the internal combustion engine by linking it to advances in the understanding of aerodynamics. The development of out-of-town superstores capitalised on changes caused by the widespread ownership of the motor car: the advantage of increased personal mobility, linked to the disadvantage of congestion in town centres. The Internet is evolving from parallel advances in computing power, networked software systems and advances in telecommunications.

The successful entrepreneur investigates and analyses change in order to find opportunities for innovation. Drucker[12] has identified seven sources for innovative opportunity.

❐ **Drucker's seven sources:**

1. the unexpected;
2. the incongruous;
3. process need;
4. industry and market structures;
5. demographics;
6. changes in perception;
7. new knowledge.

❐ **The unexpected**

A very common indicator of underlying change is the unexpected result. Unexpected success, or failure, often gives clues to underlying trends which can lead to innovation.

○ *Unexpected success*

Early computers were designed exclusively for scientific purposes. IBM demonstrated one of the first computers, which it also targeted at the scientific market. To their surprise, their established business customers showed keen interest in using this highly complex equipment for very ordinary tasks such as bookkeeping and payroll. Whilst other computer manufacturers regarded this mundane application with some disdain, IBM took this unexpected success very seriously. They developed equipment and software specifically for business customers, who in the end proved to be the most significant market for computers. By innovating in response to this unexpected interest, IBM were able to establish themselves as market leaders.

○ *Unexpected failure*

A restaurateur was initially irritated when increasing numbers of customers ordered only a jacket potato, a side dish with no main course, from his extensive menu. On investigation he found, however, that the unexpected demand for jacket potatoes could be turned to his advantage by innovating a whole range of toppings to make it a profitable, stand-alone meal which became a significant part of his lunch-time menu.

A local school was unexpectedly suffering from a decline in pupil numbers, despite its convenient location in a well populated, affluent neighbourhood, and its excellent academic record. The new head teacher investigated this unforeseen failure by talking to local parents. She found that they preferred other schools, often in the private sector, whose academic standing was no better, but which offered many more after-school activities and interests. By creating new, stimulating school clubs and societies, some even run by parents, the head teacher was soon able to report a waiting list for entry to her school.

Both the restaurateur and the head teacher based their innovations on changes to their marketplace, which were already under-way. The move towards a simple, healthier, meat-free diet, expressed itself in unusual selections from the restaurant's menu. The demand for all-round social and physical development from a child's education, not just academic results, unexpectedly affected pupil enrolments. In both cases the entrepreneur used the discovery of change through the unexpected as an opportunity for innovation.

❐ **The incongruous**

An incongruous event or result is a discrepancy between what is and what everyone expects; it occurs when there is a difference between reality, and everyone's assumption about that reality. It is also an important source of innovation because incongruity is a further sign that changes are taking place. Unlike the unexpected it is, however, more difficult to quantify; it is not likely to show up in a report of sales figures. Rather, it represents shifts in perception or attitudes.

Often the incongruity exists in the perception of customer values and requirements.

A self-employed investment consultant used an incongruous response from the small business sector to uncover a misunderstanding in his perception of customer needs. He decided to concentrate his efforts on selling investment packages to the small businessman – the successful entrepreneur who had generated some surplus cash from his or her labours, and needed an investment home for it. He expected these entrepreneurs, who had already taken considerable risks to earn money from their own business, to be prepared to take further risks to increase their surplus cash still further – only this time without all the effort of running their own business. Their response in no way matched his expectations; the risk takers did not buy his investment packages, which they viewed as too risky! This incongruous reaction gave the consultant an opportunity to innovate. By talking to these self-made entrepreneurs, he found that most of them had set up on their own, not just to make money, but more importantly to achieve independence. Once they had taken the risk to achieve that independence, they were not prepared to take a further risk, through investments, which might jeopardise it. They became, in fact, extremely cautious and conservative, demanding security for their money above all else. The investment consultant innovated by offering them a relatively risk-free package with moderate returns, which they found much more acceptable. Thus he created an opportunity from the incongruity of entrepreneurial risk takers who turned down higher risk investments.

❑ **Process need**

The importance of need as a source of innovation is captured in the proverb: 'Necessity is the mother of invention'.

Drucker highlights one particular need, the 'process need', as a major area of opportunity, because it is a very specific and easily identified need. Innovation from process need improves an existing process which is recognised as having significant limitations; it takes new, often unrelated, developments to revolutionise an existing process or way of doing something.

○ For years, there were two basic types of glass: sheet glass which was cheap but optically imperfect, and plate glass which was ground and hand polished to optical perfection and therefore expensive. There was a recognised need for cheaper, high quality distortion-free glass. But it was not until Alastair Pilkington developed 'float glass', allegedly inspired by a floating plate in his washing-up bowl, that the process need was met. Molten glass is floated on a bath of molten tin which keeps it flat and regular as it cools, eliminating the need for later labour-intensive polishing.

○ Dai Davies's invention, Letraset, likewise recognised a process need. Davies was a graphic artist, used to working to tight deadlines designing high quality presentations and artwork, usually for the advertising industry. He recognised that the process of carefully hand lettering each presentation or headline was time consuming and repetitive. So he used developments in transfer technology to transform the design process by making available easily applied lettering in a wide variety of typefaces and sizes.

In each case, it was the understanding of the need to improve a process which led to the innovation. The new knowledge required to develop the process was obviously important, but the first, crucial step was the recognition of the need in the first place. Once the need is felt, a programme of focused research can be instigated to develop the required innovation. Provided that the technology is available and the objective clearly defined and specified, such research can usually find the answer.

❑ **Industry and market structures**

Whole industry and market structures can change rapidly, sometimes after a long period of stability. Such changes offer exceptional opportunities to innovators, and considerable threat to those who incorrectly read the changes.

The structure of the printing industry has been through such a change. After a long period of stability, the basic technologies of printing changed. The pre-print activities of producing artwork and printing plates, which until the 1970s relied on photo-mechanical methods, were increasingly replaced by computer-aided technology. At the same time traditional printing methods using 'hot-metal' and letterpress were updated by more flexible offset lithography. Long training in the mysteries of the printer's art are no longer necessary. One effect in the marketplace has been the emergence of 'instant print' shops. The lower set-up costs and skills needed to start a printing business using the new technologies allowed a new type of printer to emerge. Instant print shops were an innovation in that they were located nearer the customer and offered more flexible, faster response times. This development is now being challenged by the penetration of the Internet and email which can bypass some printing applications.

Changing industry and market structures often give the small business entrepreneur opportunities to benefit from the sluggishness of larger, existing suppliers who often view structural change as threats to be resisted, rather than a chance to innovate.

❏ Demographics

Changes to the environment of an enterprise inevitably contain many possibilities for innovation, but are often hard to see, or understand, until they are past and the opportunity missed. Demographic changes, however, are clear and unambiguous, and signalled well in advance. Demography is the study of statistics of the population births, deaths, diseases, employment, education, income and the trends which these figures show. These statistic are universally accepted as key indicators of demand changes within society which are often highly predictable. A high birth rate in one year will inevitably mean an increased need for First School places four to five years later. Lower death rates and longer life expectancy will be sure to create more demand for retirement homes and old age care facilities. These new requirements create many opportunities for innovation which can be seen well in advance; yet often these key numbers are overlooked in the search for entrepreneurial ideas.

The 'Swinging 60s' gave rise to a host of innovations, many in the fashion, leisure and entertainments industry. Whilst this may have seemed like a sudden revolution in attitudes and patterns of demand it should have come as no real surprise to the student of demographics, who could have pointed to the post war baby boom, which in turn meant a dramatically increased percentage of teenagers in the population by the 1960s. Their predominance in that decade ensured that activities would reflect youthful values and demands. Similarly in the 21st century, we know that the age profile of the population has become older, with an increase in the percentage of people 70 years old and over, and a decrease in the number of young people. The alert innovator will be developing enterprises with these trends firmly in mind.

❏ Changes in perception

Some changes are not really changes at all. The facts do not change, but people's perception of the facts change, which has an equally powerful effect.

The fashion industry relies heavily on changes in perception. Clothes from an earlier generation do not change, but our perceptions of them do. We regard the trendy garments of yesterday as comically out of date today.

Changes in perception give the entrepreneur many new openings.

○ Twenty years ago, vegetarian restaurants and health food shops were viewed as strictly for a minority fringe element of the population. The food has not changed dramatically, but now every restaurant has to have at least one vegetarian dish, as our perception of what we ought to eat has shifted.

○ Today we perceive an urgent need to protect our environment, a notion that had little following a decade or so ago. Anita Roddick sensed this shift in values well before it became common policy to have green products, in creating The Body Shop.

The skilful innovator will be careful to differentiate between temporary changes in perception, or 'fads', and longer lasting developments. The entertainment industry, for example, throws up a continuous stream of new heroes, from masked cowboys to oriental warriors. Focusing an enterprise entirely on any one of these novelties would be a very short-term strategy, as young people's fidelity to any one heroic concept is extremely fickle. However there is a well established long-term need for heroes on which the innovators in Hollywood have built up a world-wide industry.

❑ **New knowledge**

The most famous innovations are often based on new knowledge, or inventions. The first telephone made by Alexander Graham Bell, the light bulb demonstrated by Thomas Edison, the radio messages of Guglielmo Marconi and the early television transmissions of John Logie Baird are all well known.

But despite the publicity, knowledge-based innovations are the most problematic and, in many respects, the least attractive to entrepreneurs.

The time between new knowledge being available and its successful development into marketable products is long. The idea of using radio waves to transmit visual information was around in the early days of radio in the 1890s, but only became practical with the first television transmission in 1926.

Innovations based on new knowledge also require not just one independent discovery, but the bringing together of several developments. Baird's first television, itself based on earlier research on radio waves, scanned an image into lines of dots of light by a mechanical method. More sophisticated, electronic systems were required before television could become an acceptable product, a decade or so after the first transmission.

The development of the Internet has followed these patterns, (as described earlier in section 3 of this Unit). The linking of computers to form an international communications network, or Internet, has been developing since the 1960s. But it took other advances such as an easy-to-use interface in the form of the World Wide Web and web browsers for this to become practically useful. Further developments which overcome current problems, such as the security of payments, are required before the full commercial potential of this innovation can be realised.

Activity 5 Finding the market

Ideally, how can small businesses make sure that their products are acceptable in the marketplace? In practice, how do they tend to develop new products and services?

5 Innovating for the marketplace

5.1 Missing the market

Creativity in business is only beneficial if it has a practical application. New product ideas need to be based on the needs of customers if they are to have any use. We have already drawn the distinction between an invention – a creative idea – and innovation which takes ideas and puts them to work. The process of implementing innovation can only happen by reference to the marketplace.

Entrepreneurs originated because of the need to shift resources from where they were under-used, or surplus, to areas where there was demand because of relative shortages. This was done through the 'marketplace', where those with a surplus – something to sell – could meet with those who had a shortage – a need to buy.

Business and commerce has its roots in this concept of the marketplace. The ancient bazaars of the Middle East, the medieval merchants of the Mediterranean and the shopkeepers of Victorian England, all based their trade on understanding what customers in the marketplace wanted, finding it for them, and making it available in an acceptable way at the right price. They were small businesses by today's standards, whose size made regular contact with customers inevitable, helping them identify with the markets they served.

One of the most common reasons given for the failure of a small business today is that it did not identify a viable market – there were insufficient customers for its products. If the origins of entrepreneurship and the traditions of commerce over the centuries are based on understanding the needs of customers, why did modern businesses 'unlearn' this fundamental principle and need retraining in customer-orientation? Some of the reasons are:

❐ Technology and other advances in human knowledge and skills have made many more new products or services possible. It is increasingly tempting to launch a new business based on an idea just because it becomes possible, rather than because there is an identifiable, sustainable demand from the marketplace. Larger, as well as smaller, organisations fall into this trap; the development of Concorde may have been a great technological advance, but it has been a very limited business success. Successful entrepreneurs from Branson to Sinclair have indulged in ideas which were temptingly possible but which did not pass the ultimate test of market demand.

❐ Modern business has become a very complicated mixture of forces and influences. A small business manager has to consider not just the demands of customers but the requirements of many other forces, including the government, employees, suppliers, banks, other financial partners, existing competitors, and potentially new competition. The owner-manager does not have time to fully consider all these influences, and sometimes it is the customer who is forgotten.

❑ The complex nature of modern business requires systems and policies to help manage and control the confusion. Order reduces the chaos of conflicting demands and makes the accomplishment of necessary tasks more likely. Unfortunately order tends to create inflexibility; ways of doing things, once established, are difficult to change. The marketplace however is constantly changing: customers' preferences change; competitive products and services come and go; technology creates new opportunities; the law imposes new constraints. The small enterprise with limited resources can be tempted to over-organise its activities so that it fails to understand and respond to these changes.

❑ As an enterprise grows, it needs more levels of management. This tends to make key decision makers, even in relatively small companies, more remote from the marketplace and the customer.

5.2 Approaches to the market

There are two theoretical extremes in how enterprises develop products or services for the marketplace: the 'product-based' approach or the 'market-based' approach as illustrated in Figure 4.2. The product-based approach implies that the enterprise is primarily concerned with product development, or the internal demands of the organisation. It can lead to inflexible, even arrogant attitudes towards the ultimate buyer of the product or service ('I wish all the people who want to shop at lunch time, would realise we have to eat as well', a store manager). It can lead also to successful products which, by chance, find a market.

The market-based approach on the other hand seeks to find out what the customer wants and is willing to pay for. It implies that the enterprise is focused around the needs of the customer, rather than its own internal requirements[13]. It does not leave success to chance as it first researches market needs, and then develops products and services to meet them.

PRODUCT-BASED APPROACHES		MARKET-BASED APPROACHES	
Stage 1	Product *idea* by firm	Stage 1	Market *analysis* by firm or individual
Stage 2	Product *developed*	Stage 2	Market *identified* and needs estimated
Stage 3	Product *sold*	Stage 3	Product *criteria* established
Stage 4	Product *adapted* according to sales levels	Stage 4	Product *developed* and tested with target market
		Stage 5	Product *marketed* to customer

Figure 4.2 Product-based and market-based approaches to the market

In practice, product development in small business is unlikely to take a totally market-based approach, however desirable that may be, for a variety of reasons, including:

❐ Owner-managers starting a business usually have a specific skill or knowledge which they wish to exploit.

❐ The business is already established and wishes to add to its existing product range without diversification.

❐ The business has established products which it wishes to sell to new customers.

A successful approach to the market is a combination of understanding the resources available and matching them to an idea for a new product or service, which fills a gap in the marketplace. This is illustrated in Figure 4.3.

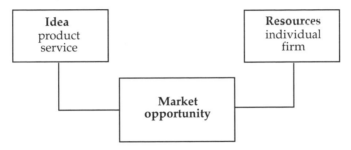

Figure 4.3 Matching ideas to resources

This summarises the matching process that takes place when an idea, based on customer demand or needs, is linked to the existing or future resources of an enterprise. It acknowledges not just the importance of the customer, but also the strengths and weaknesses of the owner-manager and their small business in relation to the market opportunity.

Activity 6 The rifle not the blunderbuss

Small businesses are tempted sometimes to appeal to everyone in general in order to increase sales, but they end up serving no-one in particular. How can they focus what they have to offer more precisely?

6 Who is the customer?

6.1 Market segments and niches

It is possible for a small business to regard customers as the focal point of its activities yet still fail.

Failure can come from an inability to define precisely who is the target customer. It is always tempting to believe that products or services can have a universal appeal, or that it is safer to offer them to as wide a market as possible.

However, there is overwhelming evidence that successful companies, large as well as small, carefully target customer groups. These companies identify sub divisions of markets – referred to as segments – and specialised subdivisions of segments – referred to as niches.

Data on hundreds of companies world-wide has been analysed for many years by the Strategic Planning Institute of Cambridge, Massachusetts, USA, in a project called PIMS (Profit Impact of Market Strategy). This study shows that firms achieve long-term profitability by selling high value-added products or services to viable market niches, and establishing a leadership position within them. In other words, it is better to have a high share of a relatively small market than a small share of a relatively large market.

This is particularly valid for small enterprises whose limited resources make the precisely targeted approach to the customer even more preferable. In reviewing strategy options for small firms, Storey concluded that *'innovation and the identification of a particular niche were key strategies associated with more rapid growth in small firms'*.[14]

The purpose of segmentation

There are also dangers in identifying closely with one group of customers. Small firms can become over-dependent on one customer or over-concentrated on a small number of them. The Bolton Report referred to the high dependency of small firms on a narrow customer base. Research[15] found that one customer accounted for over 25 per cent of the sales in a third of the companies studied.

However, market segmentation should not be confused with customer concentration. Segmentation is based on the simple truth that customers buy similar types of products and services for different reasons, which give rise to different expectations of what they are buying.

For example, people buy books for many reasons: for pleasure, for study, for reference, for presents, even for show. Each end use will require differing qualities and specifications from the books purchased, not just in the content of the book, but also its size, appearance, durability, price and so on.

The principle of segmentation categorises customers and consumers into groups with similar needs and expectations from their purchases. The more precise the definition of the customer group, the more precise can be the definition of their needs and requirements.

The whole purpose of market segmentation is to allow a small business to use its resources where they count most. Segmentation allows the small enterprise to look for the most promising openings for its special talents and advantages, a niche where its strengths will be of most value and its weaknesses of little account.

The process is to discover natural groupings amongst both customers and consumers, which match the special abilities of a small firm.

6.2 The segmentation process for a small firm

Definition of the target segments for a small business can be achieved in stages as illustrated in Figure 4.4.

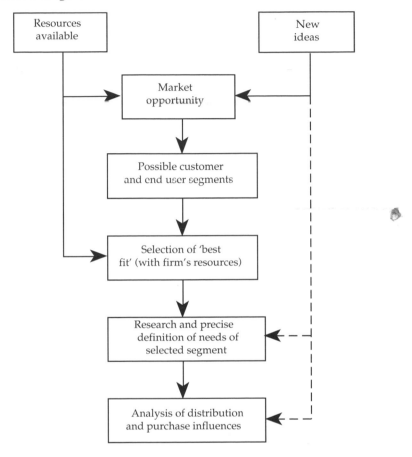

Figure 4.4 Segmentation process for a small business

A balancing of the resources available to a small enterprise with new ideas for possible innovations establishes a general definition of a market opportunity. This is refined into possible customer and consumer segments. A selection is then made of the segment which best fits with the resources available to the firm[16].

For example a small business, having focused on the market opportunity of publishing books covering business subjects, decided to further specialise in students in higher and further education as the most promising way of using its special talents and strengths.

This is one of the most crucial decisions that a small business makes, influencing how it operates and where and what it sells.

Further research into the selected segment makes possible a more precise definition of the purchasing habits and requirements of the target market. This research includes considering the distribution chain and analysing other possible major influences on the purchase decision. In some sectors, a 'decision making unit' (DMU), consisting of a number of people playing different roles in the buying process, has to be identified in order to establish customer needs. At these stages new ideas may again be considered.

The choice of the student segment by our publishing business actually determines who will be the customer, as the firm will need to sell through the established distribution channels of wholesalers and retailers specialising in student sales. Setting up a new access system to the target market would be a much harder route. The decision also reveals other influences in the purchase decision which will need careful consideration; in this case, lecturers of business studies play an important role in determining student purchases through recommended reading lists. The decision-making unit is made up therefore of: bookshop/retailer (the direct customer), student (the end user) and lecturer (influencer/specifier).

The segmentation process is important for a new business start up. It is equally important for an existing small business to understand the changing needs of its target market. If the business develops beyond its initial customer groups the segmentation process will need to be repeated.

Activity 7 Why did you buy?

Consider a small business (for example a restaurant, take away food outlet, confectioners, clothes retailer, hairdressers) that you have used on more than one occasion. What are (a) the features of the products or services offered, (b) their benefits to you, and (c) the competitive edge which attracted you back to that business?

7 Why will the customer buy from me?

7.1 The matching process

Sales are the life blood of an enterprise, providing the income upon which all other functions, from production to accounts, ultimately depend. The point of contact between the customer and the business will vary from a direct sales visit, to a retail shop in the high street, to mail order, or even word of mouth recommendations. But whatever form it takes, the sales activity represents the motive force which drives the small business on, or causes it to stall, sometimes never to start again.

Selling is essentially a matching process. Customers have certain requirements or needs. An enterprise offers products or services which have certain characteristics or features. Customers compare their needs to the benefits which these features offer them, and either accept or reject the costs associated with acquiring those benefits. Figure 4.5 illustrates this process.

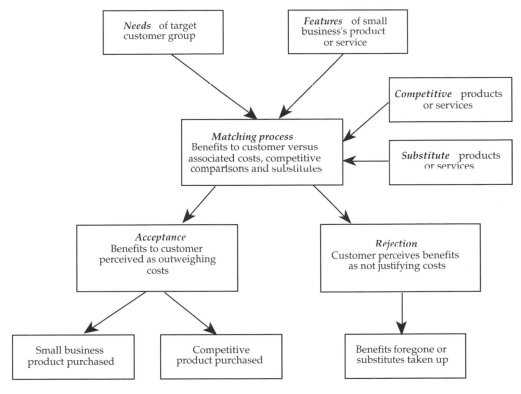

Figure 4.5 The sales process in a small business

7.2 Features and benefits

In the matching process, the customer's decision hinges on the benefits offered by a product or service, not its features.

❐ A *feature* is a characteristic of a product or service. For example, a student's text book has a soft, laminated cover; this is a feature of the product.

❐ A *benefit* is the value of a product feature to a customer. For example, the benefits of a soft laminated cover are that it is hard wearing, and therefore lasts well, whilst being light and easy to carry.

These are benefits which are relevant to students; they might be inappropriate to other customer groups, and therefore not really benefits. For example a book that was targeted at the coffee table market, for display purposes, would probably require benefits of high-quality finish and attractiveness rather than lightness and durability.

A successful small business meets the needs of the targeted customer group by ensuring the features of its products or services translate into benefits appropriate to the customer.

Price: the overused benefit

Inevitably in a competitive environment, the customer has choice. The purchase decision is not based solely on an assessment of whether the benefits on offer outweigh the costs to acquire them.

Comparisons are made with competitive products or services, and the benefits they offer. What is on offer is seldom unique, so a prospective customer usually has the opportunity to shop around and assess the purchase benefits that competitive products offer before making a choice.

Substitute products, or alternative ways of acquiring the benefits, are often also considered. Does the student purchase a book or a cassette programme, for example? Can the information required be obtained from other sources, e.g. TV programmes, articles, libraries? Competition does not only come from directly comparable products or services.

To get the sale, the small business has to offer the customer more benefits than competitors and substitutes.

It is always tempting for a small business to compete mainly on price. By offering a product or service at the lowest possible price the small business helps stimulate a purchase in the first place; it is offering benefits at the lowest possible cost of acquiring them. Low prices can be an advantage over the competition for a small firm, or they may keep consideration of substitutes to a minimum.

In some instances, a small business with low overheads can compete on price in the longer term, provided they do not grow to a size where central overheads are required. A freelance bookkeeper working from home is always likely to charge significantly less than an accounting practice with premises and office staff to support.

However, there is evidence that many small businesses compete on price when they are first set up, based primarily on the cheap labour of the owner. There is even concern that government subsidies, aimed at helping a new enterprise in its early days, may be used to gain short-term advantages by undercutting the competition. This can cause problems, sometimes terminal ones, for established businesses and the new business cannot sustain its price advantage once the subsidies are removed.

Unless a business has established economies not available to its competitors it is unlikely to gain long-term competitive advantage through pricing policies alone. As economies of scale are not usually available to a small business (because of their size), low prices are most likely to come from short-term cost savings: for example the owner does not expect a market wage, particularly in the start-up phase of the business, or little investment is made in product development or marketing. As other businesses are likely to react by lowering their prices, the small firm may find that the only result of price competition is to reduce the profitability of the total business segment. Under-pricing has certainly been a major factor in small business failures.

7.3 The competitive edge

If a small firm is unlikely to gain long-term advantages over the competition through low prices, it still has to find a competitive edge if it is to survive and grow.

A competitive edge is the means by which the small firm differentiates itself from the competition. It comes ultimately from the careful selection of a target market in which the small enterprise can offer something better than anyone else. It answers the question: *Why will this particular group of customers buy from me rather than anyone else?*

The competitive edge of a small firm can be described in terms of benefits, with two main characteristics:

i)   they are benefits significant to the target market segment;

ii) in total, they amount to a greater package of benefits than those offered by competitors.

To return to our example of the book publisher, this firm considered the needs of its target customer segment – students of business studies in higher and further education – and produced the following list of desirable benefits for books offered:

❏ easy to understand, readable contents;

❏ easy to follow (and memorise) layout;

❏ affordable prices;

❏ light and hard wearing;

❏ available when required;

❏ up to date information;

❏ texts aligned to courses taught.

When investigating how well existing suppliers met these needs, the small firm discovered two problem areas: many books covered broad subject areas, not necessarily in line with the content of specific courses; students complained that recommended texts were frequently out of stock at the beginning of term.

From this the small firm developed its competitive edge. By working closely with lecturing staff it developed innovative texts which followed courses of study, not just subject areas. By specialising in business studies it was able to concentrate on specific outlets and, by giving them a fast delivery service, to ensure adequate stocks of recommended texts at the beginning of courses.

The firm's books became the market leaders as text books in the limited areas covered. They gained a large share of a small market by understanding the target market better than any of their competitors, and offering products and services that were different in ways that were of significant benefit to the customer.

8 Case studies and activities

Case studies *Innovating for target markets*

Case 1 Andrea goes back to school

Andrea Clarey decided to concentrate her efforts on the schools market for the payroll service that she was setting up. She considered that a possible large contract from the local authority where she currently worked would make her too dependent on one customer – and there was no guarantee she would win the contract despite a considerable amount of effort that would have to go into any tender for it. Her preliminary investigations into a possible market for her service amongst primary and secondary schools had indicated that she should further target her efforts. First she had decided to concentrate on smaller schools, and primary schools in particular. Secondary schools were larger but there were fewer of them and those she called on used either the local educational authority or well established accountants to handle their substantial payrolls. Secondly, she found out that some state schools had more financial independence than others. This invariably meant they had to source their own payroll system and the smaller primary schools usually bought in the service from a local supplier.

She also felt that she could develop a competitive edge by an innovative service not offered elsewhere to her knowledge. She had stumbled upon the idea when she attended an annual meeting of parents with governors at her daughter's local school. As part of the changes in the way state schools are managed, governors had taken on more responsibilities, but also had to report back to parents once a year giving them information on such matters as the financial accounts of the school. Andrea noticed that over 75 per cent of expenditure at her daughter's school was on staff salaries and she asked the Chairman of Governors if this was normal and how it compared to other, similar-sized schools.

'Yes, quite normal,' he had assured her, 'although since schools became more autonomous we get less and less comparative information from other schools – so I can't tell you, for example, how typical the amounts we spend on administrative compared to educational costs are.'

This had given Andrea an idea. The local council where she worked had just bought a 'benchmarking' system for its services. This allowed it to compare its efficiencies in key areas such as manpower deployment and response times for enquiries with other large organisations. Andrea thought she could do something similar for schools.

'As part of my payroll service for schools, I could offer them an analysis of their costs with trends and historic comparisons,' she thought. 'Then I could offer them comparative information from other schools who are also my clients – completely confidentially of course. That ought to give me an edge over the competition.'

Case 2 Kit tracks an idea

Kit Hugos was trying to persuade his partner in their embryonic electronics business to give him the go-ahead to develop his new product idea – a personal tracking device. 'The principle is not new,' he said. 'Basically it's a radio transmitter which can be attached to a person so that their whereabouts can be tracked at all times. What is new is the size and power of the latest electronic components and circuitry. I can now design a device the size of a thumb nail which can be carried discreetly on a person and transmit their whereabouts up to fifty miles away. It can feed co-ordinates into a computer mapping system so that the precise location of the device – and the person wearing it – can be identified. It can also be fitted with an alarm system in case of problems.'

'Sounds very interesting,' his partner, Robin Davidson, said. 'But who do you see buying it – and at what cost?'

'Every time I think about this product I can see more applications. Organisations with large sites used by lots of people find it almost impossible to provide the round-the-clock surveillance that is needed for security these days. Parents are concerned about the whereabouts of their children whether they're toddlers in the park or teenagers out at night. Now they can track them on a computer screen all the time and be alerted if there is a crisis. The actual device can be made quite cheaply. We could probably sell it for less than £50. The big cost comes with the computer mapping software, which obviously has to be very local, and would need to be developed for the locality of the users.'

Activities

Ideally, how can small businesses make sure that their products are acceptable? In the case of Andrea and Kit:

i) Would you describe their ideas as innovative? If so, in what way? In what ways are their ideas potentially flawed?

ii) Who will be their potential customers and what benefits will they offer them?

iii) Do their ideas amount to a competitive edge which can sustain a business?

iv) Can you think of different target markets for their ideas? Or other innovative opportunities for their chosen services?

v) What should they do next? Advise Andrea and Kit on how they should proceed with the next stage of developing their new business.

Extended activity *Local innovation and markets*

Consider the list of local businesses you drew up for the Extended activity in Unit 1. (If you did not complete this activity, draw up a list of local businesses, large and small, involved in the food and drink industry which operate in a local community with which you are familiar.)

i) Which ones do you consider to have been innovative and in what ways?

ii) Is there a noticeable correlation between the likelihood of innovation and the size of the business in the sample you have considered?

iii) Consider three or four of the smaller businesses in your sample. Who are their target markets, and why do their customers buy from them rather than other businesses?

In conclusion

At the end of this Unit, it is recommended that you go to Section B, Planning a new venture, and complete Step 1.4, Selecting the idea.

9 References and further reading

References and further information

1. See for example, Davis, W. 'The Innovators' in Henry, J. and Walker, D. (eds), *Managing Innovation*, Sage Publications, 1991.

2. Rothwell, R. 'The Role of Small Firms in Technological Innovation' in Curran, J., Stanworth, J. and Watkins, D. (eds), *The Survival of the Small Firm*, Vol. 2, Gower, 1986.

3. Robson, M. and Townsend, J. *Trends and Characteristics of Significant Innovations and their Innovators in the UK since 1945*, Science Policy Research Unit, 1984. The data reproduced here is taken from a summary produced in reference 2 above.

4. See Reich, R. *Entrepreneurship Reconsidered: The Team as Hero*, Harvard Business Review (May/June), 1987.

5. Roddick, A. *Body and Soul*, Ebury Press, 1991.

6. The first Business and Innovation Centres were set up in 1985. They publish a newsletter, *Network*, obtainable from European Business and Innovation Centres Network (EBN), Avenue de Tervueren 188A, B-1150 Brussels, Belgium.

7. See the Small Business Service and Business Link web site on www.businesslink.org

8. Rizzoni, A. 'Technological Innovation and Small Firms: A Taxonomy', *International Small Business Journal*, 9, 3, 1992.

9. Dawley, H. and Eng, P. 'Killer Instinct for Hire', *Business Week*, 29 May, 1995.

10. See Adair, J., *The Challenge of Innovation*, Talbot Adair Press, 1990.

11. Gates, B. *The Road Ahead*, Viking, 1995.

12. Drucker, P. *Innovation and Entrepreneurship*, Heinemann, 1986.

13. For a fuller discussion of these concepts, see one of the texts on marketing which include: Kotler, P. *Marketing Management*, Prentice Hall, 1997; Stokes, D., *Marketing: A Case Study Approach*, Continuum, 2001.

14. Storey, D. *Understanding the Small Business Sector*, Routledge, 1994, p. 149.

15. Cambridge Small Business Research Centre, *The State of British Enterprise*, Department of Applied Economics, University of Cambridge, 1992.

16. For a more detailed description of segmentation see Stokes, D. *Marketing: A Case Study Approach*, Continuum, 2001, Chapter 7.

Recommended further reading

❏ Birley, S. and Muzyka, F. *Mastering Entrepreneurship*, FT/Prentice Hall, 2000. Chapter 2, 'The opportunity'.

❏ Hardaker, G. and Graham, G. *Wired Marketing: Energising Business for E-commerce*, John Wiley and Sons, 2001.

❏ Henry, J. and Walker, D. (eds), *Managing Innovation*, Sage Publications, 1991. Chapter 6, 'Entrepreneurship Reconsidered: The Team As Hero' (Reich, R.), and Chapter 14, 'The Innovators' (Davis, W.).

❏ Drucker, P. *Innovation and Entrepreneurship*, Heinemann, 1986. Section 1 'The Practice of Innovation'.

❏ Goss, D. *Small Business and Society*, Routledge, 1991. Chapter 6, 'Small Business, New Technology and Innovation'.

❏ Adair, J. *The Challenge of Innovation*, Talbot Adair Press, 1990. Chapter 8, 'Team Creativity'.

❏ Roddick, A. *Body and Soul*, Ebury Press, 1991.

❏ Stokes, D. *Marketing: A Case Study Approach*, Continuum, 2001. Chapter 4, 'Customers and competitors', and Chapter 7, 'Marketing strategies'.

❏ Barrow, C. and Barrow, P. *The Business Plan Workbook*, Kogan Page, 2001.

❏ The Which? *Guide to Starting your Own Business*, Consumers Association, 1998. Chapter 4 has useful information and advice on marketing and selling.

5 Information and help

To set up a successful new venture, an owner-manager needs information and, quite often, some help. This Unit considers what information owner-managers need about their marketplace and how they might obtain it with the limited resources at their disposal. The sources of help and advice available to small firms are examined, including a review of government policies aimed at supporting small businesses.

Contents

Activity 1 Information required

What is the key information an owner-manager need:

a) before launching a new venture?

b) after the venture has been set up?

1 Entrepreneurial information gathering

1.1 Entrepreneurial networking

To survive and succeed in the marketplace, a would-be entrepreneur needs information to help answer two fundamental questions:

i) Is there sufficient demand for the products or services of a new enterprise so that it can establish itself as a viable business?

Before start up, the prospective owner-manager can attempt to reduce the unknown risk of a new business to the level of acceptable risk by researching the marketplace. The feasibility of a new venture can only be assessed with the help of information on the market and business environment in which it will operate. This market research has two purposes[1]:

○ To develop and confirm a strategy for market entry based upon the identifiable needs of the target customer group.

○ To provide credibility to outside backers and financiers and convince them that the new venture is founded on the realities of the marketplace, not just the dreams of the entrepreneur.

ii) Can an established small business adapt to the ever-changing environment to take advantage of any opportunities that may arise and withstand any threats to its existence?

Successful owner-managers have a good understanding of the environment in which their enterprise operates. They know their customers well; they keep an eye on competitive activity; they are aware of underlying trends which may affect their business. Researchers have suggested that a key factor in business survival is how quickly new owner-managers can understand their environment, and then learn from their experience of dealing with it[2]. Such research has also shown that future growth is critically affected by how well the owner-manager stays in touch with external influences. Successful business development begins with an awareness of the total situation surrounding an enterprise, and the modification of initial objectives to suit this ever-changing environment. Adjustment to the business environment is crucial to long-term survival[3].

There are several problems facing owner-managers in their attempts to understand their environment:

- ❏ Owner-managers tend to concentrate on immediate day-to-day problems, overlooking the wider, often long-term issues.

- ❏ Small firms often operate with a relatively small customer base. Information can be over-dependent on feedback from a small number of customers, leading to a blindness about other aspects of the environment.

- ❏ Owner-managers seem suspicious of formalised market research. Accessible market information is not necessarily relevant to the position of a small firm. There is a reluctance to commission more relevant research because of its costs.

For these reasons, owner-managers tend to rely on informal information gathering methods of highly variable reliability. Even successful entrepreneurs use informal networks to keep up to date, using extensive contacts to develop a rich mental map of their environment[4].

This has been described as *entrepreneurial networking*[5] in which the owner-manager seeks feedback from people they know well about decisions they are about to make. Typically, this is done face to face, in an unplanned and opportunistic way.

It would seem that a small firm owner's approach to information gathering is often 'chaotic and opportunistic'[5]. They tend to shy away from planned programmes of market research. They do not have the time, nor often the skill, to sift through the mountain of data which could inform their business decisions. Instead, they tend to gather information 'on-the-hoof' as they go about their daily tasks.

Successful entrepreneurs have an uncanny knack of picking up the really pertinent pieces of knowledge they need, seemingly without having to process other, less relevant, information. For example, Alan Sugar took Amstrad into a wide variety of electrical household products from videos to home computers by trusting his personal 'antennae' to be in tune with what the market wants rather than using formalised research to assess customer needs.

1.2 Entrepreneurial information needs

Even an informal information gathering process has to start by asking the right questions[5]. So what does a small enterprise need to know about its marketplace?

- ❏ *Market information* is essentially about existing customers and competitors. It seeks to give a small business answers to questions including the following:

  - ○ What are the *characteristics* of existing customers and potential new customers?
    - – *Who* makes the buying decision?
    - – *What* are the differences between customer groups? e.g. between those who buy a lot and those who buy a little.
    - – *When* are purchases made? e.g. on a regular or cyclical basis.

- ○ What is the *size* of the target market?
  - – The number of customers?
  - – Volume of purchases?
  - – Value of purchases?
  - – What are estimates for the above in one year's time, and subsequently?
- ○ Who is the direct *competition*?
  - – How many competitors?
  - – How big?
  - – How successful?
- ○ What are the *substitutes* for the product or service? What choices does the buyer have in terms of:
  - – indirect alternatives?
  - – substitutes for discretionary expenditure?

❐ *Marketing information* is about those factors which can change the existing position of customers and competitors. It seeks to find out what will influence customers in their decision making through such questions as:

- ○ What benefits is the customer seeking to acquire from the product or service offered?
- ○ How will the buying decision be made? (Who will have an influence on the decision and how will this be exerted?)
- ○ Where does the customer buy existing products or services? What distribution channels are used?
- ○ What price parameters are there?
- ○ How does the customer find out about the product or service? By word of mouth? By advertising and other promotional activities?
- ○ How well do competitors meet the requirements of the target customers' group? What are their strengths and weaknesses in relation to customer preferences?
- ○ How do competitors use marketing activities in relation to the target market?
  - – What is their pricing policy?
  - – How do they promote?
  - – How do they distribute?
  - – What is their product strategy?

Such information is just as important to the developing enterprise as it is to the new business start up. Time and cost factors will restrict the volume and accuracy of answers available to these questions, but the successful owner-manager will continually be looking for answers through formal and informal methods.

Activity 2 Primary or secondary data?

Information is sometimes categorised into primary and secondary data.

a)   What is the difference between the two?

b)   What are the advantages and disadvantages of each type for an owner-manager?

2 Market research for small firms

2.1 The research process

Entrepreneurs tend to regard market and marketing research as long-winded and expensive, but there are many inexpensive and uncomplicated ways in which a small business can research the marketplace.

An example of a research process which can be undertaken by a small firm is shown in Figure 5.1. The stages of this process are:

1.   Describe the target customer segment. Any description of the customer group under investigation needs to be as precise as possible, to avoid wasting resources in gathering unnecessary data.

2.   Define research objectives: what will the information be used for once it has been obtained? What questions, if answered, will meet the aims of the research?

3.   Check existing knowledge and data: there is always a wealth of existing data available especially in an ongoing business. Some of this may not always be obvious even to the owner-manager. Customer records, sales people, sales assistants, invoice records, sales ledgers, financial statistics, these are all very important potential sources of information about the marketplace.

4.   Define new information required. What new information will be required if the questions arising from the research objectives are to be answered?

5.   Decide methods to be used to gather data. The following sections of this Unit discuss what methods are available.

6.   Collect data.

7.   Analyse existing and new data. New and existing data is usually raw information which needs collating and turning into intelligent information, i.e. data which has been interpreted and summarised.

8.   Evaluate and review strategy in the light of information gained through research: this is the stage at which decisions relating to the objectives of the research can be made. It may involve a rethink about the customer segment under investigation. Does the information support the targeting of the selected segment and, if so, how can this be best pursued? Should the firm's resources be concentrated on a different segment, in which case which one, and what research now needs to be undertaken?

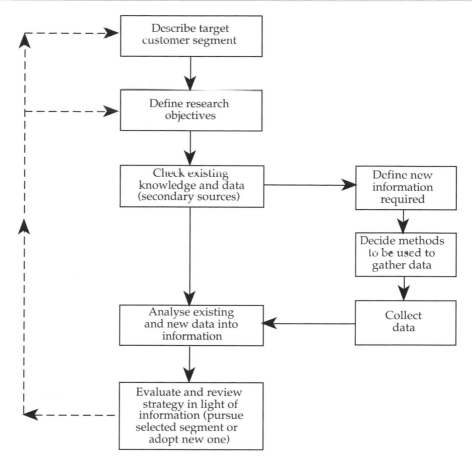

Figure 5.1 A market research process for a small enterprise

2.2 Research methods

The questions which are posed by the research objectives will determine which methods can be used for collecting the data. Data is divided into two basic categories:

❏ Primary: new data specifically collected for the project, usually through field research.

❏ Secondary: data that already exists which can be collected by desk research.

The comparative advantages and disadvantages of each type are summarised in Figure 5.2.

PRIMARY	SECONDARY
Information collected specifically for the purpose in hand	Information that already exists somewhere
ADVANTAGES	ADVANTAGES
• reflects specific need	• lower cost
• up to date	• more immediate
• individual control	• wide ranging data
DISADVANTAGES	DISADVANTAGES
• expensive	• does not meet your exact needs
• time-consuming	• often out of date
• risk of competitors finding out your intentions	• may be incomplete or inaccurate

Figure 5.2 Advantages and disadvantages of primary and secondary data

Activity 3 Secondary sources

Someone asks for your advice on how to find out about the market environment for their proposed new business. What secondary information sources would you advise them to investigate?

3 Secondary data

3.1 Sources of data for market information

Research usually considers secondary information sources first. Small firms most commonly use secondary data because it is immediate and either free or low cost. The main sources of information are:

❐ **Internal sources**

    The internal records and knowledge base of an existing small business is the obvious place to start, as it is low cost, available data and usually reliable. Most small firms have at least basic records of customers, sales and costs; they may also keep records of prospective customers e.g. from sales visit reports. Non-written information may also exist, for example from the knowledge of staff who deal with customers. One of the advantages of buying an existing business for the new entrant is that this type of internal information should exist to help them assess the risks involved.

❐ **Personal contact networks**

    We have already referred to the importance of entrepreneurial networking – the personal contacts, relationships and alliances which owner-managers develop. These can provide a rich source of informal information. Networks include suppliers, customers, local businesses, contacts in the trade, professional advisors such as bank managers, accountants and solicitors, former colleagues, friends and acquaintances. For someone starting up a new venture with few contacts in the trade, suppliers are often a good source of information: they are usually in regular contact with similar businesses and have a vested interested in helping a potential new customer get started.

❐ **Trade associations**

These may be specific to a particular trade or industry, (for example, the Federation of Fish Friers), or a locality (the local Chamber of Commerce). Both may be able to provide information and contacts for the new entrant.

❐ **Competitor sources**

Most businesses publish information about themselves, usually intended for customers, but also obtainable by other small firms. Accessible published information includes web sites, product information leaflets, reports and accounts. Trade shows and exhibitions can be good sources of competitive information; the catalogue will provide a good summary of the existing companies in the field and literature can be collected easily from one place. Franchisors give information to prospective franchisees on the prospects in their particular market, which in some circumstances can be obtained by new entrants who are not taking up a franchise.

❐ **External secondary sources**

The Internet has made access to external sources of information easy and fast, provided you know what you are looking for. Other external sources include central and local government, directories, published statistics and reports, and national and trade press articles. Government statistics and those published by other official bodies can have the disadvantage of being out of date, and not in line with exact needs. General guides, or web portals, to the information available (listed below) are a good place to start for anyone unfamiliar with the range of possible data.

Many sources of data can be referred to free of charge on the Internet or in a library. Where information has to be purchased it is still relatively low cost as the data collection is amortised over many subscribers. Trade associations, chambers of commerce, banks, universities, colleges of further and higher education and research institutions are good sources of information for specific fields. Newspapers and periodicals tend to provide more general data but can be useful for background information.

There is now a huge amount of data, much of which is available on the Internet, covering a wide range of products, markets, and companies. Listed below are some suggestions on where to start looking.

3.2 Published data

This is not intended as an exhaustive listing, but a general indication of where to start, how much information is available and of what type. For a more comprehensive list, consult the general guides given below.

General guides can be used to find out what data exists.

- ❏ ukonline.gov.uk provides a single entry point to over 1,000 government web sites containing information and details of services available. Important links for a business owner are:
  - – dti.gov.uk The DTI aims to promote enterprise and innovation and their web site is a good starting point for information, including links to other useful sites and details of their many helpful guides;
  - – businesslink.org is the web site of the Small Business Service (see section 5.4). It contains pages about government regulations, e-commerce, starting a business, and business functions such as sales and marketing;
  - – ukonlineforbusiness.gov.uk is a site to help firms exploit the benefits of information and communications technologies.
- ❏ euaffairs.com is a portal on European Union initiatives for SMEs.
- ❏ US Small Business Administration on www.sbaonline.sba.gov
- ❏ Government publications include: *Guide to Official Statistics* and a brief free guide, *Government Statistics: A Brief Guide to Sources*.
- ❏ *The A–Z of Business Information Sources* (Croner Publications), a loose-leaf directory of sources by subject area.
- ❏ *Research Index*, an index to business news and articles in UK newspapers and periodicals.

Official information on particular markets, industries and initiatives are published regularly by governments and other official organisations. These include:

- ❏ *Monthly Digest of Statistics*, monthly compendia of social and economic statistics such as population, housing, manufacturing.
- ❏ *Annual Abstract of Statistics*, as above but annual summary.
- ❏ *Abstract of Regional Statistics*, economic and social statistics for UK regions.
- ❏ *Economic Trends*, monthly economic review.
- ❏ *Key Population and Vital Statistics*, annual statistics on births, deaths and migrations.
- ❏ *National Income and Expenditure Blue Book*, (yearly).
- ❏ *PRODCOM (Products of the European Community)*, European-wide information on sales and prices of extensive range of products from alcohol to zinc.
- ❏ *UN Demographic Yearbook*, population statistics of 165 countries derived from census data.
- ❏ *Business Monitors*, government business statistics collected from over 20,000 UK firms. Particularly useful for comparing past performance, or projected performance, of a business against the industry average and for market share calculations.
- ❏ *British Business*, published weekly by the DTI with statistics on UK markets, commercial and industrial trends, and other business information.

Non-official sources of market intelligence include:

- *Market Intelligence* (Mintel International, www.mintel.co.uk) monthly reports mainly on consumer markets and products. The contents pages of reports (but not the reports themselves) are viewable on the web site.
- *Retail Intelligence* (Mintel International), specific studies of market sectors.
- *The Economist Intelligence Unit*, (EIU, part of The Economist Group, www.economist.com or www.storeiu.com) which publishes regular reports on specific industrial sectors.
- *Key Note Reports*, (Key Note Publications, www.keynote.co.uk), detailed briefs on over 100 market sectors. Their web site gives executive summaries of the reports.
- *Jordans Industrial and Financial Surveys*, (Jordan's Business Information Service, www.jordans.co.uk), comparative performance indicators in market sectors. Also provide a company search service which obtains records of limited companies from the Companies Registration Office.
- *Kelly's Business Directory* (Kelly's Directories, www.kellys.co.uk) listing of all manufacturers and distributors, by trade classification.
- *Key British Enterprises*, (Dun and Bradstreet, www.dnb.com), information on 50,000 UK companies representing 90 per cent of industrial expenditure. A list of Dun and Bradstreet's publications is available on their web site.
- *Who Owns Whom*, (Dun and Bradstreet), covers over 100,000 companies giving details of company ownership.
- Kompass, (Kompass Publishers,www.kompass.co.uk), information on products and services, plus UK companies with financial data. Also available for some other countries.

Other useful web sites: there are many web sites targeted at small businesses or new ventures, which contain both advice and information.

- Banks offer advice and industry data for SMEs; see for example www.businesspark.barclays.co.uk, www.hsbc.co.uk, www.natwest.co.uk, www.lloydstsb.co.uk
- The Microsoft web site on www.microsoft.com is a popular source of information or www.bcentral.co.uk which is the site for Microsoft's smaller business customers.
- Real Business: www.realbusiness.co.uk for an online version of this popular business magazine.
- bird-online.com offers quick and easy access to detailed information on markets and industries for SMEs.
- smallbusinessportal.co.uk is useful for research and has useful links for both advice and information.
- Smallbiz UK: www.smallbiz.uk.com aims to provide quick and easy practical help and information.
- Master Planner: www. masterplanner.co.uk for a downloadable business plan template.

- Bizwise: www.bizwise.co.uk is a portal designed for owner-managers, providing links to extensive databases on a variety of topics.
- Business Europe: www.businesseurope.com provides news, advice and case studies specifically for European SMEs.
- Success4business.com, SME portal to information and advice.
- Business Bureau: www.businessbureau-uk.co.uk is a well-established site of information and advice.
- Enterprise Zone: www.enterprisezone.org.uk
- Start-ups: www.startups.co.uk provides articles from this magazine plus some useful start-up guides to specific businesses, and documentation templates.
- Forum for Private Business: www.fpb.co.uk

Activity 4 Primary research

An owner-manager of an existing business wishes to carry out primary research into their marketplace. What inexpensive methods are available to them?

4 Primary data

Most small firms shy away from collecting primary research data, but although it is invariably time consuming to collect and collate, it need not be expensive; in some instances it can cost nothing except time. Some primary research approaches are described below.

4.1 Surveys and questionnaires

Common impressions of market research involve answering a questionnaire posed by someone with a clipboard carrying out a survey. Surveys are indeed a common form of research, but they can take many forms.

A market survey asks questions of a number of respondents selected to correspond to the target market under investigation. Its main instrument is the questionnaire, which is probably the most widely known and used market research tool. Questionnaires can be used to measure:

- buying patterns and trends (Have you purchased XYZ in last 12 months/6 months/1 month?);
- attitudes to products and services (How would you rate the performance of XYZ on a scale of 1 to 5?);
- expectations related to products and services (When you purchase XYZ, which of the following benefits is most/least important?);
- competitors' activities (Which of the following products have you purchased in last 12 months?);

❒ media exposure and influence (Which of the following journals do you read regularly?).

Small firms have tended to overlook many of the opportunities of gathering information by surveys; they have been regarded as the province of bigger companies with more resources to collect large statistically valid samples.

Contact methods

There are three principle contact methods for surveys using questionnaires, which are listed below with examples of how they can be used inexpensively by small businesses:

❒ **Personal**

The best form of research is often on existing customers or visitors to business premises. For example finding out about customer dissatisfaction is a major problem for restaurant owners, most unhappy customers say nothing at the time – they just don't come back, and then complain to their friends, thereby amplifying the damage without giving the restaurant owner an opportunity to put the damage right. A simple questionnaire, allowing customers to remain incognito, can help overcome the problem. Surveys of existing customer perceptions of a small firm can be particularly revealing and inexpensive if conducted at the point of sale.

❒ **Telephone**

Surveys by telephone can be quick and usually give high response rates. Small firms can survey their competitors' prices by phoning round for quotes on a standard item or piece of work for example.

❒ **Mail**

Questionnaires by post can be useful to reach a wider audience and remove many problems of bias through the interviewer. A small inducement may be necessary to provoke the quantity of response desired. However surveys by mail should not be confused with any form of selling, which, although tempting to mitigate the costs, will inevitably bias the results. For example, a training consultant mailed a brief questionnaire to companies in his area to find out more about their perceived training needs and intentions. Although he offered a discount voucher for forthcoming workshops as an incentive to respond to the questionnaire, he resisted the temptation to confuse his research objectives with a specific sales message about his training programmes.

Which method to choose?

These three contact methods have advantages and disadvantages, summarised in Table 5.1, which will determine which application they are best suited to. For example, if a speedy response with tight control of who is surveyed is a priority, then telephone is probably the best method. A small firm might use this route, for instance, to find out more about competitive activity to which an immediate reaction is necessary (for example, price cutting). If the need for confidentiality and impartiality is paramount, then a mail survey is usually the preferred route. This is likely to be the case when personal details, for example of health or income, are required; this might therefore be the preferred method for surveys by small firms offering financial services, or computer dating.

If the survey requires a flexible approach, allowing respondents the opportunity to comment in a qualitative, open-ended manner, then the personal interview will be necessary. This could be the case, for example, where a small publishing company wished to test various concepts for educational books by interviewing lecturers and teachers of the subjects concerned.

Table 5.1 Primary research by questionnaire

Summary of the comparative advantages of three methods

Criterion	Contact methods		
	Mail	*Telephone*	*Personal*
Quantity of data	Poor	Good	Excellent
Interviewer effect [†]	Good	Fair	Fair
Control of sample	Excellent	Fair	Poor
Speed	Poor	Excellent	Good
Response rate	Poor	Good	Good
Costs	Fair	Fair	Poor

† This refers to the possibility of interviewers biasing results because of their preconceived ideas

The structure of a questionnaire

The construction of the questionnaire in terms of wording and layout will largely determine how useful it is as a guide for decision making. Although a trained researcher should be used where possible, there is nothing to stop the small business manager drafting a valid questionnaire without expert help, provided it is kept simple and basic rules are observed.

The most common approach to an overall structure is through funnelling. This involves asking the most general questions first and then gradually restricting the focus through more specific questions, leaving the most direct questions until last. This funnel technique is used to reduce elements of bias which could come from asking specific questions up front.

The first consideration in designing a questionnaire is to define what information is required. The questions asked will flow from this and will be of two basic types.

❒ *Closed questions* are those which can attract only a limited response such as Yes/No or a rating on a scale (Do you own your own house? or, How do you rate our service: excellent, good, fair, below average or poor?). Closed questions can be used when quantitative analysis is required from the surveys and result in a very structured approach.

❒ *Open questions* are those which invite a freer response, such as an opinion or individual information (What do you think of . . . ? Which sports do you play?). They are particularly useful in researching attitudes and buying motivations.

Questionnaires often use a mix of these styles of questions. A typical questionnaire might start with structured questions to qualify the respondent (e.g. Do you live within 5 miles of this town, 5 to 10 miles, more than 10 miles?) and finish with unstructured questions inviting comments on a key aspect of the research objectives (Why do you shop in this area?).

Bias in questions

The wording of a questionnaire needs careful examination to avoid biasing the response. This can result, for example, from social pressure on respondents to answer in a certain way because of implied expectations. For example, the question, 'Do you dislike smoke from other people's tables when you are eating?', encourages a positive response, which may over-emphasise genuine objections to other people smoking in a restaurant. One word can radically change the impact of a question. Consider the following two questions for inclusion in a survey of the parents of a first school:

a)   'Do you think all after-school activities should be free of charge?'

b)   'Do you think all after-school activities could be free of charge?'

The change of the word 'should' for 'could' switches the whole emphasis of the question: 'should be free of charge' may prompt the answer yes; 'could be free of charge' may lead to more realistic replies.

Omnibus surveys

If the market to be researched is large, or there is a need for continuous information, a small enterprise can consider omnibus research. This is a service offered by research agencies who regularly conduct surveys in a specific industry or market sector. The results are then sold to subscribing companies, which spreads the costs of the research over a wider client base. Subscribers can also add their own specific requirements to the survey, which is a good way of obtaining cost effective data providing the information needed is straightforward and can be obtained from a small number of questions.

Omnibus surveys are either based on national samples of adult purchasers, or specialist populations, for example regional markets or house owners. They are particularly useful if continuous research is needed. If regular feedback from a large customer base is important, this can be obtained from surveys which are regularly repeated.

4.2   Other primary research

Other types of primary research which can be used by the small firm include:

❒   **Group discussions** (focus groups)

Group discussions or focus groups are a good example of qualitative research available to the small business. A group of people, conforming to the parameters of the target market, are invited to an informal discussion, led by a facilitator to guide the conversation around desired topics. The session is normally taped, and may also be observed. The aim is to give insights into perceptions and motivations of potential customer groups. One of the prime uses, for example, is in testing concepts for new products or services. The results are not statistical, but more unstructured and subtle, probing for reactions to various propositions. A small business can consider using them as they are not prohibitively expensive, the principle costs being that of the facilitator, an interpretative report on proceedings if required, and the recruitment of the group. For example, a small firm specialising in marketing free publications to doctors, financed by pharmaceutical advertising, conducted discussion groups of general practitioners to test the concept of a new magazine. They obtained useful feedback not only on the acceptability of the idea, but its proposed content, layout, design and name as well.

❐ **Observation**

Some opportunities lend themselves to research through observation of what is happening in the marketplace. For example, a small business owner could observe the quantity and type of shoppers using locations where he or she was interested in opening a retail unit. Competitive information can be gained from observation; the size, staffing and activity levels of stands at exhibitions and trade shows are useful indicators of competitive strengths and weaknesses. (Some owners use less open tactics such as following a competitor's delivery van to find out where their customers are!)

Where possible, observations should be quantified to ensure objectivity and comparability. For example, pedestrians can be counted at different times, in different locations, to build up a comparative audit of shopping traffic, which could give vital clues to potential demand in given areas.

❐ **Experimentation**

Experiments, or tests, are sometimes conducted in the small business field to obtain live feedback from the marketplace. A small retail chain of two or three shops might vary their marketing activities in one outlet; for instance, prices may be changed in one shop only and sales patterns compared to the other shops in an effort to gauge the effectiveness of the price change.

❐ **Geodemographic databases**

Geodemographics is a modern research tool which segments and targets consumer markets. It does this by building a profile of the population in defined geographic areas based on the latest Census and other demographic and lifestyle information. Significant socio-economic factors such as age, sex, marital status, occupation, economic position, education, home and car ownership are covered so that the population can be divided into over 50 types of demographic and lifestyle profiles.

For example, ACORN, one of the geodemographic databases, classifies the population into 54 types ranging from 'Wealthy suburbs, large detached houses' (2.6 per cent of the UK population) and 'Private flats, elderly people'

(0.3 per cent), to 'Estates with high unemployment' (1.3 per cent) and 'Multi-ethnic, large families, overcrowding' (0.6 per cent).

Significantly for small business, these population types are identified according to precise areas based on postcodes. As there are approximately 1.3 million domestic postcodes in the UK, or an average of 15 houses per full post-code, the geodemographic information can be targeted to very local areas.

For example, a small business can enter the postcodes of its customers into the system to receive a geodemographic profile of its customer base and catch-ment area. It can also locate key market segments by enquiring in which other areas potential customers in their target groups live.

Increasingly used by larger companies, geodemographic classifications are relatively undiscovered by smaller firms. As they provide precisely tailored information for localised trading areas, they ought to be of considerable value to small businesses such as retailers and consumer service firms[6].

Activity 5 Help!

A new owner-manager needs help and advice in order to set up their business. Where do you suggest they go for it? Do you know of any government schemes that might be available to them?

5 Help for small business

5.1 Why help small firms?

The small business sector has become of such economic and social significance internationally that its development can no longer be left to chance. In the UK, the Bolton Committee recognised the need to provide support, and, in the years since their deliberations, help for small business has come in many forms and from a variety of sources. Both Conservative and Labour governments have followed policies aimed at supporting small firms. Non-governmental organisations give support for specific sectors and regions. Banks and financial institutions offer help beyond just the provision of finance. European governments and the European Union have also instituted policies and initiatives to promote the development of SMEs.

Help on this scale in favour of one particular business sector seems contrary to the non-interventionist policies increasingly followed by many European govern-ments. The Conservative government in the UK moved particularly towards the use of market forces to overcome economic problems[7]. Whilst the governments and organisations responsible have not spelt out a coherent overall strategy, the rationale for actively discriminating in favour of the small firm stems from a number of beliefs about the role of the small firm.

❐ *Creation of jobs*: most European countries encourage small firms, and particu-larly new firms, as a way of reducing unemployment.

❐ *Source of innovation*: although small firms have proved to be an abundant source of inventive ideas, they can lack the resources to put them into practice without external assistance.

❐ *Competition to larger firms*: as part of an anti-monopoly policy, small firms are needed to compete with larger companies by providing alternative sources of supply.

❐ *A level playing field*: some legislation is aimed at removing the unfair advantages that large firms might enjoy over small. These include the fixed cost of implementing government regulations in taxation, health and safety, and employing additional personnel, which are a relatively higher burden for the small firm to carry. Small firms' access to external finance is also seen as more restricted as financiers prefer lending to larger companies, where the risk is less and the returns greater, (costs of setting up loans are similar for greater or smaller amounts).

In the UK, successive governments since the early 1980s have been particularly active in attempting to promote small firms with literally hundreds of measures and initiatives introduced. These have been in three main areas of financial assistance, lightening the tax and administration load, and information and advice.

5.2 Financial assistance

Various forms of direct and indirect financial assistance have been tried. Some of these have been targeted at start-up firms, but the emphasis of current initiatives is to help established businesses that need to develop. (See also Unit 13, section 2, Obtaining funds, which explores forms of finance for small firms including public assistance.)

❐ **Helping the unemployed and disadvantaged into business**

A number of schemes have tried to help the unemployed either to set up their own business or to become employed by established small businesses. The *Business Start-Up Scheme* (BSUS) and its predecessor the *Enterprise Allowance Scheme* (EAS) encouraged people to start their own business by paying them an allowance for a limited period. The Enterprise Allowance Scheme was designed to offset the loss of unemployment benefit once an unemployed person was in business by paying them £40 per week (1991/2 rate) for the first year. These schemes attracted large numbers of participants. Over 650,000 people took part in the first decade of the scheme to 1993, with entrants peaking at over 100,000 in 1987/8, and running at around 40,000 per annum from 1992 to 1994. However, they encouraged more self-employment than small business development in that for every participant in the schemes only one-third of a full-time job was created for others. Attrition rates were also high: only 50 per cent of businesses started under the schemes were still trading 3 years later according to one study[7]. This emphasises the dangers of using the 'push' motive to encourage the unemployed to start their own business.

The *New Deal* has effectively replaced these initiatives by offering training and financial assistance to seek jobs to the longer term unemployed, including jobs provided by small businesses. In doing so, it has shifted the emphasis of policies linking unemployment to small business development by focusing on creating jobs in established firms. A small business which takes on an unemployed person through the scheme receives an allowance (£60 per week in 2000), plus a contribution of £750 towards training costs.

The *Phoenix Fund* was launched recently to encourage entrepreneurship in disadvantaged communities and amongst disadvantaged groups. It allocates resources to 'Community Finance Initiatives' so that these local organisations can invest in new and growing businesses.

❏ **Helping small firms obtain bank finance**

To obtain a bank loan, an owner-manager often needs not just a good business proposition, but also some form of collateral or guarantee to support the loan. *The Small Firms Loan Guarantee Scheme* (LGS) was introduced in 1981 to help owners obtain finance from banks when they would not normally be able to do so because of lack of assets to use as security. It is intended for small businesses not able to arrange loans under normal banking policies, as, in certain circumstances, the government will agree to guarantee a bank loan, in return for which the borrowing firm pays a small interest rate premium.

The terms and conditions have varied considerably over the years. In 2001, the government, through the Small Business Service (see section 5.4), guaranteed 70 per cent of a qualifying bank loan to a new business, and 85 per cent if the firm had been trading for at least two years. Loans can be up to £100,000 (£250,000 for 'established' businesses), repayable over 2 to 10 years; there is a premium of between 0.5 per cent and 1.5 per cent payable to the government by the borrower in addition to normal bank interest rates. The scheme is available to UK companies with an annual turnover of less than £1.5 million or £5 million for manufacturers.

Currently, 4,000–5,000 firms are supported each year in obtaining loans with a total value around £200 million per annum. However, the overall effects of the scheme on the small business community have been minimal. Although the scheme may have originally encouraged some clearing banks to take the small business sector more seriously, it still accounts for less than 1 per cent of total lending to small firms.

❏ **Helping small firms attract venture capital**

In addition to bank lending, the government is keen for private individuals and companies to act as external investors in smaller businesses, and has introduced tax incentives to encourage such investment.

The Enterprise Investment Scheme (EIS), and its predecessor the *Business Expansion Scheme* (BES), were designed to attract outside investment in small businesses by UK tax payers. Under the Business Expansion Scheme investors could deduct up to £40,000 in any one year from their tax liability to match the size of their investment.

To qualify, investors:

○ could not be paid directors or employees of the business;

○ could not own more than 30 per cent of its equity;

○ had to invest a minimum of £500 and a maximum of £50,000 for at least five years.

The effect of the scheme was that a £40,000 investment made by a top-rate (60 per cent until 1987/8) taxpayer cost only £16,000 to the investor, the balance effectively coming from the Inland Revenue.

The scheme attracted not only direct investment by individuals but also BES portfolios, offered by some financial institutions who selected a range of businesses for investment, thereby spreading the risk of the investment and putting it under professional management. This also had the effect of concentrating investment in larger firms: although over £750 million was invested in nearly 4,000 small businesses through the scheme between 1983 and 1988, over half of this went to a handful of companies – less than 4 per cent of the total – which raised over £1 million each.

In 1988, the scheme was extended to include residential property let under an assured tenancy agreement. This proved such an attraction to investors that it took over 90 per cent of the funds in the following two years. The 1992 Budget announced the end of the scheme by 1993 as most of the funds were ending up in property investments and not the small enterprises for which they were originally intended.

In 1994, the Enterprise Investment Scheme (EIS) was introduced. Although similar to the BES, alterations included:

○ investments in private rented accommodation excluded;

○ investors could become directors and take some income from the business;

○ income tax relief is limited to 20 per cent, although there is still no capital gains tax if the investment is held for three years;

○ individuals can invest up to £150,000 each year, and companies can raise up to £1 million.

❑ *Venture Capital Trusts* (VCTs) were introduced in 1995, as vehicles for private individuals to buy shares in a portfolio of smaller firms. VCTs are quoted on the London Stock Exchange (LSE) and invest in smaller private trading companies. Investors in VCTs benefit from tax relief on income tax from dividends and capital gains tax on disposal of shares. The *Corporate Venturing Scheme* gives tax incentives to larger companies to invest in new or expanding small businesses.

5.3 Lightening the tax and administration load

Government policy has been to remove as much of the burden of taxation and the bureaucratic regulation of business activities as possible, claiming in the 1985 White Paper, *Lifting the Burdens*, that this was necessary to encourage economic development and growth.

Small business has been singled out for special treatment in several areas.

❐ **Taxation**

The Bolton Committee were particularly concerned that taxation policy reflected the need to encourage entrepreneurial activity and improve the liquidity position of small businesses. These concerns have been taken up in a number of ways:

○ A progressive rate of corporation tax means that smaller firms benefit from lower corporation tax rates. Rates rise from 10 per cent to 30 per cent on taxable profits up to £1,500,000. For example, the top tax rate for a company with profits of less than £300,000 is 20 per cent (2001/2).

○ Personal income tax reductions have directly affected small businesses that operate as sole traders and partnerships, as any surpluses are liable to income tax whether drawn from the business or not. (See Unit 8, Legal identities, for more information on legal forms of business and the tax implications.)

○ Inflation accounting, rather than historic cost accounting, can now be used in assessing tax liability, with a resulting benefit for most profitable small firms.

❐ **Retirement**

Measures have also improved the arrangements possible for the retirement of a small business owner:

○ *Pensions*: although still not equal to the tax-free provisions available to employees, the self-employed can now obtain tax relief on up to 17.5 per cent of earned income (or progressively higher levels up to 40 per cent, depending on age over 35 years).

○ *Capital Gains Tax*: relief on capital gains of up to £150,000, available to owners disposing of their business on retirement, is being phased out. However it is being replaced by 'business asset taper relief' to capital gains tax, which can reduce effective tax rates to 10 per cent of the gain on the sale of a business asset held for more than three qualifying years.

❐ **Tax collection**

Businesses are major collectors of Pay-As-You-Earn Income Tax (PAYE), National Insurance Contributions (NIC), and Value Added Tax (VAT). By requiring even very small businesses to act as unpaid tax collectors, the government places a very high burden on them, which for the very smallest has been calculated to cost as much as one-third of the value of the tax collected[8].

Although still a major burden there has been some mitigation:

○ *VAT*: once a business's turnover passes a certain threshold, a business has to register for VAT, and thereby charge its customers and account for VAT. This minimum threshold for registration for VAT was substantially increased in the 1991 Budget, when it was lifted to £35,000 from £25,400 in 1990. Levels have been progressively raised since and in 2001/2, the minimum level was £54,000.

VAT is normally accounted for quarterly, against invoiced sales and purchases. The Cash Accounting Scheme, which permits firms to only pay VAT on those transactions which have been paid for, and not just invoiced, and the Annual Accounting Scheme, which allows for one return only for the year with estimated monthly payments, have helped to reduce the financial and administrative costs of these procedures for many small firms.

○ *PAYE*: employers with small monthly PAYE deductions can now account for this tax on a quarterly return not the monthly basis which is normally required.

❑ **Health and safety at work**

Like all businesses, small firms are responsible for working conditions on all their premises for employees and visitors alike. The *Safety at Work Act (1974)*, the *Offices, Shops and Railway Premises Act (1963)*, and the *Factories Act (1961)* give employers extensive responsibilities, covering such areas as fire precautions, means of escape, hygiene, temperature, toilet and washing facilities, workspace and machinery safety. The government recognised the difficulties for small firms of applying these regulations in detail, by removing the requirement to prepare a written safety policy from very small firms with less than 5 employees. Health and Safety Inspectors have also been encouraged to increase their awareness of smaller firms' interests.

❑ **Disability discrimination**

Smaller employers are exempt from some of the responsibilities laid down by the *Disability Discrimination Act (1995)*. Employers are required to take reasonable steps to ensure that they do not discriminate against disabled employees in either recruiting or employing staff. This can mean that employers have to remove physical barriers and make other adjustments to their working practices. However, firms with less than 15 employees are exempt from these requirements.

❑ **DG23 in the EC**

Increasing concern that legislation and regulations from the European Commission (EC) might place unfair burdens on small business led to the setting up of the *SME Task Force in the European Commission* (DG23). This has the brief to scrutinise EC measures for any adverse effects on the small business sector.

5.4 Information and advice

The third major area in which the government has sought to help small firms is in the provision of information and advice.

❑ **The Small Business Service**

The *Small Business Service* (SBS) is the latest in a line of government agencies designed to champion the interests of small businesses. On the recommendation of the Bolton Committee, the *Small Firms Service* (SFS) was set up in 1972 within the Department of Trade and Industry, to provide information through a network of 13 *Small Firms Centres* (SFCs)[9]. In 1989/90, the responsibility for this service was transferred to *Training and Enterprise Councils* (TECs) in England and Wales, and *Local Enterprise Companies* (LECs) in Scotland, set up with the aim of improving efficiency in delivering training and other government initiatives, directed at regenerating local economics.

Not all the TECs succeeded as businesses in their own right: in 1995, South Thames TEC went into receivership. TECs' responsibilities covered large as well as small firms in their area, and they found it difficult to reach more than a small percentage of SMEs. The TEC network was effectively replaced as a small business support mechanism by the emergence of the Small Business Service and Business Links (see below).

The *Small Business Service* (SBS), which came into being in April 2000, was intended as an umbrella organisation which would promote and co-ordinate the wide range of help, information and advice available from many sources. Reporting to the Under-Secretary of State for Small Business, it operates a number of schemes and initiatives, largely delivered through a network of *Business Links* in England, *Small Business Gateway*, in Scotland and *Business Connect* in Wales[10].

❏ **Business Links**

When launched in 1993, Business Links were described as:

'a network of independent local business information and advice centres offering a range of services to the business community, designed to enhance the competitiveness of local companies. They are run by partnerships which include Chambers of Commerce, Training and Enterprise Councils, Enterprise Agencies and the Department of Trade and Industry. They will be the place to access a full range of business support services.'[11]

Business Links now operate throughout England. *Small Business Gateway* in Scotland and *Business Connect* in Wales operate in a similar way to Business Link, (to find out your nearest Business Link, consult their web site on www.businesslink.org). Business advisors, who work with local businesses to identify growth opportunities and develop a support package, are central to the services offered.

Although the DTI provided 'pump priming' funds Business Links are intended to be self-supporting as businesses are expected to pay for many of the services received. Amid some concern about the financial health of some of the Business Links already in operation, a further £100 million of public funds was allocated for the programme in the 1995 competitiveness White Paper, *Forging Ahead*.

Whereas the government's advice services had previously concentrated on start ups, Business Links 'aim particularly to help existing companies with the will to grow... Their focus will be smaller companies, usually with 10–200 employees.'[11]

❒ **Local Enterprise Agencies**

Local Enterprise Agencies (LEAs) are small, local advisory organisations, funded from private and public sources. A network of about 350 emerged during the 1980s, sponsored by local government, chambers of commerce, universities and colleges, and a mixture of private companies including banks and building societies. Although there is no set format, the primary objective is to provide help and advice to local business communities. The work of each LEA varies considerably from the provision of small premises to training courses and advice clinics[12].

❒ **TCS**

TCS, one of the schemes operated by the SBS, aims to provide the small business owner with the knowledge and expertise to tackle a particular problem or opportunity of strategic importance to their business. For example, the owner-manager identifies a project vital to their development, but it is beyond their existing technical or business competence (e.g. a design for a new product, or an export marketing strategy). So a recent graduate, supervised by a university expert with the requisite knowledge-base, works on the project for two years with up to two-thirds of the cost borne by the SBS.

❒ **SMART**

SMART is an SBS initiative to provide grants for SMEs (up to 250 employees) to improve their use of technology and to develop technologically innovative products and processes. Grants of up to £150,000 are available for technology studies and development projects.

❒ **Other assistance**

Other public and private sector bodies have echoed the national government's emphasis on assistance for small firms.

○ *Local Government* agencies offer various kinds of assistance to small firms. This can be through their *Economic Development Units* (EDUs) which offer cheap premises and relaxed planning controls. Some offer financial assistance in loans or grants to certain kinds of business, such as co-operatives. About two-thirds of all local authorities offer some type of advisory or information service.

○ *Banks* have set up their own small business advisory units which offer a range of information and advice

○ The *Rural Development Commission* (RDC), which formed in 1988 to advise the government on rural issues, have a Business Service offering a wide range of advice, and sometimes finance, to small businesses in rural areas.

○ *The Prince's Trust* is a charity that offers advice, training and finance to young people, from 14 to 30, who want to set up in business.

○ *Livewire*, sponsored by Shell, helps 16–30-year-olds to start and develop their own business. It hosts a national competition for new business start ups.

○ *Chambers of Commerce* offer a variety of support services to their members, many of whom are small businesses.

Activity 6 Does it help?

Consider how the government in the UK has tried to help small firms. In what ways do you think these measures may have helped the small business sector? How do you think they could be improved?

6 The effects of government policy

6.1 UK criticisms

Over the last twenty years or so there has been substantial growth in the types of assistance offered to small firms in these three major areas of financial assistance, lightening the tax and administrative load, and information and advice.

There is considerable debate over the impact and effectiveness of all this activity. In particular there is really no conclusive evidence that these measures have induced growth in the small business sector which would not have happened anyway. Measurement of the success of policies has been largely by reference to the numbers of small firms using a particular service – the number of loans guaranteed by the LGS, or the number of inquiries to a support agency for example – without research into whether those small firms would have existed, or survived, without such assistance.

There can be little doubt that a general environment has been developed which does encourage, rather than dampen, enthusiasm for starting and growing a small business. However, a number of important criticisms have been made of the effectiveness of government policy:

❒ **Lack of objectives**

One of the problems in assessing the effectiveness of government policy is the lack of overriding objectives and specific targets for measures which are aimed at helping small firms. Storey[7] is a strong advocate for a White Paper which would:

○ make clear the objectives of small business policy for government as a whole, not just by department; and

○ set targets for each policy measure so that its effectiveness in meeting those targets could be monitored.

❒ **Regional bias**

Most of the schemes described are nationally available. Although some special assistance does exist for regions which have high rates of unemployment or require additional development assistance for historic reasons (e.g. inner cities, docklands, mining or steel areas), the major government initiatives have an equal availability in all areas. Storey[13] in particular criticised this policy on the basis that it is regionally divisive, because it favours areas that are already better off. New firm formation rates do vary by region. For example, in the 1980s they were highest in the South West and South East, areas of comparatively low unemployment, and lowest in the North and Scotland, which are areas with traditionally high levels of unemployment[14]. This produces unequal benefits from such schemes as the Loan Guarantee Scheme, which has a much higher take-up rate in the South East than in Scotland for example.

More recent initiatives did prove more popular in the North than the South, which has thrown some doubt on the extent of regional bias. However, overall, the more wealthy Southern areas have benefited more from financial assistance.

Backing winners or losers?

Assistance to small firms is also widely spread amongst all varieties of business and industries. There is some evidence that this merely encourages the unemployed to set up in competition with existing businesses, some of which are thereby reduced to marginal levels of profitability or failure through this subsidised competition. The new business can do this because the owner-managers devote their own labour to the enterprise at below market rates and initially they are subsidised by government sponsored schemes[14].

Some commentators have suggested that policy should be more selective in assisting winners, that is small firms with a proven record of growth and the potential to create new jobs.

More recent government initiatives, such as Business Link, have moved in this direction by offering training, consultancy and advice to established businesses, rather than financial incentives for new ventures.

Confusion and overlap

A further area for concern is the sheer number of services now available to the small business owner manager, which can result in bewilderment and inefficiency. The integration of the SFS into TECs tended to add to the confused atmosphere. The DTI recognised that the profusion of support 'may actually deter firms from seeking help'[11]. This widespread muddle and overlap prompted Michael Heseltine, as President of the Board of Trade, to launch 'One-Stop' shops in 1992, now re-named Business Links, and the Labour administration to introduce the Small Business Service in 2000 as an umbrella organisation to co-ordinate all government sponsored initiatives.

6.2 European comparisons

All EU (European Union) countries follow policies in support of small firms, many similar to those in the UK. However there are differences in both the extent and emphasis of measures in individual states.

One study[15] looked at the numbers of government measures ('instruments of policy') by type of policy ('policy field') and by country. A total of 236 instruments of policy were analysed in the 12 member countries (i.e. an average of 20 per country).

- ❒ Ireland (at 28 instruments of policy), Germany (26), France (23), and the UK (23) were above average, which could be interpreted to mean they have tried to intervene in favour of small businesses at an above average rate for EC countries.

- ❒ Luxembourg (11 instruments of policy), Denmark (14), Portugal (15), Italy (17), Greece (19), Belgium (20) and Spain (20) were below average or average.

- ❒ Technology and R&D is the most favoured policy field with a variety of financial, information and training initiatives. The UK and France focus more than others on start ups, whereas Germany and Ireland concentrate more on finance. Environment and energy, and administrative simplification were the least frequent policy fields.

The authors of the study recommended that some of the policy areas, especially education, financing, information and help, technology and export policies, could be better co-ordinated within the EU. To this end they suggest an overall definition of objectives with execution of policies decentralised to national or regional authorities.

7 Case studies and activities

Case studies *Finding the market*

Case 1 Andrea investigates an old friend

Andrea Clarey wanted to find out more about her intended payroll service for schools. Her husband suggested she 'networked' among friends and acquaintances to test out the idea. She did not want to talk to the head teacher of her daughter's local school as she felt it might be too close for comfort to discuss new business ideas. Instead she called an old friend who had just become the head teacher of a large primary school, and arranged to meet her over coffee. When she finished explaining her idea, her friend looked rather blank.

'I am afraid I leave that to the school bursar. I don't really get involved in payroll matters. Although I do see the final costs of what staff at the school earn, the bursar liaises with the Education Authority's payroll service over calculations of tax and so forth and any queries that arise from time to time. Frankly it's an area I don't really want to get involved in.'

'What about my idea for information on payroll and other costs at the school, with comparisons to other schools? Is that of any use or interest to you?'

'Yes and no. I'm always interested in what other schools are doing, and my Chairman of Governors is always trying to find out how much money other schools get compared to us. But every school is different. The cost of staff varies according to age and experience, so one school might spend a lot more on salaries than another simply because it had older staff. So it doesn't necessarily mean the children are getting a better education just because more is being spent on staff costs at their particular school. So I don't know how valuable any comparative figures would be. Like all statistics, I suspect they could be interpreted in too many different ways.'

Case 2 Kit and Robin concentrate

Robin Davidson was sure that Kit Hugos's new product idea could only work in very specific market sectors.

'The key to your security device,' he told Kit, 'is not the transmitter carried on the person – that is relatively cheap and easy to make. What is difficult is the tracking software that locates the device and indicates where it is on a map. We need to digitise a map of the area to be covered, and the smaller that area is the better, in the first instance. If we try to map a town or wider area to track the general public we are talking lots of development costs and complications. Let's look at markets where people are confined to a limited area, but are still potentially at risk.'

'I have read that university campus sites and large colleges and schools have become an increasing security risk,' replied Kit. 'They are used by thousands of different students who are constantly changing in a relatively open environment. It's impossible to tightly control who goes in and out. The same could be said of conference centres and exhibition halls which are another problem area. Large office complexes are increasingly targeted for attacks and thefts. I could go on, but where do we stop? We can't investigate all these potential markets.'

'You're right. We may need to focus our efforts – and we need some help.'

Activities

Advise both Andrea and Kit on how to research their market and where to find help.

i)   What secondary sources of information should they consider?

ii)   What affordable primary research would you recommend for both of them. In each case indicate your recommended research objectives and proposed methods.

iii) Which sources of help and advice should they consider in order to take their business ideas to the next step?

iv)   What should they do next?

Extended activity *Local support*

Find out what organisations exist in your local area to support small enterprises. Contact as many as you can and obtain literature on their services. A good starting point may be your local Business Link – you can look at their web site www.businesslink.org to locate your nearest office. Your local district council or chamber of commerce may also have details of what services are available in the area.

If you were to start a small business how useful do you think you would find the services on offer?

In conclusion

Once you have finished this Unit, it is recommended that you turn to Section B, Planning a new venture, and complete Step 1.5, Researching the idea.

8 References and further reading

References and further information

1. Birley, S. and Muzyka, D. F. *Mastering Entrepreneurship*, Prentice Hall, 2000, Chapter 2 'The opportunity' has useful sections on identifying and researching business ideas.

2. See for example Watkins, D. 'Management Development and the Owner-Manager', in Webb, T., Quince, T. and Watkins, D. (eds), *Small Business Research: The Development of Entrepreneurs*, Gower, 1982. This follows the line of earlier research in identifying adaptability of the business to the changing requirements of the economy as important, whilst noting a general lack of outward-looking information gathering by owner-managers, who tended to be inward looking and focused on day to day problems.

3. See Smallbone, D. 'Success and Failure in New Business Start-up', *International Small Business Journal*, 8, 2, 1990. This paper makes the point (as we discuss in Unit 3, 3.2, 'Adjusting to uncertainty'), that firms most active in making adjustments to what they do and how they do it, especially in terms of market adjustments, are most likely to survive.

4. See Milne, T. and Thompson, M. 'The infant business development process', in Scott, M., Gibb, A., Lewis, J. and Faulkner, T. (eds), *Small Firms' Growth and Development*, Gower, 1986. Their research concluded that owner-managers are 'impatient with formality including formal market research. But the successful ones are doing the research in an extremely powerful and efficient personal contact manner'.

5. Carson, D., Cromie, S., Mcgowan, P. and Hill, J. *Marketing and Entrepreneurship in SMEs*, Prentice Hall, 1995, and Chaston, I. *Entrepreneurial Marketing*, Palgrave, 2000 (two texts which seek to draw together the disciplines of marketing and entrepreneurship which have many common points).

6. Acorn is operated by CACI information services. Another system, MOSAIC, is operated by CCN.

7. Storey, D. *Understanding the Small Business Sector*, International Thomson Press, 1998. See particularly Chapter 5, 'Public policy', in which the author spells out his long-held view of the need for coherent policy objectives to draw together the 'patchwork quilt' of measures in support of small business.

8. Sandford, C., Godwin, M. and Hardwick, P. *Administrative and Compliance Costs of Taxation*, Fiscal Publications, 1989. This study calculated that firms collecting less than £1,000 PAYE and NIC in one year incurred costs equivalent

to one-third of the tax collected. This fell to less than 1 per cent where the annual collection was more than £280,000.

9. See the *SFS Annual Report 1989/90,* Department of Employment, 1990.

10. For more information on the Small Business Service and Business Link, see their web sites on www.sbs.gov.uk and www.businesslink.org

11. *Business Link, Questions and Answers,* DTI. This booklet and subsequent newsletters publicised the new service and reported on progress in setting it up.

12. There is a useful list of enterprise agencies of various sorts in Williams, S. *Small Business Guide,* Penguin Books, 2001, References to Chapter 3.

13. Storey, D. *Entrepreneurship and the New Firm,* Croom Helm, 1982.

14. Whittinton, R. 'Regional Bias in New Firm Formation', in Scott, M., Gibb, A., Lewis, J. and Faulkner, T. (eds) *Small Firms Growth and Development,* Gower, 1986.

15. De Koning, A. and Snijders, J. 'Policy on SMEs in countries of the European Community', *International Small Business Journal,* 10, 3, 1992.

Recommended further reading

☐ Birley, S. and Muzyka, D. F. *Mastering Entrepreneurship,* FT/Prentice Hall, 2000. Chapter 2, 'The opportunity'.

☐ Williams, S. *Small Business Guide,* Penguin Books, 2001. Chapter 3 'A spot of coaching'.

☐ Brown, R., Barrow, C. and Barrow, P. *The Business Plan Workbook,* Kogan Page, 2001, especially section on A Plan for Market Research.

☐ Proctor, T. *Essentials of Marketing Research,* Financial Times/Prentice Hall, 2000. A good general introduction to research including some examples of questionnaires and case histories.

☐ Storey, D. *Understanding the Small Business Sector,* International Thomson Press, 1998. See particularly Chapter 5, 'Public Policy'.

☐ Summaries of the various government initiatives are also available on www.dti.gov.uk, and www.businesslink.org

Part II

The small business choice

This Part comprises Units 6 to 8. It explores the diversity of small business forms, looking at start ups, franchises, buying a business and the legal forms. Each Unit links to a Step in Stage II (The route to market entry) of Section B, as shown below. Each Step should be considered immediately following your completion of the relevant Unit.

Section A Exploring small business	Section B Planning a new venture
Part II The small business choice ⟶	*Stage II The route to market entry*
Unit 6 Start ups and franchises ⟶	Step 2.1 Start up or franchise?
Unit 7 Buying an existing ⟶ business	Step 2.2 Buying an existing business
Unit 8 Legal identities ⟶	Step 2.3 Selecting the form
	Step 2.4 Summary of the route to market entry

Contents

6 Start ups and franchises

This Unit first identifies the alternative routes for developing an opportunity from concept into business reality including start ups, franchises, buying a business and the possible legal forms. It then considers the two main methods of beginning a new business – start ups and franchises – in more detail. The advantages and disadvantages of each are evaluated compared to other small business forms. Unit 7 looks at buying an existing business, and Unit 8 the legal identities.

Contents

Activity 1 Which route?

As well as starting a brand new business what other possibilities are there for involvement in a small business as an owner-manager? Give some examples, where you can, of businesses in each category.

1 The alternative routes to market entry

A recurring theme of investigations into small businesses is that they do not represent a homogeneous sector at all[1]. The differences between the parts are sometimes so great that meaningful generalisations about the whole are difficult to make. This is particularly evident when looking at the choices facing would-be owner-managers who have decided on their preferred business concept and now wish to take it into the marketplace. Owner-managers can select from several different ways of pursuing their opportunity from beginning a new business to buying an existing one. The legal form of the business also has to be decided. These initial choices in turn lead to further alternatives as illustrated in Figure 6.1.

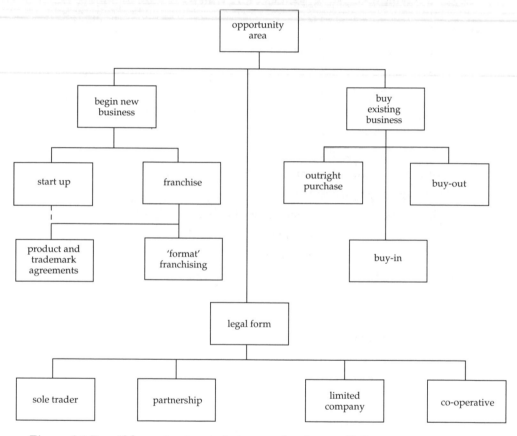

Figure 6.1 Possible routes to market entry for the small firm

Inevitably there are overlaps and areas of greyness between these various forms.

❑ **Begin new business**

   ○ *Start up*

      A business start up means creating a new business, which stands alone, and is not tied to other organisations, except in the normal course of trading. It does not mean that the idea is necessarily new, only that the vehicle which is set up to exploit it is.

○ *Franchise*

A franchise is a method for starting a new business within the framework of an existing, larger business entity. It is a legally separate enterprise operating in some way under the umbrella of another organisation.

○ *Product and trademark agreements*

A franchise can mean an agency to sell another company's products in a certain way, or within a certain territory. This may involve use of a registered trademark. It may involve distribution only (e.g. of cars), or it could include production under a licensed process. It includes straightforward agencies and more elaborate systems such as multi-level marketing. Some franchise agreements do not preclude other activities, and may thus form part of a business start up's portfolio of products or services.

○ *Format franchising*

Franchising has come to commonly mean a system for a business to set up using a complete format developed by another company, including trading name, standardised business presentation, products or services and operating systems. Some franchises have become household names, such as McDonalds, The Body Shop and DynoRod, but outlets are operated as separate legal entities by their owners.

❒ **Buy existing business**

○ *Outright purchase*

This involves buying an existing business from somebody else; although there is a new owner, the business does not start from scratch but is already trading in some way.

○ *Buy-out*

A buy-out is buying an existing business from within, rather than from the outside. Recently, this has become an increasingly popular form, as larger corporations have sold off parts of their organisations to the existing management team. Some buy-outs, such as National Freight, are large enough not to be classified as a small business at all.

○ *Buy-in*

This occurs when the existing owners accept a new partner, or shareholder, who buys into a small firm which already exists.

❒ **Legal form**

In addition there is choice over the legal form the organisation takes. There are four main legal forms possible for the small firm: sole trader, partnership, limited company or co-operative.

The rest of this Unit considers the relative merits of the principal ways of beginning a new business – start ups and franchises. Unit 7 looks at the various options for buying an existing business. Unit 8 evaluates the legal identities open to small businesses.

Each of these vehicles for establishing a new business has its particular advantages and disadvantages. The preferred choice will depend both on the nature of the opportunity to be exploited and the circumstances of the individuals who wish to pursue it.

Activity 2 For and against a start up

What do you think are the advantages and disadvantages of a business start up compared to other possible routes to market entry such as franchises or buying an existing business? As an advantage often has a corresponding disadvantage, you may find it convenient to write them down as a balance sheet with two columns headed 'for' and 'against'.

2 The start up

2.1 The wide scope of start up

The business start up means exactly what it says; it is a new enterprise, starting up and trading in its chosen field – a green field in which the seeds of ideas have a chance to grow and develop. For many new ideas there is no other option; existing businesses have not developed the idea that a would-be entrant wishes to exploit. Alternatively the new entrant may try to minimise risk in starting something new by only incurring significant liabilities after the idea has been tested in the marketplace.

In fact the scope of new businesses varies significantly, in line with the objectives of the founder, linked to their willingness and ability to invest in the enterprise. The level of risk taken in a start up ranges from virtually nothing to highly significant personal, financial and time investment. This investment can be made by an individual on their own, as the sole owner of the business, or it can be shared with others, who are either directly involved as equal partners, or less committed but still investing money, or time, in starting the business. This can be seen as a spectrum, as in Figure 6.2.

One end is typified by someone who begins in business on a part-time basis. The risk, whilst all their own, is minimal as income is generated elsewhere and investment requirements are small. The motivation may be to turn an existing hobby or skill into financial gain, or to put a toe in the water, before making the jump to full-time employment in the business.

At a higher level of risk on the spectrum is the tradesman, or professional, who decides to become self-employed, whilst keeping their liabilities low by minimal investment in equipment or overheads other than their own personal drawings and expenses.

Investment/risk		Scope of start up	Examples
	Sole risk		
Minimal personal risk with low initial investment	▼	Part-time business activity	Hobby or skill used to generate additional income or to test idea
Increased initial investment required	▼	Self-employment in existing trade or profession	Consultant or plumber using home as office
High individual risk	▼	Sole trader creating new business entity	Retail outlet, restaurant, small manufacturer
	Shared risk		
Initial investment minimised	▼	Partnership or self-employed	Accounting or other professional practice, craft partnership
Increased initial investment from partners	▼	New business organisation owned by two or more	Manufacturer, small hotel
High level of shared risk with significant up-front investment	▼	Consortium start up	High-tech company with technical, management and financial partners

Figure 6.2 Illustration of the business start-up spectrum

A start up, such as a new shop or manufacturing company, may require greater investment in capital equipment, premises, office equipment, staff in addition to the owner and other overheads. If this investment is made by a sole trader it can represent a very high level of individual risk.

Such investment can be shared, again at different levels, depending on the scope of the start up. Some new enterprises require such significant initial investment that a consortium of partners come together to share the risk. For example, a new business wishing to exploit a technologically advanced process is formed as a partnership between the full-time founders of the enterprise, a venture capital company who contribute long-term finance and non-executive management, and a bank who provide an overdraft as working capital[2].

The scope of the start up will be determined by the nature of the business, and the objectives of the owners. Businesses vary considerably in their investment requirements, from the self-employed plumber who has to buy some basic tools and an answer machine, to a capital intensive manufacturer, needing hundreds of thousands of pounds to get off the ground. The objectives of the founders in relation to the speed of anticipated growth, will also influence the investment requirements. Perhaps the objectives extend only to personal self-employment with no other staff or overheads; or maybe the scope is more ambitious, foreseeing the need to develop a team of people to cope with the business activity[3].

2.2 The advantages and disadvantages of start up

Some of the advantages and disadvantages of the business start up, compared to other methods of becoming a small business owner (such as buying an existing business), are summarised in Figure 6.3. Notice that, as is common with this kind of 'balance sheet' analysis, advantages have corresponding disadvantages. So, for example, the advantage that a start up is the creation of the owners, which gives them freedom of choice, has the corresponding disadvantage that it is unproven by anyone else. The advantage of control over decision making becomes the disadvantage that these decisions could be misplaced, as the high failure rate suggests. Starting with a clean sheet has the downside of no market share or goodwill at the out-set.

Advantages	Disadvantages
Creation of the owners: freedom of choice over what the business does, how it operates, and what its values are	*Unproven idea:* the idea may be creative, but will it work? Even after the most thorough research, a new business can only prove itself in practice
Control of the owners: personal decisions count, external influences can be minimised	*High failure rate:* the failure rate of start ups is high; less than 50 per cent survive the first 4 years. Other methods, e.g. franchising, have better track records
Satisfaction of the owners: success due to the skill and efforts of owners, which gives them heightened sense of satisfaction when (if) success comes	*Hard, lonely work:* unsociable working hours are often linked to feelings of being alone as, even in a partnership, there are no support departments and services in the firm. Entrepreneurs do it themselves
Clean sheet: the business starts with no backlog of problems; it will create plenty, but at least they will be new ones and not inherited from the past	*No market share or goodwill:* compared to buying an existing business or franchising, the start up has the problem of establishing its name from scratch; the goodwill in an established company name or loyalty of existing customers takes some time to build up
Help from various agencies: government assistance and help from other agencies is available to encourage new business start ups	*Barriers to entry:* there are many barriers to market entry. One-off start-up costs can be significant. Legislation has to be considered, premises found, accounts with suppliers opened, credit worthiness proved; these and many other obstacles have to be overcome before trading begins[4]
Match between founder and enterprise: the founders of new enterprises can ensure that their individual strengths are well used, and their weaknesses minimised, by choosing a business well matched to their own qualities and experiences	*Difficult to forecast:* with no track record, a start up is very hard to predict for financial and other outcomes
Less funds required: a start up that works costs less than buying a similar franchise or existing business	*Difficult to finance:* banks and other lenders are always keener to give money to proven concepts than to new ideas

Figure 6.3 The advantages and disadvantages of the start up as a small business entrant

> **Activity 3** Defining franchising
>
> Franchising has been used to describe a number of business arrangements and systems. How would you define franchising?

3 What is franchising?

Franchising is a business arrangement in which one party (the franchisor) allows others (the franchisees) to use a business name, or sell products, in such a way that the franchisees can operate their own legally separate business.

It can mean as little as a simple agreement to sell a company's products in a specified area. However it is now more commonly used to describe business format franchising in which the franchisor offers a complete business package[5].

3.1 Product and trademark agreements

The early forms of franchising were agreements in which manufacturers distributed their products through licensed dealers.

In the 19th and early 20th century, the Singer Sewing Machine Company, for example, sold its product in this way. Breweries, oil companies and car manufacturers all developed the distribution of their products through different forms of licensing arrangements. Under such arrangements local tenants or dealers took responsibility for sales in a given territory in return for some element of the local profit. The producers developed their products and the goodwill associated with their trademarks; the local distributor contributed local knowledge, contacts, and effort. Such distribution arrangements are still common, particularly for the marketing of drinks (soft and alcoholic), petrol and cars.

Certain manufacturing processes, particularly where a patent exists, are also licensed. The patent holder may wish to exploit their innovation on a wider basis than their own resources allow. They therefore permit other manufacturers to use the process under licence in return for a royalty. This is particularly common in international markets where local laws prohibit foreign ownership of production, or where local conditions make it impractical.

Some small businesses specialise as import agencies, often negotiating a number of agreements to import foreign goods, and act as the national, or regional distributor.

If these goods are branded, the producer will usually attempt to protect their trademark by an agreement which not only outlines the terms and conditions of trade, but also sets minimum standards covering sales and after-sales aspects.

Other forms of agreement cover the use of registered trademarks or celebrity names. The right to use well-known names, fictional or real, can be purchased under a licensing agreement which specifies how the name is to be used, and what royalties will be paid for the privilege. Many children's products, for example, are sold in the image of the latest popular hero, manufactured and distributed under a licensing arrangement with the creator. Real-live celebrities may also allow their name to be associated with a product or service under an endorsement agreement.

Although up-front payments and on-going royalties can be onerous, the small business, with no established identity of its own, can often benefit from a relevant association with an established, known name. For example, a small manufacturer of leisure clothes and equipment may seek endorsement of their products by a local sports personality, to add stature and gain new outlets.

For some small businesses, product and trademark arrangements are essential. Many public houses are tied to a major brewery, even though the business is sometimes owned by the tenant; the publicans benefit from the national marketing by the brewery, but there are restrictions on what else they can sell. A small manufacturer of toys and games will inevitably seek licensing arrangements so that their products can be merchandised using the latest cartoon characters; sales can be dramatically influenced by the well-timed launch of a product endorsed by the latest heroes.

3.2 Business format franchising

Today the word franchising is more commonly used to describe business format franchising. This is a more in-depth relationship between franchisor and franchisee than a simple product or trademark licensing arrangement.

The International Franchise Association[6] describes this type of franchise as:

> 'A continuing relationship in which the franchisor provides a licensed privilege to do business plus assistance in organising training, merchandising and management in return for a consideration from the franchisee.'

In other words, this type of franchise goes beyond the supply of products and trade names, and covers many other aspects of how the business is run. The business format offered by the franchisor can cover such aspects as:

- ❐ trade name, business style, logo, house colours;
- ❐ detailed product or service specification;
- ❐ analysis of location, and lease negotiations;
- ❐ design of premises, and purchase of equipment;
- ❐ financial advice to establish the business;
- ❐ operating systems and manuals;
- ❐ management control systems;
- ❐ training and help to set up;
- ❐ continuing assistance including research and development and management counselling;
- ❐ national and local marketing;
- ❐ centralised purchasing;
- ❐ current market research results.

This represents a complete package which allows the franchisee to use a format proven by the franchisor, whilst retaining independence as a business. There is an agreement between the two parties which sets out how the business will be run, and the obligations of both parties.

The major banks also offer specific advice and information on franchising; for certain proven franchises they will be able to offer loans more easily than for other types of new business with no track record.

Activity 4 Examples of franchises

Give some examples of franchises that you have heard of or may have used. What do you think it costs to become a franchisee in each case?

4 The franchising market

4.1 The development of franchising

Business format franchising has grown most dramatically in the USA. Originating in the 19th century, it took off in the 1950s, and now accounts for around one-third of all retail sales. Recently the development of e-commerce franchises gave the market a further boost[7].

Kentucky Fried Chicken became one of the pioneers when Colonel Sanders travelled around America teaching people how to cook chicken his way. Today, Pepsi-Cola own the Kentucky Fried Chicken chain of over 7,000 franchised outlets around the world.

Another fast food chain was started in the 1950s by Ray Kroc based on the standardised hamburger production techniques developed by the McDonald brothers. McDonalds now represent the largest group of retail outlets in the world with over 14,000 franchises in 70 countries.

In the UK, franchising is less significant but it is a fast growing sector. Wimpy was the first major franchise in the UK, developed by J. Lyons and Company from 1956. By the 1990s franchising had become the fastest growing sector among retail and service outlets, accounting for almost 4 per cent of total retail sales. The annual turnover of franchised companies was nearly £9 billion in 1999, representing around 5 per cent of total retail sales, made through 30,000 franchised outlets operated by over 600 franchisors[7].

In Europe there were over 100,000 franchised outlets by the 1990s with sales over £20 billion. In some countries penetration of franchising seems more advanced than the UK. According to the British Franchise Association[8], franchising accounts for 0.4 per cent of GDP in the UK, 1.3 per cent in France, 1.9 per cent in Belgium, and 2.5 per cent in Holland.

Canada has the highest penetration level, with 40 per cent of retail sales through franchised outlets. Franchising is growing fast in Japan and Australia, and has now begun to spread into Eastern Europe and China. The Middle East is also emerging as a growth market.

Although the best known franchises tend to be in the catering and retail sectors, the most number of franchises are in business services, as shown below in Table 6.1

Table 6.1 Franchise units by market sector

Sector	Number of units in 000s	% of total franchised units	Examples
Business services	8	25	Kall Kwik, Interlink Express
Hotels and catering	6	21	Perfect Pizza, KFC, Wimpy
Personal services	5	16	Stagecoach Theatre, Wedding Guide
Store retailing	4	14	Body Shop, Tie Rack
Property services	4	13	Dyno-Rod, Apollo Window Blinds
Transport services	3	11	Kwik Fit, Green Flag, Autoglass
TOTAL	31	100	

Source: NatWest/British Franchise Association Franchise Survey, 2000

It is still a relatively young industry: many of the franchises on offer today are less than three years old. The Internet has been a popular source of recent franchise opportunities, as well as a new promotional medium for traditional franchises. The range of franchised businesses is extremely wide. Some of the more unusual franchises offered in the UK include:

❐ Cico Chimney Linings Ltd – re-lining of chimneys and flues;

❐ Complete Weed Control Ltd – weed control service to public and private sector organisations;

❐ Cupboard Love – replacement cupboard doors;

❐ Create-a-Book – personalised children's books;

❐ Giltsharp Technology – a high-tech blade and scissor sharpening service to the hairdressing and catering industries;

❐ Mister Bagman – bag supplier to retailers;

❐ Nationwide Investigations Group – private detective agencies;

❐ Rose Elliot Horoscopes – personalised astrological profiles on computer.

4.2 How much does it cost?

In addition to the usual overhead costs of running a business, the franchisee will have to find some additional funds.

❐ **Minimum start up costs**

These include an initial franchise fee as a one-off payment to the franchisor for the privilege of becoming a franchisee. In addition, other start-up investment is required to cover the costs of buying equipment, fitting out premises, trade signs, initial stocks of materials, stationery, promotional literature, and all the other items which the franchisor deems necessary to run the business. There may be some element of profit to the franchisor in providing the new franchisee with these.

The advertised minimum finance required for some well known, and some not so well known, franchises are, at time of writing, as shown in Table 6.2 below.

Table 6.2 Profile of some franchises: number of outlets and costs

Franchise	Business type	No. of outlets	Minimum outlay
Amtrak Express Parcels	Parcel delivery	340	£20,000
Burger King	Fast food	445	£700,000
Dyno-Rod	Plumbing problems	160	£10,000
Merry Maids	Domestic cleaners	72	£10,500
Mixamate	Concrete delivery	24	£5,000
Oscar Pet Foods	Home-delivered pet food	100	£20,000
Prontaprint	Instant print and copying	220	£12,500
Perfect Pizza	Home-delivered fast food	234	£25,000
Service Master	Commercial cleaning	448	£7,700
Signs Express	Business signs	70	£16,500
Select Appointments	Recruitment agency	57	£12,500
Stagecoach Theatre	Performing arts schools	285	£10,000
The Tanning Shop	Sun tanning	163	£50,000
Wimpy International	Fast food	240	£80–200,000
Wicked Wheels	Car wheels and trim	3	£30,000

❐ **Annual charges**

Franchisors will also levy a service fee, and possibly other charges on an ongoing basis. The service charge is normally calculated as a percentage of net invoiced sales, varying from 5 per cent to 15 per cent plus, and averaging in the 10 to 12 per cent range. Where the supply of goods on a continuous basis is part of the franchise arrangement (e.g. The Body Shop and McDonalds) then the franchisor will have some level of profit in the transfer price of these goods.

Fixed charges representing a contribution to national advertising and management are also common.

> **Activity 5** For and against franchising
>
> What do you think are the advantages and disadvantages of franchising
>
> a)   from the perspective of the franchisee; and
>
> b)   from the perspective of the franchisor?

5 The pros and cons of franchising

5.1 Success and failure among franchises

Many claims are made by the franchise industry about the supposedly higher success rates experienced by franchise chains than conventional business start ups. The readiness of banks to lend money to franchisees is pointed to as evidence for a higher likelihood of success, which is often quoted to be five times as high as start ups. However, it has been argued that franchisee failures are often disguised by under-reporting from the franchisors, franchise outlets changing hands and the exclusion of 'unethical' franchises from the data[9]. Whilst franchise failure rates are on average somewhat lower than for start ups generally, much depends on the quality of the individual franchise.

Franchises vary greatly in quality, from the well-established proven formulae of household names, to new creations which have yet to establish their viability. In the USA franchising is regulated by legislation, which ensures that franchisors have to register with the authorities, completing a franchise offering circular. This is similar to a share prospectus, and contains information essential for the prospective franchisee, such as details of the history and officers of the franchisor company. In the UK such disclosures are voluntary, as is the regulation of the industry. Most established franchisors are members of the British Franchise Association, which has a code of conduct and accreditation rules, based on codes developed by the European Franchise Federation.

One of the key guiding principles is that the franchisor shall have operated a business concept with success for a reasonable time, and in at least one pilot unit before starting its franchise network[10]. The stages of setting up as a franchisor can be lengthy and expensive if the recommended route is kept to[11]:

1. *Establish basic business idea*. Testing the marketing, product/service and operational strategies should take at least 2 years with probable adjustments and modifications to the original concept.

2. *Open pilot outlet*. Another 2 years is probably required to test out a replica of the business in another location with different management to verify that it is a transferable concept.

3. *Operationalise the franchise*. This involves drawing up 3 key documents:
    - *an operating manual* – detailed guidance on how to run the business;
    - *a franchise contract* – the legal document spelling out the obligations of both parties;
    - *a franchise prospectus* – the marketing literature to attract franchisees.

4. *Recruitment and training of franchisees.* Advertising and attending exhibitions is a continuous exercise if the franchise is to grow.

This process can take 5 years if followed correctly before the first franchisee is recruited.

Many franchise concepts do not last the development course, or try to cut corners. A surprisingly high number fail or disappear once launched. A study[11] investigated the fortunes of franchises which had been advertised 10 years previously, in 1984. After 10 years, only 25 per cent were considered to be a generally successful franchise, a further 25 per cent were still in existence in some form but were not considered to be a franchise success story, and over 50 per cent had failed as a franchise and disappeared from view.

These figures have implications for franchisees as well as franchisors. The vulnerability of franchise operations can put many individual operators at risk overnight, as was demonstrated by the well publicised difficulties of the Ryman and Athena franchisees when the owning company went into liquidation.

A prospective franchisee will clearly want to know more about these aspects to protect themselves from the possibility of taking on some of the disadvantages of franchising without the compensating advantages.

5.2 Advantages and disadvantages for franchisees

❐ **Advantages for franchisees**

- ○ The business concept is proven, or should be. The British Franchise Association have laid down guidelines as to what constitutes proven, as outlined above, which includes more than just one business outlet for a short period.

- ○ The way to operate the business has already been worked out and tested. Starting up should be easier and faster.

- ○ Training and support is given including technical training, business training, site selection and choice of suppliers.

- ○ Statistically, fewer franchises fail than other business start ups; therefore it can be easier to obtain finance for the franchise. As discussed above, annual failure rates are difficult to establish precisely and success is not as assured as some of the advertising material may suggest. However one estimate is of failure rates between 5 to 7 per cent per annum, lower than for small firms generally[12].

- ○ National branding will often have been established.

- ○ Research and development, and competitive analysis, will usually be undertaken by the franchisor to keep abreast of environmental changes.

- ○ Economies of scale may apply, for example in nationally agreed terms with suppliers which take account of the total franchised business.

- ○ Economies of experience should apply, for example in knowing the marketing techniques that have worked best for other franchisees.

❐ **Disadvantages to franchisees**

○ Not your own creation. This is someone else's idea; the franchisee is implementing not creating.

○ Lack of independence. The franchisor makes the rules which the franchisee has to follow.

○ The financial costs can be considerable with large up-front fees and high royalties. Set-up costs can also be higher as they have to follow a prescribed formula.

○ The franchise may not be suited to your area.

○ The goodwill your business builds up is never all yours, as it is dependent on a continuing franchise agreement. This could cause problems when you decide to sell the business.

○ The franchisor needs to ensure regular disclosure of information by the franchisee to protect their royalties and the franchise agreement. This can become intrusive into the financial affairs of the franchisee.

○ The brand image of the franchisor can become a distinct liability if things go wrong. The franchisee is dependent on the stability of the franchisor; a national problem with the franchise can dramatically affect the franchisee who has no control over events.

5.3 Advantages and disadvantages for franchisors

❐ **Advantages for franchisors**

○ Franchising is a way of expanding a small business into a big business in a relatively short time. The burden of raising capital to develop a business concept is shared with franchisees and fast expansion becomes easier to fund.

○ Another common barrier to expansion, the recruitment, motivation and reward of key staff, is also eased; a proven opportunity usually has a queue of potential franchisees waiting to start. Franchisees tend to be motivated individuals prepared to accept rewards in line with the results of their business.

❐ **Disadvantages for franchisors**

○ Franchising inevitably means loss of control compared to a conventional branch outlet. Franchisees are more independent than a branch manager.

○ If the franchisor offers a franchise based on the recommended practices of the BFA, then it will take time, effort and resources to operate the concept as a pilot franchise unit.

○ The franchisor may take on many obligations in the franchise agreement, such as continuing commercial and technical assistance during the lifetime of the agreement, which will necessitate developing central support resources.

○ Franchisees are becoming more organised as groups in their dealings with franchisors. Their ability to exert pressure on franchisors will probably increase as the industry matures.

○ Failure of a single franchisee, through no fault of the franchisor, can do considerable damage to the reputation of the franchisor.

Ultimately the franchisor has a powerful vested interest to ensure the survival and success of its franchised outlets; without them the franchise will fail.

The self-interest of the franchisor will be best served by meeting in full its obligations to prove the idea it wishes to network, and provide the required support to ensure the prosperity of the franchisees.

Activity 6 Is it a small business?

What characteristics do franchises have in common with other small firms? How do they differ?

6 But is it a small business?

Is a franchised outlet a small business? Or should it be classified as a form of managed branch of a larger organisation?

The Bolton Committee excluded franchises from its review of the UK small business sector. One of its key criteria in defining a small business was independence from other organisations. As a franchise is not independent from the franchisor, the total franchised network could be considered as one business, rather than a collection of separate, small firms (franchisees) and one larger business (the franchisor).

In practice, all small firms exhibit differing degrees of independence. None are truly autonomous, as all will depend to some extent on forces outside their full control.

Customers can be a powerful controlling factor, particularly if a small business is reliant on a few of them. A small producer supplying a large supermarket chain, for example, may not have full control over many important operations of its business, including quality control, delivery schedule and pricing policies. Financial backers of an enterprise may also exert considerable influence on the management of a small business, particularly one that is in difficulties.

In reality the independence of small firms is not a fixed factor, but rather a point on a continuum. A firm's position on the continuum depends on a number of factors, including the level of competitive activity in its chosen market, the power of its buyers and suppliers, and its relative financial success or failure[13].

Franchisees occupy a place on this continuum, but not necessarily at the end of minimal control. Nor will all franchisees be at the same point; some will be more controlled by their franchisors than others. Indeed the perceptions of the franchisor and its franchisees over who controls what have been shown to significantly differ. A survey of three franchise networks[14] indicated that, whilst franchisors felt that their franchise contracts were strictly enforced, franchisees believed that contractual obligations were not rigorously applied. They did agree however that franchisees had the principle responsibility for hours of opening, employment of personnel, bookkeeping and quality standards, which represent a significant part of the operational running of the business.

A critical ingredient in the make-up of the relationships in a franchised network is that the franchisee operates a legally separate business. This business may be constrained by the terms of the franchise contract, but in the eyes of the law it is a separate entity. The experience of franchisors is that they need to manage their franchisees by persuasion not mandate, as the desire for independence is strong among franchisees. The degree of independence exercised by the owner of a successful franchised outlet is not so significantly different from a more conventional small business that it can be considered a totally different business type.

Many of the principles for the successful management of small businesses hold true for franchised outlets. The performance of individual outlets operating the same franchise varies more significantly than can be explained by location factors alone. Some franchisees always struggle. Others become successful owner-managers, with a chain of franchised outlets.

7 Case studies and activities

Case studies *The story so far*

In Part I, Units 1 to 5, the case studies followed the progress of two people, Andrea Clarey and Kit Hugos, as they went through the process of testing the feasibility of their business ideas. After investigating their markets more thoroughly through primary and secondary research, the decisions they made were as follows:

a) Kit Hugos researched his concept of an electronic personal safety device for specific market sectors. When he looked at the potential for the device with one university, he discovered that another company, PS (Personal Safety) was already developing a similar product for universities and children's play areas. PS's expertise was in the software to track tagging devices. Kit Hugos and partner Robin Davidson were specialists in the miniaturisation of electronic circuits and devices, and a natural partner for PS. Discussions took place, resulting in an order for Kit Hugos's new company, 'Circumspect', to design, develop and manufacture the electronic circuit which would be at the heart of the personal tagging transmitter to be worn. PS thus became Kit's first customer which allowed him to invest in a design and manufacturing facility knowing that he had some business to cover initial overheads. He gradually extended the customer base over the next few years to include companies with other applications for their specialist expertise. Circumspect became a customised designer and manufacturer of specialised electronic circuitry sold to companies with applications particularly in security and communications.

Military products featured heavily in the order book in the early years. You can pick up the story again in the Case in Unit 10, Kit Hugos cycles into trouble.

b) Andrea Clarey's investigations into her own payroll business convinced her first that market segments for payroll services in terms of different sectors did exist (such as schools and small businesses) but second that they were not large enough to sustain her business on a local basis. As her main competitive advantage was to provide a local, personalised service this seemed to be a fundamental problem. She also had misgivings about her personal aptitude to run her own small business with the accompanying pressures and risk. When an attractive job working for the payroll department of the County Council was advertised she applied. The Council was also tendering for outside work to supplement their internal service, and during the interview Andrea explained some of her ideas to them. This undoubtedly helped her get the job which she was happy to take. Her investigations into the world of self-employment had helped her to understand herself and her motivations a little better, so that she felt less discontent in her new job. She also gained some insights into small business which she was able to share with a friend, Bryony Hannam, when she talked to her about her idea for a picture framing service.

Case Bryony Hannam's picture framing idea: start up or franchise?

Bryony Hannam knew that her friend Andrea Clarey had recently investigated setting up her own business, so she decided to talk to her about her own idea. She had decided she was particularly suited to a picture framing business, and she was sure there was a need for the service in her hometown. There were other picture framers, but Bryony reckoned they fell into one of three categories:

a) small back-street traders, often working part time with long delivery times and poor choice of framing materials, although usually inexpensive;

b) art galleries offering a framing service. She was personally intimidated by the rarefied atmosphere of these, and she knew others who were similarly put off. They also offered limited choices and long delivery times as they normally sub-contracted the work to other framers;

c) high street poster shops, which targeted a young market primarily interested in posters. Although they offered other types of framing, their main business was the ready-made, clip frame.

Bryony was convinced that there was a need for a different type of framer – one who focused on the homeowner. She felt they wanted good quality framing which would co-ordinate with their interior decor. They also wanted convenience, in terms of where to shop, and a quick delivery time, with friendly helpful service from staff who related to their needs. She planned to set up in a position close to the main shopping centre, serving the local community. She also felt a location near to car parking was important as framed pictures were often bulky and awkward to carry any distance.

However, she felt constrained to go ahead because she had very little business experience and, although she was familiar with the art world, she had never framed any pictures herself.

In her investigations of the marketplace, she had discovered that she could get help from various quarters. There was no shortage of part-time business courses in the area; there were picture framing courses available from a weekend introduction to more extensive practical training. The manufacturers of framing equipment and the suppliers of materials all offered her training and advice in setting up.

She also discovered a nationally operated franchise which initially sounded very attractive. The franchise offered her a complete package for setting up as a picture framer – from the design of the retail premises and workshop, the purchasing of supplies, the craft and techniques of framing itself, through to the marketing of the business, and the management of its cash flow and other financial aspects. They could promote her outlet as part of a national operation and help her keep up to date with the latest developments in the framing world. Their marketing literature indicated they had been operating franchises for over 4 years, having set up their own framing business before that.

When Bryony read through the franchise agreement, she had second thoughts however. The financial implications were considerable. As well as an up-front fee of £10,000 she would have to pay them an on-going royalty of 10 per cent of her total sales revenue. In addition, she would still have to pay for the fitting of the premises, to their exact requirements, and find the finance for equipment and working capital which they estimated at a further £25,000. Despite assurances that finance would be readily available, Bryony wondered if she would ever be truly independent with such heavy liabilities and constraints on how she could operate the business.

When she discussed the idea with Andrea, she explained some of her investigations to date.

'This particular franchise,' she said, 'is a member of the British Franchise Association, so that gives me some guarantee of their authenticity. They have proven the business by running a pilot unit, and they are now quite well established.'

'If it's such a good deal for you, as they claim, why do they give so much away? What's in it for them?' asked Andrea. 'And if it is a good idea for you now, will it still be in 3 years' time when you have an established business but you will still be paying them royalties?'

Activities

i) What do you think is in it for them? What are the advantages for this particular franchisor?

ii) Identify the advantages and disadvantages of Bryony proceeding with this franchise compared to starting on her own.

iii) Consider Andrea's final point. How will the pros and cons change over time? Will the balance be changed in 3 years?

iv) What would you advise Bryony to do – start up on her own or take on the franchise?

Extended activity *A local franchise*

Consider a franchised outlet or business in your local area. Write an analysis of that franchise, with details of the format provided, that is the products, the logo, the trademarks and image. How successful do you believe this enterprise has been compared to similar non-franchised businesses? Ideally, talk to the owner-manager of a franchised outlet for their views.

In conclusion

Once you have finished this Unit, turn to Section B, Planning a new venture, and complete Step 2.1, Start up or franchise?

8 References and further reading

References and further information

1. For example, Curran, J. and Burrows, R. *Enterprise in Britain: A National Profile of Small Business Owners and the Self-Employed*, Small Business Research Trust, 1988. In many of his publications, Professor Curran has emphasised in particular the diversity of small businesses and the need for caution in drawing generalisations about them as a sector.

2. A special category of small firm, the new technology based firm (NTBF), has been identified by researchers looking at businesses that start up in newly emerging, and fast moving areas of technology. The role of these NTBFs is discussed for example in: Rothwell, R. 'The Role of Small Firms in Technological Innovation', in Curran, J., Stanworth, J. and Watkins, D. (eds), *The Survival of the Small Firm*, Vol. 2, Gower, 1986.

3. This theme of diversity in types of owner-managers of small business is explored in more depth in Unit 2, 2, Types of owner-managers and entrepreneurs.

   The different types of motivation for business ownership are discussed in Unit 10, 1.3, The objectives of small business owner-managers.

4. Barriers to market entry are also considered in Unit 3, 2.4, Which sector to choose.

5. This was the definition used by the Small Firms Service in their booklet *Franchising*, Small Firms Service, Department of Employment.

6. The International Franchise Association, based in Washington DC, USA, was founded in 1960 as a non-profit making body and it now represents over 400 franchisors in the USA and world-wide.

7. Keynote Report *Franchising* 7th edn, 2000.

8. The British Franchise Association, (BFA), Thames View, Newtown Road, Henley on Thames, Oxon, RG9 1HG (web site www.british-franchise.org).

    'The BFA was formed in 1977 by several leading franchisors in the UK, with the aim of establishing a clear definition of ethical franchising standards to help members of the public, press, potential investors, and government bodies to identify sound business opportunities.' (From a BFA leaflet, *Your First Steps in Franchising*.)

9. Hoy, F. 'The Dark Side of Franchising or Appreciating Flaws in an Imperfect World', *International Small Business Journal*, 12, 2, 1994.

10. The European Code of Ethics for Franchising has been adapted by an agreed Extension and Interpretation to form the Code of Ethical Conduct of the British Franchise Association. For further details see the *Franchise Handbook*, Blenheim Business Publications, 1995.

11. Stanworth, J. 'Penetrating the Mists Surrounding Franchise Failure Rates – Some Old Lessons for New Businesses', *International Small Business Journal*, 13, 2, 1995.

12. Stanworth, J. and Curran, J. 'Franchising', in Woodcock, C. (ed.) *The Guardian Guide to Running a Small Business*, Kogan Page, 1990. For a discussion on franchise survival rates see section 7.5 'Franchising for the future'.

13. The relative independence of small business types is further discussed in Unit 3, 4, Hostile and benign environments.

14. Stanworth, J., Curran, J. and Hough, J. 'The Franchised Small Enterprise: Formal and Operational Dimensions of Independence', in Curran, J., Stanworth, J. and Watkins, D. (eds), *The Survival of The Small Firm*, Gower, 1986.

Recommended further reading

☐ Burns, P. *Entrepreneurship and Small Business*, Palgrave, 2001. Chapters 4, 5 and 6 on aspects of start ups.

☐ Rosthorn, J., Haldane, A., Blackwell, E. and Wholey, J. *The Small Business Action Kit*, Kogan Page, 1991. Chapter 2, What are the options? This book has a series of work sheets to guide the new start up along its chosen course. (It is therefore a very practical book, well suited to prospective owner-managers and their advisors, and less appropriate for a student interested in a more theoretical approach.)

❐ Williams, S. *Lloyds Bank Small Business Guide*, Penguin, 2001. Section II Getting A Head Start. This is one of the best of the bank-sponsored publications on how to set up and run a small business.

❐ Felstead, A. *The Corporate Paradox: Power and Control in the Business Franchise*, Routledge, 1993.

❐ Keynote Report *Franchising* 7th edition, 2000.

❐ Hoy, F. 'The Dark Side of Franchising or Appreciating Flaws in an Imperfect World', *International Small Business Journal*, 12 (2), 1994.

❐ Spinelli, S. 'The Pitfalls and Potential of Franchising' in Birley, S. and Muzyka, F. (eds) *Mastering Entrepreneurship*, FT/Prentice Hall, 2000. Section 1 'Evaluating the opportunity'.

❐ Stanworth, J. and Purdy, D. 'Franchising and Enterprise' in Carter, S. and Jones-Evans, D. (eds) *Enterprise and Small Business*, FT/Prentice Hall, 2000.

❐ Stanworth, J., Curran, J. and Hough, J. 'The Franchised Small Enterprise: Formal and Operational Dimensions of Independence' (see reference 14 above). This paper discusses the issue of whether the franchised small business is genuinely independent.

There are also some magazines sold at newsagents, such as WH Smith, which specialise in franchising and are worth looking through to understand the scope of the system. For example, *Business Franchise* and *The Franchise Magazine*.

7 Buying an existing business

This Unit is concerned with the possibility of buying an existing business, as opposed to a start up or franchise. The opportunities for purchasing (and selling) businesses are explored, along with the main problem areas that can be encountered.

Contents

Activity 1 Why are businesses for sale?

Can you give some examples of:

a)   Different types of sellers of small businesses?

b)   Their motives for sale?

1 The scope for buying an existing business

The would-be owner-manager does not necessarily have to start a new business as either a start up or franchise. There are various opportunities to become part of an existing business. A buyer may choose to purchase an existing firm outright, or they may opt to become involved in it in some way as a partner. The sellers of existing small businesses vary from small to large enterprises, conventional to franchised businesses and from the successful to the failed.

The different possibilities arising from the intentions of a buyer, and the status of a seller, create many permutations of ways of buying an existing business, or part of it. This is illustrated in Figure 7.1 as a 'Matrix of possibilities for entry into an existing small business'.

	Seller			
	Small firm	Larger firm	Franchise	Forced sale
Buyer				
Outright purchase	✔	✔	✔	✔
Buy-in	✔	?	✔	✔
Buy-out	✔	✔	✔	✔

Figure 7.1 Matrix of possibilities for entry into an existing small business

❒ **Small firm**

The seller may be a small business person who, for one reason or another, wishes to dispose of the enterprise, or their share in it.

The reasons for the sale may include:

○ recognition of lack of success, and low probability of success in the future;

○ problems, not related to the business, which force its sale, including health problems, marital break-up or other personal issues;

○ other business activities which make a sale desirable; for example the need to raise money for another failing/succeeding enterprise, or the desire to free-up time for other business involvements;

○ desire for a career change out of small business;

○ retirement of an owner, with no family succession plans;

○ desire to cash-in on the success of a business;

○ a dispute which has led to the breakdown of a business partnership where one side cannot, or does not wish to, buy out the other.

The seller may own all of the business or only a part.

❒ **Larger firm**

Larger companies sometimes dispose of a part of their business which by itself constitutes a small firm. Again their motives will be varied, including:

○ financial targets set by the parent company are consistently not met by the small business unit. The return on the investment is considered inadequate, and there is a desire to re-invest the capital and management time elsewhere;

○ the parent company adopts a new strategy, which means that the small business unit no longer contributes to meeting group objectives. Particularly in times of recession, larger companies which have diversified into new areas of higher risk, may seek to return to what they consider to be their core business. This has motivated the scaling down of some companies, and the break-up of some conglomerates into parts which can be classified once again as a small business;

○ the parent company needs to raise money for other activities, because of financial difficulties, or for other reasons;

○ the parent company is itself taken over, and the new owners do not see the small business unit as contributing to their overall strategy, or they may wish to sell parts of the acquisition to help fund the purchase;

○ legislation may force a large company to sell some parts of its business.

❐ **Franchise**

As well as starting a new outlet in a franchise network, it is also possible to buy either the business of an existing franchisee, or a branch outlet from a franchisor. Existing franchisees may wish to sell their business for any of the reasons given for small firms above. In addition, they may simply be disillusioned with the franchise system, because it does not provide sufficient independence to the franchisee, for instance. The franchisor will have to agree to such a sale, as the franchise agreement will need to be assigned to a new owner. However, it is usually in their interests to facilitate the change of ownership for two main reasons:

○ the franchisee wishing to sell will hardly be motivated to properly manage the franchise having failed to secure a buyer because of the intransigence of the franchisor;

○ it is motivational for other franchisees to see the exit possibilities from their business; they will like to feel they are building up a capital gain, as well as ongoing income from their business. Franchisors are therefore usually keen to build up a second market for the sale of franchised outlets, providing they can approve the quality of the incoming franchisee.

Franchisors may also wish to sell off an outlet which they themselves own, and manage. This may have been an original pilot operation to prove the franchise concept. Or the franchisor may have developed as a series of owned outlets before moving into franchising, the success of which then triggers a sale of the managed outlets to franchisees.

❐ **Forced sales**

The high closure rates of small businesses unfortunately gives rise to opportunities to purchase the assets of a failed enterprise from a liquidator, receiver, or administrator. The forced sale of a business and its assets takes different forms dependent on the legal status of the failed company[1].

- ○ *Liquidation* describes the legal process of closing down a bankrupt company, and the sale of its assets to pay off as many debts as possible. The owner no longer controls the business; a liquidator is appointed who will sell off the assets of the business for the highest possible price. Insolvency has usually gone too far at this stage for there to be much interest in the on-going trading of the business. The liquidator simply disposes of the individual assets as quickly and economically as possible. Liquidation is not so much a possibility to buy a business as an opportunity to buy some assets, such as equipment, or office furniture, at low prices.

- ○ *Receivership* allows more possibilities to acquire the on-going business of a company in trouble. A receiver is normally appointed by a lender, such as a bank, who has secured their loan by a charge against certain of the company's assets, often the debtors. The receiver comes in to realise the assets in order to repay as much as possible of the debt.

  Unlike a liquidator, a receiver can keep a business trading if it is considered in the best interest of the creditors.

- ○ *Administration.* The Insolvency Act of 1986 introduced a further possibility for creditors, who might otherwise have had to force a company into liquidation.

  Before the 1986 Act, the only way of dealing with company failure where there were no specific charges on company assets, was through liquidation; potentially viable businesses were accordingly forced into liquidation because the creditors had no other process available to them for the efficient recovery of their money. The 1986 Act introduced Administration Orders, which are court orders appointing an administrator empowered to salvage as much of the company as possible, or to sell its assets on a more profitable basis than under the circumstances of a liquidation.

Whilst it would be unwise in most circumstances to buy the shares of a company in receivership or under administration, it is possible to acquire those assets of the business which enable it to continue trading, thereby in effect buying the business.

Activity 2 Who buys small businesses?

Can you give some examples of:

a) Different types of buyers of small businesses?

b) Their motives for buying?

2 Small business buyers

The intentions of the buyer add further to the scope of entry permutations into an existing business.

2.1 Outright purchase

A would-be entrepreneur may choose to buy an on-going business in its entirety, as a means of market entry.

An existing small business owner can also decide to expand by purchasing another small enterprise.

In some trades, the barriers to entry for a new start up are sufficiently high to make the purchase of existing businesses the most common route.

❐ **The case of the licensed trade**

The following has been the case for example in the licensed trades, particularly public houses. It is very difficult to obtain the necessary permission to sell alcoholic drinks from premises which do not have an existing licence, especially where this is not tied to the consumption of food, as in a pub, or a wine bar. However there is a well-established market in the buying and selling of existing licensed premises. Specialist licensed property estate agents, or transfer agents, act on behalf of owners wishing to sell the freehold or leasehold of their premises.

A buyer can find vendors in any of the seller categories listed in the matrix of possibilities for entry into small business (Figure 7.1).

❐ *Small firm*: some pubs are free houses, owned outright by the publican, and not tied by contract to any one brewer. These are bought and sold much like other small firms, often with the added attraction of having a freehold property as an asset.

❐ *Larger firms*: have also been forced to sell some public houses which they own. A Monopolies and Mergers Commission report into the supply of beer found that large brewers controlled too many of the outlets for their products. Their recommendations forced brewers to sell off hundreds of licensed outlets.

❐ *Franchise*: some pubs are sold effectively as a franchise because the publican trades from licensed premises which are tied by a lease to one particular brewery.

❐ *Forced sales*: in the early 1990s, forced sales of public houses became commonplace. Free house prices were doubly hit by the general depression in the property market and the increase in premises for sale forced on the brewers. Owners who bought when prices were much higher were affected by high interest rates, and the decline in the value of their property asset, which was usually the main collateral for loans to buy the business. This also coincided with a downturn in demand for pubs' services. Increased competition from other leisure service providers, and stricter enforcement of drink drive legislation, has led to a general decline in sales. These factors combined to cause a rise in the number of forced sales. A survey by the Business Sales Group, specialist licensed transfer agents, in 1991, suggested that one-third of free house pub sales were forced on the owners[2]. This shakeout in the industry provided opportunities for several new chains of themed pub-diners to emerge as they were able to obtain licensed properties at bargain prices.

2.2 Buy-in

Buyers may not wish to purchase an existing business in its entirety. They may instead buy into an existing business, and become a new partner, or shareholder, with those that already exist.

Again this is more commonplace in some types of small business than others. It often happens, for example, in professional practices such as accountants, solicitors, doctors and other medical practitioners such as physiotherapists. These are often large partnerships, where it is normal to have a turnover of partners who leave, or retire. In such circumstances, it is not necessary to dissolve the partnership, because the partnership agreement allows for the recruitment of another partner into the practice.

Other types of small firms, including franchises, may also wish to allow in a new partner or shareholder. For example an expanding firm out-grows the resources of the founding entrepreneur(s) who sees the need to build a team to manage the business; in order that the new team members may share the founder's objectives and commitment, they are invited to purchase into the equity of the business. A similar scenario might also arise if a small firm found itself in difficulties; the addition of different skills and capital from a new partner or shareholder represents a possible recovery strategy of the forced sale kind.

For example, a strategy between these two extremes was adopted by Anita Roddick in the early days of The Body Shop. The success of her first shop in Brighton encouraged her to open a second. She was unable to raise the necessary capital from the bank, and so instead found a new partner who put up the necessary £4,000 in return for 50 per cent of the equity of the business. It proved a very sound investment.

Buying into a business being sold off by a larger firm is also possible. This is becoming more common, especially in conjunction with buy-outs by the management (see below).

2.3 Buy-out

Buy-outs commonly refer to the purchase of a business, or a significant part of it, by its existing management. Relatively rare in the 1970s, management buy-outs have become increasingly common since the 1980s. Although buy-outs can occur from small firms and franchises and have also happened as a result of a forced sale by the parent company, larger firms are usually the sellers. Indeed many buy-outs are larger firms buying themselves out of even bigger companies. For example, MFI was bought out of Asda for £718 million.

Management buy-outs have become an important part of industrial re-organisation, and an increasingly common way for managers to become owner-managers. The USA and the UK are the biggest buy-out markets; in the UK, there are approximately 700 buy-outs each year, and only 500 in the rest of Western Europe[3]. Made possible by readily available finance from venture capital funds, buy-outs were further fuelled by some well publicised success stories, such as the buy-out of Premier Brands for £97 million from Cadbury Schweppes, in which 4,500 of the 5,000 employees bought shares at 1p each. When the company was sold in 1989, these shares were worth £5 each, turning a factory worker's stake of £10 into £5,000, and giving the managing director a reported profit of £45 million. Such large-scale buy-outs encouraged many more smaller ones.

More recently, changes in local government legislation, introducing more competition in the provision of services, have stimulated some buy-outs in the public sector as well.

For example, a local council, the City and District of St Albans, sub-contracted the management of its leisure facilities to St Albans Leisure Ltd, a company formed by the management, who had previously been employed by the council to run those same facilities. The council benefit from a fixed-cost base for the provision of leisure services, rather than unpredictable losses which they had experienced hitherto. The management team are able to market the facilities more aggressively, and believe they are financially more efficient now that they are out of local authority control[4].

But not all buy-outs are success stories. There have been many casualties. High interest rates, and falling demand in recessionary times, work against buy-outs, particularly where high levels of borrowing, and expectations of rapid growth, are typical. In the recession of 1991, the Management Buy-Out Research Unit at Nottingham University reported record levels of buy-outs in receivership.[3]

2.4 Buy-in management buy-out (BIMBO)

A variation on the management buy-out theme is the buy-in management buy-out (or BIMBO as it is sometimes called), which combines outside and inside management in the purchase of a company. The risk of buying into a company from the outside can be reduced if the existing management of the company are also involved. In theory at least, it is possible to have the benefit of a fresh approach and wider experiences from the buying-in manager(s), linked to the in-depth knowledge of the company and its markets provided by the buy-out manager(s).

The motives of the vendor follow the general lines of the larger firm as seller outlined above. Disposals often follow strategy changes brought on by financial problems or changes of ownership.

For example, Letraset grew from a small firm in the 1960s to a quoted international company in the 1970s, and then found it difficult to sustain growth in its core graphic art business. By the early 1980s it had diversified into toys, leisure and collectables, and quickly hit problems in these new businesses.

A recovery strategy involved selling three companies in the toy and leisure field to their existing management as buy-outs. But it was too late. Letraset was acquired by Esselte, the Swedish office products group. Wanting only the core graphic arts activities, Esselte promptly put up for sale the remaining unrelated business, Stanley Gibbons, the stamp dealing and philatelic publishing group. Stanley Gibbons was eventually bought by a consortium of its own internal management plus some external stamp trade specialists in an early BIMBO.

Activity 3 Buying assets

When buying a business, it is common practice to buy only the assets, and not the business entity itself. If you were buying a small business (such as a picture framing business):

a)   What types of assets would you wish to buy?

b)   On what basis would you value them?

3   Assets for sale

In buying an existing business, whoever the seller or buyer, it is important to recognise what exactly is for sale. This will depend not only on the wishes of the parties to the negotiation, but also on the legal status of the business. Sole traders and partnerships have no legal existence separate from their owners; therefore only the assets of such businesses can be sold. Limited companies, on the other hand, are separate legal bodies; they have an existence distinct from their owners. Once a limited company has been given birth it can change parents; shares can be bought and sold. However, in order to avoid inheriting unwanted or unknown liabilities it is also common for only the assets of limited companies to be acquired.

The assets of a business for sale, whether it is a sole trader, partnership or limited company, will be the focus of attention of any prospective buyer. These assets can be reviewed under several headings not all of which will appear in the balance sheet.

3.1 Tangible assets

❒   **Freehold property**

The business may own the freehold of the property from which it trades. This is often the case where the position of the property is a key factor in its success in the marketplace. Hotels, restaurants, public houses, wine bars, squash clubs and other leisure facilities will all depend on their geographic location to attract customers. If location is such an important element in the marketing strategy of a small enterprise, then it is sensible to gain security of tenure over the property by buying the freehold, or at least securing a long lease, with first option to renew. Other businesses, less dependent on location, also purchase freehold property as a long-term investment, preferring to have a mortgage on an appreciating asset rather than pay rent. Property owned by a small firm improves the look of its balance sheet, and may make it easier to raise finance at a later date.

When such a business changes hands, the property is sometimes the most valuable asset. The bricks and mortar and land of a small hotel, for example, will almost certainly be of more value than the beds, furniture, kitchen equipment and other fixtures which make it possible to trade as a hotel.

Purchasing a freehold property as part of buying a business requires all the care and caution of buying any other property. In addition to the usual checks on ownership, planning permissions, restrictive covenants, mortgages and other charges, any prospective purchaser will particularly want to assure themselves of the suitability of the premises to the business. Moving from owned premises can be a long-winded affair taking months, or even years in a slow property market.

❐ Leasehold property

Property rented under a leasehold agreement can also be a valuable asset to a business. Most independent retailers, for instance, operate from leasehold premises. The situation of those premises sometimes commands a 'premium' when the business or even just the premises, change hands. Commercial estate agents, dealing in the transfer of such properties will quote a price for the 'benefit of the leasehold interest', which in times of a strong market can be tens of thousands of pounds even for a small property with a relatively short lease if it is well situated. Any purchaser looking at the history of the leasehold property market, will understand that it is, however, more volatile than the freehold market. High premiums paid for premises can disappear to nothing in times of recession, when even reverse premiums become possible. By 1990/91 the slowness of trading in high streets caused increased closures of retail firms, such that existing tenants became prepared to pay prospective owners to take the liability of their lease from them. The owners of properties proving difficult to rent, may offer rent-free periods to new tenants as an inducement to take on a new lease.

By its very nature a lease is a declining asset, compared to a freehold which will probably be an increasing one over the long term. Its value as an asset in the purchase of an existing business will therefore depend on the desirability of the premises, and the state of the property market at the time of purchase. Thereafter the value is likely to fluctuate. Other factors which will influence the value of a lease include:

○ *Transferability.* Most leases are not automatically transferable. Landlords will want to control the suitability of any incoming tenants. Although most leases state that permission for transfer should not be unreasonably withheld, restrictions on transferability will devalue a lease.

○ *Term of the lease.* Most commercial properties are held on shorter terms than residential properties. Ten-year leases are quite common, so that a business changing hands within the term of a lease will sometimes have only a few years left to run on the lease. However, a landlord will find it quite difficult to eject a sitting tenant, and many leases provide for the existing tenant to have first refusal on a new lease. These rights can be overridden however, for example by a landlord wishing to redevelop, or use the property for their personal use.

○ *Repairs and dilapidations.* Most commercial leases are on a 'full repairing' basis; that is the tenant is responsible to pay for the upkeep not only of the interior, but also the exterior of the buildings and any surrounding land. A 'dilapidations' clause in the lease will also usually make the tenant responsible for returning the premises to the landlord in a specified condition at the end of a lease. The cost of these ongoing, and end of lease, repairs and refurbishments can constitute a considerable burden on the tenant, especially if the premises are old, and near the end of the lease. Such factors will again influence the value of a lease. In some instances (for example where a high level of dilapidations are expected soon) the lease can have a negative value as its liabilities outweigh its usefulness.

○ *Rent and provision for reviews.* Where the rent due on a property is considered to be below market levels, then this will add to the value of a lease. Most leases provide for rent reviews on a three- or five-year basis. The date of the next review, and provisions in the lease on how it is to be carried out, are also important. Many leases provide for upward only reviews, with prescribed arbitration procedures in the event of a failure to agree on a new rent. Such clauses will limit the benefit of any sub-market rent situations.

❑ **Furniture, fixtures and fittings**

Buying an existing business implies that any premises from which it operates will be fitted out and furnished. A freehold or leasehold property, when taken on from new, is usually a bare shell, adaptable to the use of the incoming tenant. The cost of these fittings, whether it be shopfittings in the case of retail premises, or partitioning and modifications for manufacturing or office premises, is usually considerable. When a business is to be sold these fixtures and fittings are an asset whose value depends on their extent, condition and appropriateness.

The type of the business will determine the nature of the furniture, as well as fixture and fittings. It is likely that those small enterprises where the customer receives a service on the premises will have a relatively high level of value in this kind of asset.

For example, a restaurant will require tables, chairs, and other furnishings and decor appropriate to its target market, which can be expensive to purchase. The value of these to prospective purchasers will depend on whether they wish to focus the business in the same way (on the same group of customers) or switch to a new theme and style which might involve a complete refit of the premises.

Those service industries where customers are not usually dealt with on the premises, and which require only a small area of office space, are likely to have a lower value in these assets. Manufacturing companies will vary, and sometimes will have spent the minimum possible on furnishings and fixtures. Higher technology firms, however, often need to invest in sophisticated fittings, for example to create a dust-free 'clean room' for certain processes.

❐ Machinery, equipment and vehicles

The machinery and equipment necessary to perform the functions of a business will invariably be acquired with it. The type and extent will obviously depend on the business and could include:

- ○ *manufacturing plant* (e.g. printing presses, automated packaging machinery), workshop machinery and tools (e.g. lathes, compressors, saws and other small tools);

- ○ *commercial equipment* (e.g. kitchen equipment, freezers, desk top publishing equipment);

- ○ *office equipment* (e.g. computers, copiers, telephones and exchange);

- ○ *vehicles* (e.g. delivery vans, fork-lift trucks, company cars).

The alternatives for evaluating these types of assets all have flaws:

- ○ the *written-down book value* will tend to be somewhat arbitrary depending on the depreciation policies of the business which may have been optimistic or cautious;

- ○ the *market value* could be a pessimistic figure as these assets tend to be worthless when sold off individually and not as part of an ongoing business;

- ○ the *replacement value* is a useful measure to appreciate what it might cost to start up an equivalent new business, but it will not take account of the age and useful life of the equipment;

- ○ the *original cost* of the equipment is again a useful measure to have in valuing these fixed assets but will not take account of inflation in new prices, nor devaluation of an asset through age.

Ownership is an important consideration in the acquisition of any assets under this heading. Frequently hire purchase, leasing or rental agreements cover such equipment, which determine who owns it and how much there is to be paid for the continued use of the equipment on an ongoing basis.

❐ Stock and work-in-progress

The vendor of a small firm will usually wish to sell the stock of the business to the new owner. This stock can be classified into three main types:

- ○ *Raw materials stock:* the materials a business buys in from suppliers which it then uses or converts into something else. For example, a picture framing business will have a stock of glass, mountboard, and uncut lengths of wood and metal mouldings for frames.

○ *Work-in-progress*; on the day of handover from one owner to the next, some jobs will be partly finished, representing work still in progress. For example, the picture framer may have frames which are not fully finished sitting on the workbench.

○ *Finished stock*; there will be a stock of product which is ready for sale to the customer, but which remains unsold or unshipped and not invoiced on the day of transfer.

The picture framer will have finished pictures awaiting collection by customers. There may also be unsold framed pictures displayed in a shop area, along with unsold ready-made frames and unframed prints.

The valuation of such stock is often more straightforward than other assets with fewer negotiating points.

The basis of valuation for raw materials stock is normally the original cost paid for the stock. If there have been price rises subsequent to the purchase of the stock the seller may wish to negotiate a higher price based on its replacement value. The buyer, on the other hand, may wish to ask for a reduced price if he/she considers some materials damaged, obsolete or overstocked and perishable. Work-in-progress is more complicated to value, but is normally valued on a similar basis to raw materials stock, with an additional amount to represent the value already added to the product.

Finished goods stock is normally valued at its selling price at the time, taking account of any overstocked positions which may decrease the value of some lines.

Stocks are normally valued on the day of transfer of the business, so that it does not represent a fixed sum of money during the negotiations. Stocks are taken over at valuation, and it is the basis only that is negotiated prior to handover.

Some types of business may need an independent valuer, because of either the complexity or the time consuming nature of the valuation of stock. The stock of a farm to be taken over will include crops already planted, requiring an expert to assess their value. A busy catering business, such as a restaurant or hotel, may have a large number of different items, some partly consumed, which require outside assistance to quantify on the day of the sale of the business.

❑ **Debtors**

Those people or companies who still owe money to a business for sale, on account of goods received or services rendered, represent a real asset in the books of any business which extends credit to its customers. The issue in valuing debtors is whether or not they will pay, and how long they will take. This uncertainty over the validity of debtors is often overcome by the vendor of the business either retaining ownership of the debtors, and collecting the money themselves after the sale of the business, or guaranteeing the amount that is collected from debtors by the new owner.

As with stocks, debtors will be valued on the date of transfer of the business to represent an up-to-date figure.

3.2 Intangible assets and goodwill

A distinction is drawn between the tangible and intangible assets of a business for sale. The assets discussed so far are tangible in that they can be physically identified and quantified. The intangible assets of a successful business will often be more important for they relate to why these physical assets have any meaning in the marketplace. The intangible assets are the sum of what makes a collection of property, fixtures and fittings, plant and equipment, and stocks work together to add value to products and services, in a way that is meaningful to customers, and profitable to the business. Figure 7.2 summarises the principle tangible and intangible assets of a business. In practice the distinction is not clear-cut; there are many areas of overlap between the types of assets, some of which have been shown.

Tangible assets	Examples of areas of overlap	Intangible assets
Property (freehold/leasehold)	Location of premises	Goodwill
Furniture, fixtures and fittings	Signage and logo	Image and reputation
Plant, equipment and vehicles	Systems and training	Employees
Stock and work-in-progress	Research and development	Intellectual property
Debtors	Mailing list	Customers

Figure 7.2 The tangible and intangible assets of a business for sale

Intangible assets only have real value whilst a business continues to trade. Once it has ceased trading, they lose most of their meaning and their worth. An unsuccessful business will tend to have fewer intangible assets as these represent the necessary conditions for success. But even a failed business will not have failed in every respect and can have some valuable intangibles, such as a skilled and loyal workforce. Even these assets soon evaporate once business has ceased, which is why the 1986 Insolvency Act introduced the concept of administration to allow struggling enterprises the opportunity to re-organise or be sold whilst trading continued.

The intangible assets of a business include:

❐ **Goodwill**

In many respects this is a summary of the value of the intangible assets of a business. It is an accountancy term which can find its way into the balance sheets of a business, but its accuracy will be determined by circumstance and not necessarily reality. If a business has recently been acquired, then the tangible assets, such as property, stocks and debtors, will have an identified value which will probably not equate to the purchase price of the business and therefore the total use of funds in buying it. In these circumstances, goodwill is a balancing figure representing the difference between the book value of specific assets, less any liabilities, and the amount actually paid to acquire them. Immediately after the purchase of a business, the amount of goodwill in the balance sheet will therefore reflect the negotiated value placed on it. But any small business which has not been recently bought or sold will not have had its goodwill valued in this way, and so it will not necessarily be reflected in the accounts.

Goodwill also occurs as a balance sheet item in relation to property. For example an existing retail business moves premises, and pays a premium over and above the value of any fixtures and fittings, to acquire a good commercial site. This premium will be reflected in the balance sheet as goodwill or intangible fixed assets. This is a first area of overlap in distinguishing between tangible and intangible assets. The value of freehold or leasehold property is not just a function of its physical attributes and associated costs, but also its geographic location in relation to the marketplace. For some small firms this will be the key factor in determining its value. A hotel near an airport or busy seaside town will be worth far more than an identical building in an area that few people visit; if external factors cause a decrease or increase in the number of visitors, then the property value will be affected accordingly. In other circumstances, the value of a property for a small firm is less significant; a manufacturing company with a geographically spread customer base may be successfully located anywhere where there is available labour.

Goodwill is a general term which attempts to value the likelihood of success and therefore the future profitability of an enterprise. When a business is advertised for sale, goodwill is often the word used to describe the vendor's valuation of this future profitability, which is added to any market value of the tangible assets.

❒ **Image and reputation**

The image and reputation developed by a small firm amongst its existing and potential customers will have a profound affect on its probability of success. An enterprise's image can be symbolised more tangibly in its logo style, the permanent signs used to advertise its presence and other fixtures and fittings which give the customer an impression of what the business is like.

For this reason a franchise network will emphasise the need to portray a consistent look in the premises of franchisees by using standard images and furnishings. But for all that, reputation is a fragile asset; the work of years to build an image of quality and reliability can be destroyed in minutes through shoddy or variable products or services.

The new owner of a small firm can become a negative influence on a well-established reputation, or provide a well-needed change to a more tarnished image.

❒ **Employees**

As well as the owner, the employees of a small business can be a crucial element in its success. Their skills, experience, and way of doing business will directly or indirectly impact on the satisfaction of customers. In part this will be truly intangible, relying on individual expertise and motivation. A more tangible aspect of this asset will be the systems which have been established to guide employees in the various operations of the business, in the use of plant and equipment and the training offered to them to improve the quality of their work, for example.

The seller of a small business often has acted as its manager and, in this sense, may have been the key employee. Their contribution to the business, and the impact of their removal from it, will be an issue that is particularly important in the sale of a small, owner-managed enterprise.

❑ Intellectual property

Innovation is a key ingredient in the success of a small enterprise. The results of innovation can become an important part of the intangible assets of a small business, classified as intellectual property. Laws protect these innovations under a number of categories[5]:

- ○ *Patents* afford temporary protection to technological inventions.
- ○ *Copyright* covers literary, artistic and musical creations in the longer term. Copyright is a right to prevent copying and covers items from computer software and databases to drawings and business plans.
- ○ *Trademarks* or brand names used in trading can be registered to protect them from infringement or passing off by other companies.
- ○ *Design right* extends protection to registered designs of products which have original features in their shape or configuration.

A small business may have created an asset from such properties in two distinct ways:

i) *As the owner of a protected intellectual property.*

For example, a small publisher usually copyrights any material which it publishes, and although this does not appear in the balance sheet, it has considerable value if the material can be reused.

ii) *As the contracted user of intellectual property.*

For example, the same small publisher also has contracted rights to publish books by certain authors who themselves own the copyright to the work.

Contracts covering licensing arrangements for products or processes protected by patents, trademarks, or design rights can form an integral part of a small enterprises activities. A new owner will therefore wish to ensure any necessary assignment of such contracts.

Past investment in research and development is a more tangible demonstration of the worth of a small firm's intellectual property, which otherwise might only be visible in its stocks of finished product, some of which may carry a brand name or be protected by patent.

❑ Customers

Customers are perhaps the most tangible of the intangible assets of a small firm; they can be observed and are often organised into a mailing list or appear in a schedule of debtors.

What is intangible is their loyalty and commitment to the business, especially if it changes ownership. The extent and longevity of the customer base will be important aspects in its valuation. A business which relies heavily on a small number of recently acquired customers has a very different asset to one with a large number of well-established clients.

Activity 4 Avoiding liabilities

A buyer of an existing business obviously wishes to avoid acquiring too many liabilities with the business. If you were negotiating to buy a small business what sort of liabilities would you look out for? Which would you definitely wish to avoid? Which might you be prepared to accept?

4 Liabilities to be avoided

Whilst wanting to retain and build on the existing assets of a small business, a prospective purchaser will wish to avoid any liabilities arising from the past activities of the firm.

The liabilities of a small business might include:

❐ trade creditors;

❐ bank and other borrowings;

❐ tax, VAT, PAYE and National Insurance contributions;

❐ lease and hire purchase agreements;

❐ guarantees or mortgages on assets.

If the business being sold is a sole trader or a partnership, then only the assets can be sold. The previous owner(s) will be left to pay off trade creditors, repay the bank or other borrowings and settle outstanding tax, VAT, PAYE and National Insurance liabilities.

If the shares of a limited company are being purchased, these liabilities belong to the company and will be transferred with it. The unknown quantity of some of these liabilities, especially those involving taxation where uncertainties can exist for several years after purchase, can be dealt with by:

❐ arranging for the vendor to give personal guarantees and warranties on the amount of future liabilities; or

❐ purchasing only the assets of a limited company in the same way as if it were a sole trader or partnership. These assets can be purchased by a shell company with no previous liabilities.

There are some liabilities which cannot be avoided, even when purchasing only the assets of a business, as some of these assets will be inseparable from certain liabilities. These include:

❏ *Obligations to employees.* When a business is sold as a going concern, even if only the assets are transferred to a new owner, employment law regards terms of employment and the period of service of an employee as continuous. Employees' contracts specifying their terms and conditions of service, including any notice period required for termination of employment, remain valid.

An employee's period of service with the former owner, is added to that with the new owner, to form one continuous period of employment. This can increase the new owners' obligations for such benefits as redundancy payments.

Where a business has contracted out of the state pension scheme and set up its own private pension fund, there is a continuous obligation on the employer to ensure that the fund can meet the minimum benefits of the state scheme.

❏ *Liabilities attached to specific assets.* An acquired asset may not be totally free of liabilities. Equipment can be subject to lease or hire purchase agreements; property or debtors may be part of a guarantee on loans. Such liabilities can be terminated by the seller before passing title to a new owner, or the buyer may agree to take on the liability with the asset.

Activity 5 What is it worth?

You own a small business (such as the picture framer already mentioned) which you wish to sell. On what basis will you decide the asking price for the business?

5 Basis of valuation of an existing business

5.1 Assets or profits

There are two basic ways of valuing an existing business, which follow the nature of the assets to be valued:

1. *Market or other valuation of the assets to be acquired.* Tangible assets tend to be valued this way. Property, fixtures and fittings, equipment, stocks and debtors, can all be physically, and separately, identified and valued.

2. *Multiple of annual profits.* Rather than evaluating individual assets, a buyer can consider the earning power of the business now and in the future. This is the usual way of assessing the value of intangible assets. If intangibles cannot be physically measured or counted, their effectiveness in the marketplace can and the usual yardstick for this is profit.

The basis chosen for valuation will depend on the mix of assets of the business, as shown in Table 7.1.

Table 7.1 The basis of valuation for a small business

Asset mix	Tangible assets only	Mix of tangible and intangible assets	Intangible assets only
Valuation basis	Market value of assets	Assets at valuation plus goodwill valued as multiple of profits	Multiple of profits
Examples	Agricultural smallholding	Small manufacturing firm	Training consultancy
	Freehold retail premises	Leasehold restaurant	Estate agency

❏ Some small businesses are *asset-rich*, and profitability becomes of secondary importance in a valuation.

For example, an agricultural business such as a small farm or smallholding is valued primarily on the going rate of an acre of land in the neighbourhood. Two farms of the same size would be of similar value, despite the fact that one may be farmed more efficiently, and therefore making more profits (or less losses), than the other. In the same way, freehold retail shops are priced according to the market value of other similar properties in the area. If the business trading from the shop is not profitable, this has little impact on the price, which will be determined more by the potential trade of the locality for any kind of retail operation.

❏ At the other end of the spectrum are businesses with no real *tangible assets* at all.

A consultancy operating from home can only be measured by its profitability, as its assets will be overwhelmingly intangible. Other small firms valued on this basis include many operating in service industries where they act as inter-mediaries between buyers and sellers, for example estate agents, import agen-cies and insurance brokers.

❏ In practice, the majority of businesses for sale are valued on the basis of a mix of tangible and intangible assets.

Even service industries accumulate fixed assets if they survive in business for long enough – fixtures, fittings and equipment for the office and cars for sales people, for example. Many businesses depend on tangible assets for their processes, and build intangible assets through the goodwill of a customer base. Most small manufacturing firms would come into this category. Other service-oriented enterprises also have valuable fixed assets in equipment and fittings, as well as intangible goodwill. For example, a restaurant will need considerable investment in its kitchen and decor, whilst its profitability will determine its full value as an ongoing business.

5.2 Multiple of profits

If intangible assets are to be judged by profitability, how much profit should be taken into account? This is normally expressed as a multiple of annual profits; for example a business making £30,000 per annum might be judged to have goodwill valued at £90,000, or three times annual profits. The size of the multiplier is a key negotiating point, which will consider the following factors:

☐ *Quality of earnings*. Where a small firm has a history of several profitable years in business (usually a minimum of three years) and can demonstrate clearly that it has a sound, continuing level of profitability, through a well spread customer base, then it can be said to have good quality earnings. It will be worth a higher multiple of profits than, say, a business which has just made an annual profit of a similar amount, which was for the first time and was dependent on only one large order. This is really a measure of risk in the likelihood of profits continuing at the current level in the future. When the risk that profits will fall is low, a potential buyer will be more easily persuaded to pay for more years of those profits.

☐ *Interest rates*. Bank interest rates will indicate the maximum multiplier that can be paid for a business, and still be worthwhile. For example, if interest rates are 10 per cent and a small firm is for sale at £100,000, representing a multiple of 10 on annual profits of £10,000 then interest payable on a loan to buy the business will cancel out the annual profits. Even a cash buyer who has no need to borrow in order to make the purchase will do as well with less risk by putting their money on deposit at a bank.

If a limited company uses its own shares to buy another business (i.e. the vendor receives shares in the purchasing company rather than cash), then higher multiples are possible because money interest rates are less relevant.

But with interest rates in the 5 to 10 per cent range, multiples of between 2 to 5 times profits are common in small firm transactions.

☐ *Rate of inflation*. Higher rates of inflation can operate in the same way as higher interest rates; the return or profits from an investment have to keep pace with inflation just to maintain its value. If £100,000 is paid for a business in times when inflation is running very high, at say 20 per cent, then profits will have to be £20,000 p.a. just to maintain the value of the original investment. This fixes a maximum profit multiplier of 5 times earnings if the money invested is not to lose its value.

5.3 Gearing

A buyer of a small business commonly uses a mix of borrowed and personal funds. The relationship between the buyer's own money and borrowed funds, or gearing, is an important influence on the risks and rewards of a purchase and therefore the price worth paying.

Higher gearing enables a buyer to purchase more for each pound of his own money invested. If the business is successful, this increases the reward. But it also increases the risk; if the profits of the business fall, the effect on the buyer's personal stake is magnified.

For example, Table 7.2 outlines two possible case studies for a buyer with £50,000 of his own money to invest.

Table 7.2 The effects of gearing on a small business purchase

	Purchase A	Purchase B
Purchase price (4 × profits)	100	200
Profit (before interest, depreciation and tax)	25	50
Personal capital	50	50
Borrowings	50	150
Interest @ 12 per cent	6	18
Profit after interest	19	32
1st scenario: profits rise by 25 per cent		
Profits	31	62
Profits after interest	25	44
Value of business (4 × profits)	124	248
Personal equity after borrowings repaid	74	98
2nd scenario: profits fall by 25 per cent		
Profits	19	38
Profits after interest	13	20
Value of business (4 × profits)	76	152
Personal equity after borrowings repaid	26	2
3rd scenario: profits fall by 50 per cent		
Profits	13	25
Profits after interest	7	7
Value of business (4 × profits)	52	100
Personal equity after borrowings	2	(50)

❏ *In Purchase A*, the buyer raises a further £50,000 to buy a business for £100,000 representing 4 × profits. After interest, the buyer is left with profits of £19,000, a rate of return on his own money invested of 38 per cent.

❏ *In Purchase B*, the buyer invests the same £50,000 from personal funds, but this time becomes more highly geared by raising a further £150,000 to buy a business for £200,000, again at a multiple of 4 times annual profits of £50,000. This time the buyer is left with £32,000 profit after interest, a rate of return of 64 per cent on the same personal investment of £50,000.

❏ *If the business goes well*, then the deal gets even better under Purchase B. The first scenario of profits rising by 25 per cent increases the return on investment, and the £50,000 invested is now worth £98,000, compared to £74,000 under Purchase A (assuming the business is still valued at 4 × profits).

❑ *If business goes badly*, the deal is worse under Purchase B, and can become disastrous sooner than under Purchase A. A profit fall of 25 per cent will still give Purchase B higher profits at £20,000 compared to £13,000 under Purchase A, but a valuation of the business on the same basis of 4 × profits shows that the original investment of £50,000 has virtually all been lost under Purchase B, and only half lost under Purchase A.

Under Purchase B a profit fall of 50 per cent will not only lose the buyer his original stake, but also put him into debt by £50,000 if the business was sold. Under Purchase A, the buyer loses his personal investment but no more.

Although higher gearing improves the rewards of success, it also increases the risks in failure. A cautious buyer will want to be very convinced about the quality of earnings before accepting a high gearing in order to make a purchase.

In the mid to late 1980s, the easier availability of loans to buy businesses helped increase the risks involved, not only by tempting purchasers to accept higher gearing, but also by increasing the price of buying a business at a time of relatively low interest rates and a booming economy.

Management buy-outs were particularly affected. By the late 1980s, the success of earlier buy-outs made the route more popular and more expensive for buyers. Higher prices meant higher gearing; gearing for large MBOs went from 1:2 (borrowings to equity) in 1981 to 5:1 by 1989.[3]

The recession in the early 1990s particularly hit those small businesses which were purchased with high gearing, through high interest rates and lower profits. Failures have made banks more cautious and gearing ratios are back to levels more common in the early 1980s.

Activity 6 Tax implications

In what ways can tax affect:

a)   the purchaser of a small business, and

b)   the seller?

6 Taxation aspects of a small business purchase

Taxation aspects are important in buying an existing business, not only in the immediate impact they may have on the total costs of purchase, but also the ongoing level of profitability thereafter.

Once a purchase price has been agreed, the next negotiating point is often the allocation of the price to the individual assets purchased. The interests of a buyer and a seller in terms of tax minimisation seldom coincide.

❐ **The buyer**

When assets are purchased, some qualify for writing down allowances which are deducted from taxable profits. The amount of these allowances varies according to the asset purchased:

○ *Plant, machinery and vehicles*: these normally qualify for capital allowances.

○ *Property*: tax relief on buildings and land is the exception rather than the rule.

○ *Stock·* stock used in the course of trading represents a cost against sales, but it is possible to make a paper profit on the value of stocks held through inflation or because of a low valuation of stocks bought with the business.

○ *Debtors*: if debtors are acquired in a purchase which subsequently are not paid, then these bad debts can be written off against profits, and any VAT paid can be reclaimed.

○ *Patents and know-how*: from 1 April 1986, new provisions were introduced in the UK to allow payments for know-how or patent rights to be written down.

These allowances apply for sole traders, partnerships and limited companies. Therefore, careful consideration is required in allocating a purchase price to the various assets acquired, as future tax liabilities will be affected. A prudent buyer will seek the advice of an accountant in this complicated area.

❐ **The seller**

The seller will also wish to carefully consider the taxation implications of a sale. Capital Gains Tax (CGT) may be a major concern. Capital gains for both individuals and companies are now taxed as income in the year in which they are made. There is an individual exemption (£7,500 in 2001/02) in any one tax year, and gains are reduced to reflect changes in the retail price index.

Roll-over relief can also apply. If business assets are sold, and others purchased within 3 years, payment of tax is deferred until the new assets are finally sold.

The 1998 Spring Budget provided for the phasing out of retirement relief, and the introduction of 'tapering' to capital gains on assets which have been held for a number of years. Business assets qualify for greater deductions of capital gains tax than personal assets. Business asset taper relief potentially reduces the CGT rate from 40 per cent to 10 per cent .

❐ **Tax losses**

If a limited company has made trading losses, which have not all been cancelled out by subsequent profits, then those losses remain with the company, and are available for use by a new owner of the shares. Tax losses can thus represent an asset which make it more advantageous to purchase the shares of a limited company rather than just its assets. However if the nature of the trade carried on by the company is significantly altered, the relief against future tax given by past losses may be denied. It is not possible to purchase a company solely for its tax losses, and carry on business in a totally new direction.

Activity 7 For and against buying a small business

Compared to a start up or franchise, what are:

a)   the advantages of buying an existing business, and

b)   the disadvantages?

7 For and against buying an existing business

How does buying an existing business, or part of it, either as an outsider, or an existing manager, compare to other routes to market entry as a small enterprise? See Table 7.3 for a summary.

Table 7.3   *A summary of the possible advantages and disadvantages of buying an existing business*

Possible advantages	Possible disadvantages
• overcomes barriers to market entry	• possibility of liabilities as well as assets
• buying immediate turnover and income	• uncertainty over records
• buying market share	• risk in intangible assets
• existing assets of property, equipment and staff in place	• historical problems in the business
• goodwill with existing customers already built up	• not all my own work
• existing track record	
• insider knowledge (especially in MBOs)	

❐   **Possible advantages**

   ❍   *Overcomes barriers to market entry.* Where there are significant barriers to market entry for a small business entrant, buying an existing enterprise may be the most realistic alternative. For example, the planning permission, and other legal permits required for restaurants, hotels, nightclubs, wine bars and public houses make market entry through acquisition the most common route.

   ❍   *Buying immediate turnover and income.* This could be important, especially when the buyer has no other sources of income.

   ❍   *Buying market share.* One of the key ingredients for a successful small business is to build a high share of a specific market. If existing businesses control a significant percentage of the desired market then it may be advantageous to buy into them, rather than compete.

○ *Existing assets of property, equipment and staff*. The costs and time required to put these into place as a start up can be considerable, and it may be more appropriate to focus resources and energy on the marketplace through an existing operation.

○ *Goodwill with existing customers*. An existing customer base is evidence of the viability of a business concept, and therefore takes some of the risk out of small business ownership. It can also provide a good platform for future growth.

○ *Existing track record*. The ability to look over the past performance of a company provides comfort not only to a potential buyer, but also to financial supporters such as banks. A business showing evidence of a good track record over a number of years is easier to fund than one with no history at all.

○ *Insider knowledge*. This advantage only usually applies to situations where the existing management is involved in the purchase. But it may also be in the best interest of existing management to be as open as possible with prospective new owners, rather than suffer the consequences of concealment at a later date.

❒ **Possible disadvantages**

○ *Buying possible liabilities with assets*. Even if only assets are purchased, liabilities can still be attached to them, for example employee liabilities. If shares in a company are bought, then liabilities will certainly exist. Liabilities can form part of an acceptable risk when they are known; the greatest problem is the possibility of liabilities, unrecognised at the time of purchase, emerging at a later date.

○ *Uncertainty over records*. A business for sale will obviously be presented in the best possible light. Sole traders and partnerships are not required to have their accounts audited, so some information may be withheld. The onus is on the buyer to ask the right questions, not on the seller to provide all the information.

○ *Risk in intangible assets*. The goodwill inherent in an existing business can disappear very rapidly if a new owner makes inappropriate changes. A previous owner-manager may represent a substantial part of the goodwill, which goes with them when they leave.

○ *Historical problems in the business*. An existing business may have some negative goodwill which is not immediately apparent. There may be a history of poor relationships with suppliers or staff, for example, which outlives the departure of the owner.

○ *Not all my own work*. Some of the satisfaction an entrepreneur gains from a new business start up derives from taking a business idea from conception to successful implementation. Buying an existing business can diminish the sense of achievement, and therefore the motivation to make it succeed.

☐ **Motives for sale**

The key question to ask in buying an existing business is: why is it for sale? A buyer needs to establish acceptable reasons why a business should be sold. If they can not, there may be hidden negative factors which may apply equally negatively to the buyer.

8 Case studies and activities

Case studies *Buying a framer*

Case 1 Bryony Hannam considers buying an existing business

Whilst investigating her idea of a picture-framing business, Bryony Hannam discovered that a framer and picture gallery was for sale, located not far from her home town. She decided to investigate further, and asked the business transfer agent handling the sale to send her the particulars. These are summarised on the following two pages.

Bryony's reaction

Bryony was excited after she had done some initial calculations: 'It's just what I'm looking for', she told her husband. 'And I won't have to go through all the trauma of starting up from nothing. The business is obviously successful judging by the sales figures. I know one of the shops, it's very similar to the idea I was working on, it's just not in this town, that's all. But of course, I could always open up another outlet here as I had planned to do, except that I will have a ready-made workshop and existing sales to keep me going from day one.'

'What about the price?' her husband asked. 'Your mother only left you £75,000. Where will you get the rest from?'

'I'm going to talk to my accountant about the price, but the bank manager has already said I can borrow the rest, with the house as guarantee of course. If the stock is £50,000, I will have to borrow £125,000 which will cost less than £15,000 per year. The profits more than cover that', replied Bryony.

'What about your salary? You will need something for your efforts, not to mention return on the money you're putting in', her husband persisted.

'If it makes the forecast profits next year, the business will still have profits of £40,000 after interest, which sounds a good enough return to me', argued Bryony.

The accountant's caution

The next day Bryony saw her accountant, who had been studying the particulars and the finances in more detail.

'I'm concerned about this forecast', he said. 'If the business makes the projected figures for next year it may be worth what they're asking. But part of that result will be down to you; if you buy it, you will be running it by then. Why should you pay for future profits? It's what the business earns now that they're selling, not what you can do with it tomorrow. If it is so sure to improve next year, why are they selling it now?'

Southgate and Co.

Business agents and valuers

On the instructions of the shareholders,

FOR SALE: ART ENTERPRISES LTD trading as GRAYS FRAMING STUDIOS

Important These particulars are confidential: staff are unaware of the impending sale.

General Established by our client some five years ago, we are now pleased to offer for sale 3 picture shops well situated in market towns, and a framing workshop, giving combined sales of £300,000 gross per annum.

Price We are instructed to seek offers in the region of: £150,000 (one hundred and fifty thousand pounds) for the entire issued shares of the company. Stock to be transferred at an additional valuation (approx. £50,000).

The retail premises There are 3 shops, all in good positions next to busy high streets in sizeable market towns.
The premises are leasehold, with terms left to run of 12, 17 and 22 years. Rent review patterns are 5 yearly, with reviews due in 2 years' time.
Each shop is staffed by a manager and an assistant.
Each shop is furnished and fitted to a high standard, with picture and frame moulding displays, carpeting and other furnishings, a desk and an electronic cash register. Sales areas in the 3 shops vary at 700, 900 and 1200 sq. ft.

The workshop The workshop of 2000 sq. ft. is situated in a small industrial estate. The lease has 16 years to run, with a rent review due next year.
The premises are comprehensively equipped with all the machinery and tools needed for the provision of a successful and efficient framing service.

Equipment includes:

- Mitre saws and guillotines
- Glass cutting table
- Mountboard cutter and trimmer
- Assorted small tools
- Pneumatic under pinner
- Dry mounting press
- Worktables, racks and shelving
- Large capacity air compressor

Staff: the workshop employs 1 manager and 2 framers.

The business The business was established by our client 5 years ago. Since that date, the business has expanded from a single unit to the current three unit operation.

The principle activities are those of:

1. *Bespoke framing*
2. *Framed and unframed pictures.*

1. Bespoke framing. The company offers a high quality framing service for customers which accounts for approximately 60 per cent of turnover. Production, according to the customer's specification, is carried out centrally and delivered back to the retail premises within a 7 day period.

Particular strengths of this service are:

- wide choice of frames and mounts
- quality of production
- level of service provided by retail staff.

2. Pictures. The company retails a range of pictures from reproduction prints and posters, limited editions, to original oils and watercolours. The majority of stock retails for between £10–£150. Particular strengths are:

- wide range of images available
- affordable prices.

Financial information Past trading results:

£000s	Current year	Prior year	Next year forecast
Sales (net of VAT)	260	180	325
Cost of materials	85	60	105
Gross profit	175	120	220
Overheads:			
Salaries & wages	90	75	100
Rent and rates	45	28	50
Other	10	7	15
Total overheads	145	110	165
Net profit	30	10	55

Net profit is before depreciation, interest and directors' salaries and fees.

The purchase price The business is for sale at £150,000 comprising:

Value of leases remaining:	£35,000
Value of equipment and machinery:	£15,000
Value of fixtures and fittings:	£10,000
Goodwill:	£90,000
Total	**£150,000**

In addition stock will be charged at valuation estimated at £50,000.

Liabilities, including creditors, borrowings and hire purchase agreements will be discharged prior to completion of the sale.

Future developments The sales forecast for next year includes a full year's trading by the third shop which opened part way through the current year. Overheads are based on actual costs plus inflation so that the forecast result is considered most realistic by our clients.

'The agents told me on the phone that the shareholders were a husband and wife team who are getting divorced and want to sell the business as a result', Bryony replied.

'Well that may, or may not, be a genuine reason for sale. You will need to find out more. Can you talk to the managers?'

'No, no-one in the organisation knows it's for sale', said Bryony.

'What about the assets, and this stock you will be buying? Do you know anything about them? How new is the equipment? Is it what you want? Is the stock right for the business when you will be running it? If not it might be better to start from scratch, and even compete with them, as it sounds from what you've said that they've lost interest in the business', suggested the accountant.

'Yes, I know I will have to check these things. The agents say I can have a tour tomorrow. I'll be introduced as a customer', said Bryony.

'The other worry I have is buying the shares. It would be better to buy only the assets, and not the company itself', continued the accountant. 'Unless there are tax losses we can use, that is.'

'I thought the particulars state that they will pay off any liabilities outside the sale', said Bryony.

'They do', replied the accountant, 'but that only applies to liabilities we know about. When you buy the shares of a company, you may be buying liabilities we don't know about – disputes with suppliers, employees, past tax claims, VAT problems – there are a lot of possibilities.'

Activities

i)   Bryony has thought of some of the advantages of buying an existing business. What others might there be for her in this proposition?

ii) What will be the problems? The accountant has mentioned several, but list some other potential pitfalls.

iii) How can Bryony find out more information as suggested by the accountant? What else does she need to find out about and how can she go about getting the information? What other advice does she need?

iv) Do you consider the asking price for the business to be a fair one? Make an alternative valuation, and suggestions for justifying this to the owners.

Extended activity *Garage for sale*

Try to obtain particulars of businesses for sale by contacting business transfer agents in your area, or by looking at advertisements in the small business pages of publications such as the *Financial Times, Sunday Times, Dalton's Weekly* or *Exchange and Mart*.

Then, assume that you work for a business transfer agent as a negotiator responsible for finding buyers for small businesses for sale. The owners of a local garage have instructed you to sell their business. It is profitable, with a good base of customers for repairs and maintenance. It also has the agency for a Japanese car manufacturer, specialising in four-wheel-drive vehicles. You have interviewed the owners, and gathered the information you require about the business.

Your task now is to write up the particulars of the business, using some of those you have obtained as a model. It will outline the nature of the business, and give basic financial information to justify the purchase price that you have put on the business.

Case 2 Bryony looks at a BIMBO

Bryony Hannam pursued her investigations into Grays Framing Studios with such tenacity that she discovered some very interesting facts. Talking to one of the suppliers helped her to find out the reason why the business had been put on the market.

'It's immoral', she complained to her husband, 'all this work I've done, only to find that the workshop manager is going to buy out the couple owning the business. It seems that they have put the business on the market just to find out what sort of price it might fetch. They intended all along to sell it to the workshop manager, not an outside buyer.'

'Did the agent know?' asked the husband.

'Evidently not, I got this from a supplier who is out of favour with the manager, but who knows what he's up to', answered Bryony.

'Well you've found out quite a lot about their business, that can't be wasted effort. But there's not much else you can do now is there?' Her husband tried to console her, knowing she had grown keen on the idea.

'Well there is something. Maybe I should talk to the manager. I don't suppose he's got all the money necessary himself; it could work to my advantage if he needed a partner. After all he's got all the inside information on the business. It would be a safer bet to buy it with him', said Bryony thoughtfully.

A week later Bryony was with her accountant again.

'That's right', she explained, 'he's only raising £20,000 from his own pocket. He's been offered the rest of the money from a finance company who would buy loan stock, with the balance as an overdraft from the bank.'

'This workshop manager seems to be quite smart', mused the accountant. 'By offering loan stock, he plans to retain a majority of the ordinary shares for himself no doubt. How much does he plan to offer did you say?'

'£100,000 plus the value of the stock', answered Bryony. 'He's putting up £20,000 for shares and the finance company will buy £20,000 worth of shares, but also put in £60,000 of loan stock, which has no voting rights, but qualifies for profits at a preferential rate. He plans to raise the £50,000 or so for the stock as an overdraft. He says it's not all necessary and can be soon reduced, especially with credit from the suppliers. So he's effectively planning on buying half the company for £20,000', Bryony summed up.

'You've certainly found out a lot. Why did he tell you all this?' asked the accountant.

'I was introduced to him by this supplier as you know, and it was soon obvious he still has two problems. First he doesn't have any experience in running anything other than the workshop, and the shop managers aren't interested. Second the finance company are making lots of demands with seats on the Board and monthly reports. He's beginning to think it will be rather like being part of a larger company, even though he will own half of it', said Bryony.

'So what is his solution?' asked the accountant.

'I suggested he might be better off with a working partner who will put up money in a similar way to the finance company, but help him run the business and expand it – open new outlets, look after the marketing. In other words me! And he's accepted in principle', Bryony beamed her pleasure.

'Ah, you're talking of a BIMBO', said the accountant, quickly adding before he was misunderstood, 'a buy-in management buy-out. They're becoming more common, and do seem to have some advantages.'

Activities

i)   What do you consider to be the advantage of this approach? What are the potential problems?

ii) What finance package made it possible for the workshop manager to realise 50 per cent of the equity, for less than 15 per cent of the total consideration?

iii) What deal, if any, do you think Bryony should strike with him?

In conclusion

Once you have finished this Unit, it is recommended that you turn to Section B, Planning a new venture, and complete Step 2.2 'Buying an existing business'.

9 References and further reading

References and further information

1.   For more information on bankruptcy and liquidation the government Insolvency Service has a number of publications, including *A Guide to Bankruptcy* (tel. 01530 272515).

2.   As reported in the *Daily Telegraph*, 14 September 1991, p. 24. The article 'Private woes in the public house' summarised the business difficulties of those involved in running their own pub.

3.   Birley, S. and Muzyka, F. *Mastering Entrepreneurship*, FT/Prentice Hall, 2000, Chapter 8 'Buying a company'. This chapter has detailed information on buy-outs based on the work of the Centre for Management Buy-out Research (CMBOR) at the University of Nottingham.

4. These, and other interesting cases, are reported in 'The Management Buy-Out Report' in *Management Week*, Management Week Publishing Ltd, 30 October 1991.

5. A useful review of patent and trademark law is in Williams, S. *Small Business Guide*, Penguin, 2001, Chapter 12 'Beating the pirates'. See also Unit 12, section 3.2 of this book.

Recommended further reading

❑   Birley, S. and Muzyka, F. *Mastering Entrepreneurship*, FT/Prentice Hall, 2000. Chapter 8 'Buying a company'.

❑   Sperry, P. and Mitchell, B. *Selling your Business*, Kogan Page, 1999.

❑   The Which? *Guide to Starting Your Own Business*, Consumer Association, 1998. Chapter 11, 'Protecting ideas and innovation'.

❑   Williams, S. *Small Business Guide*, Penguin, 2001. Chapter 9, 'Off the peg'.

❑   Clayton, P. *Law for the Small Business*, Kogan Page, 1991. Chapter 5, 'Premises', Chapter 11, 'Intellectual property: patents, copyrights and trademarks', Chapter 14, 'Bankruptcy and liquidation'.

8 Legal identities

This Unit contains information about the basic legal identities a small business can take: limited company; sole trader; partnership; and co-operative. The advantages and disadvantages of each form are identified.

Contents

Activity 1 Choice of form

What are the different legal forms a small business can take?

1 Choice of business organisation

A small business can take on four basic legal forms. The choice depends on the circumstances and objectives of the small enterprise. The first choice is between going it alone or working in co-ownership with others. Figure 8.1 summarises the basic alternatives. A limited company can be owned by one or several persons. If this is not the desired form, then single ownership has to be achieved as a sole trader and multiple ownership as a partnership or co-operative.

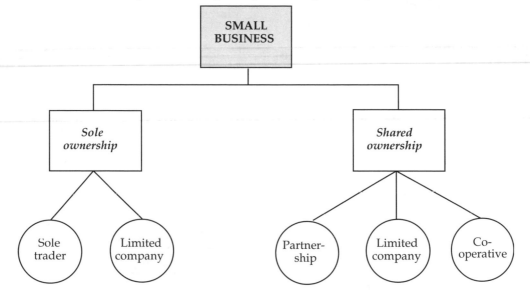

Figure 8.1 Forms of small business according to ownership

Activity 2 Company differences

A limited company is significantly different to a sole trader or partnership in several significant respects

a)   What are these?

b)   What advantages and disadvantages do these differences give to the small business owner?

2 Limited company

A limited company, incorporated under the Companies Act, is a legal body, which has a separate identity to that of its owners. It can be bought and sold as a whole, or in part, go bankrupt without its owners suffering the same fate, have legal documents signed on its behalf by a director, and employ staff. Putting business activities into a company literally gives them life as a separate legal entity. This is a key difference to a sole trader or partnership, where the owner(s) are inextricably linked to the business and not separable from it.

2.1 Responsibilities

A company needs shareholders (the owners) and directors (those empowered to act on the company's behalf by the shareholders). In small companies, shareholders and directors are often the same people, but not necessarily so. Some investors in a business do not become directors; indeed investments made under the now defunct Business Expansion Scheme specifically prohibited management involvement in the enterprise (see Unit 5 'Information and help' for more details of the BES).

❒ **Shareholders' responsibilities**

The shareholders' responsibility for the company's debt is limited to the paid-up value of their shares. Once they are paid for, the company cannot call on shareholders for more funds (unless by way of a voluntary subscription for more shares), even if it is insolvent.

❒ **Directors' responsibilities**

The responsibilities of a director extend beyond that of a shareholder. Although directors can separate their own personal assets from those of the business, this is dependent on responsible business behaviour. Where directors have been deemed to have behaved irresponsibly, they can be held personally responsible for the company's debts. In other words, there are limits to the limited liability of directors.

Directors' duties and responsibilities include:

○ *To act honestly, and in the company's best interests*: for example a vested interest in a transaction involving the company must be disclosed to other shareholders.

○ *Not to allow the company to incur debts when there is no reasonable chance of paying the debts.* Directors who knowingly allow a company to continue to trade whilst insolvent can be held personally responsible, without limit, for those debts.

○ *To have regard for the interests of employees as well as shareholders.* There are EU-inspired provisions in the Companies Act to ensure directors generally take note of employees' interests. There are also specific responsibilities under employment, industrial health, safety and training regulations; violation of these can result in proceedings against the company, and its directors in person.

○ *To comply with the requirements of the Companies Act.* This, for instance, requires proper accounts and records to be kept and officially filed on a regular basis.

As well as the possibility of fines and criminal proceedings because of improper behaviour or failure to execute duties and obligations, directors can be declared unfit and banned from directorships for up to 15 years.

2.2 The Memorandum and Articles of Association

Although commonly referred to as one, these are in fact two key legal documents, which set out the constitution and management arrangements of the company.

❑ **Memorandum of Association**

This is the company's charter which includes:

○ *The name of the company.* The name of a limited company has to be approved by the Registrar of Companies. It cannot be offensive, nor likely to be confused with an existing company. To limit its liabilities, limited must be the last word of the name of a company trading for profit.

○ *Location of the registered office.* The location of the registered office effectively establishes under which laws a company trades, and where it pays its taxes. It is the address to which official and legal notices will be sent. It need not be the company's principle place of business and for small firms it is frequently the address of the company's solicitors or accountants.

○ *The objects of the company.* The objectives for which a company has been formed, its powers and area of business, are defined in the objects clause of the Memorandum. These are normally kept very general (as in general commercial activities) to avoid activities and transactions being declared *ultra vires* (outside of the powers of the company), which may then make them the personal liability of the directors or management. Recent legislation has abolished the *ultra vires* rules for external transactions, so that third parties can now insist a company meet the obligations to which a director or senior manager have committed the company, even if they fall strictly outside of the company's objects. *Ultra vires* still holds for internal transactions, however, between directors and shareholders, for example.

○ *The limited liability of the shareholders.* This clause in the Memorandum limits the liability of shareholders to the value of their shares.

○ *The share capital and structure.* The amount of authorised capital, and how it is divided into shares, is specified. Shares are normally made up of relatively small denominations, e.g. £1, to retain flexibility in transfer and issuing of new shares.

The amount of capital subscribed for by shareholders, that is shares issued and paid for, is the issued share capital of a company.

Sometimes not all the authorised capital is subscribed for, some shares being authorised but not issued. Shareholders are still however liable for this amount but no more, in the event of liquidation.

○ *The names of signatories.* At incorporation, there must be two signatories who agree to take out at least one share each. When formed, a company has to have two shareholders, at least one of whom is a director; a company secretary (who may or may not be a shareholder) is also appointed. Share holdings can later change so that one person can own all the shares.

- **Articles of Association**

  The Articles contain detailed information about the internal management of the company. They deal with the appointment of directors, their powers and fees, and procedures for meetings. They deal with the relationships between the company and shareholders and between individual shareholders. For example, the Articles usually provide for the issue of new shares to be offered first to existing shareholders, in proportion to their existing holding, so that they can protect their percentage stake in the company.

  Likewise it is common in small companies for shareholders to give first refusal rights to the other shareholders should they wish to sell any equity.

- **Formation of a limited company**

  Forming a new limited company can take some time. Suitable Memorandum and Articles of Association and other documents must be lodged with the Registrar of Companies, and a Certificate of Incorporation obtained[1].

  It is possible to buy a ready-made company off-the-shelf. This is usually a shell company which has not traded, but is incorporated and, with a suitable name change, can be used by a new small firm.

2.3 Tax, National Insurance and pensions

As a company is a separate legal body, owner-directors are employed by it, and are therefore employees for tax, national insurance and pension purposes. As a corporate body, the company is the employer and taxable on its profits.

This means that:

- PAYE is operated even for owner-director salaries. As tax is deducted at source, this has cash-flow disadvantages over the self-employed status of a sole trader or partner who pays tax annually on a retrospective basis. Income tax is paid at normal rates.

- *National insurance contributions* are paid by directors as employees, and by the company as the employer, which makes them more expensive than for self-employed owners, but entitles the director-employee to the full range of benefits.

- *Corporation tax* is paid by the company on profits it makes, after deducting all expenses including directors' salaries. For small businesses this will usually be at a lower rate (10 to 20 per cent tax bands on profits up to £300,000 in 2001/2) which can be an advantage over self-employed owners making good profits, which will be taxed as income at the higher rates.

  Losses can be carried forward in a company to be offset against future profits or capital gains. This can represent an asset if the company is sold.

- *Pensions* can be contributed to by both employee-directors and the company. There is no limit to the contributions which a company can make free of tax to a pension scheme on behalf of employees. Director-employees can also contribute up to 15 per cent of their salary to a pension fund, with relief at their highest rate of income tax. Self-employed sole traders and partners will be more restricted, as they have no company to make contributions on their behalf.

❒ *Capital gains* made by a company form part of its profits, and are therefore liable to corporation tax with no relief, unlike a self-employed owner who can use personal relief to offset the tax due.

The principal advantages and disadvantages for a small business to trade as a limited company are shown in Figure 8.2.

A limited company has an existence separate from its owners. As a corporate body, it has independent legal and tax status.

Advantages

- Limited liability for shareholders
- Some formalised structures (e.g. directors' meetings) make management clearer
- Income tax paid only on salaries drawn; higher rates of personal tax can be avoided when profits are retained
- No limit to contributions made to a pension scheme with tax relief
- Finance easier to raise externally especially from equity
- Easier to widen ownership base
- Existence not threatened by death or personal bankruptcy of one of owners
- Possibly higher perceived status

Disadvantages

- More time consuming and expensive to set up
- Complicated and time consuming to conform to requirements of Companies Act
- Loss of confidentiality as some records are publicly filed
- Audit and accounting costs higher
- Double tax when company pays corporation tax on profits and capital gains, and shareholders are personally taxed on dividends
- Higher national insurance contributions
- As employees, directors have worse cash flow of taxes under PAYE than self-employed
- Limited liability reduced in early days as creditors seek personal guarantees from directors
- Directors can be held personally liable if company trades while insolvent

---

Figure 8.2 Limited company – summary of advantages and disadvantages

Activity 3 Going it alone

What are the advantages and disadvantages to the small business owner of becoming a sole trader?

3 Sole trader

3.1 Legal status

A sole trader is unlike a limited company in that the owner is the business; there is no legal separation between the assets and liabilities of the business and the assets and liabilities of the individual who owns it.

This makes for simpler and more informal arrangements for operating a business. It can also increase the risk for an owner, whose total possessions are now on the line with his or her business at all times.

The sole trader can simply choose a business name, and start trading. If they use a name different from their own, they will have to put their own name on their headed paper, however. The only obligation is to inform the relevant authorities for taxation and employment status purposes (e.g. Inland Revenue, and Customs and Excise)[1].

A sole trader can invest in or draw funds from the business as they think fit. However, additional resources can only be raised by loans; it is not possible to invite outside equity participation.

3.2 Tax, National Insurance and pensions

As the business will not have any separate status from the owner, the sole trader will be self-employed, and not an employee. This has implications for tax and pension provisions.

Tax is payable on any profits of the business, which are treated as if it were the income of the owner, whether they receive it or not. A sole trader cannot choose to reinvest profits for income tax purposes. If profits are made, the sole trader is taxed as if they were taken as income, whether they were drawn or not.

As profits increase so tax can be payable at higher rates (40 per cent for 2001/2). Being self-employed the sole trader will not pay tax as income is earned, but on a retrospective basis. On the preceding year basis, tax was payable up to 20 months after profits were made. From 1996–7, taxation for the self-employed changed to a current year basis.

Losses can be offset not only against future profits of the same business, but also against other income of the owner, as they are inseparable from the business. If the owner previously paid taxes under PAYE, then trading losses in the early years can be used to claw back some of these taxes paid before self-employment.

National Insurance contributions for self-employed people are payable as:

i) a weekly flat rate (Class 2 contributions);

ii) a percentage of profits (Class 4 contributions). Although this usually amounts to less than the total amount payable by company director-employees the benefits are also less: there is no unemployment benefit, widows benefit, invalidity pension, or the earnings-related portion of the retirement pension.

Pension payments are also more restricted as a self-employed person. Tax relief for personal pension payments is allowable on 17.5 per cent of net relevant earnings (which for most purposes equates to taxable profits), or higher levels for those over 35 years old rising to 40 per cent for those over 61. This compares to the unlimited, tax deductible payments which a company can make on behalf of its directors.

Capital gains can however be more favourably treated, as the sole trader's personal allowance for tax-free capital gains (£7,500 in 2001/2) is available in the event that the business makes a capital profit. A company does not have such allowances.

3.3 Setting up and record keeping

Setting up is very straightforward, requiring only notifications to the local tax and DSS (Department of Social Security) office of self-employment status. VAT registration is a further possible step, either on a voluntary basis, or because the business trades at above the minimum registration level (£54,000 per year from April 2001).

The Inland Revenue and Customs and Excise authorities require certain financial records to be kept for taxation purposes. Apart from that, the accounting requirements of the business can be determined by internal management needs. An independent audit is not a legal requirement. Records are private, and need not be revealed to anyone other than the Inland Revenue.

The individual and the business are the same. There are no legal or tax distinctions.

Advantages

- Straightforward and easy to set up; minimal legal requirements and costs
- Make all the decisions and keep all the profits
- No audit of accounts legally required
- No public disclosures of records (unless registered for VAT)
- Business losses can be offset against other income, including clawback of past PAYE
- Self-employment defers income tax, and reduces national insurance contributions

Disadvantages

- Unlimited liability, including personal assets outside of the business
- No additional funds possible from equity investment by others
- Transfer of ownership less flexible; can only sell the assets of the business
- Possible status problems perceived by third parties
- All profits taxed as personal income whether retained in business or taken out
- Self-employed national insurance entitlements have less benefits
- Tax relief on pension contributions restricted

Figure 8.3 Sole trader – summary of advantages and disadvantages

Activity 4 Joining others

What are the advantages and disadvantages to small business owners of forming a partnership?

4 Partnership

Where two or more people set up in business intending to share the profits, then the law deems that they are in partnership[1].

Regulations under the Partnership Act of 1890 provide a framework which applies unless partners specifically agree to the contrary. Some of these provisions assume that:

❏ all partners have an equal vote in how the business should be run;

❏ all partners have invested equally in the business;

❏ all partners have an equal share of profits and losses;

❏ partners will not receive a salary;

❏ partners will not receive interest on their capital invested.

Clearly these assumptions will not be the intentions of every partnership. But unless there is an agreement by the partners to the contrary, the law will assume this to be the case in the event of a dispute.

Partnerships are restricted to 20 partners, except in certain professions, such as law and accountancy.

A partnership is like a sole trader in that it is not a legal entity. It therefore carries unlimited liability. Unlike the sole trader, partners do however have to look beyond just their own liabilities. Each partner is jointly and severally responsible with other partners for all the obligations and debts of the partnership, even where they exist directly as a result of another partner's actions. If one partner fails to meet their share of the liabilities, creditors can look to the rest of the partnership to make good the deficit.

A new hybrid form of 'limited liability partnerships' (LLPs) came into effect from April 2001. The taxation treatment of individual partners is the same as ordinary partnerships but partners' exposure to the liabilities of the business is limited.

The formalities to establish a partnership follow those of the sole trader; they are simple, and legally only require the names of partners on any letterhead.

If one partner dies, retires, or becomes bankrupt, the partnership is automatically dissolved, whether or not this is in the best interests of the other partners, unless a separate written agreement is made to the contrary.

4.1 The Partnership Agreement

To regulate matters between the partners (and prevent dissolution as described above), a Partnership Agreement is strongly advised. This is not a legal requirement however; partnerships are legally, and in practice, a matter of trust between the partners. A Partnership Agreement can define some broad areas of responsibility and authority such as:

- ❐ details of the partners, and the name and nature of the business they carry on;
- ❐ duration of the partnership, date of commencement and any anticipated termination date;
- ❐ capital contributed by the partners, and any agreement on interest payable to partners for money introduced;
- ❐ calculation and division of profits: this needs to be specified particularly where partners contribute unequally, as the 1890 Act assumes they have equal rights to profits;
- ❐ management and control of the business: this is most needed where partners put in unequal amounts of time in the partnership. Where there is a sleeping partner, management partners may need to guard against future interference, and provide for their own salaries before profits are divided;
- ❐ dissolution: what happens on retirement, death or withdrawal of a partner has to be spelt out in order to prevent automatic dissolution of the partnership.

4.2 Partners' responsibilities

A partner in a business is expected by law to behave fairly and in good faith. In practice, partners will control each other to a greater or lesser extent. As all partners act for the partnership, and therefore incur liabilities on behalf of other partners, the choice of partner is an extremely important decision. It can be a decision which has effects even beyond the life of a partner, as their estate can still be responsible for partnership liabilities, unless the partner has taken public leave of the partnership by notifying their retirement to business contacts and advertising it in the *Business Gazette*.

4.3 Tax, National Insurance and pensions

As there is no corporate body to employ them, partners are self-employed. This confers the same advantages and disadvantages as to the sole trader of delayed income tax payments, reduced national insurance contribution (but with the penalty of reduced entitlements from NIC) and smaller tax-free pension contribution possibilities. Losses in the partnership can also be used to offset taxes due on other, non-partnership income.

The principal advantages and disadvantages of operating as a partnership are shown in Figure 8.4.

Two or more persons undertaking a business activity together are in partnership. There is no separate legal entity, and partners are personally responsible for all liabilities of the partnership.

Advantages
- Easy to set up
- Access to the experience of other partners
- No audit of accounts legally required
- Confidentiality is maintained, as no public access to accounts
- Losses from the business can be offset against other income
- Can be relatively easily transferred to a limited company at a later stage
- Benefits of self-employment for income tax and national insurance purposes

Disadvantages
- Partners are liable for debts, jointly and severally
- Partner's estate can still be liable for their debts after death
- Death, bankruptcy or retirement dissolves partnership, unless specific continuation provisions in agreement
- Less flexibility in transferring ownership than limited company
- High degree of mutual trust required
- Profits taxed as income, whether drawn or not
- Self-employed national insurance entitlements have less benefits
- Tax relief on pension contributions restricted

Figure 8.4 Partnerships – summary of advantages and disadvantages

Activity 5 Some examples

Can you give some examples of the types of small business which become
a)   limited companies?
b)   sole traders?
c)   partnerships?

5 Choosing the appropriate business form: sole trader vs partnership vs limited company

The choice of business identity is usually between these three forms, as co-operatives and other forms are much less common. Their appropriateness depends on the circumstances of the business and the objectives of its owners.

These can be evaluated on a number of categories which are shown in Figure 8.5.

Categories	Company	Sole trader	Partnership
Liabilities	Liability limited, but personal guarantees and directors' obligations can reduce limitations	All assets liable including those not involved in the business	Liability extends to business debts of other partners
Records and accounts	Legal accounting and audit requirements. Accounts filed open to inspection	No strict accounting or audit requirements. Records not available for public inspection	As for sole trader
Selling up	Formalities of registration, although can buy off-the-peg	No formalities except registering as self-employed	As for sole trader, except partnership agreement strongly advised to prevent problems, especially of dissolution
Raising money	Wide choice, including further equity investments	Options limited to overdraft or loan	Overdraft, loans or new partners with money
Selling up	Flexible, as can sell part or all of shares	Can only sell assets; difficult if selling part of the business	As for sole trader
Status	Possibly higher perceived status	Possibly lower perceived status	As for sole trader
Tax, National Insurance and pensions	Employee status PAYE, high National Insurance, but full benefits. Unlimited company contributions on pension. Corporation Tax on company profits. Losses retained in company	Insurance cheaper but fewer benefits. Tax-deductible pension contributions restricted. Losses can be offset against tax on other income	As for sole trader

Figure 8.5 Checklist for choosing the appropriate form

The decision of business form may be dictated by one category only. If the nature of the business is such that uninsurable liabilities are possible on a large scale, then a limited company is the only choice. For this reason, many small firms manufacturing components for other companies wish to maintain limited liability. Lawsuits instigated by end-users over a product deficiency could involve a subcontractor not involved in the final sale. When products are exported, especially to the USA, this can increase the possibility of legal problems, not within the control of the subcontractor.

At the other extreme, where a small business is offering an individual service which carries no real liabilities, or is covered by full indemnity insurance, then the advantages of the lack of formality in sole trader status will probably be the obvious route. Most tradesmen operate as self-employed sole traders or partners for this reason.

The developing business may wish to change status because of an altered environment. Growth can make it desirable to introduce the more formal structures and money raising possibilities of a limited company.

Activity 6   Why co-operative?

A co-operative business is owned and controlled by its employees for their mutual benefit. In what different circumstances are they formed? What are the principle motives of their founders?

6 Co-operatives

Co-operatives are jointly owned by their members. A consumer co-operative is jointly owned by its customers, a community co-operative by the community it serves. The most common form, a worker co-operative is an enterprise owned and controlled by all the people working for it, for their mutual benefit. It is an alternative form of business structure, where the emphasis is on the work environment and not the accumulation of individual wealth. Established in the 18th century, they were almost extinct until a revival began in the 1970s that has continued ever since.

6.1 Legal form

Co-operatives are usually limited companies, co-operative societies or, more rarely, partnerships. Governed by the Industrial and Provident Societies Acts 1965–75, registration as a co-operative requires the following principles to be adopted:

- ❐ The objectives, management and use of assets are controlled by the members.
- ❐ Membership is not restricted; it must be open to anyone who fulfils the qualifications laid down.
- ❐ Each member of the co-operative has an equal vote in how it is to be run.
- ❐ Surpluses, or profits, are shared between the members, pro-rata to their participation.
- ❐ Share capital remains at its original value. Members benefit from their participation, not as investors; co-operatives are not about making capital gains.
- ❐ Interest on loans, or share capital, is limited, even if profits permit higher payments.

A registered co-operative is a separate legal body, which has limited liability for its members, and which must file annual accounts. A minimum of seven members are required to register, but they do not all need to work full time. Registration is not mandatory however, and where co-operatives do not register, they are regarded in law as partnerships with unlimited liability.

6.2 Background

In the 18th and 19th centuries working people formed many self-help groups to cope with poverty and hardship. Co-operatives were part of this movement, and were established either from above, by those seeking to spread a philosophy of co-operation, or at the grass roots by working people themselves in an effort to improve their conditions.

Today the best known co-operative is the supermarket chain, which is a consumer co-operative. Worker co-operatives peaked at around 1,000 in the early 1900s and then declined to a very small number by the 1960s. They have since enjoyed a revival, promoted by the Co-operative Development Agency set up by the government in 1978 to give advice to anyone wishing to form a co-operative. Estimates suggest there were over 1,500 by the late 1980s, with some 300 or so being established annually. The reasons for the growth lies in the motives for establishing the various types of co-operative.

6.3 Types of co-operative

Like other small businesses, co-operatives do not constitute a uniform group. Research into the characteristics and objectives of co-operatives suggests that there are four main types[2]:

☐ *Endowed co-operatives*: some owners transfer their business to their employees, either as a philanthropic gesture or an attempt to keep the firm going, for example, if the owner has no heir. Shares are usually held in trust by the employees. This is a relatively uncommon form, the best known example of which is the chemical manufacturer, Scott-Bader Commonwealth.

☐ *Defensive co-operatives*: if an enterprise is threatened with closure, employees have formed co-operatives in a desperate attempt to keep their company alive and their jobs with it.

   Co-operatives of this type have been small in number, but have often commanded considerable publicity.

   As Industry Minister in the 1970s, Tony Benn encouraged some of the better known examples, such as Triumph Meridian and the Scottish Daily News.

☐ *Job-creation co-operatives*: in times of high unemployment, increasing numbers of co-operatives have been set up to create new jobs. Encouragement and help from local Co-operative Development Agencies, with financial support from government sponsored job schemes, have stimulated this form in recent years.

☐ *Alternative co-operatives*: this is the most common form of modern co-operative, arising from various alternative movements, emphasising social and environmental needs rather than profit. Members of these co-operatives are often from the well-educated, middle-classes, looking for a lifestyle that is different to what they perceive as the conventional rat-race. Businesses are often in craft-related industries, health products, such as wholefood distribution, or publishing and printing.

6.4 Advantages and disadvantages

The recent renaissance of co-operatives has stimulated evaluation of their success or failure[3].

Advantages

There are some obvious advantages in the high level of commitment a member of a co-operative is likely to feel towards their work.

Increased motivation comes from putting an ideology into practice, and from sharing equally in the control and rewards of an enterprise. Those working in co-operatives report a higher than average sense of purpose and satisfaction from their work.

Disadvantages

Co-operatives face the same problems as many other small businesses including the lack of management experience and other appropriate skills, insufficient finance, and difficulties in gaining access to the marketplace. But they also face additional problems:

❒ Many start in difficult economic conditions. Defensive co-operatives emerge from firms already in serious trouble. Job creation co-operatives are stimulated by recession and high unemployment. Many alternative co-operatives operate in markets which are inherently difficult, for example small health-food shops. Only endowed co-operatives have the benefit of a successful background as they are usually formed from a well-established business; it is not surprising therefore that their success rate is highest among co-operative types.

❒ Workplace democracy requires innovative organisational structures which sometimes work, but often do not. Decision making can become confused. Lengthy debates over the running of the co-operative can be an unproductive use of time. Finding people to join a co-operative and keeping the ones that have, is more difficult than conventional recruitment and retention practices, and can put an effective brake on growth.

The emphasis on social and environmental factors, particularly in alternative co-operatives, often leads to inefficient, labour intensive work practices.

Despite these difficulties, the new breed of co-operative does not seem to have a survival rate dramatically worse than small business generally. It is not necessarily a criticism that their financial performance tends to be poorer, but rather a reflection of the lower status accorded to making profits in many co-operatives.

7 Case studies and activities

Case studies *Forming a business*

Case 1 Janet and Mike take the plunge

Janet and Mike Bloomfield had come to a momentous decision. Mike had often talked of giving up his job with a large leisure group and running a small hotel in their favourite seaside town; Janet had been working as a physiotherapist for many years and wanted to set up a practice of her own. Now that the children had all left home, they were preparing to take the plunge. Mike had found the ideal hotel for sale, with under-used space on the ground floor, which would make an ideal area for Janet's physiotherapy practice.

They had found a buyer for their home and their offer on the hotel was accepted, so that their move into small business was becoming a reality.

Raising the money

The hotel was for sale freehold, and they planned to live in it themselves. They had calculated that the proceeds of the sale of their house, plus a mortgage, would pay for the hotel, but not their estimate of the necessary refurbishments Mike planned, nor the investment in fittings and equipment for Janet's practice.

❐ Estimated start up costs were (£000s):

cost of hotel	250
refurbishment	20
physiotherapy practice conversion and equipment	20
working capital	10
Total	*300*

❐ Funds available were (£000s):

net proceeds of sale of house	200
mortgage on hotel	50
other funds required	50
Total	*300*

Mike and Janet had talked to their bank manager about funding the difference. He had asked for a second mortgage on the property plus a business plan he could approve, before he would commit to an overdraft.

Then Janet's father had offered to invest in the business. He had some spare capital which he was happy to put into their venture, provided he received a reasonable income from it.

Discussing the form

Janet had been discussing the alternative legal forms of business organisation with their solicitor and she asked Mike for his views.

'We will need to make a decision soon', she urged, 'as it will affect how we buy the hotel and start to trade. Do you think we should form a company or operate as a sole trader, or in partnership?'

'Well, I assume we cannot be a sole trader as there are two of us', replied Mike.

'Not necessarily', said Janet. 'We could run our businesses totally separately, and therefore each operate as a sole trader.'

'What's the point in that, when we're both under the same roof, sharing in some of the costs?' asked Mike.

'Well', said Janet, 'I think we should know how each business is doing, and therefore keep separate records of sales and costs. If not, one might be keeping the other going without us realising it – I'm not going to subsidise you for ever you know!'

'Seriously', Janet continued, 'if one business does not do well, we don't want it to pull down everything else with it. Suppose one business did fail. If it isn't quite separate, all our assets could be liable.'

'Then we need a company to limit our liability', suggested Mike.

'I don't think so', said Janet. 'Talking to our solicitor, she says that we can operate as sole traders, with you responsible for the hotel and me for the practice. That way there are less formalities and records to keep and we can be self-employed which delays our tax payments.'

'Yes, but if we own the property jointly', Mike interrupted, 'this means that if one of us fails, our main asset is still on the line. What happens if you are sued by one of your patients?'

'I'm covered by professional indemnity insurance for any mishaps', Janet answered.

'What about your Dad, then?' Mike continued. 'If he is going to invest in our businesses, how can he put money into a sole trader?'

'Well, I think he can make us a loan, but it may be complicated to split it between us', replied Janet. 'To avoid confusion, why don't we go through a checklist of the various aspects so that we make a structured decision?'

Activities

i)   Assess whether or not you agree with Janet, that they should operate two separate businesses. If they were not married, would you advise differently?

ii) Consider Figure 8.5, Checklist for choosing the appropriate form, in section 5 above. In each category decide which would be the most appropriate form for Janet and Mike.

iii) Decide which form(s) you would recommend they choose.

Extended activity *A local survey*

Look at a copy of your local *Yellow Pages* (or equivalent business directory if this is not available).

First, consider the listings of two professional services, one involved in a profession (such as accountants or solicitors) and one offering a creative service (such as advertising agencies or designers).

Compare and contrast the incidence of sole traders and partnerships to limited companies in these categories, where this is evident from the listing. What do you think are the major reasons for any differences in the pattern which emerges?

Conduct a similar survey between two manufacturing or distribution sections, one in high technology areas (such as electronics components or electronic equipment) and one in a more artisan or craft field (such as furniture manufacturers or woodturners).

Case 2 Janet thinks co-operative

Two years on, Janet and Mike Bloomfield's move to an alternative lifestyle, running their own businesses, was proving to be a success. The hotel had flourished under Mike's experienced management, and was more than repaying the mortgage, loans and overheads.

Janet's business was also developing well, but in a way she had not expected. The demand for physiotherapy in their new location proved fickle. At times Janet had more patients than she could handle, but there were lulls in which she had insufficient custom for her services. During one of these slacker periods she decided to try a diversification for her business. For some time she had been interested in alternative forms of healing, and had several contacts practising various types of treatment and therapy, outside of the main stream of conventional medicine. She also knew that there was a growing demand for these services. What some of her practising friends lacked was proper business premises from which to operate.

The solution to her problem of fluctuating demand and their lack of accommodation seemed obvious. She invited an acupuncturist, an aromatherapist, a reflexologist, a shiatsu masseuse, a herbalist, and a homeopath to use the facilities she had developed within the hotel.

The centralisation of these services on one site proved a great success, generating sufficient business to provide all the practitioners with a living. Janet was now concerned to devise a working structure in which everyone could happily operate, and be fairly rewarded for their efforts.

'It's not the sort of business that we will ever be able to sell at a capital profit', she explained to her husband Mike. 'It's far too dependent on our individual skills to be able to sell it on. But we can make a reasonable income from it, and we all share a common interest.'

'You mean healing', said Mike.

'Not just healing', replied Janet,' we want to promote natural healing. We don't need to be pumped full of chemicals to get over the slightest ailment. We can offer a complete range of alternatives which work and have no harmful side effects. Nor do they need testing on animals. We've really a common cause, that we all believe strongly in, as well as a business.'

'Don't get too carried away with the cause', warned Mike, 'we still have the bills to pay.'

'Exactly', responded Janet, 'that's why I want to make it into a co-operative. I've asked the local Co operative Development Agency about it. They're very helpful and keen to support us, and I think it would fulfil our needs as an organisation. We'd all have an equal vote in how things are done, and equal pay, depending on how much profit we make and how many hours we work. Of course we will need to pay you a fair rent for the use of the premises', she added.

'Of course', said Mike.

Activities

i)   What would be the advantage of Janet's proposed course of action?

ii) What could be the disadvantages?

In conclusion

Once you have finished this Unit, it is recommended that you turn to Section B, Planning a new venture, and complete Step 2.3, Selecting the form.

8 References and further reading

References and further information

1.   For more information, see DTI Publications, *Setting Up in Business: A Guide to Legislation, Requirements*, URN 97/524.

2.   For a summary of this work see Goss, D. *Small Business and Society*, Routledge 1991, Chapter 5, 'Alternative forms of small business'.

3.   For a review of the background, classifications, and influences on success or failure see Cornforth, C. 'Worker Co-operatives: Factors Affecting their Success and Failure', in Curran, J., Gibb, A., Lewis, J. and Faulkner, T. (eds), *The Survival of the Small Firm*, Gower, 1986.

Recommended further reading

❐   Williams, S. *Lloyds Bank Small Business Guide*, Penguin, 2001. Chapter 4, 'Your business identity'.

❐   Clayton, P. *Law for the Small Business*, Kogan Page, 1991. Chapters 1, 2, 3, 4 and 6.

❏ Barrows, C. *The Complete Small Business Guide*, BBC Books, 1995. Section 3, Joining a co-operative, and Section 7, Choosing the legal form of the business.

❏ Cornforth, C. 'Worker Co-operatives: Factors Affecting their Success and Failure' (see reference 3).

❏ DTI, *Setting up in Business – A Guide to Regulatory Requirements*, DTI Small Firms Publications (URN 96/916), 1996. This explains the legal regulations that need to be considered when starting a new business.

Part III

The small business in action

This Part comprises Units 9 to 14. It considers how small businesses work in practice, focusing on successful strategies particularly in the areas of the management of people, marketing and money. Each Unit links to a Step in Stage III (The business plan) of Section B, as shown below. Each Step should be considered immediately following your completion of the relevant Unit.

Section A Exploring small business	Section B Planning a new venture
Part III Small business in action ⟶	*Stage III The business plan*
Unit 9 The business plan ⟶	Step 3.1 Outlining the plan
Unit 10 Successful small business ⟶ strategies	Step 3.2 Deciding the strategy
Unit 11 Management of resources ⟶	Step 3.3 Managing the resources
Unit 12 Marketing ⟶	Step 3.4 Planning the marketing
Unit 13 Money ⟶	Step 3.5 Forecasting the money
Unit 14 Further case studies ⟶	Step 3.6 Summary of the business plan

Contents

9 The business plan

This Unit looks at the when, who, why and what of business plans for the small enterprise:

❏ when they are produced or can be used;

❏ who writes them, and for whom;

❏ why they are produced, and the benefits that can follow;

❏ what they look like, the topics covered and a format that can be used.

Contents

Activity 1 Planning problems

Business plans are sometimes considered necessary only as a means to obtain funds for a new venture from a bank or other lender, rather than a vital document for the business itself. Do you agree:

a)   that formalised planning is less important for a small business; and

b)   that it is at the time of start up that it is most necessary to draw up a business plan?

1 The purpose of a business plan

1.1 Planning and performance

Many managers already involved in small business, or those considering it as a possibility, perceive the business plan, first and foremost, as a document that is produced for the bank manager, investor, or venture capital company, in order to raise money.

For this reason, small businesses that do not have an external funding requirement tend not to write formal business plans.

The reasons for this include:

❑ a lack of understanding of the process or benefits of business planning;

❑ pressure on doing, rather than thinking or gathering information, in the small business environment;

❑ the belief that strategic planning is for larger organisations and big business resources, and not necessary for smaller firms who can plan effectively on the back of an envelope.

The Keynesian concept of central control and planning of the economy at the macro level was rejected emphatically by the post-1979 Conservative government. In part this was reflected at the micro level, by the feeling that entrepreneurial management, of the seat-of-the-pants, unstructured variety, should be encouraged rather than criticised. This apparent victory for the entrepreneur over the planner, helped devalue the planning process, except as the means to the end of raising finances.

Some research evidence also cast doubts on the value of planning. One investigation[1] reported that there was no clear evidence that formalised strategic planning in small firms led to improved performance. Other studies have however linked planning to growth. Another study[2] found that small businesses which grew rapidly did spend more time in formally planning their activities. Other research[2] has indicated that it is more important to plan after start up than before setting up a new venture: no significant differences in performance were found between firms who had a written business plan at start up, and those who had not, but 93 per cent of the fast growing firms had introduced a business plan later on, compared to 70 per cent of more stagnant businesses.

The evidence suggests that formal planning is more common in businesses as they grow from small to larger firms. Whether it actually helps small firms develop into larger ones, or whether it is just a characteristic they tend to adopt when they become bigger, is less clear.

1.2 The when, who and why of planning

A business plan can be used at different times, with potential benefits for several audiences. This is shown in Figure 9.1 which illustrates when a business plan can be used, by whom, for whom and why.

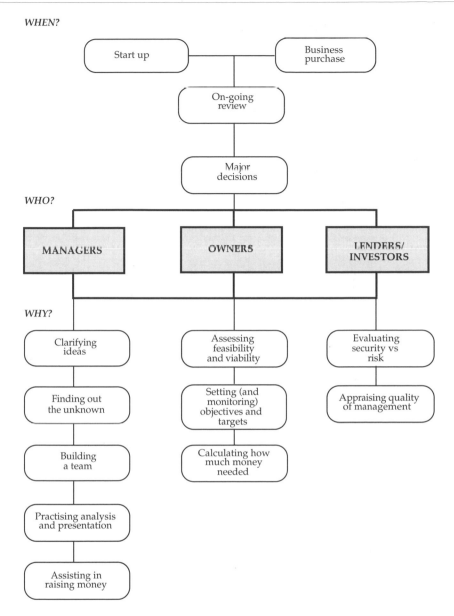

Figure 9.1 Purpose of a business plan – the when, who and why

Activity 2 Timing of plans

Can you give some examples of situations in which it might be beneficial for a small enterprise to draw up a business plan?

2 When to plan?

Business plans can be triggered by a number of events or reasons.

- ☐ *Start up.* After the concept stage of initial idea and feasibility study a new business start up may go through a more detailed planning stage of which the main output is the business plan.

- ☐ *Business purchase.* Buying an existing business does not negate the need for an initial business plan. A detailed plan, which tests the sensitivity of changes to key business variables (e.g. what if sales drop by 25 per cent ... what if overheads increase by 25 per cent ...?), greatly increases the prospective purchaser's understanding of the level of risk they will be accepting, and the likelihood of rewards being available.

- ☐ *Ongoing review.* Ongoing review of progress, against the objectives of either a start up or small business purchase, is important in a dynamic environment. 'If you do nothing, nothing will not happen', is a truism that should motivate any small business manager to periodically review their business in its constantly changing environment.

   To have lasting benefit, a business plan ought not to be a one-off document that gathers dust in a drawer once it has fulfilled its immediate purpose. It can be the live, strategic and tactical planning focus of how a small business responds to the inevitable changes around it.

- ☐ *Major decisions.* Even if planning is not carried out on a regular basis, it is usually instigated at a time of major change. Again it may be linked to a need for finance: for example, the need for major new investment in equipment, or funds to open a new outlet. It may be linked to failure, such as a recovery plan for an ailing business.

Activity 3 Who is involved?

Who might be involved

a)   in producing a business plan; and

b)   in making decisions based on it?

3 Who can benefit?

Three types of people will be interested in a business plan: the managers who run or intend to run the business on a day to day basis; the owners, or prospective equity investors; and the lenders who are considering loans for the enterprise.

- ☐ *Managers* are involved in small business planning both as producers and recipients of the plan. The management of a small enterprise are the only people likely to be sufficiently knowledgeable to produce a business plan; the small business equivalent to a corporate planning department does not usually exist. Business plans are also written to aid small business managers. An obvious conclusion, but one that is often overlooked, is that the managers themselves can be very important beneficiaries, not only of the plan, but also the planning process.

❑ *Owners.* The managers of a small enterprise may also be the owners and take a keen interest in the planning process, wearing their shareholders' hat. A plan may be intended for prospective equity partners, either a sleeping partner looking for an investment, or an active partner looking to join an existing small business. Owners may also be lenders, as in venture capital companies, who take an equity stake in return for providing loans.

❑ *Lenders/investors.* The traditional recipient of the business plan is the bank manager. It is true that the major banks all encourage the production of business plans to justify overdrafts and loans, offering literature and advice on putting together business plans. Other lenders of money, from private individuals to venture capital companies, will also expect to make their investment decision after the presentation of a formal business plan.

Activity 4 Why are plans beneficial?

Why might a business plan be of benefit to:

a)   owner-managers; and

b)   investors or lenders?

---

4 Why produce a plan?

These three groups will have some shared, and some separate, motives for using a business plan. *Managers, owners* and *lenders/investors* will all be seeking to investigate the following issues:

❑ *Assessing the feasibility and viability of the business or project.* Will it work and become commercially and financially viable? It is in everyone's interests to make mistakes on paper, hypothetically testing for feasibility, before trying the real thing.

❑ *Setting objectives and budgets.* What is the overall direction and financial target set by the plan? Having a clear financial vision with believable budgets is a basic requirement of everyone involved in a plan.

❑ *Calculating how much money is needed.* What level and type of finance is required to make the plan work? A detailed cash flow with assumptions is a vital ingredient to precisely quantify earlier 'guestimates' of the likely funds required.

Managers involved in producing the plan can, in addition, gain from the process itself in the following ways:

- *Clarifying ideas.* Putting together a business plan often acts as a powerful focus bringing together generalised and random thoughts into a clearer understanding of the concept, and how it can be made to work.

- *Finding out the unknown.* The information gathering process of a plan can uncover many interesting and relevant facts. The day to day pressure may obscure much in the business environment from a new competitor about to open; opportunities for cheaper premises or suppliers; the availablity of new equipment; successful marketing methods used by others; or useful ideas from staff.

- *Building a team.* Developing a plan can be a catalyst to promote a feeling of participation among all those involved in a small business. Contrary to popular belief, small enterprises do not necessarily benefit from their shorter communication lines by encouraging participation in decision-making processes. Some owner-managers are deliberately secretive about their plans; others leave insufficient time to effectively communicate with their staff. Even before a business has been launched, future partners may develop ideas themselves which remain unexpressed to each other.

  The business plan provides a useful forum for all people involved in a small enterprise to express their ideas and feelings, in a way which develops a spirit of teamwork among them. The separate parts can find some unity not only in the plan, but also in the process of putting it together.

- *Practice in using analysis and presentation.* A plan can be an aid to training and management development. The research and analysis involved in a business plan, with quantification into forecast profit and loss, and cash flows, is a widely used learning tool at centres of business education and also in practice elsewhere. For some would-be and practising small business managers the planning process is their first experience of market research and detailed budgeting. The presentation of a business plan to raise funds from banks or investors is good experience in selling a concept of any kind.

- *To assist in raising money.* A well presented business plan is no guarantee of raising money, but it helps. Research into why banks decline finance for small business cites inadequate information as a common reason[3]. Banks and venture capital companies receive many requests for finance. A professional-looking business plan will at least help overcome the first hurdle of gaining a hearing[4].

Lenders/investors will look to a business plan to provide them with additional information, particularly:

- *To evaluate the security offered for funds versus the risks involved.* Any source of funds for a small business will seek the security of tangible assets for their loans, and the comfort of a very high probability of receiving their money back. The assets of a business, such as its debtors and fixed assets, are likely to be investigated for their underlying quality and not just balance sheet value.

  Although personal guarantees are frequently needed from owners, these are not necessarily a passport to successful loan negotiation. Financiers will not lend money for ideas they do not believe viable, even when fully backed by security. The higher the assessment of the risk, the greater the security needed to obtain finance.

❑ *To appraise the quality of management.* A lender of loan capital will be aware that in a small business the intangible asset of the quality of its management is more important than tangible assets in guaranteeing the security of a loan. The best opportunity they have to assess the quality of that management may be in observing the production and presentation of the business plan. It is not just what the plan says but how it is put together, and communicated, that will count for or against a lending or investing decision.

Activity 5 What is in a plan?

What general topics should a plan cover? Suggest some specific headings which a plan might have to cover these topics.

5 The format of a business plan

5.1 The three key questions

What should a business plan look like, and what should be included or excluded? Many outline business plans look formidable documents, running to numerous pages filled with very detailed questions. In fact, to do its job, a business plan needs to answer three straightforward questions:

- ○ Where are we now?
- ○ Where do we intend going?
- ○ How do we get there?

❑ **Where are we now?**

An analysis of the current situation of the marketplace, the competition, the business concept and the people involved is a necessary first step. It will include any historical background relevant to the position to date.

❑ **Where do we intend going?**

The direction that is intended for the business needs to be clear and precise, if others are to share its vision for the future. As well as qualitative expression of the objectives, quantifiable targets will clarify and measure progress towards the intended goals. Identification of likely changes to the business environment will build on the opportunities outlined, and assess possible threats.

❑ **How do we get there?**

Implementation of accepted aims is what all the parties to a plan are interested in as a final result. Plans for marketing and managing the business, with detailed financial analysis, are the advisable preliminaries before putting it all into practice.

5.2 Outline of a business plan

The precise format of a business plan depends on the particular business and the intended audience of the plan. It is not possible to suggest subject headings for a plan which would have universal application, although the main clearing banks and other sources of help in the UK do make outline business plans available.

Figure 9.2 suggests an outline which follows standard practice in answering the three key questions above. Suggested topics for each section are developed as a more complete outline below.

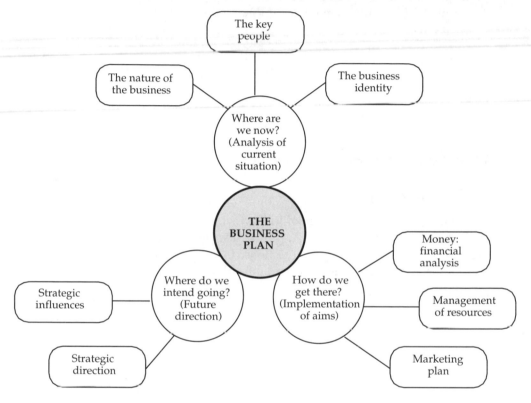

Figure 9.2 The format of a business plan

I Analysis of current situation (where are we now?)

i) *Identity of the business*

- Introduction
  - relevant history and background
  - date or proposed date for commencement of trading/beginning of a plan
- Names
  - name of business and trading names
  - names of managers/owners

•	Legal identity	• company/sole trader/partnership/co-operative
		• details of share or capital structure
•	Location	• address: registered and operational
		• brief details of premises
•	Professional advisors	• accountants, solicitors, bank

ii) *The key people*

•	Existing management	• names of the management team
		• outlines of background experience, skills and knowledge
		• why they are suited to the business
•	Future requirements	• gaps in skills and experience and how they will be filled
		• future recruitment intentions

iii) *The nature of the business*

•	Product(s)/service(s)	• description and applications
		• breakdown of product line as % of sales
		• outline of any intellectual properties, patents, trademarks, design registrations, copyrights
		• key suppliers
		• after-sales service, or guarantees and warranties offered
		• planned developments of product or service
•	Market and customers	• definition of target market
		• trends in marketplace
		• classification of customers
		• needs of customers and influences in their buying decisions
		• benefits offered by business to target customers
•	Competition	• description of competitors
		• strengths and weakness of the major competitors
		• competitive edge; the uniqueness of your business compared to the competition

II Future direction (where do we intend going?)

i) *Strategic influences*

- Opportunities and threats in the business environment
  - socio-economic trends
  - technological trends
  - legislation and politics
  - competition
- Strengths and weaknesses of the business
  - in its industry
  - in the general environment

ii) *Strategic direction*

- Objectives
  - general
  - specific
- Policies
  - guidelines and rules
- Activities
  - action plan
  - timetable of key activities

III Implementation of aims (how do we get there?)

i) *Management of resources*

- Operations
  - premises
  - materials
  - equipment
  - insurance
  - management information systems
- People
  - employment practices
  - recruitment
  - retention and motivation
  - payroll and personnel system
  - team management

ii) *Marketing plan*

- Competitive edge
  - unique selling point of business
- Marketing objectives
  - specific aims for product or service in the marketplace
- Marketing methods
  - innovation   – features and benefits
    - product mix
    - product development
  - incentives   – basis of pricing
    - margins
    - discount policy

- promotion   – methods to be used
  -     – consistency of image
- distribution – channels used
  -     – direct or intermediaries

- Research
  - confirmation of demand
  - future research planned

iii) *Money: financial analysis*
- Funding requirements
  - start-up capital
  - working capital
  - asset capital
  - timing of funds required
  - security offered
- Profit and loss
  - 3-year forecast
  - sales
  - variable costs
  - gross profit
  - overheads
  - net profit
- Cash flow
  - 3-year forecast
  - receipts
  - payments
  - monthly and cumulative cash flow
- Balance sheet
  - use of funds
  - source of funds
- Sensitivity analysis
  - break-even point
  - what-ifs
- Summary
  - main assumptions
  - performance ratios

Note on presentation: although business plans can be long, they should not be an unmanageable length for an external audience. A summary, and perhaps a timetable of activities, is advisable. Where detailed information is necessary it should be given in appendices so that the main body of the report can be kept as concise and clear as possible.

6 Case studies and activities

Case study The entrepreneur versus the planner

A small business owner, Richard Rodrigues, met a corporate planner, Kevin Watkins, for a social drink. The two were old friends, but as they had not met up for some time, they were anxious to catch up on each other's news.

Kevin was still working for a large utility company, as he had been when they last met. His work was to assist the line managers in his organisation to produce regular business plans which reflected corporate goals.

Richard's business, by comparison, was small and changing. He had owned a publishing company, which specialised in producing magazines for the medical profession paid for by advertising from drug companies.

'Yes, I think I was doing rather nicely in publishing when we last met', Richard commented to Kevin. 'That's all changed now of course. Generic prescribing came along and wiped out that business. Doctors have to prescribe non-branded drugs where possible now, so there's little point in the drug companies advertising their branded products to them. My publications were dependent on that advertising, so the day that generic prescribing came in, I went out – of the business that is.'

'You mean you've stopped publishing altogether?' asked Kevin. 'Didn't you see it coming and move into some other form of publishing?'

'Well, I heard about it of course, as it was being talked about well before it became policy', Richard replied. 'But I didn't think it would affect me the way it did. My advertising revenue dropped by 25%, which was enough to make the publication unprofitable. I had hoped I could ride the storm, but there didn't seem much point once I was losing money. If I'd had more time to develop new products, I probably could have stayed in the same business. There's still plenty of money to be made in medical publishing. But once the cash is flowing out of a business, it's like taking the plug out of a bath of water; it's hard to put it back in the hole and keep what you've got. I decided to cut my losses and do something else.'

'What did you do then?' Kevin questioned.

'I decided to do something completely different. I bought a toy company, making dolls and children's games', announced Richard. 'Want to buy it? It keeps me awake at nights with its cash flow problems.'

'No thanks. Very seasonal business, I imagine. Still you would have known that before you bought it. What's been the problem?' asked Kevin.

'You're right', said Richard, 'I did know it was a seasonal business, but I actually did a very good deal in buying it. The price was rock bottom. I didn't even have to take out any loans. It's just that so much depends on Christmas it's impossible to plan anything. My accountant checked out the reported profits and balance sheet before I bought the business, so I knew what I was getting. And the profits are there, as the previous owner said they would be. He just forgot to tell me about the cash flow. I nearly went bankrupt in the first year waiting for Christmas.'

'Didn't your business plan predict that, or at least indicate there would be some serious troughs in your cash flow?' asked Kevin.

'Like I said, I didn't need any loans, so I didn't need a business plan. I don't have a corporate planning department like yours, you know', said Richard.

'Well I don't want to push my own profession, but I think a business plan would have told you about these troubles in advance. But then I am biased', laughed Kevin.

Richard did not seem to appreciate the joke.

'If I had to put together the sort of five-year plan you produce every time I make a decision, I'd get nowhere fast. As a matter of fact, when I found out about this toy company for sale, there was another larger organisation interested. It was only by going down there the next day and making an offer on the spot that I clinched the deal. I expect your equivalent in this other company is still working on the business plans!' he retorted.

'I don't think that's fair at all', responded Kevin. 'How can you know what you're doing without some sort of plan? It doesn't have to be complicated or time consuming. And it can show how sensitive a business is to seasonal factors or more permanent changes like your last business. You know, a business plan may have helped you there too.'

'I don't think so at all', Richard said indignantly. 'What I needed then was creativity and innovation to change my business, not the straightjacket of some plan. Anyway they are only financial forecasts – crystal ball gazing. What's the point of that when you're going bust?'

'Ok, ok, so you don't believe in planning. How about objectives? Do you believe in setting those?' asked Kevin.

'Of course I do', said Richard, 'I just don't want to spend my time writing them down, that's all. You sound like the sales manager of my toy company. He's always sending me endless statistics of how he's doing compared to last year. I tell him to get out and see the customers. Don't worry about the targets, I can set those, and I'll tell you if you're not doing well. Just get out there and sell, that's all I ask.'

'Well you obviously like centralised control, at least that's something you have in common with us planners', smiled Kevin.

Activities

i)   Kevin may be right to claim that business plans could have helped Richard. In what ways do you think Richard could have benefited from a business plan in both of his businesses?

ii) Richard may be right to be sceptical about planning. What are the problems, perceived and real, in writing a business plan?

iii) Richard claims that plans 'are only financial forecasts – crystal ball gazing'. What would you want to put into a business plan to make it more meaningful in his situation? Suggest some outline headings for a business plan for Richard's toy company.

Extended activity *A bank's plan*

Most high street banks offer information on business plans with a suggested outline either in hard copy form or on a computer disc. Obtain a business plan from a local bank and study its content. How appropriate do you think the outline plan is for most small businesses? How would you improve on the structure for your own business plan?

In conclusion

Once you have finished this Unit, it is recommended that you turn to Section B, Planning a new venture, and complete Step 3.1, Outlining the plan.

7 References and further reading

References and further information

1. Robinson, R. and Pearce, J. 'Research Thrust and Small Firm Strategic Planning', *Academy of Management Review,* Vol. 9, No. 1, 1984.

2. This and other research is reported in Storey, D. J. *Understanding the Small Business Sector,* International Thomson Business Press , 1998.

3. Robbie, M. 'Small Business Requests for Bank Finance: Reasons for Decline' in Scott, M., Gibb, A., Lewis, J. and Faulkner, T. (eds), *Small Firms' Growth and Development*, Gower, 1986.

4. The major banks provide outline plans for finance applicants.

    For example, HSBC provide a template on disc or as a hard copy.

    Downloadable business plans templates are also available – see www.master-planner.co.uk

    The British Venture Capital Association suggests a Short Form Business Profile to obtain an initial expression of interest: see the BVCA Directory available from BVCA, Essex House, 12–13 Essex St, London WC2R 3AA. Web site: www.brainstorm.co.uk

Recommended further reading

- ☐ Barrow, C., Barrow P. and Brown, R. *The Business Plan Workbook*, Kogan Page, 2001.
- ☐ Johnson, R. *The 24 hour Business Plan*, Hutchinson Business Books, 1990.
- ☐ Burns, P. *Entrepreneurship and Small Business*, Palgrave, 2001. Chapter 8, 'Developing a business plan'.
- ☐ Deakins, D. *Entrepreneurship and Small Firms*, McGraw Hill, 1996. Chapter 12.
- ☐ HSBC offer a business start-up pack, *Running Your Own Business*, including an outline form for a business plan on disk. This is supported by in-depth profiles (*Business Information Guides*) of many types of businesses, and a telephone helpline.
- ☐ *The Business Start-up Guide*, National Westminster Bank. This is one of the more comprehensive bank planning guides containing a step by step approach to new venture planning.
- ☐ *Starting towards success*, Lloyds Bank business banking. This provides a business plan outline on disk and *The Lloyds Bank Small Business Guide* by Sara Williams (free if you open a business account).

10 Successful small business strategies

Although strategy is a word more commonly associated with large organisations, strategic decisions have been found to be just as significant to the success of small enterprises. This Unit describes some of the main considerations in formulating small business strategies, taking into account the diversity of motives of the owner-managers.

Contents

Activity 1 Objectives of a small business

In large businesses, growth of sales and profits is a common strategic goal, but this is not always the case in small business. Why not? What other strategic objectives might a small business have?

1 What is successful?

1.1 Success equals growth?

It is often assumed that to be truly successful a small firm must manage the transition into a larger company. Small business is, after all, the seed corn for tomorrow's larger enterprises; many of our industrial giants will disappear to be replaced by today's fast-growing small firms. Success is inextricably linked to growth. The small business owner who achieves rapid growth to enter the large business category is seen in a heroic light. Examples of successful entrepreneurs are drawn from the likes of James Dyson, Richard Branson and Anita Roddick, who had humble origins in small business, but have now moved on to bigger things.

An analysis of successful small business strategies often starts with a large company and its founders, then works backwards to see how they got there. Little attention is given to the owner-manager who has survived in business, yet remained small[1].

The size distribution of firms in the economy

Unfortunately this narrow view of success consigns most small businesses into the category of 'unsuccessful'. The vast majority of businesses do not grow beyond their classification as a small firm. Only a few grow to become medium-sized, and even fewer grow into the new, large companies of the future. Larger firms in the UK economy account for a very small percentage of the total number of enterprises. As we saw earlier, (see Unit 1, Table 1.1), 99 per cent of UK businesses fall into the EC 'small' category of less than 50 employees, and 95 per cent are 'micro' enterprises of fewer than 10 employees.

If the size distribution of firms is visualised as a pyramid, the base is extremely broad and the apex very narrow. If success means climbing from the bottom to the top, then it is rare indeed.

1.2 Models of growth stages

This view of small business success or failure has been refined into various models of the growth stages of a small business[2]. The number of stages varies, but a composite model is illustrated in Figure 10.1.

❒ **Phase 1: Concept/test stage**

   The new business idea is conceived and planned. Full-scale operations may (or may not) be preceded by detailed planning and testing in the marketplace. In some cases the business is run as a part-time operation, before the owner places complete dependence on it.

❒ **Phase 2: Development/abort stage**

   The small business begins operation and is developed to viability, or it is aborted at an early stage. This stage is typified as the individual owner-manager launching a new enterprise largely through their own efforts.

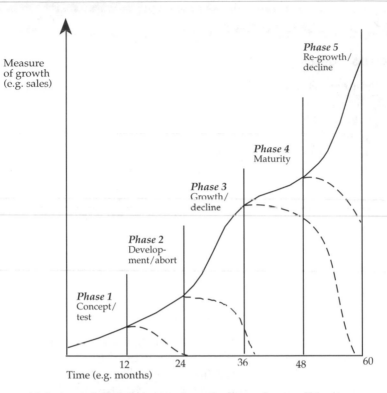

Figure 10.1 A model of the growth or decline of a small business

Some analyses indicate crucial periods when a small business will survive or fail. One such period is illustrated as the first 18–24 months, when a new enterprise will pass through the critical phase of start up, and grow to a viable size, or it will not develop satisfactorily and suffer an early exit. Business survival statistics[3] confirm this high level of early closures with only approximately 60 per cent of enterprises surviving the first 2 years (see Unit 3, Table 3.2).

❐ **Phase 3: Growth/decline stage**

The second crucial phase is sometimes shown as occurring between the second and third years of operation. The growth that can occur at this time places organisational strains on the enterprise. The one-person entrepreneurial management style is inadequate to fully sustain growth. A division of managerial tasks, the recruitment of non-owner-managers and the development of a functionally organised team are seen as prerequisites to take the business through this phase, without which it will struggle and often close.

❐ **Phase 4: Maturity**

A further stage looks at the business maturing, and going through a period of stability, when growth flattens. The small firm loses its simple structure of centralised decision-making, and becomes more sophisticated in its control systems and more bureaucratic in its procedures. In other words it takes on some of the characteristics of a larger organisation.

❐ **Phase 5: Re-growth/decline**

The identification of a further phase, sometimes referred to as the s-curve hypothesis, suggests that once a small business has established itself in the marketplace, with a demonstrable competitive advantage, profits or external investment will follow to further exploit this early success. This will trigger a second period of high growth. Without this second surge of growth, the lack of impetus in the maturity phase can turn into stagnation and decline, as competition intensifies.

Whilst these models of the various growth stages of successful small enterprises contain aspects which are indeed descriptive of how businesses develop, they overlook the statistical evidence, that most small businesses do not develop into larger organisations in this way. It is true that many do close; but others simply establish themselves and survive as small businesses, without becoming larger companies in either size or organisational structure.

It is important to follow the fate of the owners as well as the businesses, as the two are inextricably linked. There is an assumption that most owners that close down their business have been unsuccessful. But many owners do not see it that way. In a study by the Small Business Research Centre of Kingston University[4], owners were asked to rate their success as a manager of a business that closed. Over half (54 per cent) rated themselves as successful with only 14 per cent describing themselves as unsuccessful. As a further indication of the confidence of these owners, the majority tended to remain involved in running a business. The study classified owners that had closed a businesses into three broad categories:

❐ *Departing* (30%) – owners who returned to employment, or became unemployed, or out of work through ill health.

❐ *Retiring* (10%) – owners retiring from active involvement having sold or closed their business

❐ *Returning* (60%) – those who continued as business owners by opening or buying a new or similar business to the one closed, or through the existing ownership of another business.

This indicates that only a minority of owners can be described as truly departing when a business closes down, as most still wish to run their own business and are soon returning to business ownership. A model of the experiences of business owners would resemble more of a roller-coaster ride with many peaks and troughs, rather than the neat curve of the life-cycle model of a business as shown in Figure 10.1. The crucial role of the owner-manager means that success or failure of a small business can only be judged in relation to the motives and objectives of that owner, rather than any standard measure of business performance.

1.3 The objectives of owner-managers

The general purpose of the management of any enterprise has been defined as the achievement of the organisation's objectives and a continuous improvement in its performance[5]. Successful management is thus directly linked to the objectives of the organisation. If the objectives of a business include high rates of growth, then this is clearly a yardstick against which success of the management can be judged. If, however, continuous strong growth is not necessarily one of the aims of an enterprise, then success has to be measured in other ways.

As many small businesses are the psychological extension of the owner-manager, their personal motives and objectives will be crucial in assessing success or failure. Research has cast considerable doubt on whether growth is the common goal driving the small business owner forward. A survey of owner-managed businesses concluded that for owner-managers growth is only one of a number of desirable objectives and is less important than survival and staying independent[5]. Another study reported that more than 30 per cent of owners wanted their small firms to stay at their present size[7]. This echoes earlier work done at the time of the Bolton Report which suggested that many owners paid lip service to the ideal of growth, being primarily motivated by the need to preserve independence, which too much growth might threaten[8].

Clearly the motives of owner-managers for entering into the world of small business will vary, giving rise to different objectives for their business. Attempts have been made to classify entrepreneurs in terms of their personal values, in order to distinguish between some of the more obvious types, and their possible objectives (see also Unit 2, The entrepreneur and the owner-manager). Figure 10.2 illustrates some of these[9], in relation to their desire for growth.

This so-called social action view sees the small firm as a social grouping in which the attitude to growth is determined by the participant's social background, identity and desires. Passive owner-managers, who look upon growth as a necessary evil to ensure survival, will not primarily be motivated by the prospect of high profits. They will be more concerned with the intrinsic satisfaction of the job itself (*the artisan*), or by the business's ability to deliver an acceptable lifestyle, without having to compete in the rat-race of employment in larger organisations (*the isolationist*). At the other end of the spectrum are those who conform to the capitalist model of a profit seeking opportunist (*the classical entrepreneur*), which may involve attachment to the marketplace (*the marketeer*), or a specific product or process (*the technocentric*). Others may place emphasis on recognition from others, with security for themselves and their heirs (*the manager*), making them less likely to take the risks of high growth, whilst being dissatisfied with minimal growth.

The only common motive that can be attributed to owner-managers with such differing backgrounds and desires is the survival of the business itself, for a sufficiently long period to deliver the objectives sought.

Growth	Identity	Personal values
LOW GROWTH Passive owner-managers	1. The isolationist	• escapism from market economy • maintenance of acceptable lifestyle • business seen as means to an end
	2. The artisan	• personal autonomy • work satisfaction from quality of product and personal service • ability to choose workmates
	3. The manager	• seeking recognition by others of own managerial excellence • security and long-term planning
	4. The technocentric	• attachment to a given industrial process and its potential for development • managerial orientation
	5. The marketeer	• business goals ends in themselves • less importance on nature of business, more on customer satisfaction
HIGH GROWTH Opportunistic owner-managers	6. The classical entrepreneur	• great importance on profits and earnings • satisfaction from success of risk taking

Identities taken from Stanworth and Curran, Growth and the Small Firm *and Goss,* Small Business and Society[9]

Figure 10.2 Examples of personal identities and values which condition the growth objectives of the owner-managed business

Activity 2 Cause of death

In an earlier Unit, we saw that closure rates among small firms are extremely high (Unit 3, 3.1).

What do you think are the principal internal causes of small business failure? Try to classify some specific reasons into more general strategic categories.

2 Business closures

2.1 Business closure and failure

In order to understand more about successful strategies, it is necessary to look at the frequency and causes of unsuccessful small business strategy. In this sense, 'success' can only be described by looking at its opposite – failure. The management of a small firm which goes out of business after a relatively short time is often described as 'unsuccessful'. However we have already indicated in section

1.2 that owners often do not see it that way, regarding their experiences in a closed business as useful and sometimes profitable. Only a minority of those that close a business can be regarded as failed entrepreneurs, as often the business continues and the owner re-enters into business ownership. A recent study classified and quantified entrepreneurs who leave a business according to:

a) how their business performed financially; and

b) their future intentions and attitudes towards running a business.

This resulted in four categories of entrepreneurship as follows[4]:

❑ *Determined entrepreneurs* (45 per cent of those who close a business). Despite problems in their previous venture, they return to business ownership determined to do better. This is the largest group as it frequently takes more than one attempt to 'make a go of it'.

❑ *Serial entrepreneurs* (37 per cent). Having succeeded in a previous venture, they return with resources to invest in new business. This group have probably sold one business and are keen to become involved in another.

❑ *Failed entrepreneurs* (13 per cent). The problems of a previous venture discourage them from re-entering into business ownership. This represents the group who can be said to have 'failed' in that they have closed a business in financial difficulty, often leaving bad debts, and return to employment, or unemployment. However it is a relatively small percentage of those that do close down a business.

❑ *Discouraged entrepreneurs* (5 per cent). Although their previous business venture succeeded, they do not wish to repeat the experience. Often the strains of running a small business outweigh the financial rewards, so this relatively small group also withdraws from business ownership.

Therefore we should be careful not to equate closure with failure. The exit in the ownership of a business is more like a revolving door, rather than one that simply opens and shuts. Assuming that one objective of the owner is for the business to survive, we can draw some lessons from the statistics on business closures.

2.2 Frequency and timing of small business closure

In an earlier Unit, (see Unit 3, The small business environment, sub-section 3.1, Small business closure rates) we looked at the frequency and timing of small business closure rates and drew some important conclusions:

❑ *Closure rates among small firms are very high.* On average, about 10 per cent of the total numbers of small businesses cease trading each year in the UK. As there are approaching 4 million small firms in the economy, this means that on average around 400,000 go out of business each year[10]. Closure rates in the EU and USA are comparable: it is estimated that less than a quarter of all firms survive for more than a decade.

❑ *The young businesses are more likely to die than the old.* Closure rates are highest in the early years but chances of survival improve as the business matures. Up to 20 per cent of new starts are likely to disappear in the first year of trading and over 40 per cent within two years.

❏ *Small firms are much more likely to cease trading than large firms.* Failure is a key distinguishing feature between small and larger business, as medium-sized and large firms have much lower closure rates.

❏ *The very smallest firms are the most vulnerable.* Micro-firms employing less than 10 people have a much higher closure rate than those employing higher numbers of people.

❏ *Those that grow are less likely to close than those that do not.* As a firm becomes larger its chances of survival improve. Staying small is not a good survival strategy, even though, as we have seen, many owner-managers do not want to grow their business.

2.3 Critical factors in the closure of young businesses

Young firms face many problems in their formative years which threaten their survival.

❏ *External influences.* Earlier in this book (Unit 3, 1, A matter of life and death) we reviewed the external influences outside of their control. Macro-economic conditions such as interest rates and overall levels of consumer demand, and micro-environmental factors in the local catchment area or industry sector such as the intensity of competition, are important influences on whether a new venture sinks or swims.

We concluded that the small business environment varies from being hostile to relatively benign, dependent on the time period, geographic area and market sector in which the small firm operated. Because of the vulnerability of very young and very small firms, much depends on the owner-manager's ability to adapt to the surrounding changing circumstances (Unit 3, 3.2, Adjusting to uncertainty).

❏ *Internal factors.* The personal attributes, skills and competencies of the individual owner-manager are crucial to how well the business faces up to the inevitable crises that arise.

Which particular internal issues should the owner-manager be prepared to face? The list could be very long, but researchers have attempted to identify those areas which are particularly important, as some seem more critical to survival than others.

❏ One study[11] analysed events which particularly threatened the survival of small ventures. The percentages of small businesses studied experienced crises in:

  ○ marketing (38.1 per cent)
  ○ finance (32.2 per cent)
  ○ managerial (14.3 per cent)
  ○ personnel (13.0 per cent)
  ○ 'acts of God' (10.4 per cent)
  ○ no crises (18 per cent)

❑ A review of around 50 articles and five books on the subject of small business failure and bankruptcy[12] revealed six major categories of failure:

accounting; marketing; finance problems; the behaviour of the owner; other endogenous (internal) factors; exogenous (external) factors.

❑ A study of surviving small firms concluded that 'small, young organisations experience problems particularly in the areas of accounting and finance, marketing, and the management of people'[13].

❑ Researchers[14] in Britain and Europe asked financial institutions, lending to small manufacturing industries, to rank their perceptions of the major threats to the survival of small firms.

Their reasons were:

United Kingdom	1.	Availability of finance
	2.	Management capability of owner
	3.	Marketing problems
West Germany	1.	Availability of finance
	2.	Management capability of owner
	3.	Marketing problems
France	1.	Management capability of owner
	2.	Availability of finance
	3.	Difficulty in complying with new laws and regulations.

❑ The judgement of individual investors in small business, or so-called 'business angels' is interesting in that it indicates what they have discovered to be critical factors which make a venture more likely to succeed or fail. The principle reasons given by business angels for not investing are[15]:

○ Lack of relevant experience of entrepreneur and any associates.

○ Deficiencies in marketing.

○ Flawed, incomplete or unrealistic financial projections.

2.4 Management, marketing and money

There is some consensus over the areas critical to a small enterprise's chances of survival which are controllable to some extent by the owner-manager.

❑ **Management** (of resources, especially people)

The competence of the owner-manager is the ultimate determinant of survival or failure. In the early days, the founder's personal competence in selecting the right business and running it will be crucial, as the firm is likely to be indistinguishable from the owner. As the business develops, growth can be prematurely curtailed by an unwillingness or inability to draw others in to help with the management of the enterprise. Management of people is particularly important as it includes not only the personnel issues of dealing with employees, but also of managing people outside of the organisation who are also critical to its success, such as key customers, suppliers, banks and investors.

❐ **Marketing**

To have a good chance of survival, a small firm needs to answer the basic strategic question: what markets are we targeting, with what products? A common weakness in owner-managers lies in their failure to understand key marketing issues. Product and service concepts and standards often reflect only the perceptions of the owner, which may not be mirrored in the market-place. Minor fluctuations in markets can topple a newly established small firm, particularly where it is reliant on a small number of customers.

❐ **Money**

Financial difficulties of small firms arise, either because of an inability to raise sufficient funds to properly capitalise the business, or a mismanagement of the funds that do exist (or a combination of both). Access to external funds may be difficult to achieve for the new, or young, small business with no track record, especially for owners without personal assets to offer as security. Venture capital may be inappropriate for very small enterprises. Many new owner-managers, having received funds, misuse them; small businesses are notorious for their lack of proper financial controls and information.

Activity 3 What is strategy?

What do you think is meant by strategy in the small business context?

What would the main ingredients be in a small business strategy?

3 Small business strategy

With a low probability of sustained growth, and a high risk of closure, can a small business adopt strategies to improve its chances of success?

Much advice is published on how to succeed as a small business owner. There is obviously much to be gained from listening to the practical advice of those who have experience of small enterprises. But can this be formulated into a prescriptive strategy to guide the small business owner?

3.1 Some definitions

First let us be clear what we mean by strategy in this context.

A *strategy* is a *plan* or *pattern* that brings together an enterprise's major objectives, policies and activities into a cohesive whole[16]. It provides the direction necessary to allocate the resources of the enterprise in a unique and viable way, which takes account of internal strengths and weaknesses, and external opportunities and threats.

❏ *Objectives* represent what is to be achieved (but not how). Objectives can be a broad and permanent assessment of the values to which an enterprise and its chief participants aspire (e.g. to remain independent of others; to satisfy customers whilst doing and enjoying what we are best at; to make a large capital gain; to promote the protection of the environment; to work in a truly democratic and fair organisation). Alternatively objectives can be more narrow and less permanent, defining specific targets (e.g. to reach a turnover of £1 million; to open three outlets; to pay off the overdraft; to take on an extra partner).

❏ *Policies* are rules or guidelines which define the limits within which activities should occur. Again they can be broad (borrowings should be kept to a minimum, so that our house is not at risk), or more specific (we will not trade on a Sunday).

❏ *Activities* are the detailed actions necessary to achieve the objectives, within the policy constraints. They can be formalised in action plans, which specify the step by step sequence of how objectives will be achieved.

Earlier discussion in this unit around the objectives of a small firm concluded that:

❏ the personal motives of the small business owner will largely determine the objectives of the enterprise;

❏ these motives vary from the craftsman seeking an alternative lifestyle to the opportunistic entrepreneur driven by materialistic gain; and

❏ the objectives of small enterprises will also vary. High or continuous growth cannot be assumed as an objective. Even the objective of survival can be questioned; many owners close a business which has out-lived its usefulness, or in order to concentrate on another venture.

3.2 Survival strategies

These conclusions, taken with our definition of strategy, mean that there can be no prescriptive successful small business strategy, only descriptive guidelines on key strategy influences.

It is possible however to identify the basic influences on a small business strategy in relation to the objective of survival. We have established that the key determinants of survival, within the controllable environment of a small firm, are management, marketing and money.

These are illustrated in Figure 10.3 as the '3 Ms'.

These influences are shown as overlapping, as clearly they do not work in isolation.

❏ *Management* is concerned with the efficient and effective use of resources by the enterprise, in order that it can meet its objectives. Money is one of the resources for management to use, or misuse. Marketing decisions are a crucial aspect of management.

Figure 10.3 Key influences in small firm strategies for survival – the '3 Ms'

❐ *Marketing* represents the relationship of the enterprise with those customers it seeks to serve. It will determine how much money flows into an enterprise via sales to customers. It will also dictate the kinds and quantities of resources that management will need to satisfy the demand it has stimulated.

❐ *Money* enables the whole system to work. It enables management to purchase the resources it requires; it enables marketing activities to take place.

3.3 Strategies beyond survival

Beyond survival, strategies will depend on the objectives of the enterprise. However, the quality of management and marketing and the quantity of money remain as key influences on the ability of the small firm to meet its objectives, whatever these happen to be. New strategies will need to build on, rather than detract from, these primary influences. The motives of the owner-manager(s) are therefore a fourth influence to be added to the existing three.

Unlike large companies where objectives arise from the influences of a variety of stakeholders, small enterprise strategy is driven by a more easily identifiable source, often one person. This additional force in any development of strategy beyond survival is shown in Figure 10.4 – the '4 Ms'.

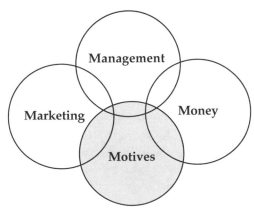

Figure 10.4 Key influences in small firm strategies beyond survival – the '4 Ms'

Again the influences overlap to represent the impact they can have on each other. For example:

❏ *Motives* can point to one strategy which is thwarted by money or marketing considerations. An owner may be motivated to run a business which is completely environmentally friendly, only to find that money does not permit this policy to be fully implemented. A restaurant owner may have personal motives to provide only vegetarian food, but finds that the marketplace does not support this strategy.

❏ *Management* considerations may indicate a strategy which is thwarted by the motives of the owner. An appropriate management structure for a growing business may never be implemented by an owner motivated by a strong desire for personal control.

❏ *Marketing* strategies may run counter to motives. An owner's desire to run what they perceive as a completely ethical business may prohibit certain sales approaches. Despite evidence of strong local demand, and competitive advantage, a trader may refuse to open on Sunday for personal reasons.

❏ *Money* influences may be diminished by personal motives. A desire to retain certain friendships may prevent rigorous pursuit of debtors. An owner with motives to promote their standing in the community may turn down the cheapest deal in favour of the local supplier.

Activity 4 Growth

If a small firm had the objective of high growth, how would its strategies be different from businesses with less ambitious growth plans?

4 Strategies for growth

Small businesses can be divided into three broad categories for strategic analysis:

❏ those likely to cease trading in the near future;

❏ those likely to survive, but which will stay very small;

❏ those which will not only survive but will also grow rapidly.

As we have seen, the vast majority of small businesses fall into the first two categories. Only a tiny minority turn into the high growth enterprises which move quickly towards medium-sized status and beyond.

However their significance to the economy is much greater than their numbers imply. High growth firms are those that provide most employment prospects: over 50 per cent of the new jobs created by small businesses are provided by the fastest growing 4 per cent of firms[17].

This section looks at some of the influences on their growth.

4.1 The entrepreneur, the firm and strategy

In a review of the evidence on small business growth, Storey[17] developed a frame-work of the characteristics of high growth small firms involving three components:

- ○ the starting resources of the entrepreneur;
- ○ the firm;
- ○ strategy.

☐ **The entrepreneur**

The success of a business is very dependent on the characteristics of the entrepreneur, but it is difficult to isolate attributes which are more significant than others, (as we have seen in Unit 2, The entrepreneur and the owner-manager). Storey suggests four entrepreneurial elements which are likely to be important influences on high growth:

- ○ *Motives.* Those 'pushed' into a small business through unemployment, or other causes, are less likely to establish high growth firms than those 'pulled' by the attraction of a market opportunity.
- ○ *Education and experience.* Higher levels of education and prior managerial experience help.
- ○ *Age.* Middle-aged founders are more likely to combine the energy and experience requirements for growth.
- ○ *Numbers.* Businesses owned by several people, rather than one individual, are more likely to have the range of skills required to cope with growth.

Other possible influences such as prior self-employment, prior business failure, gender, family history and social marginality were found to be less strong.

☐ **The firm**

The characteristics of the firm itself also have an influence:

- ○ *Age.* Younger firms grow more rapidly than older ones. A new business needs to grow rapidly to achieve a viable size.
- ○ *Size.* Smaller firms tend to grow more rapidly than larger ones. As with age, there is pressure on small firms to reach their minimum viable size, or 'minimum efficiency scale'(MES) as quickly as possible.
- ○ *Legal form.* Limited companies experience more rapid growth than sole traders or partnerships.
- ○ *Location.* As small firms tend to trade in localised markets, location can be a significant influence on growth.
- ○ *Sector.* The overall growth rate of the market or industrial sector in which the firm operates influences its development.

☐ **Strategy**

Once the firm is in business, the strategic actions and decisions taken by the owner-manager are what counts. Four strategy areas which particularly influenced growth were found to be:

○ *External equity.* Growing businesses are more likely to have obtained external funds from outside individuals or organisations.

○ *Market positioning.* High growth firms tend to occupy deliberately chosen market niches where they can exploit innovations and any technological sophistication they might have.

○ *Innovation.* New product or service introductions are key to small firm growth.

○ Growth is restricted if *non-owning managers* are not brought in. The selection, motivation and retention of a management team is important to increase the capabilities of the business.

4.2 Stages of growth

Different strategies and skills are required at different stages of a firm's life.

Setting up a new business is not the same managerial task as running an existing, fast growing one. The problems and issues seem to crop up in the same strategic areas, however.

For example, Drucker[18] puts forward four requirements for the successful development of a new venture:

1. Focus on the market.

2. Financial foresight, especially planning cash needs in advance of growth.

3. Building a top management team before it is required.

4. Careful definition of the founder's role in the enterprise.

His analysis assumes that growth is the motive force, and illustrates how the significance of marketing, money and the management of people shifts according to the stages of growth of an enterprise.

☐ *Marketing*: the need for a market orientation is paramount whilst a new firm is establishing itself. Lack of market focus is a problem typical of the very young business; failure comes quickly if there is insufficient demand, or inadequate stimulation of it.

☐ *Money*: inappropriate financial policies are the greatest threat to a new enterprise in the next phase of its growth. Here the focus has to be particularly on cash, not profits, as the growing firm outstrips its capital base.

The business will need to change its financial structure, and improve mechanisms for controlling money if it is to move smoothly into the next phase of its development.

☐ *Management*: once it is established in the marketplace, and has developed the necessary financial structure and controls, the young enterprise faces a further barrier before it can progress into adulthood. By this stage the business is too big to be managed by its founder(s) alone. It needs a management team. But a team does not form overnight; it has to be built in advance to fully function when it is needed – a brave move for a growing business with limited resources.

A corollary of the emergence of a management team is that the founder(s) then has to redefine their own role in the light of the changed circumstances. It may be that their style is not flexible enough to fit in with a broader spread of control. The only remedy may be their departure from a top executive position to an advisory role. These strategies for the high growth new venture are illustrated in Figure 10.5.

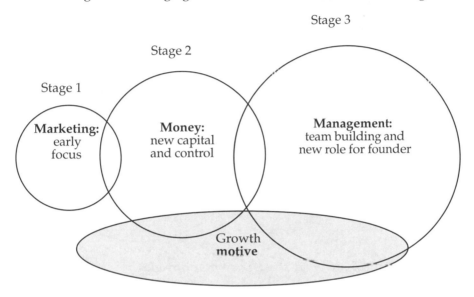

Figure 10.5 Phased influences in growth strategies

Activity 5 Emergent strategies

Strategy sometimes emerges as a pattern of activity, not deliberately conceived in advance. Can you give some examples where this may happen in small business? Consider also how these emergent strategies might then be converted into intended strategies.

5 A composite model of successful strategies

5.1 Successful small business strategies

In this and other Units the various influences on the likelihood of, first, the survival of a new venture and, secondly, its growth into a larger enterprise have been discussed. These have been divided into external and individual influences and into factors that particularly affect high growth firms. As growth is one of the key factors in survival, many of the influences on survival are similar to those that are important for high growth firms. A composite model of these influences is summarised in Figure 10.6.

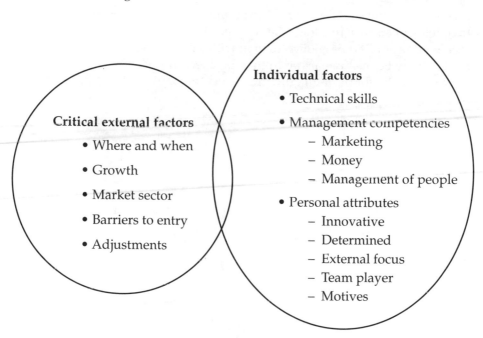

Figure 10.6 Critical factors in small business strategies

Unit 3 (section 5, Critical survival factors) summarised the external factors listed above. Unit 2 (section 6, Towards successful entrepreneurship) analysed the building blocks of successful entrepreneurship which make up the individual factors. This Unit has added the important ingredient of motives. Together these factors influence the likelihood of success or failure. The overlapping circles indicate the inter-dependence of these forces. For example, the importance of individual factors such as management competencies varies according to the sector in which the firm is set up, just as the decision on which sector to start a new venture in is influenced by personal factors and previous experience.

Few entrepreneurs develop a business in which all these factors are favourably disposed. If a complete set of favourable influences is not attainable, which are the most significant ones to get right? Research into successful small firms provides some guidance: evidence from several studies[19] suggests that the success of a small firm depends more upon the policies it adopts than the buoyancy of the markets in which it operates. External influences are less important than individual factors, particularly the management competencies and the personal attributes to cope with the small business environment. Some individuals succeed as entrepreneurs when the odds seem stacked against them, whilst others fail when the conditions for success are relatively good.

5.2 Intended and emergent strategies

Strategies can be deliberate, consciously intended courses of action. They can also emerge as a pattern with no advance deliberation. Realised small business strategies are invariably a mixture of both.

☐ **Intended strategy**

Strategy may be formulated as a deliberate plan of stated, or unstated, intentions. Some small businesses produce a business plan before start up, which sets out their intended course of action. Others do not formally document a plan, but intentions are thought through in advance in a deliberate and purposeful way.

☐ **Emergent strategy**

Some strategies are not conceived in advance but emerge as a consistent pattern during the course of events. Examples of strategies that emerge as patterns, before conversion to intended strategies, include:

○ *Marketing approaches which are often on a reactive basis until a pattern emerges.*

A small firm had no intended strategy about the size of its customer base. But one customer liked their products so much that they ordered more and more. There was no time to find other customers, as this one demanded so much attention. A strategy of concentrating 80 per cent of production capacity on one customer emerged. After a while, the owner realised the dangers in this and deliberately decided to follow a strategy of broadening the customer base.

○ *Management strategies, especially those involving people, often emerge as unplanned reactions to factors previously unknown.*

A small retailer employed mainly part-time staff, as they found that the best applicants for advertised vacancies were invariably those only able to work on a part-time basis. When this pattern was recognised, the owner consciously adopted a policy of seeking part-time staff.

○ *Money strategies are sometimes difficult to deliberately plan, except in the short to medium term.*

A small manufacturer did not intend a strategy of long-term bank borrowing. But when the owner reviewed the bank statements over a two-year period, the overdraft never fell below £30,000. A pattern of borrowing had emerged, and the bank manager advised recognition of this strategy by converting the fixed element of the overdraft into a 10-year loan.

Patterns that emerge from a small firm's activities become strategies, even though they are not formally designed that way.

☐ **Realised strategy**

In practise even the most carefully planned strategy is not fully implemented; there will be an emergent aspect to it. Emergent strategies, once spotted for what they are, often become subject to some form of planning. Strategies which are implemented, or realised, are therefore usually a mixture of intended and emergent strategies. A small business will exist somewhere on the continuum between very planned, deliberate strategies to frequently unplanned, unstructured approaches. Where exactly they fit will depend on the personality of the owner-manager(s) and the nature of the objectives of the business. An ambitious entrepreneur, who believes in the detailed planning of every move, might operate at the intended end of the spectrum. At the other, emergent extreme, might be a craftsman living day to day, content to keep their business as it is.

❐ **Adjusting strategy**

Adjustments to existing strategies are an important part of small business survival and growth, (see Unit 3, 3.2, Adjusting to uncertainty). The ability of the owner-manager to learn from any problems or mistakes and rapidly adjust their business accordingly is key to success.

An important corollary to this, is the importance of understanding which strategies can be adjusted quickly and which decisions, once taken, have longer term impact.

For example, a retailer had two strategic decisions to make when opening a second branch to their original shop. The first decision was where to locate the new shop. The second was what to stock in it. The first decision is likely to be more critical than the second as it is much harder to adjust or change if required. A shop lease may be hard to pass on, and can still remain a liability many years after the premises have been sub-let to someone else. Whilst the stock available for sale is a crucial marketing decision, the owner-manager may have more flexibility in their decision making, especially if he or she can obtain sale-or-return terms from suppliers and move stock between shops.

Strategy may seem a word more applicable to larger organisations than small. However, small businesses are similarly influenced by their strategic choices. The common perception might be that the typical small business is more often than not at the emergent end of the spectrum, whilst larger organisations are more deliberate in their strategic processes. There is little hard evidence to support this view. Some commentators view entrepreneurial strategy as more toward the intended than the emergent end of the spectrum[20]. The focused control of small enterprise certainly makes the process of formulating strategy easier than in larger organisations. The sheer size and complexity of some enterprises means that changing existing patterns to a deliberate new strategy is a difficult task. In a small business, the owner-manager can embark on a new strategy with minimal consultation and communication.

6 Case studies and activities

Case studies *Circumspect strategies*

Case 1 Kit Hugos cycles into trouble

Kit Hugos's electronics company, Circumspect, was at another critical phase in its development. In fact, recently, every year seemed to be a critical one. It had taken him the first three years after start up to grow to a viable size of around £400,000 sales, with some element of profitability. This had been too long for his partner Robin Davidson. Impatient with the lack of growth, he had sold Kit some of his shares and become very much a non-executive director.

Then in the fourth year sales had levelled off, caused, as Kit discovered, by some fundamental changes in the marketplace around him. Kit's timely investigation into the marketplace had provided him with the clues to refocus his business. His initial orders had come from industries dependent on military expenditure. Determined to reduce his reliance on this vulnerable sector, he had turned his attention to developing commercial-sector customers, where his technology base might be in demand. He had found them in the automotive industry, which was rapidly expanding the number of electronic components in domestic and commercial vehicles.

'Whereas a car today might have 30 per cent of its equipment containing electronic components, tomorrow it will be 60 per cent', one manufacturer had told him.

Focusing on this particular opportunity had required extra money to buy new equipment for his factory, and, as it turned out, to finance a new surge in growth of his business as well. His market strategy paid off, as sales climbed to over £500,000 by the end of his fifth year. Unfortunately, he then almost ran out of money. The growth put increasing strains on his financial resources and systems. Debtors grew as a percentage of sales, and up to date, reliable accounting information was very hard to find. It took Kit some time to re-establish control of his cash flow, and put in some systems to cope with a business that was no longer very small.

With a full order book, Kit was content to spend most of the sixth year working on the efficiency of his company – first the financial aspects, and then the operating systems. Quality control was something he found particularly in need of attention, as customers were becoming more and more demanding in that area. He had little time for marketing, but sales stayed buoyant, rising to over £600,000 by the end of year 6.

The improvements made meant that when he did turn his attention once again to sales in year 7, he could seek out new customers with increased confidence that he could provide an excellent service.

The trouble was that the time between arousing a customer's interest and receiving and fulfilling orders was a long one in his business of electronic design. The amount of time he had spent internally and not externally began to show through in the seventh year, when his order book had a distinctly thin look about it. Shipments flattened off, and annual sales showed no real increase over the prior year. He redoubled his marketing efforts, spending long hours travelling to see customers.

After a year in which turnover had levelled off, and his business had a definite mature look about it, sales began to grow healthily in year 8. It was at this stage that Kit sat down to review where he was going. He talked to an old friend about it one day.

'The trouble is', Kit explained, 'that I seem to stagger from one extreme to the other. Every year is crucial for different reasons. When will I have a normal business that is not in some kind of crisis?'

'What exactly has been the pattern of these crises?' asked the friend.

'Stop-start-stop-start would be the best way to describe it', replied Kit. 'The order book looks thin, so I spend my time out selling. I fill up my order book, then the supervisor in the factory yells that she can't cope unless I spend time with her, to sort out production schedules and the ordering of components. Then my accountant tells me that debtors are a bit high, and I should spend some time chasing money. So I take time out to sort out these problems. What happens? You've guessed it. The order book weakens, and I have to dash off and drum up some more business. I'm not sure if I can cope with this up and down existence much longer.'

'Have you thought of getting anyone else in to help, at a senior level I mean', suggested the friend.

'Sure, I'd love to, but the business can't afford two of us right now. A good man at director level is going to cost the company at least £40,000. That's all the profit we make right now. I need to grow the business by another £100,000 sales to afford someone. But I'm not sure I can do it on my own.'

Activities

i) Map out the stages which Circumspect has been through so far. Try to draw this as a life-cycle graph indicating the key category of problem(s) experienced in each stage.

ii) What strategies has Kit adopted at each stage to overcome the problems?

iii) What is the principal category of problem that faces Kit right now? What do you think he should do about it? Outline the strategy you would recommend that he adopt, with some specific activities.

Extended activity *A strategic case study*

Consider a successful business which has had high growth in recent years. This may be one with which you are personally familiar, or a well known large company that has grown from small roots in recent times, (such as The Body Shop or Virgin if you have been following their fortunes).

How would you summarise its overall business strategy? Try to do this by reference to the '4 Ms' of management, marketing, money and motives (or objectives of the business).

Which of its strategies would you say were intended, and which have emerged as a pattern of activities over some time?

Case 2 End of a decade at Circumspect

Kit Hugos was celebrating 10 years in business with his bank manager.

'It's quite an achievement to survive a decade in your own business. Most small businesses don't make it this far. How does it feel?' asked the bank manager.

'Oh, I obviously feel very pleased to have survived. But right now I also feel quite sad. It's rather like watching one of your own children grow up, knowing that one day they have to leave you', replied Kit.

'Surely you're not retiring?' asked the bank manager.

'No, not exactly', explained Kit, 'but I have to change something. Young managers these days don't seem to have the same approach as our generation. Take my operations director; he's just decided to give all the shop floor workers Friday afternoon off from 3pm. He says that it's modern working practice, but I'd like to know how he's going to make up the lost time, and hit his production targets.

'Oh and talking of targets, my new accountant is target-mad! We joke that if anything moves, she gives it a budget, but it's almost true. Everything we do is allocated somewhere and costed against targets. It can be useful, but it's made the whole place so bureaucratic, forms for everything', complained Kit.

'You don't have to tell me about forms', said the bank manager, 'but doesn't the business need this type of organisation now?'

'Well it didn't before I hired all these managers. I sometimes think they are just making a job for themselves. Now they want to bring in consultants to introduce total quality management. Why we need an outsider to come in and teach us the latest jargon I'm not sure', said Kit. 'I'm beginning to think I've got the wrong team. These MBAs don't seem very practical people for a small business.'

'You're not so small any more', commented the bank manager. 'Your turnover has certainly jumped up since you enlarged your management team. What do you think it will be this year?'

'Well we might even make £2 million. I suppose this is my biggest problem. We're selling more than ever, and growing by 30 to 40 per cent per annum, but I'm not getting any benefits personally. There's no more cash for me to pay myself, and I'm not getting the same satisfaction from my work. I feel they resent my interference except in technical matters where they're always asking for help. What do you think I should do?' Kit asked.

'Well, forty-eight is a bit young for retirement', joked the bank manager. 'Ever thought of selling the business?'

'My accountant tells me to wait a few more years. Although we've grown fast, the profits will not materialise for a while. We've grown the overhead very quickly and it can cope with quite a lot more volume. Just at the moment though our ratios wouldn't look too good in any sale prospectus', answered Kit.

'I'm going to have to put up with them, or put them out, I can't decide which.'

Activities

i)   Why do you think Kit is facing the problems he describes?

ii)   What do you think Kit should do about his problems? If you were Kit what questions would you be asking yourself?

In conclusion

Once you have finished this Unit, it is recommended that you turn to Section B, Planning a new venture, and complete Step 3.2, Deciding the strategy.

7   References and further reading

References and further information

1.   Curran, J. 'The small firm: a neglected area of management' in Cowling, A. Stanworth, J., Bennett, R., Curran, J. and Lyons, P. (eds), *Behavioural Sciences for Managers*, Arnold, 1988.

2.   See for example, Scott, M. and Bruce, R. 'Five Stages of Growth in Small Business', *Long Range Planning*, 20 (3) 1987. This describes the stages as: inception, survival, growth, expansion, maturity. They also suggest that crisis points fall before the next stage of development.

3.   See Part I, Unit 3, The small business environment, sub section 3.1, Small business closure rates, which reviewed some statistics on small business longevity.

4.   Stokes, D. and Blackburn, R. *Opening up Business Closures: a Study of Businesses that Close and Owner-manager Exits*, Small Business Research Centre, Kingston University, 2001.

5.   According to the Management Charter Initiative (MCI), the key purpose of management is: to achieve the organisation's objectives and continuously monitor its objectives. *Occupational Standards*, MCI, The National Forum for Management Education and Development, 1991.

6.   *A Survey of Owner-Managed Businesses*, Department of Employment, September 1990.

7.   *The Quarterly Survey of Small Business in Britain*, Small Business Research Trust, Open University (2nd Q.) 1991.

8.   See especially Golby, C. W. and Johns, G. 'Attitudes and Motivation', Committee of Inquiry on Small firms, *Research Report No. 7*. HMSO, 1971.

9.   Identities of artisan, classical entrepreneur and manager are from Stanworth, J. and Curran, J. 'Growth and the Small Firm' in Curran, J., Stanworth, J. and Watkins, D. (eds), *The Survival of the Small Firm*, Vol. 2, Gower, 1986.

Identities of technocentric, marketeer, and isolationist, are from Goss, D. *Small Business and Society*, Routledge, 1991.

10. Small Business Service, *SME Statistics for the UK, 2000*, SBS, 2001.

11. Watkins, D. 'Management Development and the Owner-manager' in Webb, T., Quince, T. and Watkins, D. (eds), *Small Business Research*, Gower, 1982.

12. Berryman, J. 'Small Business Failure and Bankruptcy: A Survey of the Literature', *International Small Business Review*, 1, 1983.

13. Cromie, S. 'The Problems Experienced by Young Firms', *International Small Business Journal*, 9 (3), 1991.

14. Watkins, D. and Morton, T. 'Small Firms in Britain and Europe: the Perceived Environment' in Watkins, D., Stanworth, J. and Westrip, A. (eds), *Stimulating Small Firms*, Gower 1982.

15. Harris, D. 'Where those Business Angels Fear to Tread', *The Times*, March 13, 1993.

16. See Quinn, J. *Strategies for Change*, Irwin, 1980.

17. Storey, D. *Understanding the Small Business Sector*, Thomson International Business Press, 1998.

18. Drucker, P. *Innovation and Entrepreneurship*, Heinemann, 1985.

19. Hall, G. *Surviving and Prospering in the Small Firm Sector*, Routledge, 1995. From his own research and a review of other studies, this author concluded that 'internal efficiency would appear more important then the general state of the environment'.

20. See Mintzberg, H. 'Opening up the Definition of Strategy' in Quinn, J., Mintzberg, H. and James, R. (eds), *The Strategy Process*, Prentice Hall, 1988. In this Mintzberg describes entrepreneurial strategy as relatively deliberate because it is the personal unarticulated vision of a single leader.

Recommended further reading

❐ O'Gorman, C. 'Strategy and the Small Firm', in Carter, S. and Jones-Evans, D. *Enterprise and Small Business*, FT/Prentice Hall, 2000.

❐ Storey, D. *Understanding the Small Business Sector*, Thomson International Business Press, 1998. Chapter 5, 'The growth of small firms'.

❐ Drucker, P. *Innovation and Entrepreneurship*, Heinemann, 1985. Chapter 15, 'The New Venture'.

❐ Cromie, S. 'The Problems Experienced by Young Firms', *International Small Business Journal*, 9 (3), 1991.

❐ Quinn, J., Mintzberg, H. and James, R. (eds) *The Strategy Process*, Prentice Hall, 1988. Chapter 1 'The Strategy Concept'.

❐ Hall, G. *Surviving and Prospering in the Small Firm Sector*, Routledge, 1995.

11 Management of resources

This Unit considers the first of the '3 Ms': management of resources. There are distinctive aspects to managing in a small, compared to a large, organisation and we examine first how impersonal resources are managed in the small firm context. The management of people, and the development of a management team, is often the crucial owner-manager role, particularly in a growing firm, and this is evaluated from a practical and a more theoretical perspective.

Contents

Activity 1 Is there a difference?

Is management of a small business intrinsically different to management in a large organisation? If so, in what ways?

1 There is a difference

1.1 The influence of smallness

How does managing a small firm differ from that of a larger organisation? We have already seen that the small business environment exerts some pressures, which can be different to the influences on larger organisations. Problems of the availability or cost of finance, the burden of government regulations and paperwork, and shortages of suitable premises, are examples of the preoccupations that might concern the manager of a small enterprise (see also Unit 3, The small business environment).

However, differences in the environment are probably as great between sectors defined by products or markets, as they are between those delineated by size of company. For example, the external influences on a large engineering company manufacturing capital equipment for industrial customers, will be very different to those on a building society offering financial services to domestic markets. Such environment differences can be just as significant as those between a large and a small company.

But the small scale of a business does bring some common problems and influences, some of which are listed in Figure11.1 below.

- Small management team
- Total management with multi-functional roles for managers
- No specialist personnel or support functions
- Scope for autocratic leadership style by owner-manager
- Informal control systems
- Closeness of working group
- Limited control of environment
- Limited resources to research the environment
- Limited market and usually small market share
- Limited product range, although flexibility within it
- Technology limited in terms of scale
- Limited leverage in obtaining financial resources

Adapted from The Small Business Challenge to Management Education[1]

Figure 11.1 Influences of small size on management

Some of these influences relate to the lack of specialist management in the firm. 'Total' management of an autocratic style and the use of informal control systems often arise from the very real pressure of time in a small business environment. Other influences reflect a sense of helplessness in the face of external forces, with no real resources to research the environment, let alone control it. All the influences imply limited resources in terms of money, marketing and management.

1.2 Total management

What sets small business management apart is the enormity of the range of issues confronting owner-managers, which they have to deal with personally. The internal structure of a small business creates the need for a different management approach. In a larger company, the chief executive is head of a team of specialists in production, finance, marketing, personnel and other functions. There will be a clear distinction between those planning the future of the business in the longer term, and those implementing the strategy on a day to day basis. The small business owner-manager has to do it all. They are generalists who will have to turn their hand to all functions from sales to production. They are the planners and the implementors, responsible for deciding strategy and making it happen and also filling out the VAT form while they're about it.

This scale and diversity of issues to be dealt with is a unique feature of small business management. Of course no manager can hope to be expert in all fields, and advice or training is often needed. However, the required skill is not always the trouble for an owner-manager faced with a multitude of problems, demanding attention simultaneously. Having the experience and understanding necessary to know how to choose which problem to deal with first is often the difficulty.

It is tempting to always tackle the most immediate first; for a small business this may mean overlooking a less obvious, but more significant problem which has a critical impact.

The juggler and the conductor

The analogy has been drawn between the owner-manager and the entertainer spinning dozens of plates on poles, all of which need attention to keep them going[2]. One false move, one touch out of sequence, and they all crash down.

By contrast, the chief executive of a larger company is likened to a conductor of an orchestra; their leadership can profoundly influence the result, but their attention can wander without stopping the orchestra from playing.

In contrast to the conductor of an orchestra, who can walk away for a while without the players stopping, the owner-manager is involved in many functions which require constant attention. The next section reviews some of the resources which are part of this difficult juggling act.

Activity 2 Management issues

The small business manager is responsible for many decisions in the early days of a new venture. How many specific decisions can you think of? List as many as possible under the headings of operations, people, marketing and finance.

(As this could develop into a major task, you may need to give yourself a time limit of, say, 2 minutes in which to write down as many issues to be resolved as possible.)

2 Use of resources

Management is about using resources efficiently in order to meet the objectives of the enterprise.

In the start-up, and early years of a small firm, the owner-manager(s) will be responsible for all significant decisions regarding:

❑ what resources are needed;

❑ where they will come from;

❑ how they will be used;

❑ how their use will be controlled and monitored.

This adds up to an almost endless combination of different responsibilities and activities. Some examples of these are shown in Figure 11.2, Management of resources in a small firm[3], which breaks the issues down into the four main areas of (a) operations, (b) people, (c) marketing, and (d) finance.

MANUFACTURING PROCESSES	MATERIALS
• equipment required	• products and services to be bought in
• costs and methods of finance	• suppliers
• operating systems and controls	• costs and credit terms
• safety regulations	• purchase order systems
• quality control	• storage systems
• operator training	• goods inward
• maintenance	
PREMISES	**OFFICE EQUIPMENT**
• location	• telephone systems
• space requirements	• office furniture
• leasehold vs freehold	• computer equipment
• rent and rates and insurance	• WP software
• maintenance and cleaning	• database software
• environmental controls	• stationery items
• enterprise zones/assisted areas	• photocopier
• security	
MANAGEMENT SYSTEMS	**LEGAL AND INSURANCE**
• accounting systems	• employers liability insurance
• financial management information	• fire and theft insurance
• stock control	• loss of profits insurance
• debtor and creditor control	• public liability
• cost controls	• professional indemnity
• order book	• key man insurance
• mail in and out	• engineering breakdown insurance
• filing	• employment law regulations (toilets; first aid; washing water; drinking water; notice board)
	• certificate display (fire and insurance)
	• company law requirements

Figure 11.2(a)   Management of resources in a small firm: some issues to be resolved – OPERATIONS

RECRUITMENT AND DISMISSAL
- job titles
- job definition
- person specification
- advertising/agencies
- interviewing
- offers/rejections
- anti-discrimination (race/sex/unions)
- written statements
- redundancy
- notice periods

POLICIES
- rates of pay
- full time/part time
- commission/bonus
- fringe benefits
- safe working environment

RECORDS AND SYSTEMS
- contracts
- personnel records
- payroll/PAYE and NIC
- lateness/sickness
- holidays
- grievance procedures
- sick pay
- maternity pay

POLICIES
- wage/salary review
- overtime
- training
- pension schemes

Figure 11.2(b)   Management of resources in a small firm: some issues to be resolved – PEOPLE

MARKET RESEARCH
- evaluation of competitors
- evaluation of customers
- evaluation of market needs
- primary market research
- secondary market research
- sales prospects lists
- enquiries logging
- customer sales records
- customer visit records
- database/mailing list
- order conversion rates

PRODUCT
- main benefits
- key features
- extended product opportunities
  (after sales service; guarantees/warranties)
- product development
- R and D
- licensing opportunities
- collaborative ventures

PRICING
- price lists
- market/competitor pricing
- variable costs
- fixed costs per unit
- gross margins/mark-ups
- discounts
- logo
- contract pricing
- price increases

PROMOTION
- direct selling
- use of agents
- advertising
- listings in directories
- direct mail
- press releases
- house style
- signage
- shop layout
- window display
- merchandisers
- selling aids
- leaflets and brochures

DISTRIBUTION
- use of intermediaries
  (wholesale; retail; mail order)
- export agents
- physical distribution & transport
- goods out system
- inspection
- packaging

SALES ADMINISTRATION
- order book valuation
- order acknowledgements
- quotations/estimates
- delivery
- payment terms and conditions
- invoice/credit note queries
- customer queries
- sales leads follow-up
- export documentation
- complaints and response

Figure 11.2(c)   Management of resources in a small firm: some issues to be resolved – MARKETING

SALES	DEBTORS
• invoicing	• statements
• sales ledger	• chasing letters
• payments procedures	• telephone follow-up
• banking (cash; cheques)	• stop supply date
• credit notes	• legal action date
• sales of assets	• write off date
• bad cheques	• debtor information (aged analysis; by customer; by product)
BANKING	TAX
• current account	• VAT
• deposit account	• PAYE
• cheque book(s)	• NIC
• signatories	• P 11 D
• statements	• Corporation Tax
• reconciliation to cash book	• Personal Tax
• bank manager relationships	• Capital Gains
• interest	• Stamp duty
• bank charges	
• credit cards	
PURCHASES	CREDITORS
• purchase orders	• credit terms and references
• authorisation of orders	• authorisation of invoices
• cost control systems	• payments system
• expense accounts	• creditor information (aged analysis; by customer; by product)
• chasing of suppliers	
• goods-in system	
MANAGEMENT ACCOUNTS	SOURCES OF FINANCE
• ledgers (purchase; sales; nominal)	• overdraft facility
• cash book	• bank loan
• petty cash	• shareholders' investment
• cash forecast	• director's loans
• management accounts (P&L; balance sheets)	• outside investors
	• venture capital
• audit arrangements	• government assistance
• filing of accounts	

Figure 11.2(d)   Management of resources in a small firm: some issues to be resolved – FINANCE

Activity 3 Where is the best location?

What factors do you think the owner-manager should take into account in locating the premises of their business?

Which do you think is the most common deciding factor in practice?

3 Operating resources

A key management area for the small business owner is the selection, acquisition, use and control of operating resources. Under this heading we include many of the impersonal resources that a manager controls, such as premises, materials, machinery, equipment and systems.

3.1 Premises

In a start-up situation, the location and type of premises is often a first considera-tion. Key questions for an owner-manager will be:

❐ **Where is the business to be located?**

Kitchen tables (and even a telephone kiosk in the case of Richard Branson) have provided many new ventures with a first, low-cost working facility. Once independent premises become necessary there are many considerations to be taken into account, such as:

○ ease of communication (e.g. road and rail);

○ availability of labour, especially for any process requiring specific skills;

○ proximity to centres of population: this is a key factor for retail, catering and hotel businesses;

○ costs of rent and rates; these still vary considerably even within relatively short distances;

○ government and local authority assistance: there are a variety of ways in which specific geographic regions try to stimulate the growth of small business. Regional Selective Assistance (RSA) offers grants for investment in some areas[4].

○ proximity to the home of the founder of the small business. Research[5] has indicated that, in practice, this is the most important consideration in deciding the location of a small firm. Very few founders move their homes in order to set up a new business.

❐ **What type of premises are needed?**

The nature of the business will largely dictate the type of premises required. Considerations will include the facilities, the appearance, the size and layout, and the physical environment of the premises.

❐ **What are the legal and financial implications?**

Taking on a lease can be a major commitment for a small business, especially for an owner-manager who may have to give personal guarantees. As well as the obligation to pay rent and rates, the tenant will normally be obliged to pay for the insurance, maintenance and repair of leasehold property (for fuller details of the implications of acquiring freehold and leasehold premises, see Unit 7, Buying an existing business).

❐ **Are the right premises available?**

Finding suitable premises has been a major problem for many small firms. In the 1970s and early 1980s, several surveys showed that difficulties over premises, particularly in inner city areas, were a constraint on the develop-ment of small businesses[6]. Armed with a study carried out by Coopers and Lybrand in 1980 which concluded that there is clear evidence that the shortage of premises has constrained the establishment and development of small firms[7], central government became increasingly critical of local government planning policies. As a result public authorities and developers have now provided many more units suitable for small businesses. It has also been shown that small firms tend to relocate quite frequently as they grow[5]; requirements can change quite rapidly from small space in a fully serviced, shared unit to larger, more independent premises. Flexibility of tenure is therefore needed, in addition to the right size of premises in a good location, with appropriate facilities. These needs have been increasingly met by local councils, Enterprise Agencies, British Coal and British Steel Enterprises (formed to promote new business activity in areas of high job losses), business centres, business parks and science parks.

3.2 Materials and equipment

Purchasing of materials and equipment is a key management activity in many small firms, especially manufacturers and retailers.

❒ **Materials**

Materials purchased fall into two basic types:

○ *Goods to be sold, either modified or unchanged.* This includes the stocks of raw materials for a manufacturer, retail stocks in a shop, food ingredients in a restaurant, and building materials in the construction industry.

○ *Consumable items, indirectly supporting the business.* This includes stationery, publicity material, and reference catalogues.

Larger manufacturing companies and retailers will normally employ specialist buyers; the owner-manager usually fulfils this role in the formative years, perhaps handing over routine ordering to an office manager or assistant as the business develops. Good management of this function can assist the small firm in a number of ways:

○ ensuring that the right material for the job is always purchased;

○ reduction in costs: time spent on researching and negotiating with suppliers can result in lower buying prices;

○ availability of stock: poor purchasing systems can easily lose sales because a manufacturer cannot produce on time, a retailer runs out of a popular line, or a construction company develops a reputation for delays;

○ reduction in stock: just-in-time purchasing policies ensure adequate availability, whilst minimising stock levels to keep down the working capital requirements of the small firm.

Despite these benefits, many owner-managers neglect the purchasing function, and fail to build good relationships with suppliers. The demands of other activities which may have more immediate effect, often take precedence; for example, the visiting representative from a supplier is put off or not seen at all, as the owner-manager struggles to keep up with other demands on their time. Alternative supply sources are often not followed up because it is easier not to change from the existing supplier.

❐ **Equipment**

The infrastructure of a small firm is made up principally of various categories of equipment, representing a key resource to be managed. These categories include:

○ *Production machinery and equipment:* this is obviously specific to the type of manufacturing process.

○ *Communication equipment:* telephone, fax and word processing systems are becoming increasingly sophisticated at the level a small business can afford.

○ *Office or retail furniture:* image as well as functionality will influence the selection of furniture for public areas of a small firm.

○ *Systems equipment:* this category represents an area of increasing expenditure for small businesses, as it includes computer hardware and software for a variety of applications, including word processing accounts, databases and stock control. Cash registers and tills for retail outlets are also often part of a wider computerised system, capable of generating accounting, sales and stock control information as well as performing the basic function of monitoring cash intake.

○ *Personal equipment:* cars, mobile telephones and portable computers are the main items of equipment that a small business manager may consider, especially if their work involves travelling to visit customers or suppliers.

❐ **Finance**

Owner-managers often buy equipment on lease or lease purchase at real rates of interest above those applying to normal bank borrowing. Commentators have therefore been critical of small firm management for its use of financial resources to acquire equipment. Whilst there are, no doubt, cases where small firms do pay more in finance costs than they need, there are often valid objections to looking beyond lease or lease purchase. It is often easier and less time consuming to arrange leasing, and owner-managers may wish to keep their bank borrowing potential available for other purposes, such as the funding of expansion or losses, for which there are fewer alternatives.

3.3 Insurance

The purpose of insurance is to minimise risks. As small firms are particularly vulnerable to one-off disasters, an important management issue will be the choice of appropriate insurance policies to mitigate the effect of misfortune.

❐ **Obligatory insurance**

In some areas there is no choice. Insurance is obligatory for:

○ *Employers liability:* insurance against claims by employees who suffer injury or illness as a result of their employment is required by law.

○ *Third party vehicle insurance:* company vehicles are subject to the same legal requirement as private vehicles, and need at least third party insurance.

○ *Specified insurances:* some contracts will stipulate a requirement for insurance. Leases for premises normally require the tenant to take out property insurance. Lease or lease purchase agreements for equipment usually insist on a specified insurance cover.

❏ **Discretionary insurance**

Other insurance is not obligatory, but more or less desirable according to the circumstances of the business and the owner-managers. They include:

○ *Fire, theft and other disasters:* covering premises and their contents, stock and goods in transit.

○ *Engineering breakdown:* equipment can be insured for the costs of repair in the case of breakdown or damage.

○ *Loss of profits:* in the event of fire, theft, breakdown and other misfortunes, a small firm can suffer not just the costs of replacement or repair, but the loss of profits whilst it is out of action. Insurance can cover these other costs of disruptions.

○ *Public and product liability:* in the event of injury to members of the public or damage to their property. Because of the size and frequency of claims in the USA, this insurance is particularly advisable for companies exporting to North America.

○ *Professional indemnity:* against claims of misconduct or negligence in performing a professional service.

○ *Legal costs insurance:* provides cover in the event of a legal dispute with customers, suppliers or employees.

○ *Key man insurance:* a small firm is usually heavily dependent on one person, or a small number of people, whose death would jeopardise the future of the enterprise. Key man insurance helps by paying a large sum so that at the very least a business can cover its debts if a key person dies.

○ *Personal insurance:* owner-managers are usually advised to take out life, permanent health and pension policies to protect their family and themselves.

Activity 4 What information does the small business manager need?

Records needed in a small firm are not just accounting ones. What other information does a small business need? Specify some general areas, with some examples in each.

4 Management information systems

To help the small business manager in their seemingly impossible task of juggling with all the important variables that could affect their business, management information systems are becoming increasingly available and affordable. Whilst manual systems are still common, and advisable in some situations, computerised systems are helping the small firm more and more to develop not only adequate records, but controls as well.

The economies of scale, available to larger firms in computerisation of important information areas, have been gradually eroded by the availability of hardware and software which has reduced in price, whilst it has increased in scope, power, flexibility and user friendliness. Quite sophisticated systems are now available to a small business to cover all major management functions. The Internet services, particularly email and the World Wide Web, are used by rapidly growing numbers of small firms.

Many owner managers, however, have learned the lesson that it is more important to keep basic records in a methodical way right from the start of a new business, than to spend time installing sophisticated systems whilst overlooking more fundamental paperwork flows, and information requirements.

Another common error is to assume that record keeping and systems are primarily financial in function. Whilst accounting records are at the heart of any small firm's systems, every other management function benefits from an information system. Figure 11.3 is a summary of areas where records are necessary, or may be desirable, for a small firm. Whilst not all these categories are applicable to every small firm, the list does appear formidable. Paperwork, especially that generated by government regulations, is a constant source of complaint by many owner-managers[8]. Unfortunately, these complaints often overlook the real benefits which can result from the use of information in all areas of small business management.

Activity 5 Harmony or conflict?

Some people believe that small businesses tend to make a happier working environment than larger organisations.

Do you agree? Which factors may help a small business to become a more harmonious place to work? Which may cause more conflict?

5 Management of people

Small firms employing up to 50 people now account for half of all UK private sector employment[9]. Although 70 per cent of small businesses employ only the owner, there are over a million that do have employees, and their role as an employer is becoming more significant (see Unit 1 'Small business in the economy', section 3 for a more detailed discussion). In these small firms, people will be the key resource. The management of other people is often the most important role played by the owner-manager. Like all other functional areas in a new start up, the owner-manager will tend to take control of the personnel function. It is also the function which the owner-manager is least likely to give up as the firm grows. Rarely is a trained human resources manager appointed from outside, as even high growth small firms tend to make do in this area. It is also the function in which owner-managers assess themselves as having the lowest level of expertise[10].

SALES
- potential customers
- sources of enquiries
- follow-up statistics
- conversion rates
- time management of sales people
- volume and value of sales (by customer; by product; by time period)
- order book value and changes
- product margins
- price movements and elasticity of demand
- effectiveness of promotions
- direct mail response/order rates
- sales by distribution agent/retail outlet

FINANCE
- cash book
- petty cash book
- sales ledger
- purchase ledger
- nominal ledger
- banking records and reconciliations
- VAT/PAYE/NIC
- budgets
- cash flow
- management accounts
- debtor analysis
- creditor analysis
- costs analysis
- sales and gross margins
- fixed asset register
- annual accounts

PRODUCTION
- productivity measures (by operators; by machine; by time period)
- wastage
- rejects
- breakdowns
- critical path for orders
- quality control
- work in progress
- goods-out

PURCHASING
- stock turn
- stock valuation
- purchase specifications
- supplier quotations
- orders and acknowledgements
- invoice approval
- goods-in
- direct material costs

PERSONNEL
- employee records
- PAYE/NIC references
- wages payments
- time sheets
- overtime
- absenteeism
- holidays booked and taken
- statutory sick pay
- statutory maternity pay
- pension contributions

Figure 11.3 Management information systems for the small firm: areas where records are necessary or desirable

5.1 Employment law

One reason for the low level of confidence of owner-managers in their personnel role is the complexity of employment law. An employee gains rights according to the length of time they are employed by a firm. Figure 11.4 summarises some of the main obligations of the owner-manager as an employer. Although at first sight, these legal rights may seem weighted towards the employee, in practice, owner-managers can employ who they want, and remove those they do not want, provided they behave reasonably. This involves abiding by the regulations, and giving employees the opportunity to explain themselves in the event of a problem[11].

Length of employment	Legal obligation of employer

Recruitment	• no discrimination because of:
	    • race
	    • sex
	    • marriage
	    • union membership
	    • disabled
	 • collect income tax and national insurance for the Inland Revenue (collect P45 or P46)
	 • written statement on health and safety (5+ employees)
	 • employers liability insurance

1 month plus	• minimum notice period 1 week (2 weeks after 2 years, and 1 week for each additional year, to 12 weeks maximum, unless contract states more) • pay guarantee payments if no work available
2 months	• provide employee with a written statement of the main terms and conditions of employment, i.e. job title, pay, hours, holiday, sick pay, notice, pension
6 months plus	• pay statutory maternity pay
1 year plus	• do not dismiss unfairly and give written reasons, which can be: incapability of doing job, misconduct, illegality of employment, redundancy or other substantial reason • do not dismiss because of pregnancy • give job back to employee returning from maternity leave
2 years plus	• give redundancy pay to redundant employees working 16 hours + (0.5 to 1.5 weeks pay per year of employment, depending on age and length of employment)

NB Since 1995, part-timers have the same rights as full-time workers in these areas

Figure 11.4 Employment obligations

5.2 Harmony versus conflict

The case for harmony

A widely held view is that the small firm provides a more motivational and happier working environment than the larger firm. This was certainly endorsed by the Bolton Report, which stated:

'In many aspects, the small firm provides a better working environment for the employee than is possible in most large firms. Although physical working conditions may sometimes be inferior in small firms, most people prefer to work in a small group where communications present fewer problems; the employees in the small firm can easily see the relation between what they are doing and the objectives and performance of the firm as a whole.'[12]

This opinion was based largely on earlier work, which had suggested that better personal relationships between employer and employee were made possible by the low level of bureaucracy in the small firm[13].

This picture of harmony within a small enterprise was contrasted to the confrontational industrial relations in larger firms – the all one happy family environment of the small firm, versus the them and us attitudes in larger companies.

Some evidence does seem to support this view. There are lower levels of unionisation and industrial action in smaller firms. One survey found that a large organisation (1,000+ employees) is 40 times more likely to experience industrial action than a micro firm (fewer than 10 employees), and that trade union recognition was much lower in smaller enterprises[14].

Less idealistic views

However there are several important challenges to this representation of harmonious working relations in the small firm.

The lack of unionisation and strike activity cannot be taken as synonymous with lack of conflict. There is considerable evidence that conflict expresses itself in different ways within the smaller firm[15].

Employees in small firms are difficult to organise into unions, because of the fragmentation of their workplaces, the larger numbers of part-time employees and higher labour turnover rates.

Unions, therefore, find it difficult to establish communications to encourage membership in the first place, especially as this is often hindered by owner-manager antipathy to unions. Where they are successful, unions then find that maintenance of membership is expensive. Conspicuous disputes and strikes may be relatively rare because of this lack of organisation of labour in small firms, but it does not mean that the incidence of grievances is any less. Research has confirmed that not only do small business employees feel as much discontent as those in larger organisations, but that employers also have high levels of dissatisfaction. Owner-managers frequently complain of the difficulties of finding and retaining staff with the right attitudes, behaviour and skills[15].

Other research has noted that working relationships are as much dependent on the type of industry and individual circumstances of a firm as they are on its size[16]. In this, as in other aspects, generalisation is difficult because of the huge variety of contexts in which small firms exist. Employment conditions in a high technology service firm (for example, a small firm dependent on individual expertise such as a design consultancy), are likely to be very different to those in a more traditional manufacturing company (for example, a small firm dependent on its production line, such as a bottling plant).

At the extreme, the small firm can be reduced to a sweatshop working environment with employees suffering low pay, autocratic management and poor conditions. Some research has concluded that market forces largely determine the likelihood of adverse working conditions. Rainnie[17], for example, studied small firms in the clothing industry, and observed the dependence of small garment manufacturers on large high street retailers. The buying power of large retailing chains, combined with intense rivalry amongst suppliers, who tended to be small firms because of the low barriers of entry into a fragmented industry, creates intense cost-cutting pressures on the owner-managers. They in turn tend to use autocratic methods, exploiting a captive labour market to keep down their employment costs and maximise their output.

Other circumstances also influence behaviour. Friendly relationships can be destroyed by external pressures exerting stress on employers and employees. A cash crisis can ruin the good intentions of all parties to enjoy their work. Partners often know each other socially before joining forces in a small business, and they believe their excellent relationship will continue to the benefit of the enterprise. Whilst this may be true in good times, the stress of less successful periods of trading can ruin relationships (including marriages) to the detriment of partners, managers and employees alike.

Expressions of conflict in small firms are more likely to take the form of employees leaving a firm, or a partnership breaking up, than the conventional form of disputes in larger firms. The higher than average level of labour instability in small firms, which experience higher employee turn over rates than larger firms, bears witness to the less than ideal working situation which often exists beneath the surface in a small firm.

Despite the possibility of problems, lower than average pay and less than ideal working conditions, many employees do still prefer to work in small rather than large organisations. Their experience will undoubtedly be conditioned by the type of management control exercised by the owner-manager.

5.3 Types of management control

The way in which an owner-manager exercises control over their workforce will depend not just on the personality of the manager, but also the disposition of power in the employer– employee relationship. Some circumstances will give the owner-manager, as the employer, relatively high levels of control over employees; in other situations, employees may be able to call more of the tune. For example, the owner-manager of a small firm requiring unskilled labour in an area of high unemployment is in a much more dominant position than the manager of a small enterprise, reliant on employees with specialist skills which are in short supply.

To illustrate this relationship Goss[18] identified four types of management control in small firms, which are shown in Figure 11.5.

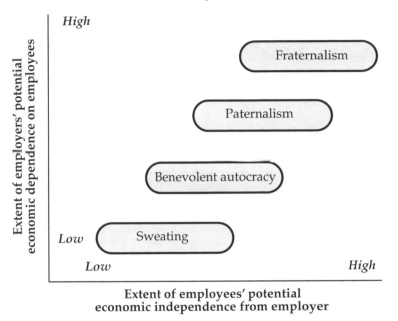

Figure 11.5 Types of management control in small firms

Fraternalism

This describes a situation where the owner-manager is heavily dependent on the skills of the employee(s) to get the job done. They in turn are relatively independent of the small firm because their expertise is in demand elsewhere. Employer and employee work alongside each other, with decisions made from a position of mutual respect. This is common in the construction and building industry and craft-based companies. For example, the owner-manager and the craftsman who work in a small joinery, specialising in the restoration of old window frames and doors, were so dependent on each other that a harmonious working relationship evolved with no formal hierarchy for decision making.

This management style is also common in some professional and high technology small businesses. For example, a private health practice, a training company or a software development business will be dependent on the skills of individuals, who can only be managed by mutual consent.

Paternalism

Where the alternatives for employees are more limited, and the employer is less dependent on them, then a paternalist management style may emerge. A clear distinction between employer and employee exists, but owner-managers are still sufficiently aware of the importance of their workforce to encourage common ties and personal relations. Farming[19] has been typified as paternalistic because of the economic situation of small farms and the traditional role of the landowner in society. Farm workers often have little choice of alternative employment, and are poorly paid. Yet the farmer is dependent on their commitment and experience, as they will be working for long hours with little supervision. Whilst maintaining a clear social and economic distance the small farmer will encourage mutual identification of aims among their farm labourers by gifts and wider community involvement.

Benevolent autocracy

This is the most common situation for a small firm; the owner-manager is less dependent on the employee, and able to exercise their influence from a position of power as an employer. However, employees are not so economically dependent on the small firm that they become totally subservient. Close links exist between employer and employee, and friendly relations exist, often on a first name basis, but this rarely extends beyond the workplace (except for an annual outing or Christmas festivity). The founder of a small electronics company, for example, chose the location of the factory to ensure a ready supply of skilled and semi-skilled labour. Although able to hire and fire more or less at will, the owner-manager was anxious to keep employee turnover to a minimum because the selection and training of new staff was expensive and time consuming. The firm developed a name in the area as a good employer, a reputation the owner was anxious to preserve by acting fairly, paying the market rate and providing reasonable working conditions.

Sweating

There are some circumstances which conspire to give the employer all the power, and the employee virtually none. We have already described the environment of parts of the clothing industry, in which fragmented suppliers, dependent on powerful buyers, exploit their labour force in order to provide a low cost, flexible service. The 'sweat shop' emerges in conditions such as these. Some workers, especially immigrant female labour, are particularly vulnerable to exploitation because they lack relevant skills in an area of high unemployment. They have little alternative but to accept low pay, and erratic employment dependent on the workload of the small firm. Their employers trade in marginal, highly competitive industries, subject to sudden rushes of orders, and then gluts of production. They survive by keeping overheads down, using poorly equipped premises and hiring and firing workers at the first indication of growth or contraction of the business.

These four examples of the types of management control are not meant to be exhaustive; there are many variations on the theme. Nor are the types mutually exclusive. In some small firms two different modes of relationship can exist side by side. An electronics design and manufacturing company, for example, employs highly skilled technicians, who enjoy an egalitarian, fraternal, relationship with the owner-manager, who is very dependent on their design expertise. The semi-skilled production operators also employed are more easily replaced, and treated in a more autocratic, although still benevolent, fashion.

What does emerge from looking at these types is that there is a highly varied pattern of management of people in the small firm. Central to them all is the owner-manager whose personal style will be conditioned by the external forces prevalent in the industry.

5.4 Personnel practices

Good practice in human resource management in larger firms relies on formalised, written procedures and longer-term planning.

Small firms tend to manage people through informal, unwritten and ad hoc practices. Much will depend on the management qualities of the owner-manager to make them work effectively.

❐ **Recruitment**

Recruitment theory advocates several formal stages to ensure the selection of the right person for the job:

○ A job description, which carefully analyses the work to be done and details the responsibilities and levels of authority of the job.

○ A person specification which attempts to match the ideal candidate to the job, reflecting essential and desirable qualifications, experience, skills and characteristics.

○ A promotional campaign advertising the vacancy to attract the best possible candidates, using advertisements and possibly recruitment agencies.

○ A short-listing and interviewing process, which is designed to find out as much as possible about the applicant, and also allows them the opportunity to find out as much as possible about the employer.

In practice the small firm tends to follow a much less structured approach.

Job descriptions and person specifications are unlikely to exist, except for management positions.

Several studies have concluded that word of mouth is the most commonly used advertising medium for job vacancies in small businesses[15]. Agencies and advertising are regarded as expenses to be avoided if at all possible, particularly as small firms are big employers of part-time staff. Interviews tend to be with owner-managers, who will be more concerned to see how well the person fits into the team than with their formal qualifications and experience.

There is evidence of some sectoral differences in this general pattern, with high technology firms, for example, more likely to follow more formal procedures[15].

❐ **Training**

Small firms have a much lower incidence of formal training, relying mainly on training on-the-job[20]. Owner-managers are reluctant to pay the price of external training, particularly the cost of losing staff for the time needed.

Although owner-managers tend to retain control over personnel matters, they also complain that people management is one of their biggest problems. Some avoid the issue altogether by remaining a one-person business, often by sub-contracting work to other self-employed people. This has the added attraction of only incurring costs when necessary. In other cases, small enterprises grow by using labour within the family rather than employing others.

5.5 The non-owner-manager

If a small firm is pursuing a strategy of growth, it needs to develop a management team. The owner-manager cannot maintain personal control over every aspect of an enterprise once it has grown to a certain size. The size at which a management structure is required will vary; some commentators have suggested that once a firm reaches 20 employees, it should begin to employ managers.

We have already examined some of the implications of this (see Unit 10, Successful small business strategies). The failure of the owner-manager to build a management team and carefully define their own role within it, can seriously threaten the growth and even the survival of a small firm. Despite this the role of the non-owner-manager has been largely neglected by researchers. A review by Curran[21] of small business research, in the fifteen years after the Bolton Report, failed to reveal a single reference to the non-owner-manager. Yet the managerial team of a small firm will be crucial to its success once it has achieved initial viability. More recent research has suggested that managers with larger company experience are more likely to help a small firm grow than those with more limited experience[22].

Not bosses but leaders

Despite the lack of detailed investigation, the management message is clear. The functions of leadership are as relevant in the small firm environment as the large. Leaders[23] are concerned with three primary functions:

○ The achievement of the task.

○ The building and maintenance of the team.

○ The support and development of the individual.

Our earlier portrayal of management in the small firm, using the analogy of the entertainer balancing plates on the ends of poles, seems to imply concentration on the achievement of the task, if the plates are to be kept up. Because the owner-manager takes on all the key roles in a small firm, the management style can become very task-oriented. There seems little time for the team, or the individuals within it, who are supporting the small enterprise. The team may not all be employed by the small firm. Financial supporters, bankers, key suppliers and customers all form part of an extended team which the owner-manager leads.

People within a small firm may also be neglected, particularly as relationships tend to rely on informal structures. The owner-manager can become so engrossed in managing the impersonal resources that they neglect the people resources. They can become preoccupied and distant, appearing as more of a boss than a leader. The appointment of managers at an early stage may be expensive (and therefore risky) but it may also represent the only way an owner-manager can fulfil the functions of leadership, and provide support for the team, as well as achieving the task.

6 Case studies and activities

Case studies *Managing restaurant resources*

Case 1 Kimberley runs into conflict

Kimberley Lawson was feeling disillusioned. Her vision of running her own happy business, removed from the hierarchy and restrictive rules of her previous employer, was rapidly crumbling. When she had bought her own restaurant a year earlier, her main aim was to get away from the politics of big business and concentrate on making her own enterprise work, with a group of like-minded people. Her background seemed ideal to make the venture successful. She had trained with a large hotel group, and gained experience in almost every aspect of catering management, from kitchen hygiene to cost accounting. She felt, after her 5 years' employment there, that she knew how to manage all the various functions that were needed to run a restaurant.

She had soon found, however, that this was not enough. She just didn't seem able to cope with all the demands on her when she had first acquired the restaurant.

'It's not that I don't know what to do', she had explained to her husband Philip, when he had enquired after noticing that Kimberley seemed particularly harassed. 'It's just that I don't know what to do first. When I worked for the Milton Group, everything was organised for you. When I was managing the coffee shop, for example, the menu had already been worked out between the marketing and the finance departments, the staff were employed by personnel, and the food ordered through purchasing. Now I have to do all that myself and manage every-thing on a daily basis as well. I don't have time to think, let alone plan ahead, and there is no one I can ask to help. Everyone else is far too busy serving customers.'

These normal problems of a small business manager were no longer her big worry however. She had eventually learned how to put priorities on her activities, and to distinguish between the most important, and the most immediate jobs, which were not always the same thing.

The real issue now was that she didn't enjoy her work any more. 'I thought running my own business would be fun not just for me, but for everyone else involved. I used to dream of working in a small firm where everyone would have the same aims, we would all know what was going on, and we wouldn't have to put up with any of the bureaucratic nonsense that we had at the Milton. What do I get instead? Hassle from him, each and every day.'

Philip nodded. He had heard similar complaints before, so he knew that the source of the trouble was one Raymond Bogaerts, master chef. He had been with the restaurant when Kimberley had bought it, and seemed like a major asset at the time. His high standards of innovative cuisine made the restaurant different to its more traditional neighbours, and had helped it to a position of high popularity.

'What's he done this time?' asked Philip.

'This time he has gone too far', raged Kimberley. 'He has refused to do what I asked, and demanded a written statement of his terms and conditions of employment. He's driving me back to the old bureaucracy just because he doesn't agree with my methods. As you know, I've suspected for some time that our waste levels in the kitchen are too high. Well now I can prove it. I've spent a lot of time analysing our food costs in relation to our prices. In theory they should be no more than a third of the menu price. They're actually over 40 per cent, simply because we are using too much food. The portions are too big; customers just cannot eat all we give them. You should see what we throw away.'

'But aren't your generous portions part of the attraction of the place?' asked Philip.

'You sound like Raymond', said Kimberley. 'He believes that we can't reduce portion sizes without losing customers. I told him that was my affair, and nothing to do with him. All he has to do is to cook what I ask. That's when he asked for a written description of his responsibilities. He says he's entitled to one, and that he doesn't like the way I've changed his job. He claims that he was always involved in any menu changes before I took over.'

'Isn't it wise to consult him anyway? He does have to run the kitchen after all', suggested Philip.

'I don't mind consulting him', said Kimberley, 'as long as he doesn't just refuse to do anything he doesn't agree with. The previous owner didn't understand menus. I do. Besides he doesn't run the kitchen. He may think he does, but I can't trust him to hire the staff any more. He fills the kitchen with part-timers that he can shout at and give work to on a favour basis as he pleases. I want professionals in my kitchen.'

Philip had heard of the chef's slave-driving tactics in the kitchen, but nevertheless tried one last effort to support him. 'Yes, but what about the costs? Aren't your staff costs a lot higher than they used to be?' he asked.

Kimberley let out a long breath before replying. 'Yes. Which is why the food costs have to come down. His way of making money is to employ inexperienced part-timers, female of course, for a pittance. My way is to pay a proper wage for trained people, who will save their extra costs by reducing waste, and generally being more professional in their work. If Raymond isn't going to accept it, he will have to go. I will make him redundant and work in the kitchen myself for a while. As I've employed him under two years, I don't think he is even entitled to redundancy money.'

Activities

i)   Many people would share Kimberley's original vision that a small business could provide a happier working environment than a larger organisation. Is this a realistic view in this particular environment?

ii) Kimberley's management style is evidently different to her predecessor's. How do you think Raymond likes to be managed? What do you think Kimberley should do? Assess her current management style, and the appropriateness of her decision to make Raymond redundant.

iii) Raymond's method of running the kitchen, with low pay and poor conditions, could be likened to the 'sweatshop'. What circumstances make it possible for these conditions to prevail in this restaurant?

iv) Two points of employment law are raised in this case:

   a)   Is the chef correct in his demand for a written statement of terms and conditions?

   b)   Is Kimberley right in thinking she will not have to pay him any redundancy money?

Extended activity *Staff assessment*

Consider a small business where you have recently been a customer which employs staff other than the owner-manager (for example a food or drinks outlet such as a restaurant, wine bar or public house considered in previous extended tasks).

How would you rate the service provided by the staff, and their general attitude to the customer?

Write a short analysis of the motivation of the staff and the type of management control which you feel this illustrates.

If you were the owner-manager of this business, how could you change staff attitudes and motivation for the benefit of the customer?

Case 2 Leading to problems

Kimberley had made progress in resolving the management problems in her restaurant. Raymond Bogaerts, the chef, had not appeared for work one day, and later telephoned to say he would not be back. Conflicts in small firms are often resolved by one person leaving the organisation.

After a moment of panic, Kimberley had breathed a sigh of relief. 'At least I can make a fresh start now that he is gone', she had thought. After a period working in the kitchen herself, she had decided that the only way to develop the business was to recruit another person to manage the kitchen. Kimberley followed the personnel practices of her previous large employer, and carefully drew up a job description and a person specification before advertising the new job. The good response enabled her to select someone she felt was the ideal candidate experienced and motivated by the thought of working in a small firm. Laura, the new head chef, was given wider responsibilities than just preparing food, so Kimberley was not too surprised when she asked to see her one morning. But the meeting was not routine; Laura had problems.

'I'm sorry to burst in on you like this, but I don't think I can manage on my own any longer', she blurted out.

'On your own?' queried Kimberley. 'I thought we had agreed to work as a team. What's the problem?'

'In a word, communications, or lack of them', said Laura. 'I need you to tell me more about what is going on. I know we agreed that teamwork is important, but I feel as though I'm working alone most of the time until something happens I don't know about, that is, like the meat delivery changing from Friday to Thursday.'

'Yes, we've been over that, and I have apologised', interrupted Kimberley, checking her watch as she was due to visit a customer that morning.

'Look, I'm not sure what you're getting at exactly, but if this business is to develop the way I thought we both agreed we wanted, then I will have to leave you to manage your area. I don't have time to do my job now that we've taken on these commercial catering contracts, let alone help you with yours. You know what to do, and you have staff of your own; can't we just get on and do it?'

'I know you're busy', said Laura, 'but I need your help now and again, and I need you to tell me what you're doing, as it does affect my work you know. I can't just get on and do it, unless I get feedback from you. Besides, it's nice to talk to someone other than the wash-up now and again.'

Kimberley smiled. 'Ok, I get the message, but not today. I have appointments to keep. I'll make a point of looking in tomorrow.'

Activities

What is your assessment now of Kimberley's management. Do you think that:

i)   She has made a mistake in her choice of kitchen manager, who does not seem very independent?

ii)   She is right to insist that, now they have agreed their responsibilities, they should get on and do it?

iii) There is anything missing in her leadership of the business?

In conclusion

Once you have finished this Unit, it is recommended that you turn to Section B, Planning a new venture, and complete Step 3.3, Managing the resources.

7 References and further reading

References and further information

1. Gibb, A. 'The Small Business Challenge to Management Education', *Journal of European Industrial Training*, 7, (5) 1983.

2. By Stan Mendham of the Forum of Private Business.

3. See also Stanworth, J. and Gray, C. (eds), *Bolton 20 Years On: The Small Firm in the 1990s*, Appendix A, PCP, 1991.

4. Regional Selective Assistance (RSA) is a scheme aimed at attracting investment in designated areas. Grants of up to 15 per cent of a project's costs are available for machinery, buildings and one-off costs such as patent rights. Further information is available from Business Links. For the Business Link in your area, ring the Business Link Signpost line on 0345 567765. Also try the DTI web site on http:http//www.dti.gov.uk/support/rsa.htm

5. See Falk, N. 'Premises and the development of small firms' in Watkins, D., Stanworth, J. and Westrip, A. (eds), *Stimulating Small Firms*, Gower, 1982.

6. Falk, N. 'Small Firms in the Inner City', in Cribbs, A. and Webb, T. (eds), *Policy Issues in Small Business Research*, Saxon House, 1980.

7. Coopers and Lybrand, *The Provision of Premises for Small Firms*, Department of Industry, 1980.

8. See for example, the Small Business Research Trust's *Quarterly Survey of Small Business in Britain*, which records significant levels of problems with government regulations and paperwork (see also Unit 3, The small business environment).

9. Small Business Service, *SME Statistics for the UK, 2000*, SBS, 2001.

10. Stanworth, J. and Gray, C. (eds), *Bolton 20 Years On: The Small Firm in the 1990s*, Chapter 10. PCP, 1991.

11. For advice on good practice in employment, contact ACAS (Advisory, Conciliation and Arbitration Service, 180 Borough High St, London SE1 1LW) who offer information and free booklets on many areas.

    See also *Employing Staff*, from DTI Small Firms Publications, Admail 528, London SW1W 8YT.

12. Bolton Report, *Committee of Inquiry on Small Firms*, p. 21, HMSO Cmnd. 4811, 1971.

13. Most notably that of Ingham, G. *Size of Industrial Organisation and Worker Behaviour*, Cambridge University Press, 1970.

14. Daniel, W. and Millward, W. *Workplace Industrial Relations in Britain*, Heinemann, 1983.

15. See Scott, M., Roberts, I., Holroyd, G. and Sawbridge, D. 'Management and Industrial Relations in Small Firms', Department of Employment, *Research Paper No. 70*, 1989.

16. See a series of articles by Curran, J. and Stanworth, J. including 'Some reasons why small is not beautiful', *New Society*, 14 December 1978 and 'Size of workplace and attitudes to industrial relations', *British Journal of Industrial Relations*, XIX, 1981.

17. Rainnie, A. 'Combined and uneven development in the clothing industry', in *Capital and Class 22*, 1984.

18. Goss, D. *Small Business and Society*, p. 73, Routledge, 1991.

19. See Newby, H. *The Deferential Worker*, Penguin, 1977.

20. Blackburn, R. 'Job Quality in Small Businesses: Electrical and Electronic Engineering Firms in Dorset', in *Environment and Planning 22*, 1990.

21. Curran, J. *Bolton Fifteen Years On: A Review and Analysis of Small Business Research in Britain 1971–1986*, Small Business Research Trust, 1986.

22. Stanworth, J. and Gray, C. (eds), *Bolton 20 Years On: The Small Firm in the 1990s*, PCP, 1991. See Chapter 11 'Managers and Management within Small Firms'.

23. See for example Adair, J. *Not Bosses But Leaders*, Talbot Adair Press 1987.

Recommended further reading

❐ Marlow, S. 'People and the Small Firm', in Carter, S. and Jones-Evans, D. (eds) *Enterprise and Small Business*, FT/Prentice Hall, 2000.

❐ Birley, S. and Muzyka, F. *Mastering Entrepreneurship*, FT/Prentice Hall, 2000. Chapter 5, 'People, families and teams'.

❐ Stanworth, J. and Gray, C. (eds), *Bolton 20 Years On: The Small Firm in the 1990s*, PCP, 1991. Chapter 9, 'Employment and employment relations in the small enterprise', and Chapter 10, 'Managers and management within small firms'.

❐ Goss, D. *Small Business and Society*, Routledge, 1991. Chapter 4, 'Employment relations in small firms'.

❐ Williams, S. *Lloyds Bank Small Business Guide*, Penguin, 2001. Chapters 20–21.

❐ The Which? *Guide to Starting Your Own Business*, Consumers Association, 1998. Chapter 5, 'Premises', Chapter 8, 'How to be an employer', Chapter 9, 'Insurance for the small business', and Chapter 10, 'Buying a computer'.

12 Marketing

This Unit looks at the theory and practice of marketing in small firms. The reasons for a limited approach to marketing in many small firms are explored, and some solutions suggested. Following an evaluation of conventional marketing methods, a new model of marketing strategies and methods in small firms is proposed.

Contents

Activity 1 Limited marketing

Some small firms do not approach marketing in a positive way, believing it to be more appropriate to large rather than small firms.

Why do you think this is so? Can you suggest ways in which marketing can be made more accessible to them?

1 Small business marketing problems

1.1 Application of marketing by small firms

In theory, the marketing methods available to a small firm are no different to the marketing methods used by larger firms. Texts on marketing in the small business generally confirm this by reviewing the elements of marketing in much the same way as more generalised marketing books[1]. Yet they frequently overlook the reality of the methods used by small firms.

Small business marketing does differ in practice. There is evidence that small firms only use a small range of marketing methods, with limited expenditures. It would seem that in practice small firms do not use the '4 Ps' (promotions, price, product and place) of the marketing mix in quite the way that some theorists would advocate.

❑ *Limited promotions.* The promotional activities of small enterprises tend to react to competitor activity or events in the marketplace.

For example, research involving small electronics and printing companies[2] revealed that respondents put little effort into marketing their businesses at all unless they lost custom; otherwise they were content to allow word of mouth to do their marketing for them. Table 12.1 illustrates the degree to which the small businesses were content to use passive methods, such as word of mouth and *Yellow Pages*, compared to more active promotional methods, such as cold calls, salespeople and direct mail.

❑ *Under-pricing.* In addition to restricted use of marketing communications and promotional methods, there is also evidence that small firms tend to under-price themselves – particularly their own labour. A report[3] on self-employed people in Britain showed that they paid themselves less on average than the comparable employed persons are paid; the self-employed person earned £6.67 per hour compared with the average wage of £7.30.

❑ *Product: less development of services.* Whilst firms in manufacturing industries may have product development records comparable to their larger company counterparts, service sector small firms (the vast majority of all small businesses), have poorer records for innovation.

Table 12.1 Small business methods of finding customers

Method	% used
Word of mouth	73
Cold calls	29
Press advertising	22
Shop advertising	17
Exhibitions	10
Salesmen	7
Direct Mail	5
Yellow Pages	15

(**NB** As more than one method could have been used, the percentages add up to more than 100. Respondents were electronic and printing firms in Kingston and Sheffield)

Source: Small Firms and Local Economic Networks[2]

❐ *Place: restricted distribution.* Small firms tend to restrict the place in which they do business. Although some distribute products nationally, most small firms do not make use of extensive distribution networks, especially as most are in the service sector. Distribution through international markets is particularly rare; a survey of small firms in all sectors of the economy revealed that 94 per cent did not export at all[4].

The marketing paradox

Many small firms maintain a paradoxical attitude to marketing concepts. On the one hand marketing is regarded as something for the larger company and of little practical use to the small business. On the other hand small enterprises show themselves to be the personification of the marketing concept. The customer orientation practices of small business, which respond flexibly and quickly to the demands of the consumer, have been held up as a model to larger organisations, private and public alike. Undoubtedly, the proximity of the owner-manager to the marketplace helps them appreciate the needs of the customer, and therefore respond to changes in demand. The same owner-manager however may have a healthy disdain for using the tools of marketing to attract more custom. Some reasons for this limited application of marketing methods amongst small business owners are:

❐ *Diseconomies of scale:* small firms are unable to commit the same pro-rata level of marketing expenditure as larger firms because of diseconomies of scale. A small firm, which does not enjoy the scale or experience economies of a larger company, will have less, as a percentage of its sales revenue, to spend on sales related activities; other expenses will account for a higher proportion of its revenue.

❐ *Lack of specialised knowledge and skills:* small firms often do not optimise their marketing approach because the owner-manager does not have experience of specialised aspects of marketing. Promotional or distribution routes may therefore be overlooked, pricing or product development opportunities missed.

❑ *Distrust or lack of interest:* some owner-managers have a distrust of marketing which they view as inappropriate to small firms. Others may not take any overt interest, as they are caught up with day to day operational details; marketing strategies emerge and limited tactics are employed, but they are not deliberately conceived as long-term activities.

The motives of owner-managers, and their attitude to growth are important factors in all these areas.

1.2 Small business marketing style

It has been suggested that all of these influences add up to a distinctive marketing style which typifies the small business sector. Carson[5] has proposed that this style has a number of characteristics:

❑ *Lack of formalised planning of marketing strategies:* small firms rely more on informal procedures, often in reaction to activity in the marketplace.

❑ *Restricted scope and activity:* small business shies away from wide ranging and expensive marketing campaigns.

❑ *Simplistic and haphazard:* owner-managers rarely indulge in sophisticated, integrated marketing approaches, relying instead on rather random and basic marketing efforts.

❑ *Product and price orientation:* the marketing mix tends to over rely on developing products at competitive prices, and be less adventurous in promotional activities, and in seeking different channels of distribution, or potential new markets.

❑ *Owner-manager involvement:* the marketing strategy of small firms tends, like all aspects in the early days, to be driven by the owner-manager. The influence of their personal skills, experience and motives will be paramount in determining the nature and complexity of marketing methods used.

Whilst all of this may sound rather critical of the marketing processes adopted by small firms, the same commentator warns that marketing theorists should not be too hasty in their judgements, just because small firm marketing approaches do not conform to standard theoretical models. Marketing has to fit around the capabilities of the practitioner to be effective; if an owner-manager's background precludes sophisticated marketing techniques, then more basic practices can still be effective.

Evolution of marketing

Marketing cannot be regarded as a static discipline in the small firm. Practices will change as the firm develops, and particularly if it grows. Carson[6] has suggested there are four stages in the evolution of marketing in the small firm:

1. *Initial marketing activity:* there is usually considerable marketing activity in the set up stages of a new business, based mainly on the products, and their pricing and delivery.

2. *Reactive selling:* as demand grows, activities are usually in response to enquiries from potential customers.

3. *DIY marketing approach:* as the firm develops the need for a more positive marketing approach is seen. Owner-managers rely on their own capabilities to implement any marketing campaigns, which tend to be disjointed and sporadic as a result.

4. *Integrated, pro-active marketing:* in the final stage the small firm emerges with more sophisticated marketing planning. The various elements of the marketing mix are co-ordinated into longer-term strategies, aimed at controlling market forces rather than being controlled by them. This usually implies the recruitment of specialist marketing management.

Whilst this is an oversimple model, which does not take account of the full variety of business types, owner-manager personalities and skills or market conditions, it does illustrate that small firms can be expected to travel along an experience curve in their marketing activities, which is likely to improve their capabilities in this area.

1.3 A summary of small business characteristics and marketing problems

It would seem that small businesses have distinctive marketing issues, related to their inherent characteristics. A summary of the characteristics of small firms which tend to give rise to marketing problems, as discussed in this and earlier units, is shown in Table 12.2 .

Table 12.2 Small business characteristics and marketing problems

Small enterprise characteristics	Marketing problems
Relatively small in given industry	Limited customer base
Resource constraints	Limited activity, expertise and impact
Personalised management style	Dependency on manager's marketing competency
Uncertainty	Lack of formalised planning; intuitive, reactive marketing
Evolutionary	Variable marketing effort
Role of innovation	Difficulty in developing and defending niches and gaps

Customer base

Small firms are, by definition, relatively small in a given industry or market. This characteristic often leads to a dependency on a limited customer base, geographically and numerically. Small firms tend either to serve local markets or to have a low share of a wider market, unless the industry is very new. A number of studies have shown a relationship between the size of the firm and the number of customers, with a high percentage of small businesses dependent on less than ten customers, and some on only one buyer.

Resource constraints

A stand-alone small firm has less to spend on marketing as a percentage of its income because of the impact of fixed costs that take up a higher proportion of revenues. Financial constraints also restrict their ability to employ marketing specialists. This led Carson[6] to conclude that the marketing constraints on small firms take the form of limited resources, limited specialist expertise and limited impact.

Personalised management style

Smaller enterprises tend to have a more personalised management style than larger firms, with the typical owner-manager involved in all aspects of management and not sharing key decisions with others (see Unit 11, section 1.1). The personality and experience of owner-managers is a dominant influence, and so their marketing competency and attitudes towards marketing are a major factor in the marketing management of a small enterprise.

Uncertainty and evolution

Small firms have to cope with an uncertain environment, which means that they have to adapt and evolve as a business to survive (see Unit 3, section 3.2). Uncertainty stems from lack of control over the market, a small customer and product base, and the diverse motivations and abilities of the owner-managers. Those firms which do survive in this uncertain environment, adjust to the new conditions in a continual process of evolution. The marketing implication of this uncertain environment and need to evolve is that short-term considerations take priority over longer-term planning. Research has confirmed that planning is a problem for marketing in small firms, which tends to be reactive in style.

Innovation, niches and gaps

Although innovation is neither a unique nor a universal characteristic of small firms, entrepreneurs in small businesses have played a key role in the innovation of new products and processes because of their flexibility and willingness to try new approaches in some areas (see Unit 4, section 1). Innovations and gaps in supply that allow small firms to occupy market niches or to serve geographically isolated areas have proven to be an important way of gaining a competitive edge. The marketing problem for small firms is how to develop innovative products and services in the first instance, and then how to defend their competitive advantage and exploit innovations to the full with limited resources. Large firms may wait for smaller enterprises to open up markets and make the mistakes, before using their superior resources to capitalise on the opportunity. Exploiting niche markets to the full can be as big an issue as developing them in the first place.

Activity 2 Entrepreneurial marketing

Small business owners follow a variety of strategies to overcome the marketing problems discussed above. Do you think that they should follow general marketing principles and practices in these attempts? Or is there a specific type of marketing more appropriate to small business?

2 Entrepreneurial marketing strategies

2.1 Perceptions versus practice

There is contradictory evidence about the efforts of owner-managers to overcome these inherent marketing problems. Too often, the best practices amongst larger firms are automatically assumed to be what is required for smaller businesses, providing they can be given the resources to adopt them. However, the marketing methods used by owner-managers may point the way to different forms of marketing that are more appropriate to small firms. For example, some researchers have reported a reliance on recommendations and word-of-mouth marketing, whilst others have noted that owner-managers devote considerable time talking one-to-one with customers. If these aspects of small firm marketing are built upon, successful marketing strategies for small firms may look very different to the traditional models used by larger firms.

The marketing activities of a small business are not always visible or obvious to an outside observer. Research by the Kingston University Small Business Research Centre[7] indicated that perceptions of what the term 'marketing' meant to small business owners did not always match what those same owners did in practice. Most owners equated marketing with selling and promoting only. Unprompted definitions of marketing focused on customer acquisition and promotions whilst identifying customer needs, and other non-promotional aspects of marketing, such as product development, pricing and distribution, were largely ignored. Many owners suggested that their business was reliant on word-of-mouth recommendations and therefore they did not have to do any marketing.

This narrow view of marketing was not borne out by what the business owners actually did. Their activities indicated a strategic marketing awareness, particularly in areas such as monitoring the marketplace, targeting individual market segments and emphasising customer services and relationships. When asked to rank their most important marketing activities, recommendations from customers was first in all sectors and sizes of small firms. However, this reliance on recommendations was not necessarily an indication of minimal marketing effort, as such recommendations were often hard won.

To an outside observer, it is all too easy to accept the owner-manager's comment that they 'do not have the time or resources for marketing', when those same owners do indeed devote much of their time to building relationships with satisfied customers who then recommend the business to others. In other words, they spend considerable time and resources on marketing, but by another name.

2.2 Relationship marketing

Marketing specialists have recognised some limitations to marketing concepts in other business contexts as well. Critics have argued that the marketing models developed originally from the experiences of large, consumer goods companies operating in mass markets do not always give rise to universal principles that can be transferred to other sectors, such as services and business-to-business markets[8]. The concept of the marketing mix and the '4 Ps' of marketing – product, price, promotion and place – were particularly criticised because they focused on short-term transactions rather than establishing longer-term relationships with customers. In response to these issues, Grönroos[8] put forward a relationship-focused definition of marketing:

> 'The purpose of marketing is to establish, maintain, enhance and commercialise customer relationships so that the objectives of the parties are met. This is done by mutual exchange and fulfilment of promises.'

In a move away from the traditional 'warfare' approach of marketing, in which the deal that overcame customer resistance was seen as the outcome of marketing activities operating in a hostile, competitive environment, relationship marketing involves increasing the emphasis on nurturing relationships, especially with existing customers, and the development of supportive market networks.

This is certainly more in tune with the language of owner-managers, who stress the importance of contact with customers and the development of on-going relationships with them. Rather than emphasising the conversion of 'prospects' into single purchase 'customers' or repeat purchase 'clients', relationship marketing aims to develop 'supporters', 'advocates' and 'partners' who actively recommend each other to a wider audience and continually seek to identify ways of gaining further advantage from the relationship[9]. This again is more descriptive of what small business managers actually do; they rely heavily on the recommendations of existing customers and other supporters to generate new business.

2.3 Entrepreneurial marketing: '4 Is' rather than '4 Ps'

This research into owner-manager practices, and these developments in marketing thinking, indicate the need for a new approach to marketing in an entrepreneurial context. Successful entrepreneurial marketing consists of a circular process: innovative developments and adjustments to products and services are targeted at identified customer groups who are contacted through interactive marketing methods, whilst informal information gathering monitors the marketplace and evaluates new opportunities, which may, in turn, lead to further innovations.

This can be illustrated as shown by Figure 12.1.

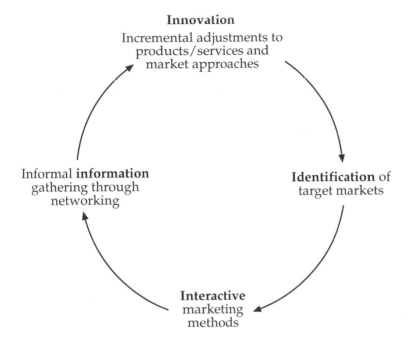

Figure 12. 1 Strategic entrepreneurial marketing – the '4 Is'

Innovation

The importance of innovation to entrepreneurship has been stressed in earlier Units (see Unit 4, Innovation and the marketplace). Some misconceptions about innovation were explored which apply equally to innovative marketing practices. In particular, innovative marketing is more likely to consist of incremental adjustments to existing products/services or market approaches, rather than larger-scale developments. Whilst a few small firms may make the big innovative breakthrough and grow rapidly as a result, the majority that survive do so by growing more slowly, through making small but regular improvements to the way in which they do business. This may mean stocking new lines, approaching a new market segment with a particular service, or improving services to existing customers – in other words incremental, innovative adjustments which together create a competitive edge. For example, an innovative restaurateur could add creative dishes to the menu, offer distinctive services to the local business community (such as accounts facilities and a high-speed lunch service), and develop special events for regular customers (gourmet clubs, wine tastings, etc.). None of these may represent a big breakthrough individually, but together they help to create an innovative approach to the marketplace.

Identification of target markets

Many successful small firms occupy 'niche' markets in which they supply specialised products or services to a clearly identified group of customers. Others find a gap in a particular marketplace for the provision of more general services.

Either way, success is dependent on identifying a particular group of customers who need the product or service on offer (as described in more detail in Unit 4, section 6, Who is the customer?). However, target markets need not be solely concerned with customers in the conventional sense of the term. Other groups of people, from suppliers to local planners, can directly and indirectly influence the fortunes of small firms, and they may need marketing consideration.

Interactive marketing methods

A selling point for a small business often lies in its ability to stay in touch with customers. Owner-managers themselves usually spend a considerable part of their working day in contact with customers. This allows them to interact with their customer base in a way which large firms, even with the latest technological advances, struggle to match.

Interactive marketing for small firms implies responsiveness – the ability to communicate and respond rapidly to individual customers. Entrepreneurs interact with individual customers through personal selling and relationship building approaches, which secure not only orders but recommendations to potential customers as well. This can be contrasted to the mass broadcasting methods, such as large-scale advertising campaigns, traditionally used by larger organisations.

Informal information gathering

Successful entrepreneurs maintain an external focus to their activities that alerts them to opportunities and threats in their environment (as outlined in Unit 2, section 6, Towards successful entrepreneurship). Their informal information gathering techniques allow them to monitor their own performance in relation to that of competitors and react to competitive threats. They are also open to new ideas and opportunities through a network of personal and inter-organisational contacts. This process restarts the marketing cycle by forming the basis for further innovative adjustments to the activities of the enterprise.

Each of these aspects of entrepreneurial marketing is discussed further in the sections that follow.

Activity 3 Resources and less risk for innovations

Two particular issues for innovation strategies in small firms are: i) where to find the resources to continually develop innovations and ii) how to protect innovations once they are launched. What solutions can you suggest for the owner-manager?

3 Innovation

Innovation has been the subject of considerable discussion in earlier units (see particularly Units 2, 4 and 10). Two particular aspects need emphasising in a marketing context:

☐ the difficulties of implementing and maintaining innovative developments with limited financial and time resources;

☐ the problem of defending innovations from pirates and predators.

Potential solutions to these issues are discussed in the following sections.

3.1 Collaborative innovation

Not surprisingly, the product idea selected by the new owner of a small business is most likely to be determined by their previous experience. According to one survey[10], 78 per cent of new owners chose a product which was the same or similar to those offered in their previous employment. This leaves most small firms with a narrow base for future product development. This implies that many businesses do not have innovative roots. We have already discussed the relationship between the small firm and innovation (see Unit 4, 1, Small firms as innovators). In terms of new product development the record is highly variable. In some sectors, the small firm is responsible for a high percentage of new products introduced. For example 58 per cent of innovations in the scientific instruments industry, between 1945 and 1983, are calculated to have come from SMEs. This compares to only 14 per cent for SMEs in the pharmaceuticals industry[11]. There are barriers to introducing innovations, just as there are barriers to entry for small firms, which vary by industry.

Another theme, previously emphasised, is the variability of motives among owner-managers, which will affect their innovations policy. Although some will show highly innovative tendencies, many others will not have the desire or capability to introduce new approaches.

The problems of innovative development for a small firm are considerable. The rate of failure of new products is high; the resources for research and development will be limited, coming in most cases from internal sources[12].

Failure of new products can easily cause the failure of the small firm if the stakes are high. For this reason, many small businesses adopt a cautious approach.

☐ *Incremental innovations*[13]: by developing new approaches within the existing framework of knowledge and experience, a small firm can more safely predict the outcome of any innovative move. The development may be of new markets, and different customer groups rather than new products.

☐ *Radical innovation:* this increases the risk significantly by taking the small firm into new technology, processes and markets, where there is little in-house information and experience. Whilst this route may produce substantial profits and growth, it also represents high risk with the future of the whole enterprise often dependent on the success of the new product.

❑ *Licensing:* a way of remaining innovative but reducing the risk is to license proven products or processes, from other companies. For a small firm, unable to invest in their own R & D, this may be an attractive option.

Licences to manufacture, or distribute new products are becoming increasingly available. A number of European initiatives, such as Business Innovation Centres (BICs) and Eureka, promote dissemination of innovations, including licensing[14].

❑ *Collaborative ventures:* the traditional British inventiveness, still evident in scientific establishments, universities and colleges, has too often stopped short of the application of new products in the marketplace. Many observers have compared Britain's innovation record to Japan's as there is evidence that, whilst the UK scores heavily in terms of pure inventiveness and research skills, Japanese industry has excelled at product development[15].

The opportunism of smaller firms has been seen as a potential positive influence in the UK to overcome this reluctance to bring new ideas into the market. The government has therefore set up schemes to encourage innovation such as:

○ LINK, which aims at bringing commerce and research institutions together with the government funding up to 50 per cent of project costs;

○ SPUR, (Support for Products Under Research), which makes grants of up to 30 per cent of the costs, to a maximum of £162,000, to help small firms develop technologically advanced products;

○ SMART, (Small Firms Merit Awards for Research and Technology), an annual competition for small firms employing less than 50 people, which awards phased grants, of up to £45,000 for the development of new technology products.

Further details of these schemes are available through Business Link.

There are mixed reports of the success of these initiatives. 'Partners in Innovation', a report[16] by the McKinsey group criticised academia and business alike (including small firms) for not making more of technological opportunities. However, it would appear that some sectors are doing better than others. The LINK initiative has been particularly well supported, for example, in the development of scientific instruments, with smaller firms playing a prominent role[17].

Innovation considerations in small firms' marketing strategy often point to a dilemma. Without new products, small firms cannot survive in most competitive markets. Yet the costs of product development, and the risks of failure, are often too high for the limited resources of a small firm to accept. The way out of the dilemma will probably involve closer co-operation and networking in joint developments between small and large organisations, in the private and public sector alike. It also indicates the need for incremental, rather than radical, innovation to both market and product approaches for the majority of small firms.

3.2 Protecting innovation – intellectual property rights

In some firms innovations form 'intellectual property' which is protected by a number of legal rights (see also Unit 7, section 3.2).

The law both restricts the use of certain names, and gives protection to the value built up by names, products and processes.

❐ *Company names:* the name of a limited company can be registered provided it is not identical to an existing company, nor can it be considered offensive or illegal. Certain words, about 80 in total, such as Royal, Windsor, National, British, University, Chemist, Trust, can only be used with the approval of the Secretary of State[18].

Sole traders and partnerships can use their own names without consent. If they choose, however, to operate under a name, other than their own, they are legally required to disclose their names on business letters, invoices, receipts and other stationery.

❐ *Trademarks:* brand names, or a distinctive mark associated with a product, can be registered with the Trade Mark Registry. Imitation of registered trade marks is a criminal offence[19]. Even where names are not registered, attempts to pass off other goods for the real thing are also illegal.

❐ *Service Marks:* registration of Service Marks, which are used to identify services as opposed to products, can also be made with the Trade Mark Registry, affording them similar protection.

❐ *Copyright:* where the product is a literary, artistic or musical creation, it can be protected by copyright, which under the 1988 Copyright, Designs and Patent Act[19] also covers computer software.

❐ *Design right:* designs for products, either initial drawings or a prototype, are also protected by design right, a new concept introduced by the 1988 Act.

❐ *Patents:* inventions of products or processes, accepted as superior to what went before, can be given temporary protection by patents. The owner of a patent can give rights to others to manufacture or sell the patented product, or use the patented process, usually granted through a licence.

Activity 4 Non-customer markets for entrepreneurs

It has been sugessted that entrepreneurs market their firms to groups other than just customers. Can you suggest who these other groups might be? Give some specific examples in each case.

4 Identification of target markets

4.1 Target marketing: bottom-up rather than top-down

If a common weakness of small firms is their over-reliance on small numbers of customers, a corresponding strength is that owner-managers often identify closely with a specific group of customers whose needs are well known to them. This is in accordance with modern marketing theories of 'target marketing', a concept which divides markets into segments of distinct buyer groups, selects an attractive segment to target, and adopts a viable competitive position within the market segment. This process of segmentation, targeting and positioning is widely used in larger consumer marketing companies and in the 1980s gained acceptance in industrial and services marketing contexts as well.

'Top-down' theory

Most marketing textbooks advocate three stages in a targeted marketing strategy, which represent a 'top-down' approach to the market[20]:

☐ *Segmentation* – division of the market into groups of buyers with different needs. The profiles of these segments are developed using demographic, psychological and other buyer-behaviour variables.

☐ *Targeting* – evaluation of the attractiveness of each segment and selection of the target segment. Companies may target many segments but need to adopt a differentiated approach to each one.

☐ *Positioning* – selection and communication of a market position which differentiates the product/service from competitors. The company's offering needs to have meaningful differences to competitive products or services, so that it occupies a distinct position in customers' minds.

This process implies that an organisation is able to take an objective overview of the markets it serves before selecting those on which it wishes to concentrate. This usually involves both secondary and primary market research with evaluation by specialists in each of the three stages.

'Bottom-up' practice

Although successful entrepreneurs do seem adept at carefully targeting certain customers, the processes they use in order to achieve this do not seem to conform to the three stages described above. Evidence suggests that successful smaller businesses practise a 'bottom-up' targeting process in which the organisation begins by serving the needs of a few customers and then expands the base gradually as experience and resources allow. Research into 'niche' marketing approaches indicates that targeting is achieved by attracting an initial customer base and then looking for more of the same[21]. The stages of entrepreneurial targeting are:

❐ *Identification of market opportunity.* An opportunity is identified by matching innovative ideas to the resources of a small enterprise. The opportunity is tested through trial and error in the marketplace, based on the entrepreneur's intuitive expectations which are sometimes, but not often, backed up by more formal research.

❐ *Attraction of an initial customer base.* Certain customers, who may or may not conform to the profile anticipated by the entrepreneur, are attracted to the service or product. However, as the entrepreneur is in regular contact with these customers, he or she gets to know their preferences and needs.

❐ *Expansion through more of the same.* The entrepreneur expands the initial customer base by looking for more customers of the same profile. In many cases, this is not a deliberate process as it is left to the initial customers who recommend the business to others with similar needs to their own. A target customer group emerges and grows, but more through a process of self-selection, and some encouragement from the entrepreneur, rather than through formal research and deliberate choice.

This process has advantages over the top-down approach. It requires fewer resources and is more flexible and adaptable to implement – attributes which play to small business strengths. It has corresponding disadvantages. It is less certain of success and takes longer to penetrate the market to full potential – weaknesses which characterise many small firms.

4.2 Identifying targets other than new customers

Small businesses survive in their changeable environment not only by success fully marketing to those who buy their products or services, but also by developing important relationships with other individuals and organisations. Suppliers, bank managers, investors, advisors, trade associations, local government and public authorities may be as vital as customers to a small business's success. Entrepreneurs may target marketing strategies at these other markets which go beyond conventional definitions of the term 'customer'. In this sense, entrepreneurial marketing resembles relationship marketing, which defines the need to develop a supportive framework around the organisation:

> 'Marketing can be seen as relationship management: creating, developing and maintaining a network in which the firm thrives.'[22]

In other words, marketing can target any organisation or individual that can have a positive or negative effect on the small firm. Relationship marketing theorists have attempted to identify these other markets more specifically in the 'six markets' model[9] as illustrated in Figure 12.2.

Figure 12.2 The six markets model

In more detail, the six markets are as follows:

❏ *Internal markets* are made up of individuals within an organisation whose behaviour and attitudes affect the performance of the business. Selling the aims and strategies of a small business to employees, shareholders and family members helps everyone concerned work towards common goals.

> For example, Perf-X, a small manufacturing firm, held informal events and social gatherings throughout the year for its 25 employees, who described the culture of the firm as that of an extended family to which they all belonged.

❏ *Recruitment markets* are made up of potential employees. The aim of marketing here is to attract a sufficient number of well-motivated and trained employees. Particularly in small service businesses, employees have become a key marketing influence on the competitiveness of the organisation.

> In order to attract the skilled workforce he needed, the owner of Perf-X held a series of open days which anyone could attend to find out more about the company. He made a point of personally welcoming visitors to demonstrate his own commitment and style of working.

❏ *Supplier markets* can be crucial to a small business's ability to service its customers. Suppliers are often vital in providing goods and services on time and at the right price. They can also be influential in passing on recommendations to potential customers.

> Most of Perf-X's new business came from recommendations from customers, suppliers and other contacts. The directors of Perf-X always welcomed visits from suppliers and took the opportunity to show them the latest developments of their business so they would be well informed in talking to others in the trade about it.

❐ *Influence markets* are made up of organisations and individuals that can influence the marketing environment within which the company competes. There are many potential such 'influencers' on small businesses, from local government planners to trade associations.

The owner of Perf-X regularly attended meetings of the local Chamber of Commerce where he made useful contacts with people involved in local public services and the professions, as well as with other business managers.

❐ *Referral markets* are sources of word-of-mouth recommendations, other than customers. Small firms may be recommended by other local businesses, professional advisors (lawyers, accountants and consultants), and friends or acquaintances who may not be direct customers of the business.

Perf-X's largest order came as a result of an introduction through a Personal Business Advisor at the local Business Link.

❐ *Customer markets* represent a continuum of relationships rather than a continuous search for new business transactions. The emphasis shifts from customer acquisition to customer retention through the development of mutually beneficial, long-term relationships. This has been conceptualised as the 'ladder of customer loyalty'[9] as shown in Figure 12.3.

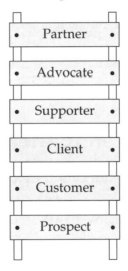

Figure 12.3 The ladder of customer loyalty

○ Prospects represent the potential market. Traditionally, marketing activities have emphasised the conversion of prospects into buyers through order-taking.

○ A customer is someone who has become a buyer and could develop a longer-term relationship with the business.

○ A client is a regular, repeat customer.

○ A supporter is a regular customer who thinks positively about the organi-sation.

○ An advocate acts positively on behalf of the firm by recommending it whenever possible.

○ A partner works together with the firm to identify further ways of working together for mutual benefit.

Thus, moving customers up the ladder is not just to secure their loyalty, but to generate new customers and business opportunities as well.

The aim of this type of marketing is to turn new customers into regularly purchasing clients, and then on to become strong supporters of the business as an active source of referrals. They help find new customers and, as partners, contribute to the development of new business opportunities.

This seems more in tune with the realities of entrepreneurial marketing which relies on identifying important customer groups and developing meaningful and long-term relationships with them.

> The design engineer of one of Perf-X's customers joked to the owner that he spent more time in Perf-X's premises than he did in his own office. The owner knew that it was probably true.

Activity 5 Entrepreneurial marketing methods

Which particular marketing methods or techniques are entrepreneurs most likely to use? Write out a list of potential marketing methods with an assess-ment (e.g. a rating out of 10) of how useful each is likely to be for a small firm.

5 Interactive marketing methods

5.1 The entrepreneurial marketing mix

Marketing strategies are implemented through marketing activities of various types which have been summarised as the 'marketing mix'. Kotler[20] defines the concept of the marketing mix as 'the set of tools that the firm uses to pursue its marketing objectives in the target market'. As these tools are numerous, various attempts have been made to categorise them into a manageable form, the most famous being the 4 Ps of product, price, promotion and place, as discussed earlier.

Entrepreneurial marketing activities do not fit easily into these existing models of the marketing mix. However, one theme does seem to run through the marketing methods preferred by entrepreneurs: they allow for direct interchanges and the building of reciprocal relationships between buyers and suppliers. Entrepreneurs prefer *interactive* marketing; they specialise in interactions with their target markets because they have strong preferences for personal contact with customers rather than impersonal marketing through mass promotions. They seek conversa-tional relationships in which they can listen to, and respond to, the voice of the customer, rather than undertake formal market research to understand the marketplace.

Interactive marketing methods imply one-to-one contact through personal or telephone selling and perhaps direct or electronic mail. Larger entrepreneurial firms may use more impersonal methods, such as advertising and PR to inform their markets, but they often rely on specific qualities of their founders to project a personal image. The personalities of Richard Branson, Anita Roddick and Bill Gates still colour our perceptions of Virgin, The Body Shop and Microsoft. In smaller firms, the ability of the owner-manager to have meaningful dialogues with customers is often the unique selling point of the business.

5.2 Word-of-mouth marketing

Entrepreneurial marketing relies heavily on word-of-mouth marketing to develop the customer base through recommendations. Research studies inevitably cite recommendations as the number one source of new customers for small firms[7]. Such recommendations may come from customers, suppliers or other referral groups. Word-of-mouth marketing has been defined as:

> 'Oral, person-to-person communication between a perceived non-commercial communicator and a receiver concerning a brand, a product or a service offered for sale.'[23]

This definition makes two crucial distinctions between word-of-mouth and other forms of marketing activity:

❐ it involves face-to-face, direct contact between a communicator and a receiver;

❐ the communicator is perceived to be independent of the product or service under discussion.

The importance of such communications is well documented in the marketing literature, which suggests that word-of-mouth is often crucial to purchase decisions in many consumer and business-to-business markets[24]. For many small firms, reliance on recommendations is no bad thing as it is more suited to the resources of their business. Referrals incur few, if any, additional direct costs; most owner-mangers prefer the slow build up of new business that word-of-mouth marketing implies, because they would be unable to cope with large increases in demand for their services.

The disadvantage of word-of-mouth marketing is that it is essentially uncontrollable. As a result, owner-mangers perceive there to be few opportunities to influence recommendations other than providing the best possible service. In practice, there may be ways of encouraging referrals and recommendations by more proactive methods which are overlooked by small business owners.

Word-of-mouth marketing communications are no longer restricted to face-to-face conversations with friends and neighbours. The telecommunications revolution means that people exchange views on their buying experiences in a number of new media including text messaging and email. Internet newsgroups (online discussion forums) now involve millions of people around the world exchanging news and views over a huge range of topics. This often includes positive or negative stories about buying experiences, or a product's performance. The scope for uncontrollable, word-of-mouth marketing communications on the Internet is enormous, and entrepreneurs will develop ways to harness this informal communications channel to their advantage.

5.3 Interactive marketing communications

The options for communicating with the marketplace are wide.

Personal methods

Direct contact with customers through personal marketing methods is often the first important step in a word-of-mouth communications chain. These methods can take the form of:

○ direct selling;

○ telephone and online selling;

○ retail selling;

○ exhibitions or trade shows.

Entrepreneurs prefer personal marketing methods for two main reasons:

❑ *A desire by the owner-manager to stay in touch with the market.* The competitive edge of some small enterprises is their rapid response to individual customer needs which is facilitated by the owner-manager's regular contact with the customer base. As many small firms are in service industries, where a more flexible response is possible, this can be an important competitive consideration over larger organisations, whose reaction time is often longer.

❑ *A belief that personal contact is the most cost effective method of promotion.* This may or may not be valid, but because owner-managers frequently do not cost their own time into the equation, this can often appear to be the case. However, as cash flow is usually the most important financial consideration of a young business, and the owner-manager's costs represent a fixed overhead, then personal selling by the owner-manager is often the only available option in the start-up phase.

Whilst personal promotional methods may be the preferred route, there is a common danger in this approach if the responsibility is always left with the owner-manager. Other pressures on the owner-manager's time may make this strategy into a purely reactive one; the internal management requirements of the small firm can leave insufficient time for long-term, planned sales approaches, and personal methods are resorted to when business looks slack.

For example, the owner-manager of a company, set up to provide commercial slide presentations, generated all the early business by personal selling. The demands of those early customers and the management of the production process soon took up all the manager's time. The business remained trapped into this narrow base, until a key account was lost to a competitor, and the owner-manager was forced out selling once again. This cycle repeated itself several times until the small firm took the decision to employ a full-time sales person. Even a retail business can develop problems when the owner-manager is serving in the shop; attention to customers can suffer because there is an urgent phone call, or an important supplier makes a visit.

Each personal promotional method involves skills and techniques which can enhance performance. These are not peculiar to small enterprises, but generic in the activity, and therefore it is not appropriate to develop these in great depth here.

However, each activity does have advantages and pitfalls which may have more emphasis in the small firm.

Direct selling

It is difficult to think of a small business owner-manager who does not have some involvement in selling, even though they may not recognise it as such. Even the self-employed plumber or builder makes a sales call when asked in for an estimate. Some owners may have a background in sales, but most owners have had no formal training in personal selling. Yet the owner-manager is most likely to be the front line sales person for the small firm.

Direct selling means face-to-face interviews with customers, usually on their premises with the objective of taking an order. It is most common in firms which sell to other businesses – manufacturers, distributors, or services. It can also be used for selling direct to consumers and is widely used by financial services and some home products, such as window and security systems.

❏ *The advantages* for a small firm often lie in the visibility of results. Direct selling is a very measurable activity where, over an appropriate period of time, results can be judged against the effort expended. Direct customer contact also emphasises the need for small firms to build good relationships with existing customers.

❏ *The pitfalls:* most experienced sales people will testify to the fact that the sales interview, or the actual moment of contact with the customer, is not the difficult part of selling; the problem is getting to see the customer in the first place. Typically a sales person will spend less than 20 per cent of their time face-to-face with a customer. The other 80 per cent is spent trying to arrange appointments, travelling to them, and on administration. Selling is more about rejection than acceptance, and rejection comes at each stage in the process. It may take ten phone calls to make one appointment, and five appointments to make one sale; that represents 50 phone calls per sale. These ratios often make selling more of a numbers game than a sophisticated technique. The most successful sales people are those who persist, and make the 50 calls to obtain one sale, rather than give up after ten calls and one disappointing appointment. Successful sales people are not necessarily those with the best presentation and sales technique before the customer.

The implications for the small business owner-manager who begins selling with little prior experience is that, like most novice sales people, they give up too soon. However, unlike most new sales people in larger companies, they have three further problems:

1. They do not have a sales manager to chase and support them. Therefore their lapses can be more permanent, as the owner-manager feels isolated by customer rejection, with no internal company support to fall back on.

2. Their lack of sales training may further decrease self-confidence, and sales approaches become even more tentative.

3. Their wide-ranging responsibilities produce a host of other more urgent things to do, as replacement activities for the lonely job of selling.

   This can result in a downward spiral, as the effort required to generate the number of sales leads to produce the final sale becomes sporadic and insufficient.

☐ *Alternatives:* there are alternatives to owner-managers performing the sales function directly themselves.

   ○ *A sales person(s)* can be employed by the small firm. The major barrier to this is cost, which is unlikely to be less than £40,000 per annum including travel and other overhead costs. For a small firm operating on a 50 per cent gross margin this implies that sales of £80,000 will be needed to cover just the marginal costs of employing a sales person before any contribution to general overheads or additional profit is made.

   ○ *Agents-on-commission* represent a way of overcoming this high fixed cost for a small firm. An agent will represent several manufacturers or distributors in a given trade, and sell their products to the relevant outlets in return for a commission (usually in the region of 10–15 per cent) on sales made. This is often an appropriate method for a new firm in a market where typically high volumes of relatively low priced units are sold through a fragmented distribution. For example, a manufacturer of gift products might appoint four or five regional agents to sell their products to gift shops, stationers and other specialist outlets.

   The advantage of this method is the rapid coverage of a large number of potential customers, at no risk to the manufacturer. The disadvantage is that there is no control over the effort in terms of amount or kind, and there is a loss of margin.

Telephone and online selling

Modern telecommunications are an essential part of the process of building customer relationships through direct contact, by making an appointment or answering an enquiry. Telesales or e-commerce can complete the whole process by taking the order.

For a small firm with limited resources, the telephone calls and emails have become an indispensable part of selling. The problems start when the objective of the communication is not clear. Use of the telephone to make a sales appointment is sometimes confused with making a sale, as the caller attempts to persuade the listener of all the benefits of the product or service during the call. This is a particular temptation for enthusiastic small business owners, who feel short of time to fully present their case at a later date. The result is often confusion of the listener, and a reluctance to take the approach further. Larger firms sometimes employ telephone sales personnel to fix appointments for other sales people to fulfil. They are trained to offer short clear reasons for an appointment which refrain from over elaboration, a technique which would benefit many small business owner-managers[20].

Taking telephone or online orders is used particularly for existing customers, who regularly place orders.

> For example, a health food wholesaler first developed outlets for its products by direct sales visits. It is not economic to make further regular visits, so customers are telephoned once a week and asked if they need to order further items. The phone call reminds retailers of the need to restock, and keeps out competitive products as the shelves are kept full. Customers can also place orders online by visiting the company's web site.

Retail selling

Small independent or franchised shops can be classified into two main types in relation to retail selling: convenience outlets, such as newsagents and confectioners, and specialist shops, varying from fashion-wear boutiques to art galleries. In both, there is a form of customer contact. In the convenience store, it will probably be no more than order taking after customers have served themselves. In the specialist outlet, the contact is more likely to involve some selling.

The advantage of a retail outlet is that it represents a (hopefully) convenient, permanent place of contact between buyer and seller. The difficulty for the specialist retailer is in recognising the line between the need to help the buyer make a decision, and maintaining a comfortable environment, in which the customer does not feel threatened or pressured.

The shop window is a key sales aid. It is often the method by which the retailer achieves contact with the customer, by tempting them inside in the first place. Larger firms, employing professional window dressers, know the importance of a regularly changed, attractive display, which is sometimes overlooked by smaller firms.

Independent retailers are a declining, but still significant, part of our high streets; the total number of independent stores declined from 450,000 shops in 1950, to 220,000 in 1980, and the proportion of retail sales from 64 per cent to 34 per cent[25]. Today, independents with one store still represent 60 per cent of the total of 350,000 retail outlets in the UK. However the sales of these independents have declined to around one quarter of total UK retail sales.

Most new entrants to small business retailing have no experience of retail selling, and so learn through practice. The variability of sales skills encountered in small shops testifies to the unevenness of that learning.

Exhibitions and trade shows

National trade shows and exhibitions cover every significant trade or industry, from lingerie and corsetry (at LACE in Harrogate) to electronic equipment (at INTERNEPCON in Birmingham).

There are also regional business-to-business exhibitions serving more varied industries on a local basis. These can represent a concentrated meeting place for a small business, and therefore an efficient way of seeing customers and competitors alike.

Exhibitions are expensive in stand costs and the time involved in preparation and attendance. They are essentially points of contact, and although orders are sometimes written during the exhibition, the key to productive use of this resource is usually in the follow up to the introductions made. Exhibition catalogues can also provide useful further information for market research, or the basis of a mailing list. Exhibition organisers usually compile a list of visitors, made available to participating firms, which can form useful data for future promotions.

A problem for small firms is often in the small size, poor presentation and out-of-the-way position of their stand, which can combine to significantly reduce the number and quality of contacts made.

Impersonal methods

Other promotional methods involve only indirect contact with customers. However, they may still be interactive if they induce a response and allow for a conversation to begin.

Impersonal methods of promoting a small firm include:

❐ advertisements in various media;

❐ direct mail;

❐ press releases;

❐ leaflets and brochures;

❐ online communications including the Internet.

Media advertisements

In practice there are two distinct types of media advertising for the small enterprise:

❐ *Directories and trade listings.* These are permanent references, outlining the products or services offered by a small firm which can be consulted by potential buyers. This form of advertising is widely used by owner-managers, who see the benefit of a permanent indication of their business in popular directories, such as *Yellow Pages* and *Business Pages*. One disadvantage is that it is quite expensive, with a display advertisement costing several hundreds of pounds for one area listing in a national directory. Judgement of which category or service, and which geographic region to enter, is sometimes a further complication and expense.

> For example, a commercial catering company with a private functions room, whose target market overlapped two geographic areas of a national directory, could not decide whether 'Banqueting Rooms', 'Conference Facilities' or 'Catering' would be their best category, and were faced with an invoice for six insertions if they wished to cover all options in both geographic regions.

❐ *Press, radio or television advertising.* There is a wide choice of media for a small firm to use on a more irregular basis, in the hope of creating or reinforcing awareness and demand for products or services.

Small enterprises are reluctant to commit expenditure on this kind of advertising. The link between advertising and sales is difficult to establish, and often requires a long-term investment to be cost effective. Small firms often therefore consider substantial expenditure on this type of promotion as a luxury they cannot afford. Detailed planning of an advertising campaign and a creative and media strategy with clear objectives, over an adequate time period, helps achieve the desired results from promotional expenditure, but it is generally rare in the small business sector.

Instead, typical small firm advertising practices seem haphazard, restricted and reactive. Often the stimulus for advertising lies with media sales people who persuade small firms to take space in an appropriate 'Special Feature' of their publication. At other times, advertising is in response to a direct competitive threat.

Direct mail

Direct mail has become an increasingly popular form of advertising over the last two decades. It is third in the national advertising expenditure league table, after press and TV[26]. The reasons for this increased popularity are particularly relevant to small business:

❐ *Direct mail is targeted.* Small firms often trade in very narrow or fragmented markets, which traditional media over-hit or miss altogether. Direct mail has been likened to using the rifle, rather than a blunderbuss, as promotional messages can be directed very specifically.

❐ *Direct mail results can be quantified.* Unlike other forms of advertising, the results of a direct mail campaign, in terms of response back from the recipients, can be measured and valued. A small firm can decide from the results whether the campaign justifies its costs.

❐ *Direct mail can be tested.* Although the set up costs of producing letters and leaflets are fixed, other costs of a mailing campaign vary with the quantity posted. It is possible to test the response from direct mail on a limited basis, before extending the mailing to the full list. A small firm can thus reduce the risks involved in this type of promotional expenditure.

> For example, a picture framing business found that advertising in the local press was either ineffective or swamped the workshop with too many orders in a short space of time. Instead the owner-manager tried direct mail to a list of existing customers and local residents on a progressive basis, to both test the response and stagger the resulting workload.

The problems associated with direct mail are:

❐ *The quality of the mailing list is crucial;* the best designed mail shot sent to the wrong people will not produce results. Finding an appropriate list can be a problem. There are a number of sources for the small firm:

○ The best list is usually of existing customers; they are, after all, known buyers of the product or service on offer, and up to date details should be obtainable. Although small firms are becoming more aware of the importance of building a customer list, and computer databases can provide an easy storage facility (note the Data Protection Act[27]), many owner-managers still overlook this opportunity, and have no systematic system for recording customer information.

○ Lists can be compiled from a number of sources, including local or trade directories, electoral registration rolls, or other official listings. An office stationery suppliers, for example, decided to target professional categories such as accountants and solicitors, which are listed in local business directories. The disadvantage was that this did not include names of partners, so that the mailing could not be personalised.

○ Lists can be purchased, or rented, from list brokers who have compiled or acquired lists of many different classifications, from sales managers to sports players. Such lists are normally rented on a cost per 1,000 basis, with a minimum charge. A potential problem for a small business is that, although lists can be localised, by breaking them down into postcodes, the result is often a small list which incurs the fixed minimum charge.

○ Lists can be geographically designated simply by the hand delivery of mail shots to specified streets or business areas. Although response from this is generally low, as the mailings are not personalised and rather random, it can be cost effective as delivery expenses are low.

❏ *Direct mail can be a fragmented and time-consuming promotional method.* An owner-manager may find it necessary to become personally involved in the various stages of a direct mail campaign, from the creation and production of letters and leaflets, to the researching of lists and appropriate delivery methods. This not only effectively increases the cost of the promotion, but also puts off some owner-managers who feel they do not have either the time or expertise to manage these functions.

❏ *Response rates from direct mail are usually very low, often less than two or three per cent.* Whilst such responses may still meet the costs of the campaign, they limit the scope of the effort.

For example, the office stationery supplier mailing to professional lists received seven inquiries from the 200 names mailed, which converted into four orders, the value of which more than justified the expense of the mailing. However, the firm soon ran out of lists to mail, and the total volume of business generated was small.

Press releases

Larger companies have long recognised the importance of good public relations, and the value that can be obtained by working with the media. PR departments and agencies can point to free advertising on TV or in the press to justify their costs to large corporations. Small firms can similarly benefit, but few make full use of the possibilities.

Local media and the trade press consume large quantities of news, and small firm activities are often newsworthy, but unnoticed. The problems are familiar: owner-managers with no time, or expertise to put together press releases, or make the necessary media contact.

Leaflets and brochures

Most small firms produce a leaflet or brochure describing their product or service. Desk top publishing has encouraged many small firms to produce more literature about themselves which, at a relatively modest cost, can now be made to look professional and business like. Small firms used to suffer considerable diseconomies of scale because of the short run nature of their publicity material. Computer graphics and laser printing technology have changed all that to the benefit of small enterprises, which now have no excuse for poorly produced literature. Whilst their general standard of graphic reproduction has undoubtedly improved, small firms still have problems with the distribution and contents of leaflets and brochures. Common problems include:

❒ *Unclear objectives:* a small firm's leaflet will typically try to be all things to all people. Whilst this is an understandable reaction to the need for economies in producing publicity material, the impact of what is produced can be considerably reduced by confusion or profusion of objectives. Brochures may be distributed by a variety of methods, and to different customer groups.

> For example, an upholsterers, selling their services mainly to hotels, decided to also target the domestic market of local householders. As they had a good stock of existing leaflets, they offered these to potential customers from this new segment. Unfortunately, householders were confused by the technical specifications in the leaflet, particularly those referring to flame-retardant materials, and British Standard Specifications.

❒ *Product, not customer, centred:* small firms often describe what they have to offer in terms of the technical specifications of their product or service, rather than by reference to what use this will be to a potential customer. Whilst there is a place for detailed product descriptions, and technical data (usually the back page) the first consideration to a reader will be the benefits they can perceive for themselves. Owner-managers, who probably have the greatest input into the contents of a small firm's leaflet, may be involved with the technology or production aspect of a small business, and therefore write literature about it from this, and not the customers', perspective.

❒ *Wasteful quantities:* small firms typically seem to have a large pile of outdated brochures gathering dust in a corner of the office. Whilst some waste is inevitable, more attention to leaflet composition and content can keep this to a minimum. Many expensive brochures contain details and prices which are bound to date rapidly. The conflict for a small firm is usually between printing enough to represent an economic order quantity, and maintaining flexibility in the content of the literature as information changes. The permutations of graphic production are now so great that it is often possible to resolve this conflict.

For example, one small enterprise, a primary school, needed a brochure every year, for prospective parents. The head teacher felt that presentation was important in the changed environment of primary schools, which had become more competitive. The annual requirement was for only 200 brochures, and some details, such as the names of teachers and governors, could change every year. This seemed to preclude the preferred four colour cover on cost grounds. A solution was found by producing a more expensive outer folder, which could be printed in larger quantities to be used over several years, into which loose sheets containing the information likely to change were inserted.

Online communications including the Internet

Bill Gates[28] forecast that the information highway would revolutionise business communications in ways that small firms would particularly benefit from. The use of electronic mail, web sites and network systems can help entrepreneurs overcome some of the inherent problems of smallness. The evidence so far is that larger firms have been first to use the new technology. Small business owners may be wise to be cautious. To date there is little evidence of profits coming from the new possibilities, except for a few well-publicised examples. However, the logic of Gates' argument is inescapable in the long term as electronic communications open up international markets for even the smallest firm, and allow the one-man band to remain in his or her virtual office wherever he or she goes.

The Internet provides a variety of new ways of communicating marketing messages. It allows computers to communicate with each other from anywhere in the world, so that they can both send and receive messages. Three types of marketing communications have become popular over the Internet with small business owners:

☐ *Electronic mail:* email can be in the form of personalised marketing messages (e.g. from an owner-manager to a client), or impersonal 'spams' (unsolicited commercial email, apparently named after a sketch in the TV programme, *Monty Python's Flying Circus,* in which everything on the menu was the same: spam). Email can be used for controllable marketing communications (e.g. newsletters from a small business to its customer base) or uncontrollable messages (e.g. positive or negative word-of-mouth recommendations by customers about a small firm).

☐ *Newsgroups:* these are online discussion forums of people exchanging news and views on their particular areas of interest over the Internet. They have become informal yet important ways of spreading positive and negative communications about products and services, including those of small businesses.

☐ *Web sites:* the development of the World Wide Web seems to offer smaller businesses an opportunity to communicate their message internationally at minimum expense. It offers an incredible combination of international coverage with individual targeting: it is already used by over 300 million people all around the world, yet it is also able to deliver messages targeted at one individual. The problem is that it is difficult to be noticed amidst the clutter of communications from millions of companies and countless individuals that have web sites.

In addition to its own web site, a small business can also use banner advertising on other firms' web sites. 'Ad banners' are the most common form of advertising on the web, so-called because they form a banner across the top of web pages, carrying promotional messages and links to the advertiser's web site. The success rate of the advertisement is measured by the number of 'click-throughs' to the advertiser. They may be paid for like more traditional forms of advertising (from small sums for relatively unknown sites, up to £10,000 per month for popular sites). Banners are also exchanged through reciprocal arrangements under which two or more organisations agree to link their sites to increase traffic to each other.

Advertising on the Internet has advantages: it can be relatively inexpensive to set up; visitors to web sites can be tracked to provide market information; it has the potential to reach audiences world-wide immediately; it can be very creative and interactive.

The significant disadvantage is that it is very difficult for an advertiser to be noticed by their target market in a relatively disorganised, unstructured system of millions of web sites. 'Visibility' of a web site is at least as important as its design. For this reason search engines that rank the list of sites according to their relevance to the user's search have become very important. Businesses need to ensure their site is ranked near to the top of relevant search lists, because users rarely bother to look beyond the first ten names. This entails constant vigilance and management to ensure that web sites are configured to the search engines' criteria for listing results ('hits') of the keyword search. As each engine uses different criteria to search its index covering millions of web pages, managing the visibility of a web site has become a skilled job.

Businesses also use a variety of offline promotional methods to increase traffic to web sites because of the difficulties in raising and maintaining visibility online. These include main media advertising through television, radio and direct mail, as well as general publicity by including web site addresses on letterheads and marketing literature.

All of these factors mean that advertising on the Internet may not be as cost effective as it may at first appear. Whilst sites can be designed and hosted relatively cheaply, maintaining sites and promoting their visibility can become more expensive.

5.4 Marketing channels

Marketing channels refer to how goods or services reach the marketplace. For any firm, there is a fundamental choice of channels: to distribute direct to end-users or through intermediaries. From this basic choice, other options then emerge as illustrated in Figure 12.4.

Direct to end-users	Through intermediaries
• Direct sales	• Agents/distributors
• Retail and specialist outlets	• Wholesalers
• Mail order	• Mail order companies
	• Retailers and specialist outlets
	• Multi-level marketing

Figure 12.4 Distribution channels

These options are self-explanatory, except for the last, 'multi-level' or 'network' marketing.

❑ *Multi-level marketing:* this rather confusing term has been used to describe a variety of ways of reaching consumers, by a chain of direct selling agents. At one extreme this includes 'pyramid selling' which is now legally regulated, as many self-employed people were duped into buying a stock of product which was being sold only to fill up the distribution pipe-line and rarely to end-users.

However, it does have its more legitimate forms. 'Party plan', for example, is a method of distributing a variety of products, including plastic containers, books and cosmetics by encouraging household gatherings at which the products are sold. This approach involves sales agents, usually operating on a part-time self-employed basis, who organise the gatherings and earn commission on the sales.

In the USA, a popular distribution system is sometimes referred to as 'multi-level' or 'network marketing'. It does involve setting up a pyramid structure of sales agents, who earn commission both on their sales to consumers and to other agents, but there is a crucial difference to the discredited pyramid selling. The agent does not need to buy stock in order to make a sale, other than for demonstration purposes; thus if final users are not buying the product the system breaks down. The promoters of this system make extravagant claims about the level of sales now being achieved in the UK, and the growth they expect. It has attracted considerable participation from self-employed business people, selling such products as water softeners and household cleaning materials[29].

Advantages of intermediaries

Small firms, with limited resources and expertise, can particularly benefit from using intermediaries. Specific advantages are:

❑ *Local knowledge and contacts of the intermediary:* small firms often base their business on the owner-manager's local know-how. Expanding into territories where it no longer applies can be risky without an intermediary to supply specific knowledge of the environment.

- ❒ *Reduced distribution costs:* a small manufacturer can considerably reduce their distribution costs by using an agent or wholesaler, thereby eliminating the need for a large number of small deliveries direct to retailers.

- ❒ *Reduced stock holding:* by shifting the responsibility for stockholding down the distribution chain, a small manufacturer can reduce their own stock holding requirements and the associated financial and space considerations.

Disadvantages of intermediaries

There are disadvantages·

- ❒ *Loss of contact with the marketplace:* a small firm relying on intermediaries for their distribution and selling will be one or more steps removed from the consumer they are seeking to serve. Their customer becomes the distributor, wholesaler, or retailer, and they must rely on them for information about customers down the chain, including the final consumer.

- ❒ *Less control over how the product is presented to the final customer:* as we have already seen, products extend beyond the physical attributes of an item. By using intermediaries, the original manufacturer is handing over control of some aspects of the extended product to somebody else. An intermediary may be providing the after-sales service and certainly the information and advice; packaging can be changed by distributors, and the presentation of the benefits of the product to the consumer is out of the control of the originator.

- ❒ *Less influence over the levels of marketing effort:* most intermediaries represent more than one supplier. They therefore exercise choice over which products receive the most effort in terms of display, promotional effort and selling time. One of the strengths of the franchise system is that it avoids this issue, by insisting on the exclusivity for a franchisor's products or services with the franchisee.

- ❒ *Less revenue per item sold:* last but not least, intermediaries cost money; although this is not a fixed cost, but a variable depending on the level of sales, loss of revenue can be substantial – commonly at least one-third of the final selling price if distributed direct to retail or up to two-thirds where agents and wholesalers are used.

All these disadvantages multiply as the distribution chain becomes longer.

Choice of channel

For a small firm the choice of distribution channel will be conditioned by a number of factors:

- ❒ *The customer:* the existing buying pattern of the target end use group will not be easy to change. A small firm will normally wish to follow traditional distribution routes for their product or services, leaving major innovations in this area to companies with more resources. However, it may be appropriate to try different channels to reach a wider audience. For example, a small manufacturer of soft toys followed the customary wholesale/retail channels for its regular production. But for special occasions, an inexpensive addition to the product could temporarily extend the market potential, which warranted innovative distribution methods. On Valentines Day, the simple addition of a message to a soft teddy bear created a new product, whose market would not be reached by traditional methods. The company found that advertising via a web site on the Internet reached a new audience for their product, which was physically distributed to respondents by post.

☐ *The product:* distribution channels need to match the needs of the product that is on offer. An electronics manufacturer, designing highly technical products, customised to client requirements, probably has no choice but to sell and distribute directly themselves. A publisher of greetings cards, sold through a multiplicity of independent retailers, probably has no option but to use a wholesaler.

Most small firms offer a service rather than manufacture a tangible product. In some cases this precludes any form of intermediary distribution. A training consultant can only really deliver their product directly themselves (although they might franchise the format). In other cases, as we have seen, the service offered is part of the distribution chain anyway. For example, a small health food wholesaler is a service company as they manufacture nothing themselves.

☐ *Finance:* there is usually a financial trade-off for a small firm in the use of intermediaries. A small business's cash flow benefits from selling large amounts of stock to distributors and wholesalers. Profitability suffers, however, because of the need to give up margin. The financial circumstances of a small firm will determine which factor predominates.

☐ *Objectives:* the marketing strategy of a small firm will indicate objectives somewhere between the extremes of high volume to wide markets, or lower volume to a select niche. The more the strategy leans towards the former, the more intermediaries will be appropriate; the more it looks like the latter, the more direct distribution will be considered.

The evidence points towards limited distribution practices in small firms. As has been emphasised before, however, the heterogeneous nature of the small firm sector makes this a far from universal rule.

International distribution

International markets are typically ignored by small firms. Surveys of small businesses in all sectors of the economy suggest that a mere 6 per cent sell any of their output outside of the UK[5]. This is despite considerable effort that has been put into providing help[30] and assistance for would-be exporters from such areas as:

☐ Department of Trade and Industry country desks, which provide information on trade with all foreign countries.

☐ British Chambers of Commerce, which issue export documentation, and may offer advice.

☐ Export Credits Guarantee Department, which arranges insurance against the possibility of non-payment.

❑ Central Office of Information offering export publicity services.

At the onset of the open European market in 1992 onwards, small firms were encouraged to look more at export opportunities. So far though, there is little evidence that there has been a change in the attitude which has regarded exports as something to explore once all home market possibilities are exhausted.

5.5 Incentives

Entrepreneurs often use incentives, particularly in the form of low prices or discounts as a way to attract business.

Much over-simplified advice has been offered on the subject of pricing for the small business. Low price, we are told, is not a sustainable competitive advantage for small firms, as they do not have the necessary economies of scale to support long-term price cutting. Price is described as the weak link in the marketing mix of a small firm because lower prices can easily be copied and beaten by competitors, particularly larger companies. Yet many small firms survive, and thrive, on prices substantially lower than their larger competitors. If you want your car serviced cheaply, or a domestic appliance mended inexpensively, you will expect the lowest price from a local trader, not a national company. On the other hand, there are circumstances where the local small firm cannot compete on price alone. Food prices will always be higher in the village general store than in the out of town supermarket. A craftsman-joiner cannot supply windows and doors at anything like the price of the national DIY chain.

In practice, price incentives in the marketing mix depends on the industry and the market. Some markets, especially those involving a customised product or service, suffer diseconomies of scale which a small firm can exploit to produce a price advantage. A small garage or appliance repair firm do not carry the over-heads, particularly in people and premises, of larger operations. The service offered by both has to be individual to the customer and cannot therefore be made more efficient by mass production techniques. In circumstances like these the small firm can establish a lasting competitive edge using price incentives.

In other industries, especially where standard products or services can be produced, economies of scale will operate, and the small firm cannot seek a competitive advantage in pricing. Food and DIY chains can use production efficiencies, and their buying power to reduce prices to levels which the local trader cannot hope to match, let alone beat. Pricing decisions may be crude processes in most small firms, but in the right circumstances low price can still be an effective strategy.

Activity 6 Entrepreneurial research

Entrepreneurs seem to have an instinctive feel for developments in their marketplace. What is the source of this? How do they keep themselves up to date?

6 Informal information gathering

The fourth element in entrepreneurial marketing strategies is information gathering through informal networks.

Networks

The dependence of marketing activities on the owner-manager makes the idea of networking particularly useful in the context of small business marketing. As owner-managers have limited resources within their organisation, they must look elsewhere for advice and information on which to base marketing decisions.

We have already seen that successful entrepreneurs build up a rich mental map of their market environment by making regular, formal and informal, contact with others in the trade, customers, suppliers, competitors, professional bodies and associations etc. They have extensive personal contact networks (PCNs) which they can tap into for market information, advice, and competitive intelligence, (see also Unit 2, 6.2).

Limitations of resources also make collaboration between organisations an important option for small businesses. Inter-organisational relationships (IORs) help supplement product development and other marketing activities which are constrained by money and other resources, (see also section 3, Innovation).

> For example, a group of small retailers were particularly affected by the closure of a nearby multi-storey car park for structural repairs which dramatically reduced passing trade to their shops. Not only did they co-ordinate their case for compensation to the local council, but they mounted a joint promotional campaign offering incentives of subsidised alternative parking and a park-and-ride service.

Marketing competency

Gathering information and making judgements based on it is a key entrepreneurial competency[31].

Competency means a person's underlying characteristic which results in an effective performance in a job. Competency comes from having the relevant knowledge, skills and attitudes to achieve the desired management outcomes. A competent marketing manager has the necessary qualities and skills to ensure an effective performance of an enterprise's marketing activities.

As owner-managers are more than likely marketing managers of their small enterprises as well, which particular competencies should they develop to ensure that they can gather, interpret and use marketing information?

❏ *Judgement*. Entrepreneurs base many of their marketing decisions on their own, personal judgement. Often decisions are based on hunches, intuition or the experience of the entrepreneur. Successful entrepreneurs develop sound judgement to weigh up the pros and cons of options.

> For example, small retailers often buy stock and decide their product range based not on any rigorous statistical analysis of historic winners and trends in

the marketplace, but on their judgement of what has sold well in the past and their feelings about what their customers will want. This is a key marketing decision relying on personal judgement based on internal information of the business.

❐ *Experience.* Experience in a particular industry sector, or of some aspects of the marketing function, greatly improves entrepreneurial marketing competency and information. An understanding of customers' buying behaviour and preferences comes from experience of a particular market segment. Specific marketing skills such as personal selling and the use of direct mail can only be developed with experience.

❐ *Knowledge.* Successful entrepreneurs have a good knowledge of their product or service range, and the individual markets in which they operate and use this as a base for marketing decisions.

❐ *Communication.* The dominant role of the owner-manager places great emphasis on their communication skills, both outside and inside the business. They are usually the front-line sales person of their organisation, handling many of the direct communications with customers. They also tend to handle communications with other key stakeholders outside of the enterprise such as banks, investors and key suppliers.

They also need to communicate with everyone inside of the organisation to ensure they can play their full part in any marketing campaign.

> For example, an owner-manager ran an advertising campaign for a new product line but did not adequately brief everyone in the organisation. When the owner-manager was out of the office, another member of staff answering the telephone was unable to answer customer enquiries competently as he was unsure of details of the new product and the promotion.

❐ *Other competencies.* Other important competencies for entrepreneurial marketing are:

- ○ *motivation* – having the desire to carry marketing plans through;
- ○ *planning* – organisational abilities to implement complex marketing activities;
- ○ *vision* – the ability to identify market opportunities ahead of time.

Successful entrepreneurial marketing very often relies on the competency of the owner-manager in these key areas. How can they improve their skills? The first stage is for the owner-manager to be aware of their level of competence in relation to marketing activities so that strengths and weaknesses can be taken into account. For example, there is little point in basing a campaign on personal selling if the owner-manager's communication competence is poor.

Secondly, these competencies represent skills which can be developed once weaker elements are identified.

7 Case studies and activities

Case studies *Grays Framing Studios*

Case 1 Marketing problems at Grays picture framing

Bryony Hannam was having marketing problems with her picture framing business, Grays Framing Studios. She found that having a partner, who looked after the production and operations in the workshop, gave her more time to spend with customers, but she did not have enough time for marketing. When they had purchased the business, the basic product and services offered were:

1. *A bespoke picture framing service*

    Sixty per cent of sales were made by providing a framing service for customers' own images, ranging from photographs to fine art. As all the operations were carried out in their own workshop, this type of business generated a good gross margin of 70 per cent: in other words the variable costs of the mouldings, board, glass and other materials involved in the framing process averaged 30 per cent of the final selling price.

2. *Framed and unframed pictures*

    As well as the framing service, a range of pictures, including inexpensive prints and posters, limited editions, original water colours and oils, were offered through the three retail shops. Although these were usually sold framed, they could be purchased unframed. The gross margin on a framed picture averaged 50 per cent, as the cost of purchasing the image lowered the profit available on the framing. However, stock costs were not necessarily a problem, as some local artists were happy to leave their work on display on a sale or return basis.

She had managed to improve the turnover of each of their three shops by offering a comprehensive design service. Many regular customers were even happy to leave the choice of moulding and framing to Bryony as they had learned to trust her judgement. However, after initial increases, sales had now reached a plateau once again and Bryony needed to consider her options for continued growth. Each of the three shops averaged approximately £12,000 turnover per month, with an average spend per customer order of £60. She studied the customer records and divided her customers into three main types:

❑ *regulars* who visited the shops and made a purchase at least once every 6 months. She calculated there were about 50 of these each month, per shop.

❑ *irregulars* who came back more than once, but only after an interval of 6 months or more. There were about 100 of these per shop, per month.

❑ *one-offs* who came into the shop to make a purchase but had not returned. There were about 50 of these per shop, per month.

Each shop was positioned between the local high streets and a car park so that convenience and passing trade were maximised. However, in one location, Bryony was particularly concerned about the effects of a new parking scheme proposed by the local planners which would reduce the number of parking places available to her customers. She had introduced new services to attract customers. Each shop now offered complimentary tea or coffee to customers prepared to linger, a concept Bryony had borrowed from a well-known book shop in New York. For larger orders, Grays Framing now made free home deliveries, a service they were keen to offer because of increased parking problems at peak times.

'If we are to grow, we need more customers,' she had explained to her partner Tony Meeham who ran the workshop, 'but it's like a leaky bucket. As fast as we fill up with new customers, we lose others who never seem to come back. None of the promotions we've tried have had any lasting effect. Most of our customers still come through recommendations.'

'Who do you think does the recommending?' Tony asked.

'Other customers mainly. But I have met customers who are sent to us from other local shops, particularly photographers – even the gallery in the high street. Some new customers come in simply because they are passing by, but prompted by what someone else has said to them.'

'Why do people recommend us? I presume our outstanding workshop quality is high up the list.' Tony smiled.

'Well, no actually,' said Bryony. 'They take that for granted, I'm afraid. They seem to like the personal service and design advice we offer in the shops. Customers get to know me or someone else in one of the shops, and trust us to advise them. The problem is that I can't be in all three shops at once, and staff tend to leave. If a customer comes in after 6 months or more, they might not recognise anyone and we have to build the relationship up all over again.'

'Do you think we should consult a marketing expert?' asked Tony.

'Mmm. Or I could go on a course. But will they know anything about the picture framing market – or the marketing problems of small businesses like ours?'

Activities

i) What marketing problems does Bryony have? Consider the list of typical small business marketing problems in Table 12.2. Which of these does she share? Does she have any others?

ii) The six markets model in Figure 12.2 describes important markets other than customers. Which individuals or organisations might fall into the six categories in the case of Grays Framing? Which do you think require marketing approaches, and in what order of priority?

iii) Consider Bryony's analysis of her customer groups. How could she use the model of customer loyalty in Figure 12.3 to improve her sales?

iv) Like many other small business managers, Bryony considers that most of her new customers come through word-of-mouth marketing. How can she actively encourage recommendations?

Case 2 Marketing innovations at Grays Framing

Initially Bryony had thought that the only way to expand the business was to increase sales through the shops. Now she had another plan. The customers they attracted at the moment were primarily householders buying pictures for home decorations. They occasionally attracted orders from businesses, however, who wanted a quantity of framing for a variety of applications. Bryony decided to focus her expansion plans on this commercial market. In talking to local businesses, she discovered that some had a need for a high volume of standard framing. A restaurant owner, for example, wanted to hang pictures in the same type of frame all over his interior walls; a local hotel had a continuous demand for framed pictures, and repairs to damaged ones.

In visiting business premises, she noticed also that many did not have pictures on their walls. Reception areas were left bare and uninviting; offices cried out for the added touch of a well-chosen picture. By probing office managers, Bryony found that many were receptive to the idea of improving the environment, but did not have the time or budget (or both) to do anything about it.

Bryony had come up with the idea of a hire purchase scheme. She would take all the problems away from the office manager, by advising them on the pictures and frames to select, and allowing them to be purchased over one year by an instalment plan.

There were a number of marketing issues to resolve. A key issue was which market to focus on first. There was a wide range of possible commercial clients: advertising agencies and design studios often needed artwork framed or mounted for display and exhibitions. Larger companies framed certificates and awards for employees. The catering industry always needed an inexpensive source of framed pictures. The office environment of most organisations, large and small, could be improved by the addition of appropriate framed art. When Bryony wrote down a list of potential customers it covered large and small firms, professional practices, local government, hospitals and schools – in fact most types of organisation in the local area.

Another issue was the pricing structure, as Bryony realised she would have to offer incentives over normal retail prices to attract commercial business. The catering industry was used to buying competitively and demanded discounts of 50 per cent or more over normal retail framing prices for substantial orders. She believed that buyers for other end uses, such as office decor and exhibitions, would be less price sensitive but that the order quantities were likely to be lower.

Her biggest concern was how to attract customers in the first place.

'We know that customer recommendations are by far the most important source of new business for our shops', Bryony explained to her partner, Tony, 'but you can't expect recommendations if you don't have the right customers in the first place. How do we break into some of these commercial markets if we don't have an existing base?'

'Perhaps we need to visit some potential customers and explain our services to them,' suggested Tony.

'I've tried that,' said Bryony. 'Two problems. First it's very difficult to get in to see anyone. You know how you always avoid seeing any new suppliers. Secondly, the few I have seen all say, "yes very interesting; when an application next comes up we'll think about you, good day." I've already wasted a lot of my time with no real orders. I feel I need more information about some of these customers, such as what prompts them to buy framing and who makes the decisions. Any suggestions?'

Activities

i)   Recommend a targeting strategy for Bryony. How should she decide on which markets to target and why?

ii) Recommend the marketing methods she should use for each of the proposed target markets, in the short and longer term.

iii) How could she find out more about the target groups? What information gathering tactics could she use?

iv) Present these and other aspects as an outline marketing plan which considers each of the 4 Is of innovation, identification of target markets, interactive marketing methods, and information gathering (see Figure 12.1). Suggest a marketing budget for your plan appropriate to the size of this business.

Extended activity *A marketing evaluation*

Consider two small businesses (preferably involved in the food and drinks industry) with which you are familiar. (See the Extended activity in Unit 1 and subsequently.)

Compare and contrast the marketing strategy of these two businesses. List their strategies under the categories of the 4 Is of innovation, identification of markets, interactive marketing methods and information gathering.

In what ways do you think they are good practitioners of marketing philosophy?

How could you improve upon their marketing strategies, and their implementation of marketing methods?

In conclusion

Once you have finished this Unit, it is recommended that you turn to Section B, Planning a new venture, and complete Step 3.4, Planning the marketing.

8 References and further reading

References and further information

1. See for example: Waterworth, D. *Marketing for the Small Business*, Macmillan Education, 1987 (in the Macmillan Small Business series); Brown, R. *Marketing for the Small Firm*, Holt, Rhinehart & Winston, 1985; Fowler, D. *Selling and Marketing for the Small Business*, Sphere Study Aids, 1984.

    One book which concentrates on the practical aspects of what is used by small businesses is Hingston, P. *The Greatest Sales & Marketing Book*, Hingston, 1989.

2. Curran, J. and Blackburn, R. *Small Firms and Local Economic Networks*, a report to the Midland Bank, December 1991.

3. *Starting-Up: A Barclays Report on Britain's Small Business Men and Women*, Barclays Bank, 1992.

4. Storey, D. and Johnson, S. *Job Generation and Labour Market Change*, Macmillan Press, 1987.

5. Carson, D. 'Some Exploratory Models of Assessing Small Firms' Marketing Performance', *European Journal of Marketing*, 24 (11), 1990.

6. Carson, D., 'The Evolution of Marketing in Small Firms, in Marketing and Small Business' (Special Issue), *European Journal of Marketing*, 19 (5), 1985.

7. Stokes, D., Blackburn, R. and Fitchew, S. *Marketing for Small Firms: Towards a Conceptual Understanding*, report to Royal Mail Consulting, July, Small Business Research Centre, Kingston University, 1997.

8. Two Scandinavian writers, Christian Grönroos and Evert Gummesson, particularly articulated these criticisms. See, for example: Gummesson, E. 'The New Marketing – Developing Long-Term Interactive Relationships', *Long Range Planning*, 20 (4), pp. 10–20, 1984; Grönroos, C. (1994) 'From Marketing Mix to Relationship Marketing: Towards a Paradigm Shift in Marketing', *Management Decision*, 32 (2), pp. 4–20, 1994.

9. Payne, A., Christopher, M., Clark, M. and Peck, H. *Relationship Marketing for Competitive Advantage: Winning and Keeping Customers*, Butterworth-Heinemann, 1995. This book summarises the principles of relationship marketing in a variety of different contexts.

10. Binks, M. and Jennings, A. 'New Firms as a Source of Industrial Regeneration', in Scott, M., Gibb, A., Lewis, J. and Faulkner, T. (eds), *Small Firms' Growth and Development*, Gower, 1986.

11. Rothwell, R. 'The Role of Small Firms in Technological Innovation' in Curran, J. (ed) *The Survival of the Small Firm*, Gower, 1986.

12. See Adams, A. and Wallbank, W. *The Introduction of New Products by Smaller Manufacturing Firms*, SRC Final Report GR/A 71072, UMIST, 1981.

13. See Adams, A. and Wallbank, M. 'The Evaluation of New Product Ventures in Small Firms', in Scott, M., Gibb A., Lewis, J. and Faulkner, T. (eds), *Small Firms' Growth and Development*, Gower, 1986.

14. Business Innovation Centres (BICS) are part of the European Business Innovation Centre Network (EBW) which promotes innovation in SMEs. EUREKA encourages collaborative R&D across Europe. Further details are in DTI, *A Guide to Help for Small Firms* URN 97/525.

15. See for example Stanworth, J. and Stanworth, C. *Work 2000 – the Future for Industry, Employment and Society*, Chapman, 1991.

16. *Partners in Innovation: Business and Academia*, McKinsey and Co. Inc. Innovation Project, 1995.

17. The *Guardian* reported on 23 September 1991 (p. 12 New Business) that 14 of the 24 companies working on projects in Link programmes developing analytical and measurement technology were small to medium-sized companies.

18. Free advice on business names can be obtained from Companies House, Crown Way, Cardiff CF4 3UZ. The DTI produce helpful leaflets, such as 'Business Names and Business Ownership', available from this address.

19. The 1988 Copyright, Designs and Patents Act reformed much of British law in this respect, and laws protecting intellectual property rights in the EU are being harmonised. There is also a European Patent Convention which allows you to obtain protection in a number of European countries without the need to apply for registration in each state. Details from the Patent Office, Newport, Gwent NP9 1RH, tel. 01633 814000. See also Williams, S. *Lloyds Bank Small Business Guide*, Chapter 12 'Beating the pirates'.

20. Kotler, P. *Marketing Management*, 10th edition, Prentice Hall, 2000. This is probably the most widely used marketing textbook.

21. Dalgic, T. and Leeuw, M. 'Niche Marketing Revisited: Concept, Applications and Some European Cases', *European Journal of Marketing*, 20 (1), pp. 39–55, 1994.

22. Gummesson, E. 'The New Marketing – Developing Long-Term Interactive Relationships', *Long Range Planning*, 20 (4), pp. 10–20, 1987.

23. Arndt, J. 'Word-of-Mouth Advertising and Informal Communication' in Cox, D, (ed.) *Risk Taking and Information Handling in Consumer Behaviour*, Harvard University, 1967.

24. Bayus, B. L. 'Word-of-Mouth: The Indirect Effects of Marketing Efforts', *The Journal of Advertising Research*, 25 (3), June/July, 1985.

25. For a survey of the problems of small retailers see Kirby, D. A., 'The Small Retailer' in *The Survival of the Small Firm*, Vol. 1, Curran, J., Stanworth, J. and Williams, D. (eds), Gower, 1986.

26. There are several good guides to Direct Marketing and Royal Mail produce useful advice. See Bacon, M. *DIY Direct Marketing: Secrets for Small Businesses*, John Wiley, 1997.

27. If information on individuals is stored on computer, then registration under the Data Protection Act is normally required. Further information can be obtained from the Registrars Enquiry Service, tel. 01625 535777.

28. Gates, B. *The Road Ahead*, Penguin, 1995.

29. For background information on multi-level, or network marketing (although not totally objective) see Hitching, F. *Boom Business of the 90s*, MGP Publications, 1993.

30. For a detailed listing of help that is available from the DTI, and other sources, see *A Guide to Help for Small Businesses*, DTI, URN 97/525.

31. Carson, D., Cromie, S., McGowan, P. and Hill, J. *Marketing and Entrepreneurship in SMEs*, Prentice Hall, 1995. This book takes an innovative approach in combining the disciplines of entrepreneurship and marketing. In particular, it stresses the need for competency development and networking.

Recommended further reading

❏ Carson, D., Cromie, S., McGowan, P. and Hill, J. *Marketing and Entrepreneurship in SMEs*, Prentice Hall, 1995.

❏ Chaston, I. *Entrepreneurial Marketing*, Palgrave, 2000.

❏ Stokes, D. 'Marketing and the Small Firm', in Carter, S. and Jones-Evans, D. *Enterprise and Small Business*, FT/Prentice Hall, 2000.

❏ Stokes, D. *Marketing: A Case Study Approach*, Continuum, 2001.

❏ Carson, D. 'Some Exploratory Models of Assessing Small Firms' Marketing Performance', *European Journal of Marketing*, 24 (11), 1990.

❏ Williams, S. *Lloyds Bank Small Business Guide*, 2001. Chapter 11, 'The right name', and Chapter 12, 'Beating the pirates'.

13 Money

This Unit is about another of the key strategic influences on a small business – money. The Unit considers the financial needs of small firms, the sources of funds available to them, and the appropriate control of those funds. Financial analysis is covered with some detailed instructions on how to construct profit/loss, cash flow and balance sheet forecasts in 21 steps. This is done using a worked example derived from the case study.

Contents

Activity 1 Financial requirements

A small firm needs finance in a variety of areas. What are the major categories of financial requirements? What does a small business need money for?

1 Financial needs – the uses of funds

Small firms need money to finance a host of different requirements. In looking at the types and adequacy of funds available, it is important to match the use of the funds with appropriate funding methods. Figure 13.1 illustrates the principal capital needs of a small firm.

A small firm needs ...			
£ *Permanent capital* • start up • expansion and development • innovation • refinancing	£ *Working capital* • debtor/creditor gap • seasonal fluctuations • bridging finance • short-lived assets	£ *Asset finance* • plant and machinery • equipment and furniture • buildings • vehicles	£ *Finance for international trade* • growth through international trading

So it requires ...			
£ *Equity capital*	£ *Short-term finance (up to 3 years)*	£ *Medium- to long-term finance*	£ *Specialist and export finance*

For which the main sources are ...			
Personal investment Venture capital institutions Public sector sources Public equity	Clearing banks Finance houses Factoring companies Leasing companies Public sector sources	Clearing banks Venture capital institutions Pension funds Insurance companies Finance houses Leasing companies Public sector sources	Clearing banks Factoring companies Export houses Finance houses

Figure 13.1 The uses and sources of funds for a small business

Permanent capital – equity capital

The permanent capital base of a small firm usually comes from some form of equity investment in shares in a limited company, or personal loans to or from partners or sole traders. It is used to finance the one-off start-up costs of an enterprise, or major developments and expansions in its life-cycle. It may be required for a significant innovation, such as a new product development. In some cases, it is required to refinance a firm that has acquired borrowings which are inappropriate to its current situation; short-term borrowings, in the form of loans or overdrafts, may need to be converted into more permanent capital as a small firm grows, or runs into problems. Equity from private investors may also be sought to take a small firm into the medium- or large-size category, or as an exit route for the original investors.

Ideally, permanent capital is only serviced when the firm can afford it; investment in equity is rewarded by dividends from profits, or a capital gain when shares are sold. It is not therefore a continual drain from the cash flow of a company, such as a loan which needs interest and capital repayments on a regular basis. Equity capital usually provides a stake in the ownership of the business, and therefore the investor accepts some element of risk in that returns are not automatic, but only made when the small firm has generated surpluses.

Working capital – short-term finance

Most small firms need working capital to bridge the gap between when they get paid, and when they have to pay their suppliers and their overhead costs. Requirements for this kind of short-term finance will vary considerably by business type.

For example, a manufacturer or small firm selling to other businesses will have to offer credit terms, and the resulting debtors will need to be financed; the faster the growth, the more the debtors, and the larger the financial requirement.

A retailer, a restaurant, a public house, or other types of outlet selling direct to the general public, will however often collect cash with the sale. If they are paying their suppliers on credit terms, the cash flow will be advantageous. In some cases, this will be sufficient to finance the start up of a small firm, so that suppliers are effectively financing the business.

However, even these types of business may need working capital to fund temporary losses, caused by seasonal fluctuations, or to cope with prepayment of expenses such as rent payable in advance.

Although short-term finance is normally used to fund the trading of a business, it is also sometimes needed to purchase assets which are short-lived, such as company vehicles which may be changed every 2 or 3 years.

Asset finance – medium- to long-term finance

The purchase of tangible assets is usually financed on a longer-term basis, from 3 to 10 years, or more depending on the useful life of the asset. Plant, machinery, equipment, fixtures and fittings, company vehicles and buildings may all be financed by medium- or long-term loans from a variety of lending bodies.

International trade finance

Exporting brings its own set of money problems. Currency fluctuations, lengthy payment terms and security of payment all give rise to the need for some kind of specialist or export finance.

> **Activity 2** Sources of funds
>
> A small firm has several options for obtaining finance. What are the major types of finance available? For what purpose is each type best suited?

2 Obtaining funds

2.1 Sources of finance

Personal investment

The majority of small businesses rely on internal funds to finance their business. Three-quarters of small firms use retained profits and cash flow from existing business to fund their development, according to the Bank of England[1]. The most important source of start-up capital comes from owner-managers themselves, although there is evidence of regional differences[2]. The level of personal owner investment is conditioned by two main factors:

❑ *Creditworthiness of the owner:* as homes are a major source of guarantee on loans and overdrafts, the higher values of properties and the rates of home ownership in prosperous regions will facilitate more borrowing to start up ventures.

❑ *Experience and awareness of sources of funds:* people who are pushed into owner-management through redundancy or other problems tend to have limited financial expertise and lower awareness of possible sources of funds.

Banks

The main source of external funding is still conventional bank lending, with around half of external finance coming from overdrafts and term loans[3]. There has been a move away from a traditional emphasis on collateral and guarantees towards the use of business plans and cash flow projections, in securing loans. However, lack of collateral is still cited by some owners as a significant barrier to growth. There is a higher reliance on overdrafts amongst UK firms than elsewhere. For example, overdrafts accounted for 56 per cent of small firm debt in the UK compared to 14 per cent in Germany[4].

Until the end of the 1970s the major banks did not differentiate small businesses as a customer group, offering them two basic products: standard overdrafts and loans. The dramatic increase in the numbers of small businesses and the self-employed during the 1980s, stimulated the main banks to develop services specifically targeted at small firms. In the early 1990s, a combination of high interest rates and the recession highlighted some tensions in the relationships between small firms and their banks[5]. Business owners complained that banks used high-handed and unfair practices in their dealings with small firms. Issues have focused on:

❑ *Interest rates and bank charges:* the range of bank lending margins to small business customers is wide, varying from 2 to 7 per cent over base rate, although the average margins were 3 to 4 per cent in 1997[1]. The Forum of Private Business has complained that bank charges can be both unpredictable and unjustifiably high.

❐ *Lack of support in problem times:* owners' complaints that banks tend to with-draw their support when it is most needed have led to calls for a code of conduct between banks and small firms. The Forum of Private Business has gone further, calling for a written contract between banks and small business customers, which would operate on the same principle as points on a driving licence, making sure that overdrafts could not be removed without a recog-nised cause.

❐ *Advice and information:* there have been complaints that borrowing was encouraged when the enterprise culture really got going in the mid-1980s, only to be unexpectedly curtailed in the more difficult 1990s. Problems have also surfaced over specific advice given by banks which has proven to be misleading, for instance over the credit ratings of customers.

Whilst many of these issues were magnified by the particular strains of a reces-sionary economy, they do point to an underlying shift in the relationships between banks and small business. This has evolved from disinterested detach-ment prior to the 1970s, through an over-enthusiastic honeymoon in the 1980s, to a slightly disenchanted, uneasy alliance since then. Most banks have made efforts to tailor their services for different types of SME activity; for example, banks have begun to recognise the importance of ethnic enterprises by making efforts to improve the cultural awareness of bank staff[1].

Although traditional bank finance remains the most important source of external finance for small firms, it is declining in importance as owner-managers diversify their ways of raising money. Bank finance represented over 60 per cent of external finance in the late 1980s; the most recent Bank of England estimate is 47 per cent[1]. Moreover the balance between loans and overdrafts has shifted in favour of term loans; the ratio of overdrafts to loans is now 30:70, compared to 49:51 in 1992. The implication is that owner-managers have a greater understanding of their financing needs as they are less prone to rely on overdrafts for requirements which need other types of finance.

Venture capital

Equity finance made up only 3 per cent of the external finance of SMEs in the UK from 1995 to 1997, according to Bank of England estimates[1]. It can be provided by banks' equity funds, venture capital funds and private individuals acting as 'busi-ness angels'.

❐ *Banks* offer a limited range of equity investment products; for example HSBC has a fund that invests in technology-based firms. In addition, all the main clearing banks sponsor the National Business Angel Network which attempts to provide links between firms that need investment and private individuals willing to provide finance in return for an equity stake (see section 2.2).

❐ *Venture capital funds* in the UK provide finance for growing businesses, usually through equity capital with some loan element. There are over 100 venture capital companies in the UK, who obtain investment funds from a variety of sources, including pension funds, insurance companies, investment trusts, regional development agencies, and private individuals. The best known is probably 3i (Investors in Industry), established in 1945 by the Bank of England[1] and the clearing banks to provide finance to growing firms.

As venture capitalists provide risk finance, their rates of return targets are high, varying from 25 to 60 per cent depending on the risk involved. The structure of any particular investment will vary, but usually involves any combination of three types of capital: equity shares, preference shares and loans. The level of share ownership required is normally less than 50 per cent with a typical stake between 30 and 40 per cent; a seat on the board of directors is also common.

Venture capitalists seek exit routes, including a public listing on the stock exchange, such as the Alternative Investment Market (AIM, see below). However, the need for clearly visible exit routes restricts the types of company in which the venture capitalist is interested. Whilst they do invest in start ups, this is not particularly favoured, unless it already seems to be a substantial business in its early days, capable of generating profits over £250,000 within 4 to 5 years; this often implies involvement in a new, high technology industry. More commonly, Venture Capital Funds are used for the expansion of already established, successful firms capable of sustained growth, or for management buy-outs.

According to the British Venture Capital Association (BVCA), the UK has the most developed venture capital industry in Europe and is second only to the USA in world importance[6]. Between 1983 and 1998, it invested £28 billion in 18,000 companies. The most common category of these investments was for expansion capital (51 per cent of companies) with start ups and buy-outs the other most popular forms of investment.

❏ *Business angels* are individuals with the means and desire to invest directly in small companies. This informal venture capital market is relatively invisible but a number of business angel networks (BANs) exist to provide an introduction service for owners seeking money and business angels willing to invest. Estimates suggest there are some 18,000 business angels in the UK, who annually invest approximately £500 million in SMEs[7].

Other forms of finance

The other main forms of finance for small firms are leasing, hire purchase and factoring[8].

❏ *Leasing* allows a small firm to obtain the use of equipment, machinery or vehicles without owning them. Ownership is retained by the leasing company, although in many cases there is a purchase option at the end of lease period.

❏ *Hire purchase* provides the immediate use of the asset and also ownership of it, provided that payments according to the agreement are made.

❒ *Factoring* is a specialist form of finance to provide working capital to young, under-capitalised businesses. The factoring company takes responsibility for collection of debts and pays a percentage (usually up to 80 per cent) of the value of the invoices to the issuing company. The company thus has immediate payment once an invoice is issued, although it pays for this service by not receiving the full value of the invoices.

Export finance

The most important step in financing international trade is in ensuring full and prompt payment.

❒ *The Export Credits Guarantee Department (ECGD)* of the DTI provides credit insurance that gives cover in the event of non-payment by an overseas customer. The ECGD offer a variety of insurance schemes, which a small firm can assign to a bank, or other lending body, in order to obtain export finance.

❒ *Export houses* offer a wide range of services to exporters including finance.

2.2 Public initiatives

Successive governments have acted to assist the funding of small businesses with several schemes (see also Unit 5, section 5.2, Financial assistance, which has summaries of some of these schemes).

Small firms' Loan Guarantee Scheme

The Loan Guarantee Scheme (LGS) was introduced in 1981 to help small firms with a viable business proposal to obtain finance when they could not meet lending banks' conventional requirements for security. In certain circumstances the government will agree to guarantee a bank loan, in return for which the borrowing firm pays an interest rate premium.

The terms and conditions have varied considerably over the years. Currently, the scheme is open to new and existing UK companies with an annual turnover less than £1.5 million (£5m for manufacturers). The government, through the DTI, guarantees 70 per cent of a qualifying bank loan to a new business, and 85 per cent if the firm has been trading for at least 2 years. Loans can be from £5,000 up to £100,000 (£250,000 for 'established' business over 2 years), repayable over 2 to 10 years; there is a premium of 1.5 per cent (reduced to 0.5 per cent if the loan is taken at a fixed rate of interest) payable to the DTI by the borrower in addition to normal bank interest rates[9].

By 1994 over £139 million of loans, to more than 36,000 small firms, had been guaranteed by the scheme from its introduction in 1981. From 1994 to 1998, approximately 6,000–7,500 firms were supported each year in obtaining loans with a total value of £200–300 million[1]. However, from 1996 the number and value of loans guaranteed has been falling year on year. The overall effects of the scheme on small business financing remain minimal as the total value of loans made under the scheme still accounts for less than 0.5 per cent of total bank lending to small firms.

The Enterprise Investment Scheme (EIS)

The need for the investment of permanent capital from private sources as equity in small business prompted the government to introduce the Business Expansion Scheme (BES) in 1983. This was not targeted originally at investment by the owner-manager, as the scheme specifically precluded investors from being directors, or employees of investment, in small firms, but by individuals who would remain as investors, not as managers. The incentive for this investment was generous tax relief to help compensate for the higher risks involved. Investors could deduct up to £40,000 in any one year from their tax liability to match the size of their investment. The scheme attracted not only direct investment by individuals, but also BES portfolios, offered by some financial institutions who selected a range of businesses for investment, thereby spreading the risk of the investment and putting it under professional management. This also had the effect of concentrating investment in larger firms. In 1988, the scheme was extended to include residential property let under an assured tenancy agreement. This proved such an attraction to investors that it took over 90 per cent of the funds in the following two years. The 1992 Budget announced the end of the scheme by 1993 as most of the funds were ending up in property investments and not the small enterprises for whom they were originally intended.

In 1994, the Enterprise Investment Scheme (EIS) was introduced to replace the BES. It excludes private rented accommodation and encourages a more participative role by removing the prohibition on investors to become directors. Tax incentives are less generous as relief is limited to 20 per cent, but the ceiling on investments has been raised to £100,000 per individual in any one year.

Venture Capital Trusts (VCTs)

VCTs are vehicles for private individuals to invest in smaller firms. VCTs are quoted on the London Stock Exchange (LSE) and invest in smaller private trading companies. Investors in VCTs benefit from tax relief on income tax from dividends and capital gains tax on disposal of shares.

National Business Angel Network

Venture capitalists have substantial funds under management which, together with the relatively fixed costs of investigating and setting up investments, has pushed them into seeking investment above significant threshold amounts. For example, the British Venture Capital Association (BVCA) lists over 100 full members in their directory[6]; only 20 per cent of these have minimum investment levels below £100,000 and over 50 per cent state a minimum investment level of over £500,000. As other common sources of funds from banks and other lenders tend to be for amounts up to only £100,000, this has led to the notion of a so-called 'equity-gap', for investment amounts from £100,000 to £250,000.

The government has recognised the importance of 'business angels' in providing informal investment to small companies, especially of smaller amounts. The DTI and the major banks have sponsored the development of a national brokerage service, the National Business Angels Network (NBAN)[10]. This is an introduction service which brings together businesses and potential investors who typically would have from £10,000 to £250,000 available for investment. Investors are charged an annual fee of £85 which includes the monthly NBAN Bulletin and access to the 'Bestmatch' web site. Companies are charged £175 for entries in the NBAN Bulletin and web site. Companies also need to use the services of an NBAN Associate who may charge fees for the work they do.

Secondary equity markets – the Alternative Investment Market (AIM)

One source of capital for the developed small or medium-sized firm is via a listing on a securities market, which allows shares in the company to be bought and sold by individuals and institutions. It also provides important exit routes for venture capitalists and business angels.

- ❒ *The Unlisted Securities Market (USM)* was launched in 1980 to give smaller companies, with a minimum three years' trading record, access to a stock market.

- ❒ *The Third Market* was launched in 1987 aimed at regulating the existing over-the-counter market, trading in higher risk shares of smaller or younger companies with a minimum of only one year's trading record. The Third Market did not last long, closing in 1990 when it was combined with the USM.

  The USM proved to be a qualified success initially, with over 400 companies listed at the end of 1990. However its initial popularity waned as a listing was expensive, with a minimum of around £100,000 costs for the simplest introduction method, and the market did not perform well for investors, ending its first decade of operation below its opening index of 100. It finally closed in 1994.

- ❒ *The Alternative Investment Market (AIM)* The closure of the USM increased concerns that the stock market did not have a vehicle which closely met the need of small firms, to raise new equity finance, or for owner-managers to realise some of the fruits of their labours by selling shares. To meet these criticisms the Alternative Investment Market (AIM) was launched in 1995 by the LSE. It has grown rapidly to a listing of over 300 companies by 2000 with a total market capitalisation of £10 billion. Although it is generally considered a success, AIM is still an expensive and time consuming route to the equity markets for many SMEs. AIM listed companies are obliged to produce detailed financial statements before listing, and to produce half-yearly reports and annual accounts thereafter[11].

Other public sources of finance

There are a number of other public sources of finance for the small business:

- ❒ *EU funds* are available in certain areas affected by the decline of a particular industry, such as coal mining and shipbuilding.

- ❒ *Regional Selective Assistance (RSA)* is available in designated Assisted Areas. It provides grants of up to 15 per cent of the costs of new investments, such as the purchase of plant, machinery and buildings.

- *British Steel (Industry) Ltd* provides financial support for small firms in traditional steel industry areas with loans and equity investments from £10,000 to £150,000.

- *The Rural Development Commission (RDC)* has limited funds available to promote small rural firms with specific projects or grants to convert premises.

- *Tourist Boards* encourage the growth of the tourist business, partly by offering loans and grants for specific projects likely to enhance the tourist trade in the UK.

- *The Prince's Trust* is a charity which provides finance (as well as advice and training) to young people to set up and develop their own business. It is supported by funds from the EU, national and local government, as well as companies and private individuals. The Trust has helped over 17,500 businesses through a combination of loans and bursaries to unemployed people aged 18–25, or up to the age of 30 if they are disabled. Each year it gives approximately £2,500,000 in bursaries, £6,000,000 in loans, and helps around 3,000 young people.

- *The Small Firms Merit Award for Research and Technology (SMART)* and Support for Products Under Research (SPUR) are SBS/DTI packages which give technology-based SMEs opportunities to gain financial awards and grants.

- *The Department of Trade and Industry (DTI)* also publishes a *Guide to Help for Small Firms* (URN 97/525, HMSO) which contains details of the financial assistance on offer. See also the SBS web site on www.businesslink.org.uk

Activity 3 Financial issues

Small firm are faced with a variety of financial issues, some of which are more common at different stages of their life cycle, such as during the start-up, growth or decline stages. Can you give some examples of these issues? At what life cycle stages are they likely to be most common?

3 Control of financial resources

3.1 Financial problems

If the first hurdle for a small firm is to ensure the availability of the appropriate amount and type of funds, the next step is to optimise the use of those financial resources by effective planning and control.

The Bolton Committee was critical of many aspects of the financial management of small firms, reporting that information was often so poor that management frequently learns of an impending crisis only with the appearance of the annual accounts, or following an urgent call from the bank manager[12].

Fast growing small businesses have particular problems in controlling their finances. Growth brings frequent changes to the internal structures and external environment of a small firm. It is often difficult to ensure that financial control systems keep pace with the changing circumstances. For example, a small firm, which historically traded directly with consumer markets, expanded by setting up distributors both in the UK and overseas. This led to the development of debtors, as the distributors were given credit, and a rapid increase in stocks which were needed to service the new outlets. The small firm did not have control systems in place to cope with these new demands and soon ran into liquidity problems.

The small business is likely to be confronted by a variety of financial problems as it advances through its life cycle[13.] Table 13.1 illustrates some of the potential issues in each stage.

Table 13.1 The financial life cycle of a small firm

Stage	Likely sources of finance	Financial issues
Conception	Personal investment	Under capitalisation, because of inability to raise finance
Introduction	Bank loans, overdrafts	Control of costs and lack of information
Development	Hire purchase, leasing	Overtrading, liquidity crisis
Growth	Venture capital	Equity gap, appropriate information systems
Maturity	All sources	Weakening return on investment
Decline	Sale of business/liquidation	Finance withdrawn. Tax issues if business is sold

In the early stages, the lack of track record can hinder raising the required money, and lead to an under capitalised business.

As the business begins to trade, it will have little experience on which to base forecasts for planning purposes, and vital information may therefore be lacking. Costs will be incurred as the company finds its feet, for which there may be inadequate control systems at this stage.

Once full development gets underway and sales grow, over trading can result, with debtors and stocks increasing rapidly as the negative cash flow builds up into a liquidity crisis.

If growth continues, and requires further funding through investment in equity, it may be difficult to raise the required amount if less than £250,000, because venture capitalists shy away from these small investments.

Finally the business matures and although cash flow at this stage is positive, profitability levels off, and return on investment may worsen. As maturity turns to decline, the business may be sold, or go into liquidation; new partners may buy into the business in an attempt to kick it back into growth. Overdraft facilities and other renewable finance, may be withdrawn at this stage as confidence wanes. If the business is sold, taxation of any capital gain requires careful consideration by the vendor.

Is there any relief from this rather gloomy picture of a small firm staggering from one financial crisis to another? It would be easy to say that adequate forecasting and the appropriate control systems can minimise the problems. The reality is that most small firms do experience financial stress at various moments in their history. It is also true, however, that these problems are often exacerbated by inadequate planning and control.

3.2 Cash flow, debtors and stocks

Financial management in a small firm starts with the management of the cash flow. Cash is critical to survival, representing the lifeblood which enables all the activities of a firm to be undertaken.

It is easy for the fragile cash resources of a small business to become locked up in unproductive areas, such as debtors, work-in-progress and finished stocks. Any areas where funds can become locked-up require effective management to minimise the extent of the lock-up.

Debtors' control

Debtors can hurt a small business in two major ways. Firstly, they absorb cash and effectively increase the funding requirement of a small firm. Secondly, the longer a debt is alive, the greater the risk of a bad debt. Particularly in recessionary times, the risks of having invoices which go unpaid are high. The impact on a small firm can be disastrous, even causing the failure of the business in a domino effect as one firm falls after another.

These problems are not unique to small firms, but they can be accentuated by the smallness of an operating unit in any of the following ways:

❑ The costs of chasing slow payers or bad debts may be greater than the amount of money being pursued. This is a particular problem for companies with a large number of small customers.

   For example, a small mail order firm sells products priced under £50 on a 30 day trial basis, as part of its marketing approach. It quickly generated over one thousand customers in this way, and found that considerable time and money had to be spent to control a sales ledger with this profile.

❑ The time taken to establish the credit worthiness of a potential customer may be longer than the sales process. Keenness to win an order, and not to jeopardise it by lengthy credit checks, may cause an owner-manager to accept imprudent credit risks.

   For example, the owner-manager of a small manufacturing firm was short of custom and losing money as production operatives and expensive equipment stood idle. A large order from a company not previously known to the owner-manager looked like their saviour: it returned the factory back to full capacity following a hasty negotiation. Unfortunately the order increased the firm's cash problems, as the customer had liquidity difficulties of their own and proved to be an extremely reluctant payer.

❑ A small firm may not have the control systems to identify individual debtor problems before they become critical. An essential part of any management accounting system is an analysis of debtors by their age, as well as their amount, so that appropriate action can be triggered to chase up slow payers. This rigorous pursuit of payment, which gradually escalates the tone of requests from polite reminder to threat of legal action is an unfortunate but essential element in small business management today. To be done effectively, accurate information on customers' indebtedness is required on a very regular basis.

For example, a small business set up a debtor control system using a series of standard letters which were sent to customers once the age of their debt passed a certain number of days. These letters were triggered by information from the computerised accounting system which produced an aged debtor-analysis. The firm was not large enough to employ full-time accounting staff, and therefore used an external bookkeeper who came in near the end of each month to process invoices and payments. Unfortunately this system generated considerable confusion and aggravation, as the information on customer payments was invariably out of date. Customers became irritated by threatening letters after they had actually paid. Also, so much time was wasted chasing payments received but not entered into the system, that serious problems were not attended to as they developed.

Management of stock

Stock represents a poor investment for a small firm's financial resources. Stock surpluses earn no money, and risk deterioration if not used quickly. However the consequences of running short of stock can be even more punitive; if orders go unfulfilled, or are even lost because of stock shortages, the effect on the cash flow can be disastrous. Stock management is therefore about balance, and the optimisation of resources; weighing up the risk of running out versus the costs of playing it too safe. Stocks need controlling in three areas:

❑ *Raw material stocks* represent what a manufacturer needs to produce its own products and services.

❑ *Work-in-progress (WIP)* is stock which is currently being worked on, but is not yet saleable as finished items.

❑ *Finished stock* is ready for sale, but either awaiting shipment to a customer, or unsold.

Keeping all these types of stock to an optimum level is a difficult balancing act, particularly in industries where demand is unpredictable, and often short lived. The fashion and toy industries, for example, are notorious for developing severe cash problems because of the difficulties of stock management. Fast moving clothes can suddenly become virtually unsaleable as fashions change. Toy products still on the shelf after the Christmas rush may have to wait until the following Christmas season to be sold.

Liquid assets and current liabilities

A good measure of the health of a small firm's cash position comes from an estimate of its liquid assets and current liabilities: that is its assets which can quickly
be turned into cash, and liabilities which should be paid in the short term (12
months). Table 13.2 illustrates the items normally found in such an estimate. If a
small business's current liabilities (B in Table 13.2) exceed the total of liquid assets
(A in Table 13.2), then problems may be just around the corner unless corrective
action is taken.

Table 13.2 Liquid assets and current liabilities

£000s		Current year	Prior year
Assets	Stock and work-in-progress	90	110
	Debtors	220	270
	Cash in bank	20	0
A. *Total liquid assets*		330	380
Liabilities	Trade suppliers	140	180
	Other creditors (VAT/PAYE)	125	130
	Overdraft	25	100
B. *Total current liabilities*		290	410
C. *Total assets less liabilities* (**A** – **B**)		40	(30)

In the example above, the business was heading for a financial crisis as short-term
liabilities exceeded liquid assets by £30,000 in the prior year. The owner-manager
took remedial action by collecting money faster, thereby reducing debtors, and
cutting back on stocks. This facilitated paying down some of the liabilities such as
creditors and the overdraft, resulting in an improvement in the solvency of the
business in the current year.

3.3 Costs and pricing

Deciding prices by calculating costs and adding what is judged to be an adequate
element of profit, is probably the most common method in use by small firms.
Marketing theorists frown upon this approach, as it does not always maximise the
price that could be charged. Costs, they argue, should not be directly linked to
prices, which should be determined by market forces; costs help to determine how
well a business has done in terms of the profit generated by its pricing decisions,
but this should be the extent of the relationship between the two. In practice,
however, most small firms will use certain costs as an important element in their
pricing decision. Pricing in small firms is more likely to be based on a compromise
between an estimate of what the business needs to cover its costs and a view on
what the customer expects and competitors are charging.

A common issue for small firms is to understand the costs they incur – not just
their extent – but the different types:

❏ *Fixed costs* refer to business expenses which do not vary with the level of trading. They are the overheads of a small firm, such as rent, rates, insurance, heating, lighting and most salaries. A small manufacturer, or retailer will have the same costs to pay for premises and full-time staff whether they have sales of £500 or £5,000 per week. As all fixed costs have to be recovered eventually from sales, a crucial element in the pricing decision is the volume of sales that can be allocated to cover these overheads.

If a small manufacturer or retailer has fixed overheads of £2,000 per week, and sales estimates vary from 1,000 to 5,000 units per week, the allocation of fixed costs will range from £2 to 40p per unit.

❏ *Variable costs* are expenses which do change in direct proportion to the level of trading. They are the costs of raw materials for manufacturing, or the costs of stock that a retailer will sell, and are sometimes referred to as the cost of sales or cost of goods sold (COGS). Most small firms that use stock in significant quantity will have a clearer idea of what these costs are in terms of a mark-up or a gross margin (although the two terms are sometimes confused).

❏ *Mark-up* relates the selling price of an item to its variable costs. It takes the costs of the unit as the starting point, and represents how much is added to reach the selling price. It is often expressed as a percentage of the variable costs.

If a retailer buys from a supplier for £20 + VAT and sells to the customer for £50 + VAT then the mark-up is £30, or 150 per cent (on top of the costs of £20). If the price is increased to £60 + VAT, the mark-up is £40 or 200 per cent.

This can be expressed as:

$$\% \text{ Mark-up} = \frac{\text{sales price} - \text{variable cost}}{\text{variable cost}} \times 100\%$$

Mark-ups are used particularly in the retail trade, where variable costs are usually a very significant but known factor in the price of an item. To ensure that its prices reflect up to date suppliers' prices, a small retailer may, for example, operate a standard minimum mark-up, which it simply adds on to suppliers' invoices as a first step in a pricing decision.

❏ *Gross margin* also relates the sales price of an item to the variable costs, representing the difference between the sales price and the variable costs. However, it takes the sales price as its starting point, and expresses how much of the sales price is left after deducting variable costs; it is often expressed as a percentage of the sales price.

In our previous example, a small retailer selling an item for £50, which had been purchased for £20, would have a gross margin of £30 or 60 per cent of the sales price. If the sales price is increased to £60, the gross margin of £40 is 66 per cent or two-thirds of the sales price.

This can be expressed mathematically as:

$$\text{Gross margin} = \frac{\text{sales price} - \text{variable cost}}{\text{sales price}} \times 100\%$$

Gross margins are particularly useful where the variable costs of an item may be difficult to precisely allocate, but an average overall margin is targeted. For example, a small manufacturer, or retailer, selling several products, budgets for a gross margin of 50 per cent. Each month, their management accounts report total sales and variable costs and therefore a gross margin. This will be an average of the margin of all products, which gives a first indication whether prices are in line with costs.

Break even analysis

A useful concept for the small firm which relates costs, prices and volumes is a break even analysis. This begins with an analysis of the fixed and variable costs which can be illustrated graphically as in Figure 13.2.

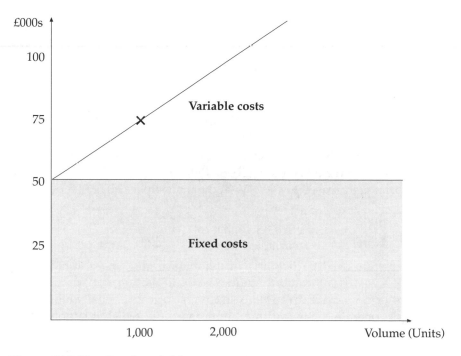

Figure 13.2 Fixed and variable costs

In this example, the fixed costs of overheads and salaries are £50,000 p.a. and variable costs are £25 per unit.

If 1,000 units are produced, the costs will be:

Fixed costs	£50,000
Variable costs (£25 × 1000)	£25,000
Total costs	£75,000
Therefore total costs per unit	£75

If 2,000 units are produced, the costs will be:

Fixed costs	£50,000
Variable costs (£25 × 2000)	£50,000
Total costs	£100,000
Therefore total costs per unit	£50

This information can be used in a number of ways:

1. A manufacturer, with the cost profile just described, looks at market prices and decides that £50 per unit is the maximum price obtainable.

    A revenue line can now be added to the graph, as in Figure 13.3, to form a break even analysis.

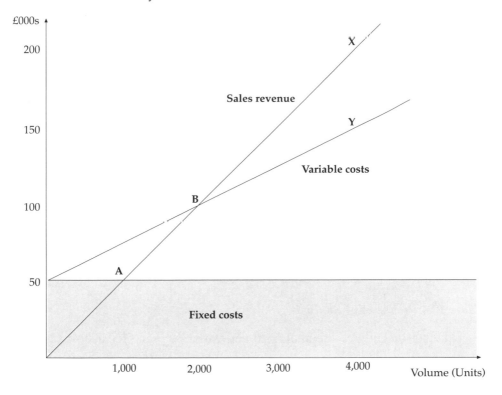

Figure 13.3 Break even analysis

This shows that, at a price of £50 per unit:

A =   volume where fixed costs covered (1,000 units)

B =   Break even volume (2,000 units)

X =   Sales target for the product (£200,000 or 4,000 units)

XY = Profits (After deducting the fixed and variable costs, this equates to £50,000. After deducting only variable costs this is £100,000 or a 50 per cent gross margin)

A break even point can be calculated by using the following formula:

$$\text{Break even volume} = \frac{\text{Fixed costs}}{\text{Gross margin per unit}}$$

In our example, break even $= \dfrac{£50,000}{£25} = 2,000$ units

2. Another small firm with the same cost profile is operating in a less competitive situation where there are no firm market prices. The firm believes it can make 2,000 units a year and would like to make a £50,000 profit on those sales. It can now plot what price to charge, as in Figure 13.4.

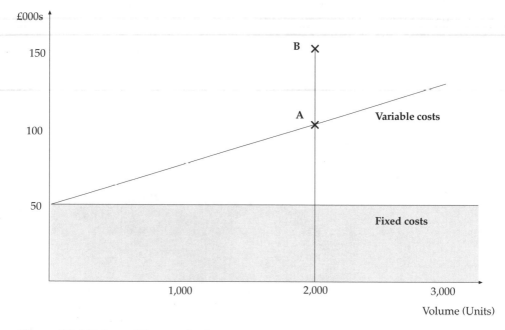

Figure 13.4 Price setting analysis

At 2,000 units,   A =   total of fixed and variable costs (£100,000).

                   B =   revenue needed to make £50,000 profit and therefore the price per unit. (£75 per unit or £150,000 divided by 2,000 units.)

3. A retailer is planning to open a new shop unit. Because they buy their products from suppliers with known prices, they can predict a gross margin of 50 per cent on their current pricing policies. They also know that the fixed costs of the new shop in rent, wages etc. will be £50,000 p.a. They have a break even point of sales of £100,000 if they continue with their existing prices. If they believe this to be unlikely to be achieved, they have the choice of increasing their prices, to achieve a better gross margin and therefore lower break even point, or of dropping the venture altogether.

Customised pricing

Another variation of cost plus pricing is customised pricing. In this method, the customer effectively dictates the price, and the producer then works out what can be supplied for that price.

For example, a large supermarket chain is looking to buy a product which it will sell as an own-brand (i.e. under its own name). The end-user price has to be just lower than the brand leaders (say £2) and the supermarket has strict gross margin targets for this category of products, (say a minimum of 30 per cent). The supermarket buyer will be sourcing a product at a known price therefore (no more than £1.40p in our example). A small firm wishing to bid for this business will attempt to tailor a product and a minimum order volume to match this price requirement.

Time and materials

Many small businesses are in a service sector business, where the key cost element will be the time spent on the job. These include domestic services such as plumbing, building and repair work, landscape gardening, tree felling and many more. Garages, secretarial services, freelance trainers, business consultants, solicitors and accountants also base their charges on time spent, plus any additional expenses incurred. The problems for a small firm in calculating time and materials include:

❐ *Hourly rate:* surprise is sometimes expressed by customers at the hourly rate charged by a service organisation. Plumbers and mechanics charging £30 per hour, and partners in accountants and solicitors charging themselves at £150 per hour, all cause eyebrows to be raised. In fact small firms often undercharge for their services, forgetting the hours of travelling, selling, administration or preparation that they will need to spend, which are unpaid and bring down their average hourly rate. Evidence that small firms under-price their labour has already been quoted with the average self-employed hourly rate below the employed national average.

❐ *Time:* where a fixed price is required for a quotation then an estimate of the total time necessary for the job becomes a key pricing decision. This would be typical of a builder quoting a fixed price for a specified job.

❐ *Materials:* materials are expected to be invoiced at cost in most service situations, but this can overlook some of the hidden costs in obtaining the materials, such as the time taken to source and buy the materials, and the travelling costs involved in picking them up. To overcome this, materials are often charged at a full retail price, although discounts or wholesale prices were obtained.

Discounting

Discounts are a pricing mechanism commonly used by small firms. The use of discounts includes selling off old or damaged stock, rewarding customer loyalty, launching a new product or service, and matching a competitor's price. These are often valid reasons for giving a discount which are to the benefit of the business.

However discounts, special offers and sales to help improve demand and cash flow are also misused by small firms, who overlook the real increase in volume that is required to make up for discounted prices.

For example a retailer, averaging a 50 per cent gross margin on sales, offers a 20 per cent discount off all stock for a limited period. Sales volume jumps by 50 per cent from the normal level of 10,000 units for the month to 15,000 units; but the owner-manager would be mistaken to believe this has been a successful promotion, as the following calculation reveals:

	Normal Trading	Special Offer	Offer Break Even
sales units	10,000	15,000	16,666
average price per unit	£1	80p	80p
total sales	£10,000	£12,000	£13,333
cost per unit	50p	50p	50p
total cost	£5,000	£7,500	£8,333
gross margin	£5,000	£4,500	£5,000

Although sales volume has increased considerably and sales revenue is also up by 20 per cent, the effect of the discount more than takes away this advantage, and less gross margin is made during the period. In fact, for the offer to break even at the gross margin, sales volume would need to increase by 66.6 per cent, or two-thirds up on normal trading. If small retailers calculated the real increase in volume they needed to recover the discounts they gave, then there would almost certainly be a drop in the number of 'Special Sales' that we see in our high streets today.

The corollary of this is that price increases can support relatively higher drops in sales volume before they have a negative effect on the gross margin. A small firm operating on a 40 per cent gross margin, can support a 20 per cent loss of volume for a 10 per cent increase in prices before its realised gross margin is affected. It is more profitable to sell fewer items at a higher price.

4 Case studies and activities (1)

Case studies *Calculating cash and profits*

Case 1 It all adds up for Susan

The first case is inserted earlier in this Unit so that you can verify your calculations as Kal Kulate's cash flow and profit and loss account are shown in subsection 5 below. (It is obviously beneficial for you to attempt it on your own first.)

Susan Howells had found that mathematics homework in her household was a traumatic experience. It started when her children were asked by their school to do simple sums at home, and then learn their multiplication tables. This proved a stressful time in the Howells' household until Susan invented a series of games which turned a duty into fun. Her children liked her mathematics games so much that they introduced them to their friends. Requests for Susan to produce more copies of the games soon followed.

Over the next few years, Susan developed this experience into a small business. Working from home as a sole trader, she built up a respectable turnover in her children's activity games, based on making mathematics more fun. Towards the end of the third year, she decided it was time to set up her business on a more permanent basis in separate premises. Her family certainly agreed; they would be pleased to have their kitchen and living room back for their own use when the piles of Susan's products and literature left.

Susan explained her plans to her accountant. 'I want to set up from January 1st next year as a limited company, 'Kal Kulate Ltd', using my brand name. I have found some new premises for a small workshop and storage facilities, where I can employ the staff I need. But I will have to buy some new equipment. We need to become more organised and efficient in our production, which means buying more benches, tools and the like. I have had a preliminary talk with my bank manager, who was encouraging, but said I had to produce a cash flow forecast in order to apply for a larger overdraft. Unfortunately I've no idea where to start, although he did give me some leaflets, with outline headings for a forecast. Can you help?'

'Yes, of course', replied the accountant, 'but you will have to do quite a lot of work to provide the information. A cash flow forecast is quite simple really. It tries to estimate how much cash will be coming into and going out of your business each month. From this we can judge what you can afford to invest in new equipment, and to risk in new overheads such as your premises.'

'Well, I've done a rough calculation of my profit for the year, and it looks as though I can more or less break even after paying myself some sort of salary. But that's not the same as a cash flow forecast is it?'

'No, it's different', replied the accountant, 'although one can be derived from the other. In fact it's usually easier to do forecasts of profit and cash at the same time. They use a lot of common information. The crucial difference is that a profit forecast looks at the difference between your sales and your costs at the moment those sales are made, or those costs incurred. It calculates a profit, or loss, based on invoices as they are sent, or received, not on when they are paid. The cash flow is only concerned with cash when sales and purchases are actually paid for.'

'Right, I think I see what you're getting at', replied Susan, 'but I'm sure it will be even clearer when we have the figures in front of us. Exactly what information do you need?'

'Here is a list of the headings we're looking at. I think you should spend a few days working on this information, and then we can talk about it again.'

A week later, Susan returned to see the accountant, and brought the information he had asked for with her. It is summarised on the following page.

'This is a very good start', replied the accountant, 'we should be able to produce a profit and loss, and cash flow forecast and balance sheet from this information. How are you going to finance your capital purchases of £21,150 by the way?'

'Well if I pay cash there are some real bargains at the moment', replied Susan, 'so I thought I would use an overdraft at the bank.'

Kal Kulate Ltd: profit and loss/cash flow input information

1. Sales forecast. Total net sales for year: £211,500

£s	Jan	Feb	March	April	May	June
	19,000	13,000	14,000	20,500	15,500	20,000
	July	Aug	Sept	Oct	Nov	Dec
	15,500	17,500	17,000	18,000	21,000	20,500

2. *Materials used*: raw materials purchased are estimated to represent 50% of the net sales value sold in the month.

3. *Production wages*: wages of production operatives will be £3,000 per month in total, including employers NIC.

4. *Overheads*: overheads are estimated as follows:
   - Salaries of directors and administrative staff £2,000 per month in total
   - Rent £12,000 per annum
   - Rates and insurances £500 per month
   - Publicity £500 per month
   - Other costs £1,000 per month

5. *Bank interest*: it is assumed there will be an overdraft of £15,000 at 10% p.a. interest, plus bank charges of £1,000 per annum.

6. *Depreciation*: depreciation will be based on fixed assets of £18,000 net costs depreciated over 3 years, or £6,000 per annum.

7. *Receipts*: sales will be invoiced with VAT at 17.5% and paid for in 60 days, or during the second month after invoice date (January invoices paid in March etc.).

8. *Payment of overheads*: purchases will be paid for on the following basis:
   - Materials used, publicity and other costs 60 days from date of use, or during the 2nd month after receipt of invoice. These costs will all be subject to VAT at 17.5%.
   - Rent will be paid quarterly (March, June, Oct and Dec).
   - Rates and insurances will be paid monthly by standing order.

9. *VAT*: will also be added to some purchases when they are paid for. This will be at the rate of 17.5% and apply to materials used, publicity and other costs.

10. *VAT due*: Kal Kulate Ltd will be registered for VAT from January 1 and will need to submit VAT returns for each quarter, and pay any VAT due during the month following the quarter end. (The first quarter will be January to March with payments due in April.)

11. *Capital*: Capital Assets which total £18,000 plus £3,150 VAT will be paid for in January.

12. *Opening position*: Kal Kulate's opening cash balance will be nil, as it is not intended to bring any cash forward into the new limited company. Shares will be purchased for £5,000 in December, which will be used to pay for any initial costs, such as prepayment of rent and legal charges.

However, debtors and creditors will be brought forward as follows:

Debtors:	Nov sales £20,000 + VAT
	Dec sales £20,000 + VAT
Creditors:	Nov and Dec purchases at 50% of the above sales + VAT
	Nov and Dec publicity and other costs at the monthly rate of £1,500 + VAT.
Prepayments:	Rent will be paid for in advance, with the first quarter paid for in December, prior to incorporation.

13. *Stocks* will equate to one month's sales, i.e. the materials needed for one month's sales (50% of the relevant month's sales value).

Activities

i) Can you prepare the profit and loss and cash flow for Kal Kulate Ltd from this information?

ii) Looking at the profit and loss account, and the cash flow forecast, why is there only a small profit for the year, yet a larger positive cash flow?

iii) Using the cash flow forecast, make some recommendations for Susan's borrowing strategy. Is she right to want an overdraft to finance her new equipment?

iv) Can you produce a projected balance sheet for the end of the first year (December) from this information?

5 Financial analysis

5.1 Management accounts and forecasting

Small firms differ greatly in their approach to the provision of accounting information, and the use of forecasts and budgets for planning and control of the business. Some studies suggest that there is a considerable gulf between small entrepreneurial companies aiming for high growth, and firms who have no great ambitions to grow other than that required to survive[9]. Whilst there are less differences between the provision of historical accounting information, the entrepreneurial small firms make much greater use of forecasted financial information than the passive firms. This illustrates the greater perceived need for forecasting during times of change, than during periods of relatively stable sales.

The three most widely used financial summaries are the profit and loss account, the cash flow, and the balance sheet.

❑ *The profit and loss account* shows how a business is doing in terms of sales and costs – and the difference between them of profit or losses. It is a moving picture and can be used to forecast, and monitor, results on a monthly basis or for a longer period.

❑ *The cash flow* is perhaps the most important summary for a young firm as it indicates the movement of cash into and out of the business. Similar to the profit and loss account, it differs in the important respect of reflecting credit given to customers and received from suppliers, as well as the amount of money invested in a business, or borrowed by it. Because of their importance, cash flows are used on a very regular weekly or monthly basis.

❑ *The balance sheet* is a snapshot, rather than a moving picture, as it represents a summary of what money has been spent by a business, and what it has been spent on. It is usually an annual summary of the use and sources of funds in a company.

5.2 The 21 steps to profit and loss, cash flow and balance sheet forecasts

Although they are different forms of financial analysis, a series of steps can be used to build up a set of forecasts of profit and loss, cash flow, and the balance sheet. This can be done manually, but a computer spreadsheet is a highly useful tool, as it allows for regular modifications and sensitivity analysis (for example to project the effect of a drop in sales or a rise in costs).

The following 21 steps are explained with a worked example of Kal Kulate Ltd, the company in Case 1 of section 4 above.

Note: each step (on the following pages) can be related to the profit and loss, cash flow and balance sheets of Kal Kulate Ltd at the end of this subsection.

Profit and loss

STEP 1

Estimate *likely sales turnover* for the forecast period, based on historical precedent and research in the marketplace. Also work out any output VAT element on those sales.

STEP 2

Work out what *materials* will be used to make the goods needed to achieve the sales estimated in Step 1. This can only be accurately calculated by taking the opening stock, adding all the purchases in the period, and deducting the closing stock (see Step 14). Although this is done on a regular basis to verify actual profits, forecasts usually assume a percentage usage based on historical data.

Example: Kal Kulate Ltd – Step 1

Month	Net sales	Output VAT	Gross sales
	£	£	£
1	19,000	3,325	22,325
2	13,000	2,275	15,275
3	14,000	2,450	16,450
4	20,500	3,588	24,088
5	15,500	2,713	18,213
6	20,000	3,500	23,500
7	15,500	2,713	18,213
8	17,500	3,063	20,563
9	17,000	2,975	19,975
10	18,000	3,150	21,150
11	21,000	3,675	24,675
12	20,500	3,588	24,088
TOTAL	211,500	37,015	248,515

Example: Kal Kulate Ltd – Step 2

For example, Kal Kulate had an established pattern of materials costing 50% of the net sales value. So sales of £19,000 in January would require £9,500 (50%) worth of materials to make them.

STEP 3

Work out the *wages* and other employment costs of those involved directly in production. This should include gross wages, plus employer's national insurance.

Example: Kal Kulate Ltd – Step 3

Kal Kulate employed 3 full-time and 2 part-time operatives who together were estimated to cost as follows:

	£
Gross wages	33,000
Employer's national insurance	3,000
Total (12 months)	36,000
Total (1 month)	3,000

STEP 4

Work out the *overheads* of running the business. These will normally be the fixed costs and include:

- ❐ the salaries of directors and non-production staff;
- ❐ rent, rates, insurance and other premises costs;
- ❐ telephone, postage, printing, stationery, accounting and other office costs;
- ❐ advertising, exhibitions, selling, commissions and other publicity costs.

Example: Kal Kulate Ltd – Step 4

Kal Kulate grouped their fixed costs as follows:

	£
Salaries of director and office manager	24,000
Rent	12,000
Rates and insurance	6,000
Other costs including energy, stationery, postage, accounting and sundry costs	12,000
Publicity costs including advertising and exhibitions	6,000
Total (12 months)	60,000
Total (1 month)	5,000

(Salaries, rent, rates and insurance do not attract VAT for cash flow purposes.)

Note: some of these costs will attract VAT which needs to be added to the cash flow, but excluded in the profit and loss account.

For ease of calculation later on, it is wise to group costs where possible into those which do, and those which do not, attract VAT.

It is also easier to identify significant costs at this stage which may be on a different payments cycle to other costs, as this will make transference of those items to the cash flow simpler. (For example rent, which has no VAT, and which is often paid quarterly, can be identified separately from other premises costs, some of which include VAT, and are paid on a monthly basis.)

STEP 5

Calculate interest on borrowings and other bank charges.

Interest and bank charges will clearly vary with borrowing levels, usage of the bank account and national interest rates which will not be known at this stage. An estimate based on the likely average level of borrowing and known interest rates can be made, which should be kept pessimistic as change in this area can be swift.

Example: Kal Kulate Ltd – Step 5

Kal Kulate's overdraft was thought to average up to £15,000 with 10% p.a. interest so that the following allowance was made:

	£
Interest	1,500
Bank charges	1,500
Total (12 months)	3,000
Total (1 month)	250

STEP 6

Depreciation is calculated by taking the expected life of the fixed assets of the business and writing them off progressively over that period, by making a charge to the profit and loss account.

Example: Kal Kulate Ltd – Step 6

Depreciation was based on new assets of £18,000 (plus VAT at 17.5% of £3,150). These were depreciated over 3 years, giving an annual depreciation charge of £6,000, or £500 per month.

Cash flow

STEP 7

Work out how quickly sales will be turned into cash, that is when debtors are going to pay their invoices. Receipts from customers include any VAT which has been invoiced to them.

Example: Kal Kulate Ltd – Step 7

Kal Kulate's customers were invoiced on 30 days' credit. In practice most took longer than this, and 60 days were allowed for payment in the cash flow. In other words, it was assumed that January's gross sales would be paid for in March, February's in April and so on. The receipts at the beginning of the year in January and February were November' and December's sales of the previous year which were both £20,000 + VAT (£23,500).

STEP 8

Work out when overhead costs and interest will actually have to be paid for. Some costs are paid for in the same month, for example salaries and wages. Others are paid on a regular credit basis, for example materials used, and other overhead costs. Some important overheads are paid quarterly, for example rent.

Example: Kal Kulate Ltd – Step 8

The pattern of Kal Kulate's payments were as follows:

- Materials purchased, publicity and other costs – 60 days
- Salaries and wages – same month
- Rent – quarterly (March, June, Oct, Dec)
- Rates and insurance – same month by monthly standing order
- Interest and bank charges – quarterly (March, June, Oct, Dec)

For example:

In January and February, purchases of materials used in November and December of the previous year are paid for. In March, purchases of materials used in January are paid for and so on.

Publicity and other costs are ongoing costs, estimated to be the same each month. In January, the costs incurred in November of the previous year are paid for; in February, the costs from December are paid for and so on.

STEP 9

Work out the VAT paid on invoices for overhead costs. Some purchases attract VAT, which has to be added to the amount when it is paid. Although salaries, wages, rent, rates and insurance do not attract VAT, most other costs do.

Example: Kal Kulate Ltd – Step 9

Kal Kulate paid VAT on their purchases of materials and on their publicity and other costs. VAT paid on these purchases was therefore worked out at 17.5% and included as a separate item.

For example, in January £10,000 of materials and £1,500 of publicity and other costs were paid for. As the invoices would have had VAT added, the payments must include this amount (£11,500 × 17.5% = £2,013)

(It can be added to the individual amounts, or, as in Kal Kulate's cash flow, noted as a separate line.)

STEP 10

Work out how much VAT is due to be paid to H M Customs and Excise on the quarterly returns. This is calculated by totalling the *output* VAT added to sales invoiced in the quarter and totalling all the *input* VAT added to purchases invoiced to you in the same quarter. The difference between the total output VAT and the input VAT is paid to the government in the month following the end of the quarter.

Example: Kal Kulate Ltd – Step 10

Kal Kulate's VAT calculation looked like this:

	Jan/March	*April/June*	*July/Sept*	*Oct/Dec*
	£	£	£	£
VAT outputs	8,050	9,801	8,751	10,413
VAT inputs:				
Materials used	4,025	4,900	4,375	5,206
Publicity & other costs	788	788	788	788
Capital equipment				
(VAT element)	3,150			
Total inputs	7,963	5,688	5,163	5,994
VAT due	87	4,113	3,588	4,419
	(Due April)	(Due July)	(Due Oct)	(Due Jan of following year)

Output VAT represents the VAT element on the sales invoiced in the period. (For example see Step 1 VAT: Jan = £3,325, Feb = £2,275, March = £2,450, so the total Jan–March = £8,050.)

... continued

Example: Kal Kulate Ltd – Step 10 ... continued

Input VAT represents 17.5% on the costs of materials, publicity and other costs, on receipt of invoices not when they are paid. (For example see Step 2: materials used in Jan = £9,500, Feb = £6,500, March = £7,000. Total for the period Jan–March = £23,000 x 17.5% VAT = £4,025.)

VAT due represents the difference between output and input VAT. It is payable one month after the quarter end, which in Kal Kulate's case was April, July, October and January (following year).

(No VAT was payable in January of this year, as Kal Kulate only registered for VAT at this time.)

STEP 11

Add in any capital purchases, including VAT, which are to be paid. If they are to be financed by hire purchase, then put the deposit and the repayments in the cash flow.

Example: Kal Kulate Ltd – Step 11

Kal Kulate purchased £18,000 plus £3,150 VAT worth of equipment from its working capital, so this appears as a lump sum of £21,150 in the month of January.

STEP 12

Calculate the monthly cash flow by subtracting total payments from total receipts for the month.

Then work out an opening and closing balance for each month which represents the cumulative cash position of the business.

Example: Kal Kulate Ltd – Step 12

Kal Kulate starts with a clean sheet as it is a new limited company formed from the on-going trading of a sole trader. The opening balance is nil, as no cash is transferred, but during the first month (January) receipts from debtors total £23,500. The total of payments out, including £21,150 on capital equipment, is £40,163. So the cash flow for the month is negative (£16,663). The closing balance of January is the opening balance for February. There is a positive cash flow of £4,487 during the month of February, so that February's closing balance is £12,176 (£16,663 – £4,487 = £12,176). This negative position is effectively Kal Kulate's overdraft at the bank.

The balance sheet end of year

STEP 13

Work out the end of year value of fixed assets by taking away the depreciation charge from the total fixed asset costs.

Example: Kal Kulate Ltd – Step 13

	£
Fixed assets costs, excluding VAT	18,000
Depreciation during year	6,000
Net balance sheet value	12,000

STEP 14

Stocks are entered into the balance sheet at cost, less any provisions for damaged, or slow moving and obsolete stock.

Example. Kal Kulate Ltd Step 14

Kal Kulate valued their stocks at the beginning and end of the year to verify not only the closing value of stocks, but also the materials used during the year (in Step 2). The company's policy was to hold approximately one month's usage of stocks, and the forecast position was as follows:

Opening stock(Jan)	Purchases	Closing stock(Dec)	Materials used
£10,000	£106,000	£10,250	£105,750

STEP 15

Estimate the total amount, including VAT, owed to you by customers at the end of the period. These debtors should be reduced by any debts where there is a good chance they will not be paid.

Example: Kal Kulate Ltd – Step 15

Kal Kulate assumed they would have 2 months of debtors at the year end; i.e. sales for November and December would not be paid so that debtors would be:

	£
November sales	24,675
December sales	24,088
Total	48,763

STEP 16

Estimate the total amount owing to trade suppliers, including VAT. This liability is entered as trade creditors.

Example: Kal Kulate Ltd – Step 16

Kal Kulate assumed they would pay for materials purchased 2 months after purchase; i.e. at the end of December, they would owe for materials used in November and December + VAT, so that trade creditors would be:

	£
November	9,000 + VAT
December	8,500 + VAT
Total	17,500 + VAT = £20,562

STEP 17

Estimate how much money is owed to other creditors for other supplies, for example telephone, electricity, office supplies. Also include any tax collected but not yet paid, for example VAT, PAYE and NIC.

Example: Kal Kulate Ltd – Step 17

At the end of December, Kal Kulate estimated they would still owe for November and December purchases and the October/December VAT quarter.

		£	£
Other costs:	November	1,500 + VAT	
	December	1,500 + VAT	
		3,000 + VAT	= 3,525
VAT Oct – Dec (see Step 10)			= 4,419
Total			7,944

STEP 18

Estimate any borrowings from banks and other sources such as overdrafts or loans. For an overdraft, this should be the figure shown as the cash flow projection.

Example: Kal Kulate Ltd – Step 18

Kal Kulate's cash flow showed a negative cash position of £7,714 at the end of December which effectively represented their overdraft.

STEP 19

Calculate net current assets of the business by deducting current liabilities from current assets.

Current assets (Step 14 + Step 15) represent the assets of a business which can be realised in the short term normally within 12 months.

Current liabilities (Step 16 + Step 17 + Step 18) represent what the business owes, and can be made to pay for, in the short term normally the amounts due within 12 months.

Example: Kal Kulate Ltd – Step 19

Kal Kulate's current assets of £59,013 (stock of £10,250 and debtors of £48,763), less their current liabilities of £36,220 (trade creditors of £20,562, other creditors of £7,944, and a bank overdraft of £7,714) gave net current assets of £22,793.

STEP 20

Calculate net assets by adding fixed assets to net current assets. This represents one measure of the worth of a business.

> *Example: Kal Kulate Ltd – Step 20*
>
> Kal Kulate's fixed assets totalled £12,000 (£18,000 less £6,000 depreciation) which when added to their net current assets (£22,793) gave a net position of £34,793.

STEP 21

Add in share capital – the amount paid for the shares of the company. Add in reserves of profits (or losses) retained in the company. (This figure should balance with the net assets when added to the share capital.)

Together these make up the capital and reserves of the company, which represents what would theoretically be left to distribute to shareholders should the company be wound up at the balance sheet date (it is therefore sometimes referred to as Shareholders' Funds.)

> *Example: Kal Kulate Ltd – Step 21*
>
> Kal Kulate was set up with £50,00 capital subscribed for shares. This does not appear in the cash flow forecast, as it was put into the company before the beginning of the forecast period.
>
> The reserves carried forward represent this year's profit, plus profits retained in the business since it was started. In this forecast balance sheet, it is a balancing figure which, when added to share capital, equals the total net assets of £34,793.

Example: Kal Kulate Ltd: forecast balance sheet

	Step no		£	£
FIXED ASSETS		cost	18,000	
		depreciation	−6,000	
	13	book value		12,000
CURRENT ASSETS	14	stocks	10,250	
	15	debtors	48,763	
			59,013	
CURRENT LIABILITIES	16	trade creditors	20,562	
	17	other creditors	7,944	
	18	bank overdraft	7,714	
			36,220	
NET CURRENT ASSETS	19			22,793
NET ASSETS	20			34,793
CAPITAL AND RESERVES	21	share capital	5,000	
	21	reserves	29,793	
	21			34,793

(See pages 352–3 for examples profit and loss and cash flow.)

6 Case studies and activities (2)

Case studies *Calculating cash and profits*

Case 2 Susan miscalculates

It had been a hectic year for Susan Howells. She had completed her first trading year as Kal Kulate Ltd, and felt really proud of her achievements. She had exceeded her sales targets by 30 per cent in the year, and had considerably increased her customer base.

She was therefore very disappointed when her accountant painted a very different picture. He showed her some preliminary accounts showing actual performance against the budget which they had put together at the beginning of the year.

'I can't believe it', said Susan, looking at the figures he showed her (see page 354).

'I've sold far more than I thought possible but made less money. What's gone wrong?'

'Before I answer that', said the accountant, 'perhaps we had better have the rest of the bad news. Your debtors have grown considerably in the last year. This aged analysis gives you the breakdown.' The accountant handed Susan the debtors report (see page 354).

'I know the problem', sighed Susan, 'it's partly the big customers who never seem to pay on time, and partly the smaller ones who never seem to pay at all. Our small customers are a particular problem as some of them are very old debts now, and I'm worried they may even go out of business.'

'Yes, there is certainly that concern', said the accountant, 'and also your cash. You are very near your overdraft limit now. Apart from the interest costs, the bank will be getting nervous unless you can reduce your borrowing.'

'I have been trying to collect the money', said Susan, 'but some of these debts are such small amounts. I wonder if it's worth the cost of writing them letters and telephoning. I know they all add up to a lot of money, but each one individually is quite small.'

Activities

i)   Why is Kal Kulate making less than budgeted profits when its sales are 30 per cent up? How can it improve profitability?

ii)   The debtor issue is a common one for small firms who do not have the resources to pursue a large number of customers for payment. What steps could Susan consider to improve her cash flow?

Example: Kal Kulate Ltd: profit and loss and cash flow

Step no.		Jan	Feb	March	April	May	June
	PROFIT AND LOSS						
1	SALES:						
1	Gross	22,325	15,275	16,450	24,088	18,213	23,500
1	VAT	3,325	2,275	2,450	3,588	2,713	3,500
1	Net	19,000	13,000	14,000	20,500	15,500	20,000
2	MATERIALS USED: (50%)	9,500	6,500	7,000	10,250	7,750	10,000
3	Production wages	3,000	3,000	3,000	3,000	3,000	3,000
	Gross profit	6,500	3,500	4,000	7,250	4,750	7,000
4	OVERHEADS:						
4	Salaries	2,000	2,000	2,000	2,000	2,000	2,000
4	Rent	1,000	1,000	1,000	1,000	1,000	1,000
4	Rates & insurance	500	500	500	500	500	500
4	Other costs	1,000	1,000	1,000	1,000	1,000	1,000
4	Publicity	500	500	500	500	500	500
	TOTAL OVERHEADS	5,000	5,000	5,000	5,000	5,000	5,000
5	Bank charges and interest	250	250	250	250	250	250
6	Depreciation	500	500	500	500	500	500
	PROFIT/LOSS	750	−2,250	−1,750	1,500	−1,000	1,250
7	CASH FLOW RECEIPTS[A]	23,500	23,500	22,325	15,275	16,450	24,088
8	PAYMENTS:						
8	Purchase of materials	10,000	10,000	9,500	6,500	7,000	10,250
8	Salaries and wages	5,000	5,000	5,000	5,000	5,000	5,000
8	Rent	—	3,000	—	—	—	3,000
8	Rates and insurance	500	500	500	500	500	500
8	Publicity and other costs	1,500	1,500	1,500	1,500	1,500	1,500
8	Interest	—	—	750	—	750	—
9	VAT PAID	2,013	2,013	1,925	1,400	1,488	2,056
10	VAT DUE	—	—	—	87	—	—
11	CAPITAL	21,150					
	TOTAL PAYMENTS[B]	40,163	19,013	22,175	14,987	15,488	23,056
12	CASH FLOW[(A–B)]	−16,663	4,487	150	288	962	1,032
12	OPENING BALANCE	—	−16,663	−12,176	−12,026	−11,738	−10,766
12	CLOSING BALANCE	−16,663	−12,176	−12,026	−11,738	−10,776	−9,744

Example: Kal Kulate Ltd: profit and loss and cash flow

July	Aug	Sept	Oct	Nov	Dec	TOTAL (12 months)
18,213	20,563	19,975	21,150	24,675	24,088	248,515
2,713	3,063	2,975	3,150	3,675	3,588	37,015
15,500	17,500	17,000	18,000	21,000	20,500	211,500
7,750	8,750	8,500	9,000	10,500	10,250	105,750
3,000	3,000	3,000	3,000	3,000	3,000	36,000
4,750	5,750	5,500	6,000	7,500	7,250	69,750
2,000	2,000	2,000	2,000	2,000	2,000	24,000
1,000	1,000	1,000	1,000	1,000	1,000	12,000
500	500	500	500	500	500	6,000
1,000	1,000	1,000	1,000	1,000	1,000	12,000
500	500	500	500	500	500	6,000
5,000	5,000	5,000	5,000	5,000	5,000	60,000
250	250	250	250	250	250	3,000
500	500	500	500	500	500	6,000
−1000	—	−250	250	1,750	1,500	750
18,213	23,500	18,213	20,563	19,975	21,150	
7,750	10,000	7,750	8,750	8,500	9,000	
5,000	5,000	5,000	5,000	5,000	5,000	
—	3,000	—	—	—	3,000	
500	500	500	500	500	500	
1,500	1,500	1,500	1,500	1,500	1,500	
—	—	750	—	—	750	
1,619	2,013	1,619	1,794	1,750	1,838	
4,113	—	—	3,588	—	—	
20,482	19,013	20,119	21,132	17,250	21,588	
−2,269	4,487	−1,906	−569	2,725	−438	
−9,744	12,013	7,526	−9,432	−10,001	−7,276	
−12,013	−7,526	−9,432	−10,001	−7,276	−7,714	

KAL KULATE LTD. *Profit and loss budget vs actual*

12 months	Budget	Actual
Sales (net)	211,500	274,950
Materials used	105,750	154,970
Production wages	36,000	44,990
Gross profit	69,750	74,990
Overheads:		
Salaries	24,000	26,100
Rent	12,000	12,000
Rates and insurance	6,000	5,800
Other costs	12,000	12,850
Publicity	6,000	7,770
Total overheads	60,000	64,520
Interest and bank charges	3,000	3,790
Depreciation	6,000	6,000
Profit before tax	750	680

KAL KULATE LTD. *Debtors report summary (Dec)*

	£
Current month	30,110
One month	30,840
Two months	13,219
Three months	4,990
Over three months	1,105
Total	80,264

Extended activity *The cost of money*

Try to find out the availability of various types of finance and its costs. For example, a local bank can usually provide information on commercial loans, and overdrafts, with rates of interest and any fixed costs charged for the facility.

From the information you have gathered, why is it important to match the type of borrowing to the use of the funds? Can you give specific examples of what you would use the different types of finance for (e.g. loan, overdrafts, lease etc.)?

In conclusion

Once you have finished this Unit, it is recommended that you turn to Section B, Planning a new venture, and complete Step 3.5, Forecasting the money. This concludes Stage III, so you are then ready for Step 3.6, Summary of the business plan.

7 References and further reading

References and further information

1. Bank of England, *Finance for Small Firms*, 7th report, January 2000.

2. Mason, C. and Lloyd, P, 'New Manufacturing Firms In A Prosperous UK Sub-Region: The Case Of South Hampshire', in Scott, M., Gibb, A., Lewis, J. and Faulkner, T. (eds), *Small Firms' Growth and Development*, Gower, 1986. Page 26 draws some interesting comparisons with other studies.

3. Hughes, A. 'Finance for Small Firms: A UK Perspective', *Small Business Economics* 9: 151–66, 1997.

4. HMSO *Competitiveness: Helping Business to Win*, CM 2563, HMSO, London 1994.

5. This and other aspects of the relationship between banks and small firms was reported in the *Guardian*, 16 September, 1991, p. 12.

6. *British Venture Capital Association (BVCA) Directory*. The BVCA Directory is available (free of charge) from The British Venture Capital Association, 3 Catherine Place, London SW1E 6DX, www.bvca.co.uk

7. Mason, C. and Harrison, R. 'Public Policy and the Development of the Informal Venture Capital Market: UK Experience and Lessons for Europe', in Cowling, K. *Industrial Policy in Europe*, 1999.

8. DTI *Hire Purchase and Leasing*, DTI Small Firms Publications, URN 98/547, 1998.

9. DTI, *Loan Guarantee Scheme*, DTI Small Firms Publications, URN 94/628, 1995.

10. Details of the National Business Angels Network are on their web site www.bestmatch.co.uk

11. More information about AIM can be obtained from the London Stock Exchange, Old Broad Street, London EC2N 1HP, and on www.londonstockexchange.com

12. Bolton Report, *Committee of Inquiry on Small Firms*, HMSO, Cmnd. 4811, 1971.

13. See Hutchinson, P. and Ray, G. 'Surviving the Financial Stress of Small Enterprise Growth', in Curran, J., Stanworth, J. and Watkins, D. (eds) *The Survival of the Small Firm*, Vol. 1, Gower, 1986.

Recommended further reading

❏ Birley, S. and Muzyka, F. *Mastering Entrepreneurship*, FT/Prentice Hall, 2000. Chapter, 3 'Finance'.

❏ Burns, P. *Entrepreneurship and Small Business*, Palgrave, 2001. Chapter 12, 'Financing small firms'.

❏ Jarvis, R. 'Finance and the Small Firm' in Carter, S. and Jones-Evans, D. *Enterprise and Small Business*, FT/Prentice Hall, 2000.

❏ Bank of England, *Finance for Small Firms*, 7th report, January, 2000.

- Barrow, C. and Barrow, P. and Brown, R. *The Business Plan Workbook*, Kogan Page, 2001, especially Phase 5: 'Forecasting results', 'Phase 6: Business controls' and Appendix 2: 'Sources of finance'.
- Stanworth, J. and Gray, C. *Bolton 20 Years On: The Small Firm in the 1990s*, PCP, 1991. Chapter 4, 'Banks and the Provision of Finance to Small Firms' and Chapter 6, 'The Small Firm Equity Gap Since Bolton'.
- Williams, S. *Lloyds Bank Small Business Guide*, Penguin, 2001. Section V.
- Storey, D. *Understanding the Small Business Sector*, Thomson International Press, 1998. Chapter 7, 'Finance'.
- DTI *A Guide to Help for Small Firms*, DTI Small Firms Publications (URN 97/525).

14 Further case studies

This Unit contains three case studies which reflect different stages in the life cycles of small businesses. These are longer than the cases in other units as they are intended to integrate some of the principles of small business management across topic areas. Case study 1 concerns a high-tech company before and after start up. Case study 2 is about the development issues facing an established company. Case study 3 illustrates the problems of a mature family company on the death of its founder.

The principal organisations and characters featured in these cases are fictional and no likeness to real people is intended. However the cases represent realistic contexts and summarise the realities of the relevant marketplace and industry.

Further data gathering can be done to support the information given in the case. This is a definite requirement for Case study 2, and would also be particularly useful for Case study 3. In both cases, relevant market reports and trade information are readily available.

Contents

Case study 1 *Starting up Eocha Ltd*

Case 1 The business proposal

Introduction

In the USA, Robin Poques would probably have been called a 'business angel'. In the UK, he was better known as a private investor in small businesses. To date, his entrepreneurial activities had provided him with a reasonable living, but he was still searching for the big breakthrough – a business opportunity which would grow to a size that could be floated on the stock market and make him not only rich, but also celebrated as a successful entrepreneur. He frequently received introductions and business plans for proposed ventures from a variety of sources. The majority he rejected as not viable, or not capable of the fast growth he was looking for. Recently he had been introduced to two business people who proposed to start up an electronics business which seemed to meet most of his criteria, and he needed to make an investment decision. He studied the written plan he had received from Eocha Ltd.

Private and Confidential

EOCHA Ltd BUSINESS PLAN

Background

Eocha Ltd is a start up product design and prototyping company. The company has been formed with significant equity funding from its founders and an opportunity exists for third-party investment. Eocha will work in certain niche areas of high-technology product design that offer opportunities for knowledgeable, independent designers. The founders' know-how will facilitate the custom design of products by utilising all aspects of micro-electronics technology. In particular it will utilise micro-electronics technology to turn low-tech products into 'smarter', high-tech innovations. All products will be custom designed and built to prototype stage for other companies in a wide range of industries. Eocha will concentrate initially on applications with smaller volumes, yet high added value, or in areas which traditionally have not used electronics extensively. The company will not attempt to compete with high volume electronics manufacturers who have their own research and development departments. Rather, it will complement growth companies wishing to innovate by offering them a high-grade design and problem-solving service. Eocha will sell primarily a design service, rather than a product, in a way which will differentiate it from competitors and allow for high profit margins.

The people

The founders of the company are Dr Charles Appleton and Edwina Oaks. Dr Appleton will act as Chairman and Managing Director, with responsibility for the overall strategy of the company and production. Dr Appleton is well known in the academic, industrial and investment world as a leading authority in micro-electronics. Edwina Oaks will act as General Manager, with specific responsibility for sales, marketing and administration. She currently has senior management responsibility for new product design in a large, UK company.

The founders previously worked together in Appletech Ltd, a contract design company founded by Dr Appleton. In the three years they worked together, Appletech expanded rapidly. However, as a result of an abortive move into high volume production of their own products, prompted by Appletech's external investors, both Dr Appleton and Mrs Oaks left that business. This plan is designed to bring their skills together again in the development of a specialist operation. A third-party investor(s) is sought to both invest in the business and contribute to its strategic planning and administration. However, it is intended that the founders are in a majority on the board of directors, to allow the company to be run by individuals who fully understand its operation. The two founders bring sufficient breadth of experience and knowledge to manage the company in the early stages.

A crucial area of development will be the recruitment of innovative staff, including engineers and designers. Individuals have already been identified and discussions are continuing concerning their joining the company. The founders' knowledge and reputation is seen as a significant factor in the recruitment of key staff within the industry.

Full Curricula Vitae of the founders are available on request.

The market

More and more products, from flight simulators to fishing rods, are becoming 'smarter', that is they can record more information, and make more decisions about their utilisation, without human intervention. The development of the Silicon Integrated Circuit (SIC or, more commonly, microchip) was the key enabling technology of this trend. But SICs, or 'chips', do not function on their own. For many years there has been a thriving industry in the design of circuits that connect together SICs and other electronic devices to produce useful circuits, systems and products. For example, a SIC does not easily handle the high powers and voltages of the everyday electronics world, so specific adaptations have to be made in order for microchips to be used in many applications. The falling price and increasing power of SICs is increasing the number of applications that can successfully use them, and this trend will continue to increase the demand for 'smart' products. Customised silicon microcircuits are now used extensively in many industries, including telecommunications, instrumentation, security, aerospace and the military. Significant demand exists for the design of new products incorporating such circuits, which has been estimated at £300 to £400 million in Europe, with higher figures for North America. The increased complexity and power of the SIC has increased the demand for electronic products designed for specific customer requirements by 20 per cent per annum throughout Europe in recent years. The reduced size and price of products using electronic circuits is usually accompanied by enhanced performance and reliability, so that their integration into product design is becoming a competitive 'must' in many industries.

The opportunity

The opportunity is to build a substantial, medium-sized firm over the next few years. Specifically, this firm will specialise in the design and prototyping of new products utilising the latest technologies in electronic circuitry designed for specific customer requirements. It will design such products using computer aided design software. It will purchase the necessary components to build prototypes of such circuits and products, including the SIC and other devices. However, Eocha will add considerable value through the design and interconnection of the devices in the circuit in such a way as to meet customer specifications of the final product. The founders have extensive knowledge and expertise in this area of micro-electronic applications in new product design.

Initial customers have already been identified from the founders' existing contacts. Due to the wide application of the technology, no specific industry area will be pursued above others in the longer term. In the short term it is known that innovative applications exist in several markets, including kitchen appliances which will become increasingly 'smart' in the next few years.

The difficulties

Although Eocha is aiming for a niche share of the overall new product development market, one of the difficulties will be the slow build up of work inherent in custom design; 6 to 18 months are common lead times from initial customer contact through to design of an initial prototype. The financial projections and capital requirements reflect this.

Substantial capital investment is required for the necessary equipment and facilities. This is partly offset by a low requirement for working capital, as products are made to order and not stocked in advance. Both of these factors are reflected in the cash flow forecasts.

Increasingly, the manufacture of these innovative products takes place outside of Europe around the 'Pacific Rim'. Strategic alliances will be sought with companies in Asia and elsewhere to provide them with the design resource at the leading edge of technology which they do not always possess themselves.

In summary

Particular strengths are:

❏   founders with proven track record in the technology area;

❏   growth demand for high-technology product design;

❏   close links with research institutions;

❏   low capital investment in relation to the micro-electronics industry.

Particular challenges are:

❏   slow initial build up of client base due to customised nature of the business;

❏   high capital investment compared to lower technology design companies;

❏   the need for strategic alliances with manufacturers outside of Europe.

The investment

Initially 100,000 £1 ordinary shares are being authorised. Sixty thousand will be issued at par to the executive founders (40,000 to Dr Charles Appleton and 20,000 to Edwina Oaks). An investor and non-executive director will be offered the balance of shares (40,000) at £2.00, the premium reflecting the commitment and expertise of the executive founders. A £50,000 overdraft is sought from the bank, secured against the sales ledger. In the first instance, hire purchase will also be used to purchase some capital equipment.

Summary projections

End of year	1	2	3
	£000s	£000s	£000s
Sales	120	450	700
Gross profit	96	360	560
Overheads	110	270	420
Operating profit	(14)	90	140

End of year	1	2	3
	£000s	£000s	£000s
Cash flow			
Accounts paid	197	417	610
Capital spend	141	40	75
Received	(72)	(398)	(675)
Funding required	266	59	10

Key assumptions

Sales should build up rapidly once the initial lead time is taken into account. There is no reason why this expansion should not continue after Year 3, providing the appropriate technical staff can be recruited.

Gross margins are calculated to average 80 per cent, as the costs of materials at the design and prototyping stage are low compared to the indirect costs, particularly staff costs.

Overheads include the costs of all staff and directors, as well as premises, administration, finance and marketing costs.

Cash flow assumes a time lag between invoice date and payment of approximately 60 days in the case of both debtors and creditors.

£140,000 is received from shareholders' investment in year 1 as part of the funding of the operation.

Hire purchase is used to purchase equipment, although a percentage deposit (30 per cent) has to be found from internal funds.

The decision

Robin Poques had already had one meeting with the founders whom he judged to make an innovative, technically competent team. He was concerned about their business management capabilities, but he felt he might himself have a role to play in this area. He also knew other investors were interested in backing them, so he did not have much time to make a decision.

Activities

i)   How well do you think the founders have presented their case? How would you advise them to improve the layout or content of their plan?

ii) How would you assess this business proposition in terms of its strengths and weaknesses as a new venture?

iii) What other information or clarification would you now seek if you were Robin Poques?

iv) Assuming you have to make a decision in principle based on what is presented here, advise Robin Poques on whether he should invest or not.

Case 2 Two and a half years later

Start up

At the beginning of its third year in business, Eocha seemed on course to meet its original objectives. Turnover had risen quickly to over £450,000, and the company had made a small profit as forecast in the original business plan. The three shareholders seemed to make a good team. The executive management of Charles Appleton and Edwina Oaks was complemented by Robin Poques as a non-executive director and 40 per cent shareholder who advised on financial and administrative matters.

The crisis

However, half-way through the third year, the loss of one significant customer prompted a crisis. Two key customers accounted for more than 60 per cent of sales, and when one of them decided to take the design of new products in-house rather than subcontract the work to Eocha, the planned expansion of the business was threatened. There were insufficient short-term sales to justify the overheads which had been built up on expectations of higher levels of turnover. The bank, which had been very supportive earlier, made it clear that further loans or an increased overdraft would not be considered without personal guarantees from the directors.

Personal issues

To make matters worse, Robin Poques found that he was caught increasingly in the middle of a running battle between the two executive directors. Appleton blamed Oaks for not foreseeing the loss of an important customer and for failing to take the necessary steps to replace the lost sales ahead of time. Behind the business argument, Poques knew that there was a personality problem. Appleton found Oaks' thorough, but time-consuming, efforts to build relationships with their customers increasingly frustrating, especially when the need for new business became urgent. He also become irritated by her habit of taking time off to look after her young children when they were ill and away from school. After his own marriage had broken up a year earlier, he had thrown himself into the business with even greater intensity and lack of tolerance for those that did not share his long working hours. Poques admired his commitment and expertise but, like others in the business, he found him increasingly difficult to work with. He recalled the last board meeting at which Appleton had directly challenged Oaks' sales methods:

'You need to spend more of your time out there, knocking on doors and finding new customers, not visiting the ones we have already got.'

Edwina Oaks had grimly defended her strategy: 'I know we need to find new business, but that takes time. If we treat our existing customers properly, we will not only get more sales from them, but also new business through their recommendations to other firms.'

'It's too late for that. We need new sales now. If we wait any longer, there will be no Eocha for your customers to recommend,' Appleton had said.

Poques tried to arbitrate between them, but now he felt he had to take sides. The internal wrangling was distracting them from the real issues. The drop in sales had drained their cash to the point where they had exceeded their overdraft limit. The bank had declined to extend it without personal guarantees from the directors. Appleton had refused to give such guarantees, or invest any new funds in the business, on the basis that he did not have enough confidence in the board. Oaks was threatening to leave unless she received the full backing of at least a majority of shareholders. Poques was beginning to think that the business could only afford one of the two executive directors right now – both financially and emotionally. As the shareholder with the casting vote, he had to decide on the next steps.

Appendix

Summary of results

End of year	Yr 1 Actual £000s	Yr 2 Actual £000s	Yr 3 Forecast £000s
Sales	110	459	384
Gross profit	77	312	307
Overheads	121	290	339
Net profit	(44)	22	(32)
Cash flow			
Accounts paid	190	430	410
Capital spend	148	34	55
Received	(230*)	(380)	(395)
Funding required**	108	84	70

* Includes £140 share capital in year 1.

** Currently met by bank overdraft (£50,000) and hire purchase.

Activities

Advise Robin Poques what to do next. In particular:

i) Analyse the situation of Eocha after two years of trading compared to its original business plan. Draw up a list of current strengths and weaknesses, compared to those in the plan. In which areas do they seem to have succeeded? Where have they been less than successful? (It is useful to reconsider Unit 10, sections 4 and 5 in particular, in answering this.)

ii) List the critical problems that need addressing.

iii) Draw up a list of possible options to tackle the problems.

iv) Recommend a course of action.

Case study 2 *Development strategies at Maldini Pizza*

Introduction

As part of a partnership initiative between local business and higher education, Jane Stuart, a university student, was working on an assignment with a small business owner. Her brief was to produce a business plan for a local restaurant owner, Peter Maldini, which would inform the next stage of development of his company. She had collected the internal data by visiting the restaurant and talking through the key issues with the owner. Before investigating external factors in the marketplace, she reviewed her briefing notes on the situation so far.

The business concept

Peter Maldini, owner and creator of Maldini Pizza, refers to his restaurant concept as 'designer pizza and pasta'. He has one restaurant in the centre of town which opened two years ago, and has been very successful, even developing something of a cult following. The food is not unusual – a variety of pasta and pizza dishes that can be found in other restaurants of this type. The prices are not expensive, with a variety of starters at £2 to £3 and large pizza and pasta dishes at £5 to £6. What is different is the decor and the presentation. The food is presented on beautiful tableware with large white dishes and silver cutlery. The decor is modern Italian in style, with much stainless steel and glass in evidence. Ceilings are high which, linked to minimalist decorations and white walls, gives a feeling of spaciousness. The toilets summarise the tone of the place. The washbasins are steel set in a glass surround with walls of white Italian marble tiles – stunning! Some of the dishes do reflect this style as the pasta comes in unusual shapes and colours and there are authentic Italian oils and dressings on the tables. The food, like the decor, is simple but of high quality – what Peter Maldini described as 'classically modern'.

Many of the waiting staff are Italian or French, adding to the continental feel, and wear large white aprons over black clothing. They are well trained, welcoming and relaxed. However, they are also efficient. The owner insists they follow detailed instructions on the structure of their work with clear rules on customer service, such as maximum waiting times for orders and regular checks on customer satisfaction.

Peter Maldini was brought up in England, although he is a regular visitor to Italy. He describes his mother as 'very English' and his father as 'very Italian'. He is certainly proud of both backgrounds, which are reflected in his business. His aim is to merge Italian style and food under the 'Maldini' brand, and make it appealing to the UK market.

Development ideas

He has a number of ideas about how to expand his business:

i) He is considering opening another restaurant in a similar, mid-sized affluent town as a pilot for expansion. He is unclear whether any future outlets after that should be as a franchise operation or owned outlets under management. The fitting out of the current restaurant cost £300,000 including equipment and refurbishment, so that expansion will require considerable capital. He believes he could grow quite rapidly to 10 or more restaurants, which would give him economies of buying and flexibility of staffing. However, he would not personally like to manage a chain bigger than that as he feels it would lose the 'personal touch'.

ii) He believes he can offer other products under the Maldini label which emphasise Italian style and cooking. For example, he has investigated importing a range of cooking utensils, and Italian food ingredients which he would sell mail order to his restaurant customer base. He reckons his restaurant attracts over 40,000 paying customers per year, which, discounting children and those who come in more than once, equates to about 15,000 adults. He has collected a mailing list of around 5,000 regular customers during the first two years' trading.

iii) He is thinking of launching the 'Maldini Room Service' targeted at lunch/dinner parties and business entertaining. Busy people can order from the full menu and have the meal delivered in insulated containers, and served onto his Italian tableware, in their home or office. He developed the idea from catering firms operating in big cities who provide a corporate dining service without the need for in-house kitchens. He calculates that there are about 700 local businesses within a 10 mile radius who would be interested in eating on their own premises from time to time, at a cost of £15 – £20 per head including delivery.

The financials

He was quite familiar with the basic accounting information for his restaurant, although he does not produce regular, detailed management accounts. He would plan new restaurants on the same sales and cost profile as the first one.

Sales: the present restaurant had sales of £300,000 in Year 1 and £400,000 in Year 2. Maldini is expecting it to stay at this level, except for rises in line with inflation and new business developments. The average customer spend per head is £12. Seasonal fluctuations during the summer and at Christmas mean that August and December sales are usually two-thirds up on the average £30,000 per month turnover.

Costs of food and drink: he calculates a gross profit by subtracting costs of food ingredients and drink – wine, beers, soft drinks etc. – from the sales total. The menu is priced to give an average 80 per cent gross profit on food dishes, and 60 per cent on drink. As food sales are higher than drink (the ratio is normally 70:30) this gives an overall margin of 75 per cent for restaurant sales.

Staff costs: he employs mainly part-time staff, on one daytime and one night-time shift, each with a manager. As they open seven days a week, this adds up to a lot of staff. He thinks it is equivalent to about 15 full-time staff, although he has over 40 employees on his books. In total, staff costs are £14,000 per month including employment costs. Waiting staff keep their tips, so their earnings can be quite high at no extra cost to the restaurant.

Premises costs: rent, rates, insurances, heating, light and other costs relating to the premises are running at £4,000 per month.

Office and publicity costs: accounting and administrative costs are not high, although they do have occasional publicity costs such as a mailing to their customer list or the printing of a new menu – in all £2,000 per month.

Profitability: my initial calculations indicate a profit contribution of 15 per cent of sales, although this does not include drawings for the owner, depreciation and interest. He does not seem to have any substantial current borrowings as I believe he funded the initial set up costs from savings and a legacy. However, any expansion would have to be funded separately and finance costs built into the equation.

Cash: the cash flow of the business is broadly in line with profitability. Sales are paid for immediately, except for a slight delay on credit card sales. The biggest cost area, staff salaries, is also paid for in the same month in which it is incurred. Other costs – food and drink, premises, office and publicity costs – are paid for within 30 days on average, that is the month after the cost is incurred. Although Maldini has to watch out for theft and non-payment, he says that cash follows profits as he does not have much money tied up in stock or debtors.

Marketing

Although Maldini has plenty of innovative ideas, and seems to know his target market well, he does very little to promote his business in traditional ways. He claims that customers come to the restaurant by word-of-mouth recommendations. As long as he provides the atmosphere, service and food they need, they will sell the restaurant to their friends, he claims. He does mail a newsletter to his list of regular customers to inform them of special events and menu additions, especially at Christmas. His high level of sales seems to justify his methods – he said that none of the restaurants he worked in before opening his own generated sales of more than £250,000 per annum.

His customers seem to come from a variety of age groups, but this is not really a family restaurant so younger children are rare. It attracts plenty of 25- to 35-year -olds, but also a slightly older group of over 50-year-olds. Plenty of women diners are in evidence, and the menu caters for vegetarians particularly well.

There is a lot of competition. Maldini has noticed a substantial increase in the number of local restaurants recently, especially of the less formal, cafe/diner type owned by national chains. However, he has also noticed that people are eating out much more, a habit he believes will continue to grow.

The business plan

Jane Stuart headed back to campus to the library and her computer. She knew that there were several market reports on the restaurant and catering industry, as well as magazines and journals, which would give her the overall market data she needed. She also recognised she would need local information on population and business trends, not to mention competitive restaurants and services. However, the biggest question mark in her mind was how to develop the business. Should Maldini follow up more than one of his ideas to keep his options open, or focus his efforts in one direction only?

Activities

Write a business plan for Maldini's restaurant in either outline or complete form. To do this you will need to:

i) Complete the external information gathering by investigating the overall restaurant market and a local geographic area. You can assume the restaurant is in an area convenient to you, and collect local demographic and competitive data on that basis.

ii) Summarise the key data you have, including a financial summary of the position of the restaurant before expansion. This should give you a clearer picture of the current profitability and cash flow on which to base future expansion.

iii) Consider the options for growth. You need to recommend a strategy to Maldini and incorporate this into your plan.

iv) Write up and present the final report.

Case study 3 *Succession issues at Mackay Golf Ltd*

Introduction

Duncan Mackay founded Mackay Golf in 1948, when golf was beginning to emerge not only as a professional sport but also as a lucrative, international business. He built up the company gradually over the years, specialising in high quality clubs and accessories for the discerning player who was prepared to pay a little more for hand-made Scottish golf equipment. By the 1990s the company had grown to employ over 70 staff with a turnover of £4 million and net profits of £200,000. The company survived 50 years in business, but the founder did not. He died after a heart attack on one of his favourite courses, a month before the planned half-century celebrations. His widow, family and colleagues were left to contemplate the next steps for the business.

The family

For the first 35 years of the business, Duncan Mackay seemed a typical, family-business owner. He married his childhood sweetheart, Mary, and their only son, Malcolm, joined the company on completion of his business and finance degree. Malcolm proved an asset not only for his aptitude at sales and marketing, but also for his love of golf. A regular participant in amateur tournaments, Malcolm was a well-known figure in many club-houses.

But 15 years before his death, Duncan turned his family and business world upside down by leaving his wife for his secretary, Isabel Stuart. After an acrimonious separation and divorce, Duncan re-married and had a second son, Kenneth, by Isabel. Although Malcolm stayed on in the business, he found relationships with his father difficult through the strain of these family pressures and he used every opportunity to spend more time on the golf course.

The shareholding of the business had become equally complicated. Duncan and Mary Mackay were the original shareholders in 1948 with 50 per cent of the shares each. When Malcolm joined the business, his mother transferred 30 per cent of the shares from her name to his in recognition of his contribution to the business and her own lack of involvement. Duncan's will came as a shock, particularly to Malcolm. He left 40 per cent of the company's shares to his second son Kenneth, to be held in trust by his mother, Isabel, until he was eighteen. The remaining 10 per cent went to Bill Warren, General Manager of Mackay Golf.

The management

When Kenneth was born in 1985, Duncan Mackay was 60 years old. He promised his new wife that he would shorten his 65-hour working week to spend more time with his new family. He hired a manager, Bill Warren to take over some of the responsibilities. Bill had enjoyed a successful career in the leisure industry in a variety of administrative and management posts. He was drawn to Mackay Golf for the quality of life offered by its location, the promise of shares in the business at some future date, and the opportunity to run a smaller company. He was happy to leave Malcolm to manage the sales effort with customers as his own strengths lay in running an efficient operation back at base. Bill had been running the administrative, financial and production functions of the business for the last decade or more, advised by Duncan.

The market

The sports equipment market is still sufficiently fragmented to allow smaller companies such as Mackay Golf to survive in an increasingly competitive arena. Golf is the largest market for personal sports equipment and is growing quite strongly as the population ages and more golf courses are built. The UK market for golf equipment probably exceeds £200 million, with an estimated 3.5 million regular and 1.5 million occasional players. However, it is also the most competitive sports equipment sector, with strong branding linked to high levels of promotional expenditure, particularly on endorsements. This has favoured the larger suppliers of well-known, international brands. Imports have increased substantially in the 1990s, mainly from the USA, Taiwan and Hong Kong. Traditionally strong European export markets for UK golf producers have been undermined by the strength of the pound.

Mackay Golf sales had declined for the two years prior to Duncan's death. Although their products were widely respected as quality leaders, their distributors in the USA and Europe were concerned at their high prices, lack of point-of-sale material and publicity in the retail outlets, and low investment in R&D for new products.

The shareholders' meeting

Soon after Duncan's death, the shareholders of Mackay Golf met to review the situation. After rather strained formalities, Bill Warren opened the meeting.

'I know we all have Duncan's passing on our minds, but I am sure he would have wanted us to take decisions based on what is best for the business. It seems to me we have two basic options: one is to carry on and hope we can fight our way through the difficult competitive situation we are in. The second option is to sell the business so that shareholders can realise what is still a valuable asset before it devalues any further.'

Isabel nodded her agreement to the second option. 'I for one would like to realise some capital. Duncan did not have many assets to leave in his will after the divorce settlement,' she said, looking pointedly at Mary Mackay, 'which is why he left me and Kenneth the shares – it's all we have.'

'This is very defeatist talk.' Malcolm could restrain himself no longer. 'If you feel like out Bill, that's OK. I'll happily take over the helm totally now. It's what Dad wanted originally anyway. I strongly believe we can survive and grow. We have made good profits in the past and we can again – which will give you the money you need in dividend payments, Isabel. Selling now is admitting defeat, and we would not get the best price for the business.'

'And I know it's not what Duncan would have wanted. This was his life's work,' said Mary.

Activities

You have been called in to give objective advice to the shareholders on what they should do.

i)   Summarise the problems faced by Mackay Golf Ltd. (A SWOT analysis may be a good way of presenting the issues facing the company.)

ii) Outline the options as you see them. Are there others which Bill Warren did not mention?

iii) Recommend a course of action which takes account of the management needs of the business, but also recognises the family situation.

Section B

Planning a new venture

How to use this section

1. This section contains three 'Stages' each sub-divided into a series of 'Steps'. The three Stages concern the planning of a new venture, from the creation of an idea for a new business through to the development of that idea as a business plan, in Steps which match up to the themes in the Parts and Units of Section A of the book.

2. Each Stage is linked to the Parts I, II and III of Section A. Each Step links to a Unit in Section A: for an overview of the layout of the book see the Preface.

3. The Stages and the Steps should be undertaken in the sequence of the book, and preferably after the reader has studied the appropriate Unit in Section A.

4. In summary, the three Stages are:

    Stage I   *The feasibility study* – five Steps linked to Part I, Units 1–5 and one Summary Step.

    Stage II   *The route to market entry* – three Steps linked to Part II, Units 6–8 and one Summary Step.

    Stage III *The business plan* – five Steps linked to Part III, Units 9–13 and one Summary Step.

5. The Stages and Steps develop an idea from the category of 'unknown risk' to 'reasonable prospects' in Stage I, to the selection of a 'suitable vehicle' in Stage II, and to a level of 'acceptable risk' in Stage III.

The plan of Stages and Steps shown overleaf illustrates this progression.

Stage I: The feasibility study

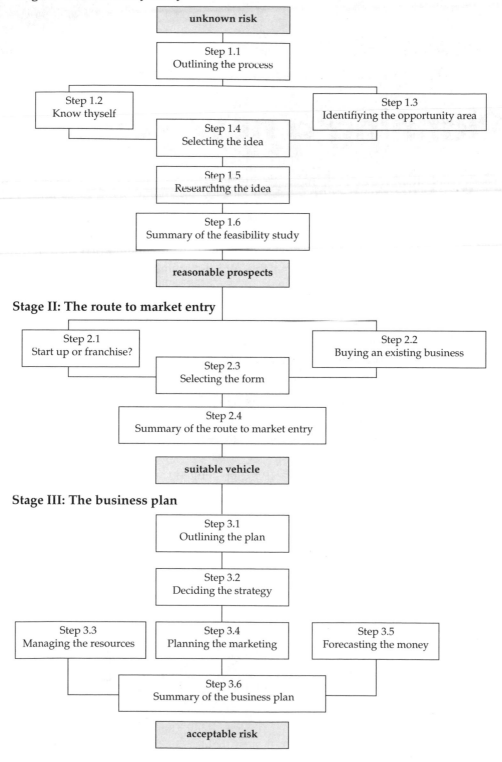

unknown risk

Step 1.1
Outlining the process

Step 1.2
Know thyself

Step 1.3
Identifiying the opportunity area

Step 1.4
Selecting the idea

Step 1.5
Researching the idea

Step 1.6
Summary of the feasibility study

reasonable prospects

Stage II: The route to market entry

Step 2.1
Start up or franchise?

Step 2.2
Buying an existing business

Step 2.3
Selecting the form

Step 2.4
Summary of the route to market entry

suitable vehicle

Stage III: The business plan

Step 3.1
Outlining the plan

Step 3.2
Deciding the strategy

Step 3.3
Managing the resources

Step 3.4
Planning the marketing

Step 3.5
Forecasting the money

Step 3.6
Summary of the business plan

acceptable risk

Stage I   The feasibility study

Step 1.1 Outlining the process

Summary of what is required

1. Review Part I, Unit 2, Small Business in the Economy.
2. Consider the process described below to develop an idea for a new venture and to assess its viability

The objective of Stage I is to decide on an idea for a new business venture and to assess the viability of that idea in the marketplace.

The first Steps take you through the process of formulating an idea, which when first identified will be in a position of unknown risk. You may already have an idea in mind, but it is still advisable to undertake all of the steps to assess if it is really suited to you.

Further Steps ask you to research more closely the feasibility and practicality of the idea. By the end of Stage I, you should be able to judge whether or not the idea has reasonable prospects.

The Stage is organised into 5 Steps and a Summary Step, as shown below.

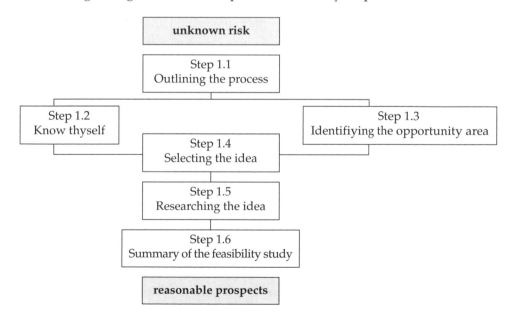

Step 1.2 Know thyself

Summary of what is required

1. Review Part I, Unit 2, The entrepreneur and the owner-manager.
2. Analyse yourself in terms of:
   - ❏ personal objectives;
   - ❏ personal resources;
   - ❏ clues from the past;
   - ❏ your 'speciality'.

Before undertaking this task

First complete your review of Unit 2 in Section A, Part I, The entrepreneur and the owner-manager.

Know thyself: personal requirements and qualities for success

Starting up a new business venture on your own is not like applying for a job in an existing organisation. There are no selection interviews, no-one to tell you what to do or how to do it. It is a green field in which you can choose what seeds to plant, what to build, and what role you wish to play.

In deciding what to do with your green field the most important influence is you: what you want from it and what you start with.

The starting point in thinking about any new venture is therefore some personal analysis which attempts to answer the following questions:

Personal objectives	How will you know if you are being successful?
	Where do you want to go in the future?
Personal resources	Where do you start from?
	What are your personal strengths, weaknesses and resources?
Clues from the past	What can you learn from your past?
	What lessons have you learned that may help take you from where you are now to where you wish to go?
Your speciality	What are your unique qualities that could help you reach your personal objectives?
	We are all different and therefore unique in some way. How can you use your uniqueness to give you enjoyment and satisfaction?
	Can you identify special talents you find most satisfying in practice?

Use the following worksheets to help you think about these questions.

It is important to establish these personal parameters for success as criteria against which to judge ideas for any new venture. As you develop ideas you will be asked to evaluate them according to your personal objectives and talents.

The level of commitment needed to make a new enterprise succeed is rooted in its ability to meet your personal requirements and in its potential for personal fulfilment through use of your special qualities. If your personal needs are not met, the motive force to make innovations succeed in practice will be lacking.

Personal objectives

Write down what you want in your life in the short, medium, and long term:

	In 1 year	*In 3 years*	*In 10 years*
1. What do I want to be?			
2. What do I want to do?			
3. What do I want to have?			

Personal resources

Assess where you are now. Summarise what you have to offer (strengths) and what you need to learn or minimise (weaknesses), in terms of technical skills (what you can do, knowledge of specific products or markets), management competencies (specific business skills in areas such as finance, marketing and human relations), and personal attributes (your personal characteristics in relation to key entrepreneurial characteristics such as innovativeness, determination, external focus and team leadership).

	Strengths	*Weaknesses*
1. Technical skills		
2. Management competencies		

3. Personal attributes

Clues from the past

Review your past life, and write down some specific moments when you felt purposeful, and focused in a way that gave you satisfaction at the time and in retrospect. Also look at times when you felt less directed and adrift.

Personal qualities used/misused

Satisfying moments:

_____   _____

_____   _____

Dissatisfying moments:

_____   _____

_____   _____

What clues do these give about what you want, what you have to offer now and what you wish to avoid?

Your speciality

Make an assessment of your knowledge, skills and qualities to try and discover some things in you that are unique and give you enjoyment and satisfaction. Review your personal objectives, personal resources, and clues from the past. Select those qualities and talents that you feel make you stand out from the crowd. These are the talents that give you the greatest sense of enjoyment and satisfaction when you use them well.

My special talents are:

1. _____

2. _____

3. _____

4. _____

5. _____

6. _____

Step 1.3 Identifying the opportunity area

Summary of what is required

1. Review Part I, Unit 3, The small business environment.
2. Define your opportunity area in a short sentence.
3. List the sources of opportunity by identifying supporting trends.
4. Give some initial ideas with specific examples of possible opportunities.

Before undertaking this task

First complete your review of Unit 3 in Section A, Part I, The small business environment.

The opportunity area: definition

The second task in our feasibility study is to identify an opportunity area. This is a general area of opportunity which not only has the potential to fulfil your personal requirements, and use your personal strengths, but which can also give rise to new solutions to problems in the external environment or novel ways of meeting market needs.

An opportunity area is a focal point for ideas for your new enterprise. It is a single focus which concentrates creative thinking into one opportunity area; it is however general enough to allow for plenty of different specific ideas at this stage.

The key criteria for your opportunity area:

❏ *personal requirements:* has it potential to meet your personal objectives and aspirations identified in Step 1.2?

❏ *personal qualities:* will it offer the opportunity to build on your personal strengths and unique qualities and not over expose the weaknesses identified in Step 1.2?

❏ *innovation:* can it contain new solutions to specific problems, or fulfil identifiable needs in the external environment in a new way?

❏ *viable innovation:* does it represent longer-term developments and trends in the social, technological, economic and political environment or could it be a short-term fad?

Description: define your opportunity area in a short sentence which links products, services, technology or resources, to market needs or problem areas.

> *Examples of opportunity area definitions*
> *   Healthy foods acceptable to younger people.
> *   Training programmes to support the public service manager in a changing environment.
> *   Desk top publishing for fast, creative presentations.
> *   Personal and accommodation protection for elderly people.

Sources of opportunity

What are the underlying trends in the environment which give your area potential opportunities? What are the supporting trends in social, technological, economic, political or legal developments? Why may these provide market opportunity? Summarise why your selected area is a good source of potential opportunities.

> *Example of a source of opportunity: 'personal and accommodation protection for elderly people'*
> - Demographic trends show increasing percentage of the population will be 70 years plus in 1990s onwards.
> - Rapidly increasing crime rates against the elderly, seen as soft targets.
> - Conventional sheltered accommodation using permanent staff increasingly expensive and difficult to recruit wardens.
> - Increasing numbers of elderly who are active and not dependent on others for normal living, but need protection and psychological support.
> - Technological developments in building and personal protection devices which are expensive on individual basis.
> - Trend to decentralise emergency systems for elderly; public services offering hot-line systems for elderly to call for help from their independent living accommodation, rather than live in homes with permanent help available.
> - Increasing numbers of retired people as owner occupiers of houses.
> - Decreasing percentage of young population and therefore people resources to look after elderly.

Initial ideas

Give some first examples and ideas of new products or services which could provide you with an entry point to exploit the opportunities offered by the opportunity area.

> *Examples of initial ideas: personal and accommodation protection for elderly people*
> - Personal security warning devices, whistles to electronic alarms.
> - Individual housing security devices, user friendly for elderly.
> - Impersonal sheltered housing: flats for elderly in electronic surveillance security accommodation.
> - Help service for elderly on subscription basis, clearing house for approved services, e.g. plumbers, transport, etc.
> - House conversion service, specialist conversions of larger premises owned by elderly, to small accommodation with rental/sale of surplus.

Step 1.4 Selecting the idea

Summary of what is required

1. Review Part I, Unit 4, Innovation and the marketplace.
2. Build on ideas by creative thinking within your opportunity area.
3. Make a short list from these ideas by elimination and evaluation against key personal and business environment criteria.
4. Assess the competitive edge.
5. Rate the benefits sought by customers, and offered by you.
6. Select a final idea.

Before undertaking this task

First complete your review of Unit 4 in Part I, Section A, Innovation and the marketplace.

Build on ideas

The next step is to select one idea, by first expanding your base of possible opportunities as widely as possible, and then narrowing it down by reference to your own objectives and to the benefits it offers to targeted customers.

Expand on your list of initial ideas by creating as many thoughts as possible relating to the opportunity area identified in Step 1.3. The aim is not to come up with the best idea.

The objective is to produce a large number of new, imaginative ideas. These can be later discarded, or built on to produce something creative and practical. (Refer to Unit 4, 3, Misinterpretations of innovation)

Creative thinking comes from seeing or making new connections. These connections are often between existing ideas or concepts that are too far apart for one person to visualise together.

The basis of *'brainstorming'* is to use a group of people to build on one another's ideas, so that these improbable connections are made. If you can work with others to develop your list of ideas, then do so. If you cannot, write down as many ideas as you can on your own.

Use the following guidelines if working in a group to brainstorm ideas:

- generate as many ideas as possible the more the better;
- improve and build on each other's ideas: as well as suggesting new ideas, try and develop someone else's ideas by proposing improvements or ways of combining ideas;
- encourage long shots: crazy-sounding ideas can often spark off original and practical thoughts;
- encourage rather than criticise others: praise other group members' ideas to encourage them to come up with more rather than turning off their creative tap by adverse comments;
- always record all ideas on a sheet of paper or a flip chart.

Make a shortlist

The large number of ideas which you have generated within your opportunity area now need sorting and shortlisting.

It usually helps to group them into different categories or types. If any are still half-formed, try and build them into something practical or group them with others to see if there are any possible new combinations. From this list, first eliminate any that you consider cannot be translated into productive use (i.e. they are totally impractical).

Next, review each remaining idea against the key criteria established in Steps 1.2 and 1.3.

❐ *Personal requirements* How well does it fit with your personal objectives and requirements?

❐ *Personal qualities* Will it offer you the opportunity to maximise your strengths and unique qualities?

❐ *Innovation* Does it meet identifiable needs in a new way?

❐ *Viability* Is it supported by longer-term trends or could it be short lived?

Decide on a short list of three or four ideas which you believe will best meet these criteria.

Assess the competitive edge

Before final selection of the one idea you wish to test through the feasibility study, it is necessary to first ensure you will have a competitive edge in the marketplace by considering your target customers and the benefits you will offer them. Again it is useful to have group feedback where possible or invite others to comment on your short-listed ideas in relation to the marketplace.

Use the 'Domestic markets checklist' to describe your targeted customer if you are selling to domestic or consumer markets.

Use the 'Industrial markets checklist' to describe your customer if you are selling to industrial markets or other businesses. Note: it is important to identify the person(s) who makes the purchase decision. Also use these checklists to consider the benefits which these customers seek from the type of product or service you are offering. When you have identified the benefits the customer is seeking, consider how well these benefits are met by existing products or services and give them a rating between 0 to 10.

Finally use the competitive edge checklist to identify your competitive edge: specify the benefits of your product or service, and how important these are to the customer, compared to competitive offerings.

Identifying your target customer

Decide if you will be selling to largely domestic or industrial markets. Then use the appropriate checklist to specify your customer target. (They are for guidance only; you may wish to add other parameters or you may feel some are not relevant.)

Checklist
Domestic markets: target customers

Sex   Male ☐   Female ☐

Age group Under 15   ☐
            15–25   ☐
            25–40   ☐
            40–65   ☐
            Over 65   ☐

Type of employment

Managerial ☐   Manual   ☐   Office/Clerical ☐
Housewife ☐   Self-employed ☐   Retired   ☐
Other (specify) _____

General

Income range _____

Householder or Rented Accommodation _____

Area of residence _____

Lifestyle/personality type _____

Interests and hobbies _____

Socio-economic grouping _____

Benefits target customer seeks from my product or service	*Existing product or service provision**
1 _____	☐
2 _____	☐
3 _____	☐
4 _____	☐
5 _____	☐

*For each benefit stated, how do you rate existing products or services available to the target customer? Use a scale of 0 to 10 where 0 = benefit not provided and 10 = benefit fully provided.

381

Checklist
Industrial markets: target customers

Sector/Industry type: _____

Legal identity: Limited ☐   Partnership ☐   Charity ☐

Size of organisation: Turnover range _____

                         Number of employees _____

Location of companies: Geographic area UK _____

                         Overseas _____

Job title of decision makers(s) for my product or service: _____

Frequency of purchase: _____

Benefits target customer seeks from my product or service	Existing product or service provision*
1 _____	☐
2 _____	☐
3 _____	☐
4 _____	☐
5 _____	☐

* For each benefit stated, how do you rate existing products or services available to the target customer? Use a scale of 0 to 10 where 0 = benefit not provided and 10 = benefit fully provided.

Rate the benefits sought by customers, and offered by you

What are the principal features and benefits of your product or service?

	Feature	Benefit
1.	_____	_____
2.	_____	_____
3.	_____	_____
4.	_____	_____
5.	_____	_____

How do your target customers rate these benefits? Indicate for each benefit which you think is the most important in their buying decision, the second most important and so on.

In the Domestic markets checklist or the Industrial markets checklist you have also indicated how you rated existing products or services available in terms of benefits sought by the target customer.

Comparing these two ratings of the relative importance of benefits to customers, and your assessment of the competitive delivery of benefits, what will be your competitive edge?

What will you be offering that is better than the competition and valued by your target customer?

My competitive edge is:

1. _____

2. _____

3. _____

Select a final idea

Carefully evaluate each idea once again.

Consider which idea best fulfils the two key criteria of i) your personal objectives and special talents and ii) a competitive edge in the marketplace.

Make a decision and select one idea to test through a feasibility study.

Step 1.5 Researching the idea

Summary of what is required

1. Review Part I, Unit 5, Information and help.
2. Set research objectives.
3. Find out more about the customer.
4. Find out more about the competition.
5. Find out more about the environment.
6. Report back.

Before undertaking this task

First complete your review of Unit 5 in Section A, Part I, Information and help.

In Step 1.4, you selected an idea and identified the target customer group. The next stage is to refine the idea by finding out more about the target customer segment, the competition you will face, and the characteristics of the environment in which the market operates.

This can only be done by carrying out some preliminary research. Use checklists 1 to 4 to structure the research, carry it out and report back.

Setting the objectives for research

The overall objective of the research is to provide you with more information to assess the feasibility of your idea as a viable enterprise. It is suggested that this is structured around two specific questions to which you may wish to add more:

(a) What opportunities and threats exist in the marketplace now, and in the future, for my idea?

(b) How much will the customer buy from me in my first three years of trading?

These research objectives can be looked at in relation to the customer, the competition and the environment.

Checklist 1: researching the customer

I   What specific questions do I need to ask about the target customer segment?
- ❐ What is the size of the total market?
- ❐ How many individual customers are there?
- ❐ Will I be dealing with more than one customer segment?
- ❐ How often do they buy?
- ❐ How much do they buy at one time?
- ❐ Do they buy randomly or at specific times?
- ❐ Do some customers account for a high percentage of purchases?
- ❐ If so which ones, and what percentages?
- ❐ What percentage of the market can I expect in Year 1? Year 2? Year 3?
- ❐ What are the existing distribution channels and structure of the market?
- ❐ Other questions

II   Which research methods can I use to find out some answers?

Secondary research:

_____

_____

_____

Primary research:

_____

_____

_____

Checklist 2: researching the competition

I   What specific questions do I need to ask about the competitors in my target market?
- ❐ Who are the competitors?
- ❐ What percentage of the market do they have?

- ❐ What is their estimated sales turnover?
- ❐ How long have they been in business?
- ❐ Is the market stable or changing, with new competitors entering and/or leaving?
- ❐ What is the competitive edge (or main benefits) of the principal competitors?
- ❐ How profitable and efficient are they?
- ❐ How do customers rate the principal competitors?
- ❐ Are they active in the marketplace?
- ❐ If yes, in what ways?
- ❐ Other questions

II Which research methods can I use to find out some answers?

Secondary research:

_____

_____

_____

Primary research:

_____

_____

_____

Checklist 3: researching the environment

I What specific questions do I need to ask about the environment of my target market?
- ❐ What are the boundaries of my target market?
- ❐ What are the social trends?
- ❐ What are the economic factors?
- ❐ What are the political factors?
- ❐ What are the technological trends?
- ❐ What are the demographics of the market?
- ❐ What will be the key external influences in the marketplace in the next three years?
- ❐ How will these influences affect the competition?
- ❐ How will these influences affect me?
- ❐ Other questions

II   Which research methods can I use to find out some answers?

Secondary research:

_____

_____

_____

Primary research:

_____

_____

_____

Checklist 4: reporting back

Collect together the research you have done, and see how it matches up against your research objectives. In particular, answer the questions below as best you can:

❐   What does my information suggest will be my likely sales turnover?

	Year 1	*Year 2*	*Year 3*
Pessimistic	_____	_____	_____
Optimistic	_____	_____	_____
Most likely	_____	_____	_____

❐   What information have I found out about the market that represents opportunities and/or threats?

○   Short-term and long-term trends representing opportunities and/or threats?

○   Competitive opportunities and threats?

○   Customer opportunities and threats?

○   Other?

○   How docs my information meet other research objectives that I set myself?

Step 1.6 Summary of the feasibility study

Summary of what is required

1.   Define the proposed business or enterprise.
2.   Check the 3 Ms of management, market and money for feasibility.
3.   Calculate the risk.
4.   Decide on future research requirements.

The conclusion of your feasibility study should only be undertaken when Steps 1.1–1.5 are complete, as they form the basis for this final Step of the study reviewing the proposal and checking for feasibility.

Define the proposed business or enterprise

You should now be in a position to write down, in simple terms, the nature of your proposed business or enterprise. While this should be a brief statement of one or two sentences, it should be precise and not vague, covering the main features of the business. It should answer such questions as:

❐ What will you sell?

❐ Who will be your customers?

❐ How will you reach the marketplace (in terms of distribution and communication)?

❐ How will you obtain products, or provide services?

❐ What methods or technologies will be involved?

For example, a manufacturer might define their business as:

'The design and manufacture of printed circuits sold directly to manufacturers of electronic instruments, using CAD and CAM techniques to add value to components purchased from industry suppliers.'

A service business might describe themselves thus:

'The provision of high quality training courses to the small business sector in South East England, largely in conjunction with Training and Enterprise Councils conducted from rented premises in the Farnborough area.'

The value of this exercise is to look at the scope of your idea again and give it some initial parameters. It should enable you to question the nature of the business, so that you understand more precisely what you are trying to do.

Check for feasibility

Successful strategies for small business rely crucially on three factors:

Management   dealing with the influences of the small business environment.

Market   matching customer needs to the strengths of the enterprise.

Money   financial foresight to ensure sufficient ongoing resources.

Before moving to the next stages of selecting the route to market entry and detailed planning of the business, you need to review your strengths and weaknesses in these three crucial areas. Look back at the relevant tasks (1.1–1.5) and summarise your idea in relation to these 3 Ms, using the 'Feasibility checklist' for a successful small enterprise strategy. Quantify the risks using the checklists given in 'Calculating the risk', below.

Management: Objectives – Strengths – Weaknesses

❐ What are your personal objectives? What are the objectives of the enterprise?

❐ What are your own, and your team's, strengths in relation to the opportunity you have identified?

❐ Which weaknesses will need to be addressed and when?

❏ How will you deal with the influences of the small enterprise environment?

Market: Opportunities – Threats – Barriers

❏ What are the opportunities and threats posed by your chosen marketplace?

❏ Who is your intended customer (precisely) and what is your competitive edge?

❏ What are the competitive threats?

❏ What are the barriers to market entry?

Money: Sources – Rewards – Risks

A more detailed financial appraisal of your business idea is necessary at this stage, which should include a break-even analysis from initial estimates of costs and sales. Some additional guidance for these calculations is given below in 'Calculating the risk'. Your financial analysis should answer the following questions:

❏ What are the likely financial rewards or benefits of your idea likely to be in the short and medium term?

❏ How quickly will you make a profit?

❏ What are the financial risks?

❏ What is the probability of survival and success?

❏ How much money will you need, and what are the likely sources of finance?

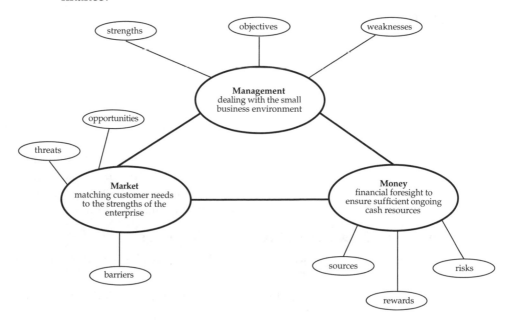

Calculating the risk

One indicator of risk is the break even point of the business: the level of sales required to cover the variable and fixed costs of doing business. If the level of sales needed to cover costs looks high compared with your estimates of market demand, then the risk of failure is obviously high. If, on the other hand, even your pessimistic sales forecast more than covers costs, then the risk looks much smaller.

At this stage, costs and sales can be approximate estimates. More detailed planning comes later, in putting together a full business plan. Here you need a first appraisal of how feasible your new enterprise looks in practice. Is the probability of success high enough to merit taking it to the next stage? Can you overcome the barriers to market entry?

Estimate the start-up, fixed and variable costs of operating the enterprise for years 1, 2 and 3.

❐ *Fixed costs* remain almost unchanged whatever you sell. They are fixed in the sense of not being altered by the volume of goods or services you sell.

❐ *Variable costs* vary according to the volume of goods or services you produce. In practice the distinction is not usually clear cut: some items are semi-variable. Often fixed costs are only fixed to a certain level of sales; above that they too increase; for example, more equipment, or staff, would be needed to cope with higher levels of demand.

❐ *Start-up costs:* estimates need to be made over the first three years of the business in order to establish a pattern of profit or loss. In the first year, particularly, these will be one-off costs associated with establishing the business. As such, they need to be identified separately from the ongoing fixed and variable costs of the business.

Inflation over the three years can be dealt with by calculating all figures at today's prices, i.e. assume that you will be able to increase your prices in line with the inflation of your costs.

Fixed costs and overheads

Fixed costs are usually the overheads of the enterprise. Use the following checklist to estimate your overheads for the first three years. Your list of costs will inevitably be different; this is intended as a prompt so that you don't leave out any important cost areas.

	Year 1	Year 2	Year 3
Salaries and wages: include employer's on-costs (i.e. any costs of employment in addition to salaries and wages which are paid by the employer, e.g. employer's National Insurance contribution.)	_____	_____	_____
Rent and rates: include other premises costs e.g. heating, lighting, repairs and maintenance	_____	_____	_____
Office costs; e.g. telephone, postage, stationery, printing	_____	_____	_____
Publicity: e.g. advertising, promotions, leaflets, exhibitions	_____	_____	_____
Legal and professional costs: e.g. bank charges, insurances, legal/accounting charges	_____	_____	_____
Travel and entertainment: e.g. petrol, car rental	_____	_____	_____
Financial costs: e.g. interest, depreciation	_____	_____	_____
Total overheads	_____	_____	_____

Variable costs and gross profit

Net sales value less variable costs is often called gross profit. As a percentage of sales this will vary considerably depending on the type of business. A manufacturing company for example might have considerable variable costs in its raw materials and consumables used in production. Some labour costs could also be variable if arranged on a part-time basis, which could be varied quickly with the level of demand. The gross profit in such a manufacturing company could be less than 50 per cent of the net sales value.

In a service company, the variable costs will be considerably less. There may even be no really variable costs, only semi-variable or fixed costs, for example in a consultancy firm. In such cases the gross profit as a percentage of sales will be very high.

Usually it is possible to establish a gross profit as a percentage of sales on an on-going basis. Once sales are estimated for a given period, the gross profit can be calculated.

One-off start-up costs

A new enterprise will inevitably require some one-off expenditure which will not be repeated on an annual basis. This may include the legal costs of setting up a company or the acquisition costs of premises, for example.

You need a rough estimate of these at an early stage to:

❏ Determine if it is feasible to raise this money.

❏ Calculate any interest payments to include in your fixed costs.

Break even analysis

Once fixed costs and variable costs are known, a level of sales can be calculated to meet the level of costs. For example, if you estimate your fixed costs for the year as £50,000 you will obviously require a gross profit of £50,000 to break even. If you also know that your gross profit is 50 per cent of your net sales, then your break-even sales value will be £100,000.

What will be the break-even point for your business? Review your fixed costs and your gross profit to arrive at an approximate level of sales which represents break even.

Sales forecasts

As part of Step1.4 you were asked to identify your customer and as part of Step 1.5 you were asked to estimate how much that customer was likely to buy from you and why. As a continuation of this exercise estimate your sales for the first three years as follows.

	Year 1	Year 2	Year 3
Pessimistic	_____	_____	_____
Optimistic	_____	_____	_____
Most likely	_____	_____	_____

Compare your sales figures in the above categories, with the break-even point for your business. Consider the implications of these calculations on the viability of your enterprise.

Decide on future research

Assuming that you have concluded from your study that your idea is worth pursuing, this is the time to consider future research needs for a more detailed business plan.

In Step 1.5 you began researching your idea to provide basic information to test for viability and progress the concept.

In the next detailed planning stage, what more will you need to know? What research objectives do you have now? What questions will you need answering to develop an in-depth plan for your enterprise?

If your conclusions are that the idea is not worth taking further then consider what modifications can be made to make it more feasible. First ideas are often changed, sometimes radically, in the light of further information and analysis.

If you consider that you need to start again because your idea now seems highly unrealistic, even with modification, then this in itself is a valuable learning experience. In order to progress through the next two Stages, without the need to start all over again, consider investigating a franchise, or buying an existing business, rather than going back to the beginning of a brand new venture.

Stage II The route to market entry

Introduction

In Stage I, The feasibility study, you developed a business idea from a situation of unknown risk to a position of reasonable prospects.

In Stage II you further develop the idea by deciding on an appropriate route to market entry. This involves exploring the possibilities of the new venture as a start up, a franchise, or buying an existing business.

If your feasibility study showed that prospects were not reasonable, then you can consider alternative routes using established ideas with proven track records.

You are also required to consider the legal identity of the venture. The Stage is organised into 3 Steps and a Summary Step, as shown below.

Stage I: The feasibility study

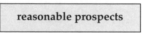

reasonable prospects

Stage II: The route to market entry

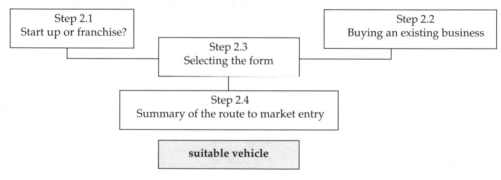

Step 2.1 Start up or franchise?

Summary of what is required

1. Review Part II, Unit 6, Start ups and franchises.
2. Investigate the advantages and disadvantages of a new business start up.
3. Consider the possibilities of the franchise system – either as franchisor or franchisee – for your business idea.

Before undertaking this task

First complete your review of Unit 6 in Section A, Part II, Start ups and franchises.

Review start ups

Consider a new business start up as an option. Conduct an audit of the advantages and disadvantages of this option for your specific idea, carrying out any necessary research.

Review franchising

Consider the development of your business idea using a franchise network with you as the franchisor. List the advantages and disadvantages.

Consider taking up a franchise as a franchisee as a possible way of developing your idea. Do suitable franchises exist? Obtain details of a franchise in a business area similar to your own and list the advantages and disadvantages of this course of action.

(Information on what franchises are on offer is available from (i) two national exhibitions held each year in Birmingham and London, (ii) in magazines such as *The Franchise Magazine*, and (iii) in publications such as *The UK Franchise Directory*, and *The Franchise Handbook* – see Unit 6.)

If your conclusions from Stage I, The feasibility study, were that your idea did not represent reasonable prospects, then it is particularly important to look at alternative routes to market entry.

Step 2.2 Buying an existing business

Summary of what is required

1. Review Part II, Unit 7, Buying an existing business.
2. Consider what type of business you could consider buying (all, or part of) that would be consistent with the development of your business idea.
3. Obtain information on suitable businesses for sale.
4. Evaluate the advantages and disadvantages of the specific business(es) offered for sale.
5. Decide if this is the appropriate route of market entry for you and your business idea.

Before undertaking this task

First complete your review of Unit 7 in Section A, Part II, Buying an existing business.

Review buying a business

Before committing yourself to a business start up, it is worth considering buying an existing business. Consider what types of business for sale would help the development of your business idea. This does not necessarily mean that the businesses you think of buying are trading in the market or style you have chosen. For example, if your business idea is a themed cocktail bar and restaurant, it may be beneficial to buy a restaurant with a very different appeal to the one you have considered. The advantages will be that some of the barriers to entry will be more easily overcome (such as licensing permissions), and equipment, for food preparation and storage, could still be appropriate for a different end product. Even if you are considering a totally different business, it is worth looking for some assets that may be useful. If your business involves retail premises you will certainly need to consider taking over the lease of an existing retail outlet, then changing it over to your use rather than waiting for the right new premises to become available.

You may also wish to consider not just an outright purchase, but buying into an existing business, with or without the participation of the existing management.

If your original idea did not look feasible from your initial analysis, is there an established business which you could consider buying instead? Are there businesses for sale in an area of interest to you?

Information on businesses for sale

Once you have decided the type of business to look for, obtain information on suitable opportunities. There are a number of sources to consider:

Business transfer agents

There are listings of local and national agents in *Yellow Pages*, *Business Pages* and *The Thompson Directory*. Business Transfer Agents act rather like estate agents in that a seller will register with them, and provide details of their business for sale; in the event of a sale the seller pays the agent a commission.

Most agents will send particulars of specific businesses for sale on request.

Some specialise in local businesses, others in a particular trade, with confectioners, tobacconists and newsagents (CTNs), and licensed premises firm favourites because these change hands relatively frequently.

Christie & Co. (Head office 2 York St, London W1A 1BP) are perhaps the country's leading transfer agents, dealing with the licensed trade (pubs, wine bars, restaurants), CTNs, hotels, residential nursing homes, the retail trade including fast food outlets and other commercial property.

Commercial estate agents also provide details of available commercial property including some which are offered as going concerns.

Periodicals and newspapers

National and local press often carry business opportunity sections. These include:

❏ *The Financial Times* (especially The Management Page on Tuesdays);

❏ *The Sunday Times* (Business to Business in the Business News);

❏ *Dalton's Weekly* (especially for retail outlets, pubs, hotels and restaurants).

Organisations

Accountants, solicitors and government agencies all assist in the transfer of businesses. Some are organised into nationwide services:

❏ *ABN (Accountants' Business Network):* most large accountancy practices participate in this service of linking buyers and sellers from their client network. Contact the local office of Price Waterhouse, Arthur Anderson, Peat Marwick McLintock, and other national accountancy firms.

❏ *The Business Exchange* (21 John Adam St, London WC2N 6JG) is a database of family-owned businesses for sale in the £800,000 to £15 million price range fed in by accountants, solicitors and actuaries.

❏ *The National Business Angels Network* is a nationwide business introduction service, which aims to put 'business angels' (individuals with capital to invest in smaller business ventures) in touch with ventures which need investment and vice versa. See their web site www.bestmatch.co.uk

Evaluate the advantages and disadvantages

Having obtained what details you can of a business for sale, or an opportunity of investing as a new partner, consider the merits of this as an option for pursuing your business idea. Use the information in the Section A, Unit 7, Buying an existing business, on general advantages and disadvantages to help you in your evaluation.

Decide

Decide if you wish to choose this method of market entry for your particular idea, and if you do, how you will investigate it further.

Step 2.3 Selecting the form

Summary of what is required

1. Review Part II, Unit 8, Legal identities.
2. Review the forms of small business organisation now open to you.
3. Consider the advantages and disadvantages of each option.
4. Decide on the appropriate business form for your organisation.

Before undertaking this task

First complete your review of Unit 8 in Section A, Part II, Legal identities.

Review legal form

The appropriate business form limited company, sole trader, partnership or co-operative will be conditioned by the route you have selected. For example, if you have decided to buy an existing business, it may be that you will be acquiring shares in a limited company, which dictates your choice.

A franchisor may also prescribe the legal form you adopt. If the business is to be co-owned, you obviously cannot operate as a sole trader.

The first step is therefore to review the options that are now open to you.

Evaluate the alternatives

Use the Checklist for 'Choosing the appropriate form', (Figure 8.5), and further details in Section A, Unit 8 'Legal identities', to assess the advantages and disadvantages of each form open to you against each of the categories shown. Are there other conditions which are not listed?

Decide

Decide on the most appropriate form of organisation for your small business, and note your reasons.

Step 2.4 Summary of the route to market entry

Summary of what is required

1. Review the possible routes to market entry for your business idea. Choose the appropriate route.
2. Review the possible legal identities which your idea can take. Choose the appropriate legal format for your idea in the chosen route.

By the end of this task, you should have identified the method you will be using to exploit the opportunity you have identified in terms of:

1. The route to market entry;
2. The legal identity.

The route to market entry

Now that you have a specific idea to develop as a small enterprise it is important to consider the options you have for entering the marketplace. Do you have to begin a brand new business? Would it be more appropriate to buy an existing business?

If you are starting a new business, does it have to be a start up, or are there franchises available?

☐ Review the options outlined in Unit 6, Figure 6.1, 'Possible routes to market entry' and list those available to you.

☐ Consider the advantages of the options available for your specific idea, which you have outlined in Steps 2.1 and 2.2.

☐ Decide on the appropriate route to market entry which you wish to pursue at this stage.

The legal identity

The legal identity you wish to adopt sole trader, partnership, limited company, or co-operative will be conditioned by the route you have selected. For example if you have decided to buy an existing business, it may be that you will be acquiring a limited company, which effectively limits your choices. A franchise may also prescribe the legal format you adopt.

This step is therefore to:

☐ Review the legal identity options that are now open to you.

☐ Conduct an audit of the advantages and disadvantages of each of the types available to you.

☐ Decide on your legal identity.

Stage III · The business plan

Introduction

Stage I, The feasibility study, developed a business idea from a situation of unknown risk to a position of reasonable prospects.

Stage II, The route to market entry, identified a suitable vehicle for market entry for the idea.

Stage III, The business plan, takes this idea (with reasonable prospects and an identified route to market entry) to a position of acceptable risk by more detailed planning. This involves researching and writing up a business plan, which uses the information gathered in the first two assignments, but develops it further by looking at the overall strategy as well as management, marketing and money plans.

The Stage is organised into 6 Steps, including a Summary Step as shown below.

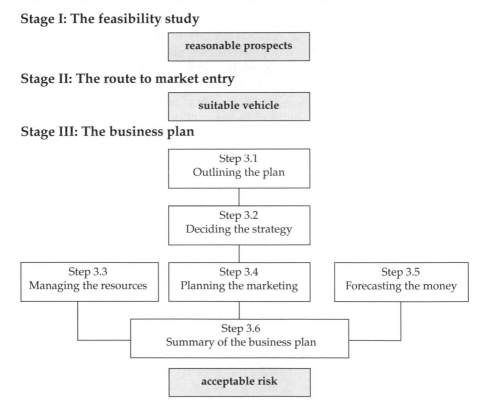

Stage I: The feasibility study

reasonable prospects

Stage II: The route to market entry

suitable vehicle

Stage III: The business plan

Step 3.1
Outlining the plan

Step 3.2
Deciding the strategy

| Step 3.3 | Step 3.4 | Step 3.5 |
| Managing the resources | Planning the marketing | Forecasting the money |

Step 3.6
Summary of the business plan

acceptable risk

Step 3.1 Outlining the plan

Summary of what is required

1. Review Part III, Unit 9, The business plan.
2. Consider the outline of headings which a business plan should cover.
3. Decide the format for your plan.
4. Complete the 'Where are we now?' sections by transferring information from Stage I, The feasibility study, and Stage II, The route to market entry.

Before undertaking this task

First complete your review of Unit 9 in Section A, Part III, The business plan. This Unit gives general and specific information on the when, who, why and what of a business plan. In particular consider the suggested outline for a business plan given in Unit 9, 5.2, Outline of a business plan.

Decide the format

Evaluate how your business plan can be organised to answer the three fundamental questions:

❑   Where are we now?
❑   Where do we intend going?
❑   How do we get there?

Decide on the outline headings for your plan, i.e. adopt the outline format given in Unit 9, 5.2 , Outline of a business plan, or amend it as appropriate to your specific idea.

Where are we now?

The feasibility study of Stage I and the methods investigated in Stage II should have given answers to cover the first sections of the outline format, in answer to the question 'Where are we now?'.

Transfer this information into the business plan. This should cover the first three sections in the suggested outline format:

(i)   The business identity

(ii) The key people

(iii) The nature of the business

This information should not be lengthy, but should give a concise summary of what the business idea is, the vehicle intended to take it to the marketplace, the key people involved in it and the nature of the marketplace and competition.

Step 3.2 Deciding the strategy

Summary of what is required

1. Review Part III, Unit 10, Successful small business strategies.
2. Confirm personal motives for entry into a small enterprise.
3. Set general objectives.
4. Set specific objectives.
5. Define policy.
6. Draw up a timetable of key activities.

Before undertaking this task

First complete your review of Unit 10 in Section A, Part II, Successful small business strategies.

Completion of this step should answer the question, Where do we want to be in the short and long term? It is setting out the strategic direction and parameters of the enterprise.

Confirm personal motives

The first step is to re-examine personal motives for entry into a small enterprise. You will have distinctive motives and expectations. Now is the time to confirm what these are, as they will be crucial in determining the strategies and objectives of the business. Go back to Steps 1.2 and 1.3 in Stage I to check your self-analysis, and the fit with the opportunity as you have defined it.

Are these personal motivations still valid?

Are there new, or additional factors which you should now consider before translating these into business objectives?

Set general objectives

What are the general objectives of the enterprise? General, in this context, means broad in scope and timespan. For example, general objectives could specify overall economic goals (e.g. to achieve sales in excess of £1 million and profits of £100,000), industry goals (to develop a particular process), lifestyle goals (e.g. to provide a satisfying and democratic place of work), environmental goals (e.g. to produce products which are environmentally safe), market goals (to achieve market leadership in a given segment) and so on. (For more examples, see Section A, Unit 10, 1.3, The objectives of owner-managers.)

Clearly these general objectives of the enterprise will be strongly linked to your personal motives as an individual.

The general objectives are:

1. _____

2. _____

3. _____

4. _____

Set specific objectives

What are the specific objectives of the enterprise? Specific means narrow in scope and timespan. For example, specific objectives could detail sales and profit targets for years 1, 2 and 3. They could quantify the number of outlets to be opened by year, the number of employees or partners by which an enterprise grows each year, the size of the customer base, the number of new accounts to be opened in each year, the percentage market share targeted by year, the number of new products, and other quantifiable goals.

The specific objectives will build into the general objectives set earlier.

Specific objectives are:

1. _____

2. _____

3. _____

4. _____

5. _____

6. _____

Define policy

What will be the policies of your enterprise? What general rules, or guidelines will you set for yourself? For example, will you have money policies (e.g. to be risk adverse, to extend no credit, to carry 90 days' stock, to borrow only against the assets of the business, to lease equipment rather than purchase it outright)?

Will you have management policies (e.g. to employ only young/experienced/part-time staff, to pay salespeople commission only, to allocate responsibilities between partners in a predetermined way, to operate a shift system, to pay staff bonuses)?

Will you have marketing policies (e.g. not to quote on the basis of price alone, or never be knowingly underbid, to maintain a specific product mix, to spend a fixed percentage of sales revenue on advertising, to use agents on commission, and not employ salespeople, to sell direct to consumers, to distribute via wholesalers)?

Financial policies include:

1. _____

2. _____

3. _____

Management policies include:

1. _____

2. _____

3. _____

Marketing policies include:

1. _____

2. _____

3. _____

Draw up a timetable of key activities

The final step in setting the parameters of strategy is to timetable some activities. What are the key stages that need to be followed in setting up this enterprise, in what order and by when?

What is the target opening date?

What has to happen before this and when (e.g. negotiation of finance, registration of company, acquisition of premises/equipment/staff, training of staff)?

What has to happen immediately after this and when (e.g. marketing campaign, production initiation, further training, targeted first order, delivery and invoice date)?

Timetable of key activities

Date/Month   Activity

_____   _____

_____   _____

_____   _____

_____   _____

_____   _____

_____   _____

_____   _____

_____   _____

_____   _____

_____   _____

_____   _____

_____   _____

_____   _____

Step 3.3 Managing the resources

Summary of what is required

1. Review Part III, Unit 11, Management of resources.
2. Complete the management section of the business plan by:
    (a) planning operations;
    (b) formulating a people plan.

Before undertaking this task

First complete your review of Unit 11 in Section A, Part III, Management of resources.

Summarise your operations plan

Outline your plans for premises, materials, equipment, management information systems and other appropriate operating resources.

Summarise your people plan

(a) Outline how you plan to manage other people within your new venture, at the beginning and as it grows.
(b) Consider how you will recruit, retain and motivate staff. How will you ensure a team spirit emerges and endures?
(c) What will be your employment practices and how will you operate payroll and personnel systems?

Step 3.4 Planning the marketing

Summary of what is required

1. Review Part III, Unit 12, Marketing.
2. Complete the marketing section of the business plan by:
    (a) completing your analysis of the marketing environment;
    (b) setting marketing objectives;
    (c) outlining marketing methods;
    (d) producing an example of promotional literature.

Before undertaking this task

First complete your review of Unit 12 in Section A, Part III, Marketing. This task is to complete the marketing section of the business plan.

The marketing environment

Marketing research should now be completed, so that the marketing environment is now understood. Earlier Steps should have done so already, but check that the following questions have now been answered:

(a) What is the market size, and the discernible trends?

(b) What is the nature and extent of the competition?

(c) What other trends in the technological, economic, and political environment will be important?

Marketing objectives

What are you aiming to do in marketing terms?

Specify marketing objectives for your enterprise. These should clarify the relationship you wish to achieve between your product or service, and the target market. In other words:

(a) They should summarise the product or service offered: for example 'office equipment and supplies'.

(b) They should identify the target market: for example 'offices in a 25-mile radius'.

(c) They should be measurable: for example 'gain 10 per cent market share', or 'achieve sales of £500,000'.

(d) They should be time specific: for example 'within two years'.

Marketing strategies

Outline the marketing methods you will use to achieve these objectives.

(a) Innovation:

- ❒ What are the products or services offered?
- ❒ What is different about what is offered compared with competition?
- ❒ How will new products be found and protected?

(b) Identification of target markets:

- ❒ Who precisely is the customer?
- ❒ Why will they buy from you?
- ❒ What other market types are important?
- ❒ How will customer relationships be developed?

(c) Interactive marketing methods:

- ❒ What personal and impersonal promotional methods will you use?
- ❒ What incentives will be offered?
- ❒ How will you overcome traditional small business problems in relation to stimulating recommendations?
- ❒ Will you distribute directly, or through intermediaries?

(d) Information gathering:

- ❏ How will you find out more?
- ❏ What networks will you utilise?

Marketing communications

In order to illustrate the benefits of the product or service on offer, it is most helpful to produce an example of promotional literature, such as a draft leaflet or brochure. This need not be a graphic masterpiece, but should attempt to illustrate how the competitive edge of your business will be put across to the target customer group.

Step 3.5 Forecasting the money

Summary of what is required

1. Review Part III, Unit 13, Money.
2. Complete the money section of the business plan by:
   (a) assessing the amount and type of funds required by your business;
   (b) completing profit and loss and cash flow forecasts for the first year in detail and the second and third years in at least outline form;
   (c) completing the balance sheet for the first year;
   (d) considering the financial policies and control systems the business will need.

Before undertaking this task

First complete your review of Unit 13 in Section A, Part III, Money. This task is to complete the money section of the business plan.

Financial requirements

You should now be in a position to assess the funding requirements of your business idea. In particular, you need to establish how much of the different types of finance you will require, and the likely sources.

- ❏ How much *permanent capital*, in the form of equity or personal investment, will be available?
- ❏ How much short-term, *working capital* is needed, and where will it come from?
- ❏ How much finance is required for *assets*, and what are the likely sources?
- ❏ If you are planning on *international trade*, how will this be financed?

Financial forecasts

Financial forecasts need to be undertaken to cover the first three years of the business:

❑ profit and loss and cash flow forecasts:

○ for year 1 by month;

○ for years 2 and 3 as a summary for each year as a minimum. It is preferable to complete forecasts for these 2 years by quarters (and it may be easier to continue the monthly forecasts for year 1 if a spreadsheet is used).

❑ projected balance sheet:

○ an opening and closing balance sheet for year 1;

○ end of year balance sheets for year 2, and year 3, are optional, but very informative about the development of the business.

Financial policy and control systems

In your financial analyses, you will have made a number of assumptions which will effectively form policies for your business, covering such important areas as:

❑ Debtors: what will be your average debtor period?

❑ Creditors: how soon will you pay your suppliers?

❑ Margins and costs: what relationship will these bear to sales turnover?

❑ Stocks and work-in-progress: what levels will these run at in relation to your sales?

It is important to list these assumptions as an appendix to your financial forecasts.

How will you ensure these policies are implemented? Consider what financial control mechanisms and information you will require to ensure you can carry through your assumptions.

Step 3.6 Summary of the business plan

Summary of what is required

1. Review Part III, Units 9 to 13.
2. Review Stage III, Steps 3.1 to 3.5.
3. Write up the business plan.
4. Write a summary.

You should now be in a position to write up your business plan. Before you do, review Units 9 to 13 in Section A, Part III, and Steps 3.1 to 3.5 of Stage III.

Presentation of your final business plan should take into account the need for:

❑ *Conciseness:* make your plan as concise as possible for an external audience such as financiers. Keep the main body of the report for essential information only, using appendices where possible to enlarge on assumptions or research.

- ❏ *Presentation:* good presentation is seen as a sign of organised management, a quality you will need as an owner-manager.
- ❏ *Enthusiasm:* your plan should be interesting to read, as your enthusiasm for the project needs to show through. If you cannot be enthusiastic about it, then no-one else will be!
- ❏ *Realism:* optimistic plans fool no-one except the writer. Where there are major uncertainties, identify them. Do not try to cover them up as they will look worse if discovered by the reader.
- ❏ *Illustration:* where possible show examples by use of sample leaflets, photographs of products, locations etc. Pictures speak a thousand words.
- ❏ *Summary:* you will need to make a short summary of your plan; this is commonly found at the front of the document.

Index